TOWARDS IRELAND FREE

The West Cork Brigade in the War of Independence
1917–1921

Ireland unfree shall never be at peace

P.H. Pearse

TOWARDS IRELAND FREE

The West Cork Brigade
in the War of Independence 1917–1921

Liam Deasy

edited by
John E. Chisholm, University College, Dublin

RᏨB

Royal Carbery Books

Royal Carbery Books Limited
PO Box 64, 2 Bridge Street, Cork

Trade distributors:
The Mercier Press,
PO Box 5,
5 French Church Street,
Cork

First published in 1973
This edition 1992

ISBN 0 946645 14 0

Printed in Ireland by Litho Press, Midleton, Co. Cork

CONTENTS

EDITOR'S NOTE

My function in preparing the present volume for publication was to put literary form on an extensive collection of unpublished manuscripts supplied to me by Liam Deasy, dealing with the role of West Cork in the national struggle for independence between 1917 and 1921. By far the greater number of the manuscripts contained notes from the pen of Liam Deasy himself, while the remainder contained statements written by comrades who soldiered with him during the war years.

In the actual composition of the book, Liam Deasy and I worked together in closest co-operation, so that there is not a single fact narrated that does not either derive directly from him or meet with his approval. So far as the plan of the book is concerned I must take responsibility. It was dictated by a number of preoccupations, namely, my concern to weave into the narrative all the facts which Liam Deasy wished to appear, to throw into relief events that he considered to be of special significance, and to include reference to as many as possible of the people he wished to have mentioned; and my design to show, in their origin and gradual evolution, the causes that led to the extraordinary achievements of West Cork in the struggle. To the extent that was possible, I endeavoured to preserve the style of writing found in the manuscripts supplied to me, but I am conscious that all too often it is my own style which prevails. Whenever manuscript material is quoted in the story, it is reproduced with only such minor alterations as were necessary to correct more serious grammatical errors, or to remove ambiguities.

In an endeavour to fill some lacunae in the accounts put at my disposal, I undertook a work of research in the West Cork area among surviving participants in the war, and was fortunate in being able to draw upon the documents and the memories of many of those who took a leading part in the events of the period recorded. It would be impossible to enumerate and to thank individually all those who co-operated with me in my research, but acknowledgement is made in Appendix I to those who allowed me to consult and quote from documents in their possession. To all the great-hearted people of West Cork who helped me my sense of obligation is very real.

John E. Chisholm

2 November 1972

PREFACE

This book is my humble tribute to the memory of the men and women who gave their lives in the fight for Irish independence, and in particular to the Volunteers, Cumann na mBan, and the people of West Cork who fought so gallantly and worked so hard in the struggle between 1917 and 1921.

My aim in the record has been to tell the story of the resistance to foreign rule that was made in the area in which I was born and reared, and in which I had the good fortune to play a part as a Volunteer, namely, my native district of West Cork. Published material dealing with the events that occurred in the area of my special interest was incomplete, and in consequence what I have written is almost entirely from my own memory and from the memories of over sixty comrades who took part with me in the struggle. The account is factual, and all temptation to alter the facts or to exaggerate them has been rigorously avoided. What may be lost as a result in romance will, it is hoped, be more than compensated for by an honest, unadorned narrative of heroic deeds that occurred in fact rather than in fancy.

From the many people to whom I am indebted for assistance in compiling my story I must single out for special mention the late Major Florence O'Donoghue who spent much time with me on the locations of the military actions and from whose notes and books I have freely drawn. To Father Tim Lyne, S.D.B., a very close friend since 1921, I am deeply indebted not only for the fact that he prompted the undertaking of writing the story, but also for the ceaseless efforts he made to encourage me in the task, for the moral pressure he exerted to ensure my perseverance, and for his constant assistance in assembling the facts. I am particularly grateful to the Rev Dr John Chisholm, C.S.Sp., University College, Dublin, who in 1969 showed interest in my work and volunteered his assistance. I gladly accepted the offer, and on my request he kindly consented to edit the work. While the facts narrated are entirely my own and those of my comrades, the form and general presentation of the story are the work of Dr Chisholm. My thanks are due to him for the work of research he spontaneously undertook to supplement my efforts, and for the meticulous care he took to ensure accuracy down to the smallest detail in the narrative. For any factual errors or omissions that may be found to occur in the record my memory is responsible, and I offer my sincere apologies in advance.

I wish to express my gratitude to all my comrades and the many other collaborators who made this story possible. It is my regret that it was impossible to make mention of them all, and I offer my sincere apologies to the many dedicated men and women whose names do not appear. At any rate, it is my hope that this record will perpetuate the memory of the wonderful effort made against immense odds by an amazing and very fortunate generation of young Irishmen and women to win freedom for their country. If this hope is fulfilled then the work of all my friends and myself will not have been in vain.

LIAM DEASY

2 November 1972

CHAPTER 1

THE SEED IS SOWN

My story begins in a small hamlet that fringes the west bank of the river Bandon, nearly half-way between Kinsale and the town of Bandon itself. The hamlet is called Kilmacsimon Quay, and my story begins there because it was there that I was born—in 1896—and because it was there, as I grew from childhood to teenage, that I first came to know and value the ideals for which the West Cork Brigade was later to fight so gallantly and with such singular success.

Like so many youngsters of my age and circumstances, I was reared in an environment in which Faith and Fatherland were seen to be all-important. My father and mother were of humble stock, and from both sides of the family I acquired, almost unconsciously, the legacy of strong nationalist feelings that had passed from generation to generation of my forefathers. Stories about Ireland's fight for freedom in previous generations were told repeatedly at our fireside, while songs and ballads commemorating victories or defeats were frequently heard at our gatherings.

At school we were denied anything like an adequate and impartial course in Irish history. Indeed, to the best of my recollection, the little history we were taught formed part of the prescribed English course, which seemed calculated to impart a British loyalist view of our Irish past. Nevertheless, the songs we were taught to sing at school, such as 'The Harp that once through Tara's Halls', 'The Minstrel Boy', and others by Thomas Moore had the effect of rousing in us sentiments of a vague nationalist kind. Then, too, our teacher strove constantly to rid us of the attitude of servility and subservience towards the landed gentry which was encouraged by this class, and in its place he endeavoured to plant a sense of self-respect and independence.[1]

If we learned little Irish history in the national school the deficiency was in great measure supplied at home. The Battle of Kinsale, for instance, was fought only a few miles from where I grew up, and was often discussed on a winter's night. The fearsome massacres of Cromwell were well known to us from local tradition,

1. The national school teachers in West Cork during the time I was at school, namely from 1901 to 1910, could, in general, be called nationalist in outlook. Many later gave evidence of their nationalism by their activities in the Gaelic League, the G.A.A., and in the Volunteer movement.

as indeed were the Rising of 1798, the ill-fated Insurrection of 1848, and, above all, the Fenian Rebellion of 1867. In this latter connexion, the story of the Manchester Martyrs was told and retold at our fireside, and it aroused all the more interest in that two of the Fenians involved were associated with our district. The young Protestant patriot, William Philip Allen, who was one of the three Fenians to be executed, came from Bandon, while Captain Timothy Deasy, one of the two who escaped, was linked through his parents with Colliers Quay a few miles up-river from where I lived. Small wonder that it seemed almost as serious to me to miss the annual Manchester Martyrs' anniversary ceremonies in Bandon on 23 November as to miss Mass on Sunday.

Politics was part of the atmosphere I breathed during my boyhood, and as a consequence of the lively discussions that took place in my home I found myself at an early age with an avid interest in the political tussles that were the order of the day. Besides, the system of local government then in existence brought politics to our doorstep. The candidates for election to our Rural District Council, to the Board of the Poor Law Guardians, and to the County Council were fairly evenly divided in their allegiance between William O'Brien with the All-for-Ireland League he founded in 1909 and John Redmond with the United Irish League that was founded in 1900, after the Parnellite Split. The elections were, in most cases, closely contested. House to house canvassing took place, public meetings were held, and feeling ran high.

The keen political rivalry between the O'Brienites and the Redmondites which I witnessed in my native district during the years between 1909 and the outbreak of the first world war was peculiar to County Cork for the reason that nowhere else, save perhaps in North Louth, was the sway exercised by O'Brien so strong as in Cork City and County. And it may well be that the interest in political affairs roused throughout Cork by the struggle between the two opposing parties of the O'Brienites and the Redmondites helped to stimulate the extraordinary enthusiasm and drive that Cork City and County showed later in the Volunteer movement during the War of Independence.

With a background such as mine, it was only natural that when, at the age of thirteen, I left my native Kilmacsimon Quay to seek work in Bandon, I should have been attracted to the nationalist organisations that were then taking shape in the town. The first of these to catch my attention was the Gaelic Athletic Association (G.A.A.) that had been founded just over twenty years earlier—in

1884—to promote traditional Irish sports and to discourage foreign games. It is true that this organisation was not directly concerned with political ends, but by emphasising the distinctive character of our Irish games it tended to strengthen us in our nationalist spirit, and to give us a stronger sense of national identity. About this time my allegiance was also won by the Gaelic League that had been founded in 1893 to 'de-Anglicise' Ireland, mainly by promoting the revival of our native language. The effect of this movement was similar to that of the G.A.A.; by introducing us to our distinctive literary culture—and it should be remembered that in our national schools at the time we learnt little about the Irish language[2]—it helped to strengthen our patriotic feelings and to give us a sense of national unity that powerfully influenced us in the years that lay ahead.

It may seem strange that one with a background such as mine did not immediately yield to the attraction of the Irish Volunteer movement which was launched in Dublin in 1913 'to secure and maintain the rights and liberties common to all the people of Ireland'. I had indeed followed closely the developments that led to the founding of this new military body as a people's army, and was aware of local efforts being made to start branches in the Bandon district. But my activities in the G.A.A. and the Gaelic League at the time were so absorbing as to prevent my feeling any immediate urgency about joining the new movement. Besides, I felt that by being actively engaged in the two organisations mentioned I was already serving my country in a useful manner.

Somewhat later an unexpected setback occurred which further delayed my entry into the Volunteer movement. In the course of 1915 I fell ill with what appears to have been a form of tuberculosis, and was invalided as a result for more than a year. By the time I recovered and was able to resume my work in Bandon, the Rising of Easter Week was at hand. Nevertheless, between 1913 and 1916 I continued to take an interest in the fortunes of the Volunteer organisation. I was aware of the efforts made by John Redmond, leader of the Irish Parliamentary Party, to gain control of the organisation once it took definite shape, and of the split he caused in it when, on 20 September 1914, just after the outbreak of

2. In fairness to our teacher in the national school at Ballinadee, it should be remarked that, if we left school with a poor knowledge of Irish, it was due rather to our lack of enthusiasm for the language at the time than to his efforts. He endeavoured to teach us how to read and write elementary Irish.

the Great War, he announced publicly at Woodenbridge, County Wicklow, that the Volunteers should be prepared to fight as members of the British forces. From the two divided segments of the Volunteer organisation were formed the National Volunteers who followed John Redmond and the Irish Volunteers who opposed him. Some time later I can recall seeing the National Volunteers under arms guarding the bridges in Cork City to allow the withdrawal of most of the British regular troops stationed there for service against the Germans in France. Perhaps it was the scandal of the split that also helped to defer my association with the Volunteers until some time later.

I was almost twenty when the Rising of Easter Week 1916 took place. Like the majority of youths of my generation I was roused by this event to a pitch of enthusiasm I never before experienced. Day by day during the fateful week I followed with quickening pulse the news—mainly rumour—of the development of the fight in Dublin, and when the end came after six days of fighting all hope of breaking the bonds of British thraldom in our generation seemed lost. News of the aftermath was received in dazed and muted silence. Thousands were arrested. The bulletins announcing the execution of the sixteen leaders appeared. Many were tried and sentenced to years of penal servitude. The vast majority were interned without trial in camps in England and Wales. The last flicker of hope appeared to be extinguished.

During the months that followed the Rising of Easter Week, the depression caused by the executions was replaced by a gradually-awakening optimism. The lead was set by the Irish Volunteers, and as the ranks closed once more the words of Pearse pronounced at the grave of O'Donovan Rossa, the Fenian hero, were being fulfilled : 'Life springs from death, and from the graves of patriot men and women spring living nations.' The spirit of the nation was not dead. Slowly, almost imperceptibly, yet inexorably as a flowing tide, it rose, and with its rising the nation was reborn.

In face of the rapid change of feeling that was occurring in Ireland, and the mounting demand for the release of prisoners taken after the Rising, the British Government found that the risk involved in liberating the prisoners would be less than that arising from detaining them any longer. Accordingly, on 22 December 1916, six hundred untried prisoners were released from Frongoch Internment Camp in Wales, and arrived to a tumultuous reception in Dublin on Christmas Eve. The demand for the release of the sentenced prisoners continued. In fact, it assumed such proportions, and became such an embarrassment to the Government in the eyes of the world, that all political prisoners were released on 15 June 1917. The hills of Ireland then blazed with bonfires. Towns and villages everywhere were *en fête* to welcome the returning heroes who were made to march at the heads of columns of men with bands playing and flags flying. Never before was seen such a welcome for men who only a short time before were seen off to prison with jeers and abuse after the failure of a great fight for freedom. In many towns the released men spoke, and when they did so they gave voice not to the sufferings they had endured, but rather to their conviction as expressed in the historic words: 'Ireland unfree shall never be at peace'.

For us of the younger generation all this was a lesson in patriotism, more eloquent than anything we had hitherto experienced. The lesson was one of which we had often heard in childhood, but until this time had never fully understood. We were actually seeing Irish patriots with shaven heads and their convict caps set at a jaunty angle, and on the caps was marked in red figures the number which had replaced their identity in prison. It was a sight to set the pulses tingling, and was more appealing to us than any oratory no matter how eloquent, and called to mind the words of the old ballad:

A felon's cap the noblest crown
An Irish head can wear.

In consequence of the events that occurred in the decisive week of the Easter Rising of 1916, and more particularly of the events that followed it, thousands of young men all over Ireland, indeed thousands of men of all ages in the country, turned irrevocably against the English Government and became uncompromisingly dedicated to the cause of obliterating the last vestiges of British rule in Ireland. I was one of them. My comrades of the West Cork Brigade were others.

CHAPTER 2

REBELS MUSTER IN A LOYALIST TOWN

Bandon at the time I joined the Volunteers early in 1917 was not very different in appearance from the Bandon of today. The general disposition of streets, buildings and bridges was the same, though the British military barracks on the rise at the north-western entrance to the town is now no more than a few crumbling walls, and the Old Dispensary off Shannon Street—now renamed Oliver Plunket Street[1]—in which we held our Volunteer meetings has recently been demolished. Despite the changes, despite the disappearance of houses here and there, and the appearance of new ones, and the obvious change in the vehicles to be seen in the streets, the town still retains some of the allure it had over fifty years ago.

Socially, however, the Bandon I knew in 1917 was very different from that of today. With a population of close on 5,000, as compared with 3,500 today, the town was a busier place than it is now, and the impress of its historical past on the people was more pronounced. From the early seventeenth century Bandon had served as an armed base to protect the English planters who occupied the rich lands of West Cork following the Elizabethan plantations. And when Bandon was incorporated in 1613, one of its first acts was to pass a by-law to the effect 'That no Roman Catholic be permitted to reside in the town'.[2] It is significant that Oliver Cromwell was enthusiastically received in Bandon on his arrival there just a few months after the terrible slaughter he wreaked on the inhabitants of Drogheda in 1649. For his part Cromwell was favourably impressed by Bandon, and described it as 'a fine sweet town, and an entire English plantation, without any admixture of Irish'.[3] Perhaps it is even more significant still that as late as 1862 a respected Bandonian could write, 'A truly great day for Ireland was 14 August when Oliver Cromwell, the new Lord Lieutenant, landed in Dublin'.[4] The descendants of the old English settlers in Bandon changed little in their loyalties with

1. I shall retain the older name, Shannon Street, because it was by this name that the street was known to us at the time of which I write.
2. Cf. G. Bennett, *The History of Bandon* (Cork, 1862), p. 29.
3. *Perfect Diurnal*, 29 January 1650, quoted by Denis Murphy, S.J., in *Cromwell in Ireland: A History of Cromwell's Irish Campaign* (Dublin, 1897), p. 242.
4. *The History of Bandon*, p. 150.

the passing of the years, and it comes as no surprise to learn that at the time of which I write they could scarcely have been more opposed to the Volunteers and the cause of Irish freedom for which they stood. Then, the solid merchants of the town were particularly prosperous during the Great War years, and in consequence were—with a few notable exceptions—anxious to maintain the *status quo,* and to avoid any trouble that could damage their business. Finally, a big number of the townspeople had close relatives in France and elsewhere fighting in the British army. Sympathy with these relatives and appreciation for the substantial weekly sums being sent home by them were powerful factors which militated against the popularity of our movement. And yet the paradox is that this unlikely town with its strong core of inveterate loyalists, its formidable military garrison of approximately two hundred British soldiers, and its force of nearly thirty pro-British policemen of the Royal Irish Constabulary (R.I.C.) became the centre of the premier battalion of the rebel West Cork Brigade.

* * * * * *

The Bandon Company of Volunteers had succeeded in recruiting about thirty members by the time I joined the ranks towards the beginning of April 1917.[5] This was a sizable number in view of the widespread hostility of the loyalists in the town, and was a tribute to the zeal of the leaders. Of these latter several were already well known to me through contacts made at Gaelic League meetings, and I can recall in particular Pat O'Dwyer, who was Company Captain, and also Hugh Thornton, Seán and Bill Buckley, Willie Walsh, Jimmy Hayes, Con O'Leary, and the redoubtable Flor Begley—all pre-1916 Volunteers.

We paraded twice weekly in an old disused three-storey building known as the Old Dispensary in a cul-de-sac off Shannon Street. Each parade began with a roll-call, after which we were instructed for a half-hour in the elementary principles of military drill, such as numbering-off, forming fours and marching. The space available in the Old Dispensary was indeed limited, but we had to make the best of it in the absence of alternative locations. As rifles were unavailable we used hurleys, spade handles, or even newly-cut saplings for our drilling exercises. The only weapon available was

5. The Volunteers in Bandon were at first a section attached to the Ballinadee Irish Volunteer Company that was founded very early in 1915. In January 1916 two Bandon Volunteers, Pat O'Dwyer and Flor Begley, went to the headquarters of the Cork Brigade in Sheares Street, Cork City, to register the Bandon Volunteer unit as an independent Company.

a revolver and we experimented with it in order to learn the technique of loading and taking aim. Target practice was out of the question because we had no ammunition and because the noise of firing would have meant betraying our activities to the ever-vigilant attention of the R.I.C. After drill practice, the Company would stand at ease while the Captain read any official communications he received from higher quarters or gave his men news of Volunteer activities in other parts of the country or while he addressed them on other matters of general interest.

Dismissal of the Company parade did not mean the immediate departure of the Volunteers present. It was rather the prelude to a discussion in which each one could freely express his views or put forward questions in his own right. The topics discussed normally centred round developments connected with Volunteer activities that had occurred in the country since the previous meeting. And the sources supplying information for our discussions were, of course, the daily and weekly newspapers, but more importantly confidential reports of a verbal kind dealing with Volunteer activities that were unknown to reporters and consequently not published in their papers.

Even now, after a lapse of more than fifty years, I can recall the thrill of those early parades—the feeling of high adventure, the sense of dedicated service to the cause of Ireland's freedom, the secret rendezvous, and the gay comradeship—all were to me and my companions like signs of the return of the Golden Age of Ireland's ancient chivalry. It is true we were but a tiny group in Bandon at the time—thirty of us in a town of close on five thousand inhabitants. What, I think, made the difference was the fact that we knew we were supported by thousands of groups similar to ours throughout the thirty-two counties of Ireland, all with identical aims and objectives, all imbued with a unity of purpose which was inspired by principles for which the patriots of Easter Week had died.

I still remember the spirit of the men at our Volunteer meetings. We drilled and planned in the firm hope that the day would soon come when we would challenge the great power of Britain to battle. There was no doubt in our youthful minds about the ultimate outcome of the unequal struggle. Without arms and hopelessly outnumbered we were still gripped by a supreme faith in the justice of our cause. We had the faith that moves mountains. Ours was the belief expressed by Thomas Davis when he wrote :

Freedom comes from God's right hand,
And needs a godly train,

And righteous men must make our land
A nation once again.

The Quest for Arms Begins

From the beginning of my association with the Volunteer movement I was conscious of the fact that we were an army without
arms, and that there was no question of waiting until arms would
be supplied to us before starting the struggle. I was aware, as indeed
were my comrades, of the need of securing arms by local initiative
and even by individual personal endeavour. No responsible leader
of my acquaintance left us under any illusion on this all-important
issue : we were never led to believe that our parading and training
were a preparation for a time of military action when arms would
somehow be given to us. On the contrary, we saw clearly that we
ourselves would have to go out with bare hands and wrest from an
armed enemy the weapons we would later use against him in our
efforts to drive him from our shores. In the event, the drive to
procure arms and ammunition was in evidence as early as 1917,
though no well-defined policy or method to deal with the problem
had as yet emerged. The methods employed depended on circumstances and were many and varied, a fact that is sufficiently illustrated by the following incidents which occurred in 1917.

A merchant vessel named *The Norwegian* was torpedoed by a
German submarine off Galley Head, nineteen miles west of the Old
Head of Kinsale. As the vessel did not sink, an attempt was made
to beach it on Red Strand, but it ran on a submerged rock some
distance from the shore and became a total wreck. Before the
arrival of the British military, a group of local men salvaged a
numbers of rifles from the wrecked vessel, and when this became
known to some Volunteers of the Clogagh Company, they approached one of the men, a local farmer, who had salvaged six of the
rifles, and offered to purchase them. Unfortunately for himself the
farmer demanded an exorbitant price, whereupon three Volunteers
from Gaggin, Mick, Eugene, and Bob Walsh, took the law into
their own hands, and carried out a raid to secure the arms. Despite
the attention they got from two barking dogs, the brothers succeeded, after a long midnight search in a hayrick, in securing all
six service rifles for their Company at Clogagh. Next day Flor
Begley and I had occasion to call at Mick Walsh's home, and there
we were told the news of the raid in strictest confidence. The sight
of the rifles and the thrill of handling one of them for the first time
is something that I can still vividly recall. Incidentally, at a later

date two other Volunteers, Frank Hurley of the Mount Pleasant Company and Dan Canty of the Newcestown Company, purchased two other rifles from those salvaged at Red Strand for the sum of five pounds each. This was a substantial sum of money in those days, and the fact that the Volunteers in question paid it from their own pockets meant a big sacrifice for them.

News of these acquisitions spread rapidly throughout the Battalion and had an interesting sequel. An old Fenian whose memory was jogged by the talk about the rifles came forward to relate that, after 1882, when the Fenian cause seemed hopelessly lost, he, together with three companions, had dumped fifty rifles in a certain field in Knockbrown, off the Bandon-Timoleague road. On hearing this, a group of Kilbrittain and Clogagh Volunteers dug parallel and cross trenches in the field indicated, in the hope of locating the Fenian rifles, but without success. A similar story about hidden rifles was told by another Fenian, and a search was made in a field he indicated at Oldcourt in the Ballinspittle area, but again without success. It is, of course, very questionable whether these guns, had they been found, would have been of any use, but at least the two incidents are some indication of the strength of the Fenian movement that had existed in West Cork, and of the spirit of the men who were continuing the Fenian tradition in my day.

Some time after the above-mentioned events, my brother Miah made friendly contact with a member of the crew of a coal boat that was discharging coal at Kilmacsimon Quay. The man was the gunner on the boat, and while the cargo was being unloaded he showed Miah over the vessel and explained the mechanism of an anti-submarine gun that was bolted down on the fore deck. On another occasion he took my brother below deck and showed him a service rifle, explained its use and finally allowed him to fire several shots at passing seagulls. This information was duly transmitted to a Volunteer of the Ballinadee Company who with two others boarded the ship in the early hours of the morning she was due to sail. Following my brother's instructions they had little difficulty in locating the rifle and making away with it without being observed. When the loss was discovered Miah was closely questioned by the R.I.C. but he had established a perfect alibi and was not arrested. Such were typical methods used to procure the vitally-needed arms for the struggle that lay ahead. More widely-organised methods were soon to follow.

Bandon Volunteer Pipe Band

Traditionally, it was to the sound of warlike music played on pipes that our Irish soldiers marched and fought in times past. As early as 1581, Vincenzo Galilei, father of the famous astronomer Galileo, could write : 'The bagpipe is much used by the Irish. To its sound this unconquered, fierce, and warlike people march their armies and encourage one another to feats of valour.'[6] And we know that the Irish fought to the sound of music at the Battle of the Boyne in 1690, and also at Fontenoy in 1745.[7] Could it be that the Volunteers of our day would break with such a tradition and think of going to battle without the skirl of pipes and the sound of beating drums? At least one Volunteer in Bandon did not think so.

All credit for the idea of forming a Volunteer band in Bandon goes to Flor Begley, a native of Bandon town. He argued—and when he did so it was always with vigour and effect!— that the formation of a band would rouse great enthusiasm among the Volunteers, that it would have a good effect on their morale, and give them prestige in the eyes of the people. Unfortunately, the sum of money required to purchase the instruments that would be necessary amounted to no less than a hundred pounds, a formidable sum in those days and well beyond the resources of our Company in 1917. It is understandable that our senior officers could provide no financial assistance for the project, but it is to their credit that they did not reject it out of hand. Instead they gave their approval to the formation of the band, but left it to the ingenuity of Flor Begley and his friends to raise the necessary funds. This Flor proceeded to do with his customary energy and determination. First of all, some friends among the business community of Bandon were approached for contributions, but as these friends were very few, it was necessary to range further afield in search of money. Then it was decided to organise a raffle in aid of the projected band, and this met with complete success. Tickets were sold in many districts both within and outside Cork County, and it was through contacts made by the Volunteers in jails and internment camps after the 1916 Rising, and particularly through a Volunteer named Joe McGuill of Dundalk, whom Flor Begley's brother had befriended in Richmond Barracks, Dublin, that most of the tickets were sold.

Within three months the required sum of money was to hand,

6. Cf. Wm. H. Grattan Flood, *A History of Irish Music* (Dublin, 1906), p. 106.

7. Cf. *The Oxford Companion to Music* (London, 1960), p. 68.

and with it nine sets of pipes of the kind known as war pipes, two side-drums, and one bass drum were bought.[8] Eager young men from the ranks of the Volunteers, and boys from Fianna Éireann[9] now came forward to join the band and to learn to play the instruments, while a skilled piper named Seán Daly, who was in employment at Upton Industrial School, four miles away from the town, agreed to be bandmaster and to train the pipers. He put his heart into the work and gave regular lessons on practice chanters with the aid of written music in the Old Dispensary off Shannon Street where the Volunteers held their meetings. The music selected for the band naturally contained a predominance of military airs and marching tunes, such as 'O'Donnell Abu!', 'Kelly the Boy from Killane', 'The Men of the West', and 'The Boys of Wexford'. So great was the enthusiasm and application of the players, and the efficiency of their teacher, that the band was able to make its first public appearance on the anniversary of the Manchester Martyrs on 23 November 1917. It was given a rousing reception by Volunteer sympathisers in the town, and gained immediate popularity— so much so, in fact, that it drew the largest crowd ever present at the anniversary celebrations that year. Flor Begley's dream of a Volunteer pipe band had become a reality and was already proving its worth.

The name given to the band was Bandon Volunteer Pipe Band, and this it retained even though later, when the West Cork Brigade was formed, it was looked upon as the Brigade Pipe Band. It was the only band which the Volunteers had in West Cork, and for this reason it was in frequent demand in different parts of the area. At the time of its formation, it was clearly understood that the band would be based in the town of Bandon, and that it would be the property of the Bandon Battalion, then known as the Tenth Battalion of the Cork Brigade, later as the First Battalion of the Third Cork Brigade.

The British authorities disliked the band intensely, and on many occasions individual members of the R.I.C. threatened to halt it by

8. Most of the instruments were bought from Denis McCullough, a Volunteer officer of Belfast who had been imprisoned in July 1915. He later transferred his business to Dublin.

9. This was a militant organisation founded by Bulmer Hobson and the Countess Constance Markievicz in 1909 'to re-establish the independence of Ireland'. Cf. Bulmer Hobson, 'Foundations and Growth of the Irish Volunteers 1913-1914' in *The Irish Volunteers 1913-1915*. Edited by F. X. Martin, O.S.A. (Dublin, 1963), p. 20. In practice, the Fianna operated very much like a junior arm of the Volunteer movement.

force, if it dared to march through the town on its way to proscribed meetings, say of the G.A.A. or the Gaelic League organisations In face of these threats, the Volunteers had recourse to a simple ruse. Whenever it had been decided that the band would attend a banned meeting on a Sunday—and it was on Sundays that meetings of the kind were most conveniently held—a point was made of parading in such wise as to meet the people coming from the twelve o'clock Mass in the town. This was done deliberately so that, if the R.I.C. wished to use their batons on us as a deterrent, they would have had to do so under the eyes of a large congregation leaving the church. As an added precaution, some of the Volunteers who were neither pipers nor drummers—and I was one of them—marched with the band so that if trouble started they could take the brunt of it. In point of fact, rather than risk rousing the hostility of the people and losing face, the R.I.C. never interfered, though they conveyed veiled threats to the younger members of the band in an effort to intimidate them.

The Bandon Pipe Band played a colourful and heart-warming role in the activities of the Volunteers throughout the early years of the struggle. It helped greatly to sustain the morale of the men, and to rouse them to deeds of valour. But when the tempo of the battle quickened and many of the Volunteers were forced 'on the run', it was necessary to dissolve the band temporarily, and to hide the pipes and drums in a safe place until quieter times of peace came to the land. But on one historic day at the climax of the struggle the warlike notes of a single Volunteer pipe were heard above the fray, and the piper who played them was none other than Flor Begley, the founder of the band. But more of that anon.[10]

Sinn Féin and the Irish Republican Brotherhood

Meanwhile activities multiplied in other directions. The Volunteers who had returned from Frongoch and other British internment camps and jails on the 22 December 1916 and during the following months were fired with enthusiasm for the immediate reorganisation of pre-1916 Companies in their native districts, and for forming new ones where previously none had existed. Besides, those leaders who had evaded arrest after the Rising, men such as Tom Hales, Captain of the Ballinadee Company, and Denis Lordan,

10. The Bandon Volunteer Pipe Band has survived to the present day. During the war years 1939-45, it was handed over on loan to the Local Defence Force, now known as Fórsa Cosanta Áitiúil (F.C.A.). It was stipulated then that the band should be based in Bandon. It was and still is.

Captain of the Kilbrittain Company, had already taken steps towards this end. Lordan, for example, had been giving practically all his time to the reorganisation of the Volunteers in Bandon town itself and also in the surrounding areas, and it was as a result of his efforts that Companies were reformed in Kilpatrick and in Mount Pleasant area. Conspicuous also in this effort at reorganisation in the Bandon district was Hugh Thornton, a Volunteer who had recently come from Dublin to Bandon.

At the same time, the Republican Clubs (that merged with Sinn Féin from October 1917) were spreading throughout the country, and West Cork was by no means overlooked in the development. The fact that by this time the Republican Clubs had evolved from being a kind of passive resistance movement to British rule, which Sinn Féin was when founded by Arthur Griffith in 1905, into being the political wing of the revolutionary movement for independence assured it full support in West Cork. It gained great influence, and Clubs were formed everywhere in conjunction with Volunteer Companies. In fact, in most districts Volunteer and Sinn Féin membership lists were almost identical.

In furtherance of its aim, Sinn Féin strongly supported the drive for the revival of the Irish language, and Irish classes sponsored by the Gaelic League were encouraged. *Feiseanna* (competitions) and *aeraíochtaí* (open-air entertainments) were held throughout the area as often as possible in order to intensify the national spirit of the people. Every opportunity was availed of to hold large public parades of Volunteers. On Sundays, several Companies would march to some pre-arranged point, and conduct training exercises there, and on the anniversary of the death of any local Fenian, Companies of local Volunteers made it a point of marching to a locality associated with his name. Public meetings were generally held on the occasion of such anniversaries, and addresses by some prominent local men were given. These parades and route marches served as a means of attracting considerable numbers to the ranks of the Volunteers and to membership of the Sinn Féin organisation. Further, the G.A.A. was vigorously promoted, and Companies of Volunteers in different areas formed hurling and football teams, and organised inter-Company matches very frequently. In the arrangement and conducting of social activities incidental to the national movements, such as *feiseanna, aeraíochtaí,* hurling and football matches and dances, there was perfect understanding and full co-operation between all the different movements, whether Sinn Féin, the Volunteers, the Gaelic League, or the G.A.A. At the various gatherings support was invariably solicited for the national movements, and every effort was made to recruit new members. Particularly memorable in this connexion was an *aeraiocht* held in Clonakilty in the summer of 1917. A huge crowd assembled and was addressed by the Countess Markievicz.[11] She spoke with telling effect of the significance of the struggle for independence and of the necessity of supporting the Irish Volunteers and Sinn Féin in that struggle. She did not speak in vain, and moved many a man to rally to the cause.

At the back of all these activities hovered the guiding spirit of the Irish Republican Brotherhood (I.R.B.).[12] This secret oathbound revolutionary movement had remained faithful to the aim propounded by its founder, James Stephens,[13] in 1858, namely the overthrow of British rule in Ireland by physical force. It had inspired and directed the Rising of 1916, and though many of its leaders had been executed for their part in Easter Week, it was still effective. Every organisation in the country that could influence the cause of national independence was the object of its vigilant attention and sometimes of its secret control.

Early in 1917 the I.R.B. extended its activities in the West Cork area, and became an influential force there. Quietly and patiently it began to exert an ever-increasing influence in the Volunteer movement and also in the G.A.A. and the Gaelic League. My first contact with the Brotherhood was made in the course of 1917 through Tom Hales, the most active leader in the founding of the Volunteers in the Bandon district from 1914, and now Commandant of the Bandon Battalion. Shortly after my enrolment in the Bandon Company, he spoke to me about the I.R.B. I was impressed by what he said, particularly by his account of the role the I.R.B. would play in the struggle for independence, and its determination to achieve complete freedom from English rule by physical force. Accordingly, I accepted his invitation to join the organisation there and then, took the oath of secrecy, and promised observance of the rules.

11. Constance Gore-Booth (1868-1927), who became Countess Markievicz, was born of a Protestant landed family at Lissadell, County Sligo. An ardent and active nationalist, she was one of the leading figures in the Rising of 1916. See above, footnote 9.

12. I.R.B. influence in the G.A.A. and Gaelic League was greater in the period before 1915-1917 than it ever was subsequently. The change was due to the large influx of new members into these movements who were not members of the I.R.B.

13. Cf. Desmond Ryan, *The Fenian Chief* (Dublin, 1967), p. 91.

To the various activities such as drilling, parading, and holding public meetings, which incidentally served to intensify national feeling in West Cork, must be added the political triumphs of the separatist movement. These had their part to play. Thus, news of the success of the Republican candidate, Joe McGuinness, in a by-election in South Longford on 9 May, following that of Count Plunkett in North Roscommon three months earlier, caused great excitement among the Volunteers in Bandon, and the momentous victory of Eamon de Valera over the Irish Party candidate in the East Clare election of 11 July had a similar effect.

The concluding months of 1917 were marked by several events which, in one way or another, helped to increase interest in our cause. Among them must be mentioned the startling news that reached us on 25 September announcing the death while on hunger strike of Thomas Ashe, a hero of 1916 whose death was really due to the treatment he received in jail because of his Republican activities. During the five days between his death and the funeral to Glasnevin cemetery on 30 September we conducted slow marches through the streets as an act of mourning. Like the blood sacrifices that followed the Easter Rising of 1916, this event had its effect in winning many more adherents to the separatist cause.

The Sinn Féin Annual Convention (*Ard-Fheis*) that met on 25 October held great interest for us. We had been subscribing to a special fund to pay the expenses of our delegates to the Convention, and eagerly awaited news of its deliberations. The election of Eamon de Valera as President of Sinn Féin at this Convention caused great elation. It was now felt that the renewed struggle for independence had found its natural leader and that through him it would be given its true direction. A few days later, i.e. on 28 October, de Valera was elected President of the Volunteers, and so gained leadership of both the civil and military wings of the Irish separatist movement. At the same time, the I.R.B. leader, Michael Collins, secured a position of importance on the Executive of the Volunteers as Director of Organisation, and so assured the influence of the I.R.B. in the military movement.

Soon after news of these favourable events reached us, it was announced that de Valera was to pay his first visit to Bandon during the following month. The prospect of this visit provoked the liveliest enthusiasm. When the great day came, de Valera was welcomed by massive crowds, marching men, cyclist groups, and, most striking of all, many horsemen from rural areas paraded for the event. It was indeed a memorable day. It helped to create a strong sense of confidence in the nationalist movements that were stirring, and to bring the eventful year 1917 to a close on a note of great optimism.

CHAPTER 3

THE MENACE OF CONSCRIPTION 1918

The year opened quietly. To keep the Volunteer organisation active and enthusiastic was a problem, now that the exciting events of 1917 were past. And this problem was all the greater in areas where little or no variety could be introduced into the habitual form of military training that was alone possible, namely elementary drill practice. This did not satisfy the more eager and energetic Volunteers who had looked forward to action. The result was that Company Commanders and Battalion staffs had difficulty in maintaining their numbers, not to speak of increasing them.

In March 1918 I was instructed by Tom Hales, senior officer of the Bandon Battalion, to organise a Company of Volunteers in Innishannon, which was four miles down the river from Bandon town. At the time, I was well known in this parish through G.A.A. activities that had led me and a few companions to found the Valley Rovers Hurling and Football Club there six years earlier. I had remained an active player on the teams, and had formed solid friendships with my team mates. Now to see what prospects there were of founding a Company of Volunteers in the parish I sounded some of the more important members of the club, and finding that they considered the prospects favourable, reported the matter to Tom Hales who took immediate action. The Company was organised, and I was duly elected its Captain. I continued to work in Bandon after my appointment, and cycled to Innishannon two nights each week to instruct the Company in the elementary principles of drill in the football fields which we had at Bally-mountain and Dromkeen. Recruiting caused no problem, and within a short while eighty per cent of the Valley Rovers players became Volunteers.

A decisive turn of events occurred at this time which accelerated the activities of the Volunteers—and indeed all the nationalist movements—in a spectacular way. England had been faring very badly in the war with Germany and its allies. Failure at Gallipoli in Turkey was followed by more serious reverses in France and catastrophic losses in manpower. Reinforcements became such an urgent necessity that the British Government decided to apply military conscription to Ireland in the spring of 1918. It is true that Ireland had been excluded from the Conscription Act of 1916, but this would have to change. On 16 April a new conscription bill was rushed through Westminster not only raising the age of exemption, but also empowering the British Government to extend conscription to Ireland by an Order in Council.

The effect was electric. The threat of conscription so galvanised the Irish people as a whole—excluding, of course, the Unionists of Ulster—that there was complete unanimity among them in their determination to resist conscription by every means possible. A great wave of nationalist enthusiasm spread over the country. Political differences were temporarily submerged in face of the common danger, and in Innishannon, for instance, where the O'Brienites and Redmondites were so bitterly opposed, all differences were dissolved in the Volunteer organisation. Young and old flocked to the ranks of the Volunteers, and showed open defiance and disregard for the many prohibitions and decrees that were being constantly issued by the Government.

As tension grew throughout the country in face of the conscription threat, the need for arms was urgently felt on all sides. Orders were issued by the Battalion Commandant instructing all Companies to collect all available fire-arms in their districts. In compliance with this order, I arranged at a weekly meeting of the Innishannon Company for the collection of shotguns and ammunition from friendly neighbours, and led a party to seize them from those who were unwilling to offer them voluntarily. As a result, twenty-five shotguns were collected in our district, but very little ammunition. Such, however, was the local enthusiasm that a primitive ammunition factory was set up in a farm-house at Ballymountain where Dick Twomey, Quartermaster of the Innishannon Company, specialised in filling empty cartridges with large shot that could be very effective at close range. Incidentally, it was at this time that we had our first casualty, and the victim was Twomey himself who lost the index finger of his right hand when a cartridge with which he was experimenting exploded. I still shudder to think of the risks our men took during these early days to manufacture ammunition. Particularly dangerous were the bombs that were improvised by filling one-pound paint tins with shrapnel and gunpowder, and exploded by means of lighted fuses. It could indeed be said that some of the ammunition we manufactured was more dangerous to ourselves than to the enemy. Shortly after the unfortunate accident at Ballymountain, one of the Volunteers of the Company announced that he was in possession of a .22 rifle and 300 rounds of ammunition. This was welcome news and afforded the opportunity to conduct live target-practice that was of great value to the men in preparing them for the military engagements that lay ahead.

In all, the arms acquired at this time by all Companies of the Bandon Battalion from private holders amounted to two hundred shotguns and a limited quantity of ammunition. One of the raids to seize arms had a near tragic ending. Mick Crowley of Kilbrittain was the victim. He had called to the house of a well-known loyalist at Ahiohill to collect shotguns, and had been refused admittance. Thereupon he forced an entry, and rushed into the spacious hall of the dwelling. The owner, who was standing at the head of the stairs, fired immediately with a shotgun, and Crowley received the full charge in the chest and fell seriously wounded. He had to be hurriedly removed to a safe place and given medical attention. No reprisals were taken on this occasion beyond the firing of a few shots at the ceiling of the hall by one of Crowley's infuriated friends.

Hugh Thornton and Denis Lordan were particularly active at this time training and organising Companies of the Battalion, the former taking responsibility for Companies on the south side of the river Bandon, and Lordan those on the north side. Lordan also occupied himself by making buckshot and loading shotgun cartridges with it. As he had to use old expended cartridges, because they were the only ones generally available, it was necessary to recharge the caps with powder fulminate of mercury as replacements for the caps could not easily be obtained. Lordan found time also for reconditioning the guns which had come into the possession of the Volunteers, whether old pattern rifles or shotguns. In order to add to the effectiveness of the latter, a type of home-made bayonet was invented, and Con Lehane, a blacksmith who had to go 'on the run' in 1918, was commissioned to manufacture them in quantity. A portable forge was organised for him, and this was moved from one Company to another so that he could continue his work and at the same time avoid arrest. The steel for the bayonets was obtained principally from pins of hay-rakes.

An event occurred in March of this same year, 1918, in the townland of Snugmore near Kinsale, which serves as an indication of the temper of the Volunteers at the time, and also shows the spirit of active co-operation that existed between the different Companies that became very pronounced as the struggle gained momentum. A farmer named Dennis had been evicted from his farm at Snugmore, whereupon the Companies of Kilbrittain and Ballinadee were mobilised to co-operate with the Ballinhassig and Kinsale Companies in staging a vigorous protest against the unjust eviction. With horses and ploughs they broke up a considerable amount of the evicted farmer's land to prevent its being used for grazing by a 'grabber'.[1] While this work was in progress, two armed R.I.C. men arrived on the scene to note what was happening. At a given moment, they separated from each other, presumably in an effort to glean as much information as possible about the leaders of the operation, and when this occurred one of them was overpowered and his rifle taken from him. Immediately both policemen left to report the matter at their headquarters. Later in the evening a contingent of soldiers arrived from Kinsale, and with fixed bayonets charged the crowd and dispersed Volunteers and ploughmen in all directions. Two men were arrested, one being Tadhg Lynch, Secretary of the local Sinn Féin Club as well as Captain of the local Volunteer Company. He was charged with seizing the policeman's rifle, and was sentenced to twelve months imprisonment. It is sad to relate that the drapery business which Tadhg Lynch had in Kinsale suffered so much in consequence of his imprisonment that it never recovered.

Following this incident, martial law[2] was proclaimed, and there was intensive raiding in the Bandon and Kinsale districts. Early one morning in May, a party of approximately ten R.I.C. men armed with carbines, under a Sergeant Brennan, arrived at Knocknacurra near Bandon to arrest Seán Hales, Captain of the Ballinadee Company, who had been recognised at the ploughing incident at Snugmore two months previously. Leaving some of his men on guard outside, Sergeant Brennan and three others entered Hales's house, but Seán resisted arrest, and as he was a powerful man weighing over sixteen stone, he was able to cause the police some difficulty. Thereupon the sergeant sent one of his men to Bandon for reinforcements, while a member of Seán's own household dispatched news of what was happening to his brothers, Tom and William, who were in a neighbouring house at the time. These, together with some supporters, closed in on the house, and when their movements were observed some of the R.I.C. men on guard outside became nervous, and two of them actually laid down their arms, refused to take any further part in the affair, and resigned from the force.

Meanwhile, Seán, seeing his would-be captors momentarily dis-

1. This was the term used to designate a person who took over property from which a tenant had been evicted.

2. The author uses the term 'martial law' in a general sense to designate various orders which gave full powers of arrest without warrant, etc., to the Crown forces.

tracted, made a dash through the back door of his house, and was well across the adjacent field before the police realised he had made his escape. One of the R.I.C. men attempted to fire on Seán as he ran for cover, but he was prevented from taking accurate aim by being pushed by one of his own comrades, and Seán evaded capture. Thenceforward this brave Volunteer was 'on the run'.

For several months after Seán Hales's escape police and military raided his home. On one occasion in the month of July, when the military were making one such raid, they suddenly came upon two of Seán's brothers, Tom and William, together with Denis Lordan who had been hiding material that was intended for use in manufacturing shotgun bayonets. The three Volunteers made a dash for cover, and the military immediately opened fire without even calling upon them to halt. Fortunately, the fence they used for cover was a narrow stone wall, and they could hear the whistle of bullets ricochetting from it as they dashed for safety. Although they were pursued for about threequarters of a mile, they finally succeeded in making their escape. The first newspaper to publish an account of this raid and the act of 'shooting to kill' of the military was the *Southern Star* which appeared weekly in Skibbereen. As a result of publishing this information, the newspaper was suppressed by the British authorities.

During the months following the passing of the Conscription Act wholesale arrests of leaders of the Volunteers, Sinn Féin, and other nationalist movements were attempted by the British Government. To avoid arrest it became customary for a number of the more prominent Volunteers in adjoining Company areas to meet together at night and sleep in unoccupied labourers' cottages or farmyard outhouses, and to post armed sentries for protection. The hardships incurred by this necessity were very great, and some Volunteers succumbed to the rigours of exposure. Among these was Lieutenant William Hurley of Kilbrittain Company who contracted pneumonia and died. He was given a military funeral, including a firing party, and this despite the fact that the area was under martial law. All Companies of the Bandon Battalion were mobilised and paraded at the funeral. There was no interference by the British authorities.

The months that had followed the Conscription Act of 16 April witnessed a series of proclamations of various kinds that were calculated to curb the growth of nationalist movements and to counteract the wave of resistance that the menace of conscription had created. Thus on 15 June County Cork and a number of other counties became 'proclaimed areas'. Three days later certain districts, including Cork, were proclaimed as 'Special Military Areas' under the Defence of the Realm Act, and orders were issued prohibiting public meetings, including fairs. Then on 4 July Sinn Féin, the Volunteers, the Gaelic League, together with other organisations, were condemned as illegal, and persons attending meetings organised by these bodies were declared liable to prosecution. To crown the series there appeared on 5 July an order prohibiting 'the holding of or taking part in any meetings, assemblies, or processions in public places within the whole of Ireland', and this was intended to apply to sports meetings as well as to *feiseanna* and *aeraíochtaí*.[3]

The reaction to these decrees and prohibitions in West Cork was similar to that which prevailed generally throughout Ireland, namely to ignore them, in so far as possible to act as though they did not exist, and even deliberately to defy them. Thus, the reaction of the Central Council of the G.A.A. was typical, and serves as a good illustration of the general mood. At a meeting of the Council held on 20 July at 68 Upper O'Connell Street, Dublin, the Secretary, L. J. O'Toole, reported on an interview he had with the Dublin Castle authorities in which he was informed that football and hurling matches could not be played in the future without an official permit. After a short discussion the Council unanimously decided that 'no permits would be asked for under any conditions; and provincial councils, county committees, leagues and clubs were to be notified accordingly; and also that no member was to participate in any competition if any permit had already been obtained ...' It was further decided 'to arrange for Sunday, 4 August, at 3.00 p.m. (old time) a series of matches throughout each county, to be localised as much as possible ...'[4]

The response was overwhelming. In defiance of the ban of 4 July, and in compliance with the decision of the Central Committee of the G.A.A., fifteen hundred hurling or football matches were played that Sunday of 4 August in Ireland. In Innishannon itself we had arranged to meet Ballymartle hurling team, and cycled the four miles to the team's ground at the Rising Sun. We were followed the whole way by members of the R.I.C. from Innishannon who insisted that we were acting against the law in playing. Despite their insis-

3. Cf. D. Macardle, *The Irish Republic* (Dublin, 1951), pp. 256-57.
4. I am indebted to Seán Ó Síocháin, Secretary-General of the G.A.A., for permission to use the above extracts from the *G.A.A. Central Council Minute-book* for the years 1911-1925.

tence, and despite the fact that they remained with us during the match to collect the necessary evidence to convict us for this our first breach with the law, we played the match. No prosecutions followed. We had gained a moral victory, and the conviction that 'unity was strength' crystallised in our minds and hardened our resolve.

11 November brought the end of the Great War, and with it the menace of conscription became a thing of the past. With this threat removed there was naturally a decline in the enthusiasm of a number of the Volunteers, and a falling off in the ranks. But this did not seriously affect the morale of those who remained. On the contrary, these felt that it was now that the real test was coming, and to meet it active preparations and reorganisation began.

Through the example set by many staunch Volunteers in the different Company areas, and especially through the efforts of members of the I.R.B., the spirit of the movement gradually became more intense than ever. An organised army whose units were everywhere receiving a strictly military formation was being slowly shaped and brought under the disciplined control of a G.H.Q. in Dublin. Of this army the company was the basic unit, and this normally corresponded with a parish district. Nevertheless, when necessary a company could be divided into sections each under a section commander. As the number of companies increased in an area they were formed into a battalion under the command of a commandant and battalion staff. Later still battalions went to form a brigade, which in the beginning could represent a whole county.

When the Volunteers were being formed, far-seeing men, especially those of the I.R.B., realised that from the movement an army could in time be developed that could be made pass from defence to attack, and strike a blow for the freedom of the country. To realise this objective was a difficult task, but able and determined men were not lacking, and under their patient and relentless effort and sure guidance the Volunteer movement worked towards the desired goal.

Towards the end of 1918 I was appointed Adjutant to the Bandon Battalion and this appointment spelt the end of my direct connexion with the Innishannon Company. My new appointment necessitated nightly visits to the different parts of the Battalion area, which extended from Newcestown in the north to Barryroe in the south west, and from Crossbarry in the north east to Kilbrittain in the south. Such journeys were made on my bicycle. There were thirteen Companies in the Battalion,[5] and when the conscription threat had passed and enthusiasm had somewhat waned we had still three hundred Volunteers on our rolls. This made Bandon Battalion numerically the largest one in the West Cork area, with Castletownbere next and Bantry third. By the end of 1918 it was decided that the Cork Brigade, which up to that time was co-extensive with County Cork, had developed to such a point that a division of it into three brigades was imperative. The division was one of the first things to be put into effect in the new year.

*   *   *   *   *   *

The year 1918 ended on a note of political triumph for Sinn Féin that more than compensated for the temporary waning of interest that followed the end of the Great War on 11 November. The British Parliament was dissolved on 25 November and the campaign for the general election was begun immediately. Sinn Féin now stood for the complete independent sovereignty of Ireland, and was vowed to use 'every means available to render impotent the power of England to hold Ireland in subjection by military force or otherwise'.

The results of the election were announced on 28 December and revealed that Sinn Féin had swept the country. More than two-thirds of the electors who voted had voted for Sinn Féin and for the principles of the Proclamation of the Provisional Government of Easter Week 1916. Of the thirty-two counties of Ireland, twenty-four returned none but Sinn Féin candidates, and even in Ulster five of the nine counties polled a majority for Sinn Féin. As one writer remarked, 'It is doubtful if in the whole history of parliamentary institutions a decision so nearly unanimous had been given to one party.'[6] The stage was now well and truly set, and as the dawn of 1919 approached, we felt we were at the threshold of a new and decisive era in the history of our people. The tide of hope was rising.

*   *   *   *   *   *

Hitherto we have dealt at some length with the Bandon Battalion. Perhaps at this juncture, on the eve of the formation of the

5. Ballinadee, Kilbrittain, Timoleague, Barryroe, Clogagh, Bandon, Mount Pleasant, Crosspound, Innishannon, Newcestown, Quarry Cross, Kilpatrick, and Ballinspittle.

6. Cf. D. Macardle, *The Irish Republic*, p. 267.

West Cork Brigade, it would be opportune to introduce the reader to the other five Battalions which are soon to be fused together with the Bandon Battalion to form one co-ordinated fighting unit. We shall begin our survey with the Beara Battalion in the extreme west and work our way eastwards through the Bantry (Fifth), Skibbereen (Fourth), and Dunmanway (Third) to the Clonakilty (Second) Battalion. We shall sketch the development of each to the end of 1918. Thereafter we shall recount the activities of the Brigade as a whole from the time of its formation at the beginning of 1919.

CHAPTER 4

THE BEARA BATTALION

The Beara Peninsula, forming the western boundary of County Cork, extends southwest of a line drawn from Glengarriff to Kenmare River, and is a district extraordinarily rich in antiquities and in history.[1] Through the centre of this peninsula, and extending to its apex at Dursey Head, runs a striking range of mountains for about thirty-five miles. Several of the higher peaks rise above two thousand feet, while deep lateral glens and precipitous slopes drop from the main central range either to Kenmare River in the north or to Bantry Bay in the south. This rugged, mountainy peninsula with its indented coastline of cliffs and bays, and many valleys, was ideal terrain for guerilla fighting, and from its fastnesses was to appear a band of intrepid Volunteers who played a vital role in the heroic struggle to come.

In November 1915 a number of men from the parish of Eyeries, five miles north of Castletownbere, made their way to Liverpool with the intention of emigrating to the United States. However, at the port they were turned back, and on their return journey, two of them, Seán O'Driscoll and Pat Mullins, contacted Terence MacSwiney, Vice-Commandant of the Cork Brigade, in Cork City. As a result of their conversations with him, they began the organisation of a Volunteer Company in Eyeries as soon as they returned home. Christy O'Connell, who was later to become one of the important leaders of this Company, was one of the founder members.

On New Year's Day 1916, Terence MacSwiney paid a visit to Eyeries, and found that the local Volunteers had already built up a Company of about thirty men. He was particularly struck by the fine spirit that was evident among them, and future events were to prove how genuine that spirit was. The Company Officers elected were Seán O'Driscoll, Captain, Dan Harrington (Causkey), First Lieutenant, and Robert O'Dwyer, Second Lieutenant. James McCarthy, who was president of Sinn Féin in the area, was by virtue of his office also considered Commanding Officer of the

1. The peninsula has for long been the happy hunting ground of antiquarians who have gone there to study the wealth of evidence available pointing to a very early civilization, and even to traces of prehistoric man. For interesting historical references, see the *Journal of Cork Historical and Archaeological Society* for the years 1908 and 1909.

whole peninsula. The Company strength increased rapidly during the following months, and developed into four sections at Urhan, Inches, Ballycrovane, with Eyeries as the centre. Each section soon had between thirty and forty men.

As there were no ex-service men among the Volunteers in the district, they were obliged to initiate and conduct training as best they could among themselves. To help in this regard, the Company Captain attended an officers' training course at Cork Brigade Headquarters in Sheares Street, Cork City, during the month of January 1916 and when he returned to Eyeries, he made full use of the knowledge he acquired. The only arms held in the Company were a seal rifle, eight or ten shotguns, and three revolvers, with very little ammunition for any of the weapons.

When mobilisation orders for the 1916 Rising were sent out on Good Friday, 21 April, by the Cork Brigade Commander, the Eyeries Company was instructed to march to Kenmare on the following Sunday, 23 April, and there await further orders.[2] Accordingly, after Mass on Easter Sunday morning, the full Eyeries Company paraded, and were warned of the seriousness of coming events, and the opportunity was offered to anyone who wished to withdraw to do so. A few, for various reasons, elected to return to their homes, and the remainder, about eighty officers and men, set out on the twenty-five mile trek to Kenmare.

Passing through Ardgroom, the Volunteers reached Lauragh, a village in County Kerry, about twelve miles from Eyeries, and there a halt was made. While the main body rested at Lauragh, a cycle patrol of six men was sent in advance to Kenmare with a dispatch, only to return with the news that plans had miscarried, and that the Volunteers were to return home. It was now late on Sunday evening. Rain had been falling and the men were soaked, hungry, cold and dispirited. They had brought no food with them, and there was very little to be had locally, with the result that most of the men had nothing to eat. They spent the night in the parish church at Lauragh, and returned to their homes tired and hungry the next day.

A small gunboat came into Coulagh Bay during Easter Week,

2. The mobilisation orders were sent out by Tomás MacCurtain, and were delivered at Eyeries by Freddy Murray who cycled from Cork on Good Friday, a distance of ninety-four miles. Having spent the night with the Volunteers at Eyeries, he continued on his bicycle the next morning, and eventually reached Headford Junction, sixty miles away. There he caught the evening train to Cork, and reported back to headquarters on Holy Saturday night.

and kept the village of Eyeries under cover with its guns. The following week a party of military came from Bere Island, surrounded the village and searched all the houses, but as they found no incriminating evidence, no arrests were made. An R.I.C. party went to the house of Joe Foley, a Volunteer living at Ardacluggin, and searched for the rifle he was known to possess. Failing in their efforts they demanded that Joe should produce the weapon, and when he refused to do so he was arrested. After his arrest, someone who knew where he had hidden the rifle brought it—without his knowledge—to the R.I.C. in the hope that he would be released if it were surrendered. Joe was not released, but was interned in Frongoch Internment Camp. He was the only one arrested in the Eyeries area immediately after the Rising.

Despite the general feeling of disappointment which was inevitable after the failure of the plans at Kenmare, the Volunteers of Eyeries continued to organise and to drill secretly on Sunday nights among the hills. Arms were scarce in the district, and the only reliable weapons now available were three revolvers and about half a dozen shotguns.

In the early autumn of 1917 Charlie Hurley came from Bandon to work in Castletownbere, and he quickly organised a new Company there. Sufficient indication of the esteem in which he was held in the town is found in his immediate election as Captain of the new Company. The influence of his natural genius and courage was soon in evidence, and nine months later, when the Beara Battalion was formed, he was elected its first Commander. There was a big increase in the numerical strength of the Companies in the spring of 1918 when the British Government threatened to enforce conscription in Ireland. At this time the peninsula was reorganised, and independent Companies were formed at Adrigole, Bere Island, and Rossmacowen, while the four sections of the Eyeries Company were formed into four independent Companies, namely at Inches, Ballycrovane, Ardgroom, and Eyeries itself.

An Attack on the R.I.C. Barracks at Eyeries, 17 March 1918

The Volunteers at Eyeries decided to hold a parade on St. Patrick's Day, 1918, and to march from their village to Castletownbere. It was arranged that Charlie Hurley would meet the Eyeries men there with his Company, and parade with them through the town. It was planned that a few picked men of the Eyeries Company would unobtrusively drop out of the ranks on the way to the assembly, slip back to the village, and approach as closely as

possible to the R.I.C. barracks without being seen. There they were
to lie in wait till the door of the barracks was opened, and then
rush it.

At this time there were four R.I.C. men stationed at Eyeries—a
sergeant named Nugent and three constables. Two of these, namely,
the sergeant and a constable, had gone to Castletownbere with the
object of keeping the activities of the Volunteer parade under
observation. This meant that there were two constables to be
contended with in the barracks. The Volunteers mustered five men
for the attack, namely Joe Foley, the veteran who had been
arrested after the events of Easter Week 1916 and was now
released, Seán O'Driscoll, Con O'Dwyer, Peter O'Neill, and Christy
O'Connell. Joe and Seán had one .45 Colt revolver each with five
rounds between them. Christy O'Connell had a .32 revolver and
two rounds of ammunition. The other two Volunteers were
unarmed. The five hastily donned improvised disguises and silently
approached the barracks. Four members of the party remained at
the east gable-end of the building while Christy O'Connell was
sent around to the front to reconnoitre. It was arranged that he
would knock at the door, and, in a voice resembling that of the
sergeant, ask the constable inside to open to him. As Christy got
close to the building, the door unexpectedly opened, and a policeman came out. Christy describes the encounter as follows :

At the door, I came face to face with the barrack orderly
whose name, I think, was Dalton. He also saw me with my
suspicious disguise, and to turn to tell the others would be
fatal. I whipped out my little gun, and ordered, 'Hands up!'
In return, he swiftly pointed his right hand at me, and I
pulled twice on the trigger. There were two dull clicks—my
two rounds were duds. There was no shot from his side either
—it was his finger he was pointing at me, thinking I would
mistake it for a gun in the dark. Then he backed in quickly to
slam the door, and I hurled myself at him with full force.
There was a step down inside, and the force of the impact
sent him reeling into the hallway. Again I ordered, 'Hands
up!' and this time he obeyed. It was with mixed feelings I
stood there in the hall, holding up this giant R.I.C. man. I
can still picture him—fair complexion, broad shoulders and
deep chest, a man of splendid physique—and the light from
the table-lamp in the dayroom shining through the open door.
I was thrilled at having taken this symbol of British imperialism, as it were, by assault, anxious that my comrades should

come to my assistance and fearful every moment of getting a clatter from Cahill (the other constable) whom we expected to be there. Luckily, we learned later, he had gone out for a drink, and that was probably why Dalton had opened the door, anxious for his return before the sergeant got back.

At last, my pals, sensing there was something wrong when I did not report back, came bursting in. Joe Foley and Seán O'Driscoll, with revolvers drawn, took charge of Dalton. Con O'Dwyer, Peter O'Neill and I rushed upstairs where we expected to find the arms. It was so dark now that we could not find our way round; we had no matches, and flashlamps were unknown to us at that time. Then I thought of the table-lamp in the day-room, and ran down for it. We had lost a lot of time and though Jim McCarthy and my brother, Dave, were on the look-out, the others would be in on us at any moment. With the lamp, I passed by Joe, Seán, and the captive at the foot of the stairs, forgetting that I had given him a good chance of recognising them. With the aid of the lamp, we found the rifles, took them from the racks and rushed out into the darkness while Joe and Seán covered our retreat.[3]

It is difficult now to appreciate how electrifying the effect of this incident was in the Beara district, and how powerfully it boosted the morale of the Volunteers there who were being gradually prepared for more desperate engagements as the struggle developed. With the four rifles and the ammunition captured at Eyeries many more raids could be planned and attempted. Where these raids were successful the stock of arms and ammunition was increased, and made possible yet greater successes. Even where the raids failed they at least provided the Volunteers with valuable experience for the future campaign.

A few weeks after the raid on Eyeries Barracks, Charlie Hurley, Captain of the Castletownbere Company, assisted by Billy O'Neill, carried out a daring raid on a British patrol boat, *The Flying Fox*, which was stationed at the pier. Armed with revolvers, the two Volunteers boarded the boat, seized two rifles, and made off with them before the alarm was raised. But the rejoicing of the Volunteers was short-lived. It appeared that some of the crew of *The Flying Fox* were local men whose jobs were in jeopardy if the rifles were not returned. For this reason, the Canon at the local parish

3. I am indebted to Christy O'Connell for this account, and also for much of the information concerning the early history of the Volunteer activities in the Eyeries district.

church appealed to the raiders to restore the rifles, and the Volunteers reluctantly agreed to do so.

About the same time, a small group of unarmed Volunteers of the same Castletownbere Company under their intrepid Captain, Charlie Hurley, carried out another daring operation, this time an ambush on a party of armed military. Jeremiah McCarthy, a local Volunteer, observed three soldiers leaving the town and going in the direction of Furious Pier. He immediately alerted Charlie Hurley and Billy O'Neill. Thereupon the three Volunteers hastened to Rodeen Cross where they took up a concealed position in the narrow laneway near the main road, and waited for the soldiers to come along. It was still daylight and local people were passing by, but the Volunteers could not be seen from the main road. Presently the military appeared, and each Volunteer was assigned a soldier whom he was to overpower and disarm. The soldier assigned to Charlie was nearest in line as the trio approached the fatal crossroads. Ironically enough the song he was singing as Charlie jumped on him and brought him crashing to the ground was 'Johnny, get your Gun!' But this soldier was merely carrying a parcel, and was unarmed. The other two, however, were carrying rifles, and these were swiftly snatched from them by the Volunteers. Bearing their precious prize of two rifles with them the three Volunteers took off across the fields, and as they ran, Charlie Hurley remarked, 'There is no Canon with us today!'

Raid on the Barracks of the Royal Engineers at Bere Island, 5 June 1918

Eugene Dunne, an Intelligence Officer in the Adrigole Company, was also an employee of the Bantry Bay Steamship Company, acting as their shipping agent on Bere Island. For centuries, this island had been a heavily fortified fort guarding Bantry Bay, one of Britain's important naval bases. From the civilian storekeeper on the island, Dan Coughlan, Dunne learned that there was a large quantity of gun-cotton in the stores of the Royal Engineers on the island. In his weekly report at the Volunteer meeting of the Adrigole Company, Dunne gave particulars about the gun-cotton, and also suggested that it could possibly be captured. Immediately, a meeting was arranged with the Captain of the Bere Island Company, Con Lowney, and it was decided to raid the stores for the explosive.

The raid began at 12.30 a.m. on 5 June 1918. The store was situated about fifty yards from the barracks of the Royal Engineers, and Dunne was stationed on the look-out half-way between the store and the barracks. A duplicate key provided easy access to the store, where the raiders found fifty-two boxes, each containing fifty-six pounds of gun-cotton, primers, and detonators. Each box had to be conveyed by hand from the stores to the pier, a distance of two hundred and fifty yards, where they were loaded into Volunteer Tim Moriarty's boat. When the boat was loaded to capacity, there were still six boxes of gun-cotton, two coils of electric cable, and one large bag of black powder remaining over. Rather than leave this small balance of the spoils the raiders dumped them in an old store owned by John Houlihan which stood beside the pier. While the raid was in progress, Dunne heard foot-steps coming from the direction of the barracks towards the store. Passing the warning to the Volunteer on guard at the door of the store, he himself lay flat by the side of the road. It was a tense moment for him when he recognised Staff-Sergeant Herbert of the Royal Engineers coming straight towards him. Fortunately, the sergeant passed by without noticing anything amiss.

When everything was in readiness, the members of the crew who were drawn from the Bere Island Company, rowed the boat with its precious cargo across the harbour to Bunnow where Volunteers from the Companies of Adrigole and Rossmacowen were waiting with transport to convey the booty to a prepared dump in the Adrigole area. In charge of this latter operation were Acting Battalion Commander Michael Crowley and the Captain of the Castletownbere Company, Billy O'Neill. The cox of the boat was John Houlihan of Rerrin, and the importance of his task may be judged from the fact that there were several British destroyers and other vessels at anchor in the harbour that night, while searchlights frequently swept the water.

The importance of this capture of gun-cotton for the future campaign not merely in the Beara Peninsula, but throughout West Cork as a whole is hard to exaggerate. As a result of acquiring it the Volunteers were later encouraged to plan and carry out an ambitious series of attacks that had a decisive effect on the future course of the struggle. But we have to wait until the early months of 1920 before these developments can be seen to take shape.

Meanwhile, during the course of August 1918 the R.I.C. stationed at Eyeries attempted to arrest Con O'Dwyer, a Volunteer of the local Company, but they were obstructed by a group of Volunteers, and prevented from carrying out the arrest. As a result, a force of British military—the King's Own Yorkshire Light

Infantry—was moved into Eyeries before the end of August, and there commandeered a private house. Within a week of the arrival of this force, all the Volunteers involved in preventing Con O'Dwyer's arrest were taken into custody, and brought to Victoria Barracks in Cork City. There they were charged with obstructing the R.I.C. in the fulfilment of their duty, found guilty, and sentenced to eighteen months' imprisonment with hard labour. At the same time, the Captain of the Eyeries Company was charged with illegal drilling on St. Patrick's Day when he took charge of the Volunteers' parade that marched to Castletownbere. He was also found guilty, and sentenced to a term of imprisonment.

Undismayed by the imprisonment of some of their most dynamic comrades, the Volunteers in the Beara Peninsula continued to hold their normal parades and drilling exercises. In September, members of the Eyeries Company carried out an attack on an R.I.C. patrol in their area, while some members of the Inches Company devoted their attention to a military convoy operating between Castletownbere and Eyeries. The convoy consisted of a horse-drawn wagon bringing supplies from the town centre to the military garrison which had been stationed at Eyeries since the previous month. Every day at approximately the same hour the wagon made its way northwards towards Eyeries village with two armed soldiers in the wagon itself, and two armed officers walking some distance ahead.

On 26 September a party of four Inches Volunteers, each armed either with a rifle or revolver, lay in ambush on the sides of the road at Bealnalappa, and waited for the convoy. But as the wagon drew near the ambush position, a man driving a sow appeared on the scene, and the leader of the ambush party, Corney O'Sullivan, called the attack off that day. On the following day, the Volunteers were in position again, but this time two women put in an appearance at the critical moment, and again the ambush had to be postponed. On the third day, however, fortune favoured the patience of the Volunteers, and the road was clear as the wagon drew alongside the position. Immediately the Volunteers jumped up and ordered the soldiers to surrender. One of them made an attempt to resist, but thought better of it, and put up his hands. At that, one of the Volunteers climbed into the wagon and captured a Lee-Enfield rifle with a sling of .303 and a Webley revolver with its ammunition.

The Bealnalappa ambush was indeed a minor affair, but it prepared the way for greater ones. Indeed it was by an accumulation of painstaking and courageous efforts of this kind that the strength of the Battalion in the Beara Peninsula was gradually increased, arms were acquired, experience and confidence gained. From these small beginnings were to emerge the spectacular developments of 1920 which will be recorded in their proper place later in our narrative.

CHAPTER 5

THE BANTRY BATTALION

'The time has come to give up forming fours, and learn to shoot straight.' These were the closing words of a public speech delivered by Terence MacSwiney at Drimoleague in West Cork on the Saturday week before the Rising of Easter Week 1916. A group of fifteen Volunteers from Bantry had travelled the thirteen miles to the town in a horse-drawn wagonette that morning to attend the Volunteer rally. At a later committee meeting that evening Terence MacSwiney gave orders for a mobilisation on Easter Sunday.

Bantry folk had good reason to be responsive to Ireland's national aspiration towards freedom. For long their lovely bay had been exploited by the British, and made serve as a bastion to defend English domination in Ireland. A large military and naval base had been established there since the eighteenth century, and grim reminders of Britain's hated thraldom were everywhere in evidence. Two French expeditionary forces had endeavoured to land there at different times in the hope of furthering the Irish cause, but ill-fortune attended them both. The first of these sailed into the bay in 1689 but was engaged by the British fleet and was defeated. The second, which included Wolfe Tone, came in 1796 and was scattered by an untimely storm. Nevertheless, the spirit of resistance never left the air in Bantry, and in 1822 during the Tithe War a bloody battle was fought in the Pass of Keimaneigh.

In 1909 a branch of the Ancient Order of Hibernians (A.O.H.) —American Alliance—was founded in Bantry, and functioned as the most nationalist body in the town up to the time of the formation of the Irish Volunteers in December 1913. In fact, it was this local branch of the A.O.H. that introduced the Volunteer movement into Bantry, and supplied it with its first officers and with most of the fifty recruits who enrolled at the beginning.

During the winter of 1913 and the following spring, training exercises were conducted regularly in the Town Hall, with an ex-British soldier as instructor. No arms were available at the time, and the training consisted mainly of close order and extended order drill and marching. Numbers steadily increased and rose to a maximum of one hundred and fifty. Following the split in the Volunteer organisation caused by Redmond's unfortunate speech of 20 September 1914 there was a considerable dwindling in the ranks of the Volunteers in Bantry, and by the end of 1915 the strength of the Company had fallen to about twenty, and remained so up to Easter 1916.

On the fateful Easter Sunday of the Rising, the Bantry Company paraded after the first Mass, and then sixteen of them, in accordance with instructions, proceeded to Kealkil with a day's rations and whatever arms were available. There they were to join forces with the Ballingeary Company and await instructions from Seán O'Hegarty, a member of the Cork Brigade Executive who was to take charge. The Bantry Volunteers duly arrived in Kealkil, and there joined with the Ballingeary Company only to be dismissed a few hours later after some close order drill, and instructed to return to their respective areas. No members of the Bantry Company were arrested after the episode, but interest waned and numbers fell.

In the early months of 1917 the Irish Volunteers were reorganised in Bantry, a Battalion Commander was elected by popular vote, and in the same manner an entirely new staff of officers was chosen for the local Company. These latter were, Ralph Keyes, Captain, Robert Lynch, First Lieutenant, Michael Crowley, Second Lieutenant, Michael Harrington, Adjutant, and Jack O'Mahony, Quartermaster. The Company then became the 'A' Company of the Fourteenth Battalion, Cork Brigade. Immediately, the Company gained in strength. Young men in increasing numbers were attracted to the movement, and displayed a keen interest. Close order drill was practised in the Town Hall on three nights weekly, and when the days grew longer route marches were organised on weekday evenings. New Companies were formed at Glengarriff, Coomhola, and Kealkil.

A Petrol Strike in Bantry Bay and an Election Victory in Clare

About April 1917 a U.S. transport ship *en route* for England with a large quantity of petrol in metal drums was torpedoed off Mizen Head. Soon afterwards a considerable number of the drums were seen floating into Bantry Bay, and the fishermen from Whiddy Island, unknown to the British authorities, were quick to salvage them, and hide them safely on the shores of their island. Two months later, the Bantry Volunteers received an appeal from the Cork Sinn Féin Executive requesting that a supply of the petrol be transferred via Cork City to County Clare to help transport in a very important by-election there. Immediately, the local Volunteers set to work and succeeded in bringing a hundred gallons of the petrol from the shores of Whiddy Island by boat to a point on the mainland named Beach about two miles along the southern coast from Bantry. The oil had been brought in two-gallon cans, and these were now wrapped in potato stalks and packed in large sacks with some potatoes in the bottom and on top to serve as a camouflage. When the sacks were ready they were sent by rail to Cork. Little did the R.I.C. officers in Bantry suspect that the sacks of 'potatoes' being carried past their barracks by one of the local Volunteers were, in fact, sacks of petrol that would have their part to play in the historic victory that Eamon de Valera, the Sinn Féin candidate, was to win in East Clare over the popular and well-known Irish Party candidate, Patrick Lynch, K.C., on 11 July 1917.

On 7 October of the same year, an *aeraíocht* was held in a field at Newtown. There Michael Collins, the Countess Markievicz, and Gearóid O'Sullivan addressed a large gathering. The Countess appealed for recruits to form a branch of Fianna Éireann, and from the many who came forward nine were selected as having the required age. These formed the first branch of the Fianna in Bantry and indeed the only branch that was formed in the whole of West Crk, excepting Bandon. During the war years that followed, the boys of this unit proved to be a valuable adjunct to the fighting forces as scouts, dispatch-riders, and general helpers with intelligence and supply duties. Ernest Blythe, too, was in the area at this time, and cycled round with the Battalion Commander, Dan O'Mahony, and Company officers visiting the Companies at Kealkil, Coomhola, and Glengarriff. He then continued on his way to the Beara Peninsula where he did valuable work visiting already-existing Companies and organising new ones.

The conscription threat of 1918 had the same effect in Bantry as it had elsewhere throughout the country. It sent unprecedented numbers of young, and not so young, men flocking to the ranks of the Volunteers. In Bantry the ranks were swollen to such a degree that it became necessary to increase the number of sections that formed the Company there from four to seven. It was a strong Company in numbers, but not in arms; it had one hundred and seventy-seven members, but its arms consisted of but one rifle, and that a .22 miniature, eight revolvers, and about a dozen shotguns. To remedy a desperate situation the Volunteers had recourse to desperate measures.

In January 1918 the barytes mine at Derryganaugh was raided, and a quantity of gelignite, together with fuses and detonators, was taken. A primitive factory was next set up at Jack O'Donoghue's of Gurteenroe, and there hand-grenades of a sort were improvised. These were made by putting sticks of gelignite with fuses attached in tin canisters filled with pieces of scrap iron. One section of the Company actually began the manufacture of the traditional '98 pikes by attaching eight-foot ash handles to forged-iron heads. As in the old days these primitive weapons were made secretly at night by a local blacksmith. At the same time a number of loyalist houses were raided for shotguns. These activities helped to keep up the morale of the Volunteers, but something more was needed.

In February a section of Volunteers was mobilised to attack a troop train coming to Bantry, but the operation had to be abandoned for lack of firearms. Then in March, the Company Captain was informed by a Volunteer who was a clerk at Bantry Railway Station that a wagon had arrived from Cork with a case of rifles and a supply of provisions for the British military on Bere Island. The matter was immediately investigated, and it was found that two soldiers had been placed on guard at the railway station. Further investigations showed that the soldiers were there not to guard the wagon, but rather an eighteen-pounder field-gun that was to be drawn to Mizen Head in the hope of blowing a German submarine that was causing trouble there out of the water. Nevertheless, the soldiers' presence caused a problem as they were stationed only thirty yards from the wagon containing the case of rifles.

In order to keep the attention of the two soldiers directed elsewhere while the Volunteers were breaking the seal and opening the wagon, two members of Cumann na mBan were detailed to keep the soldiers in conversation. Everything went according to plan; the seal of the wagon was broken, and the door opened. But to the great disappointment of the Volunteers, the precious case of rifles was missing, though the provisions were there. Later it was discovered that the Cork City Volunteers had intercepted the case of rifles, and had commandeered them for their own use. It was obvious that Bantry was not the only place with an efficient intelligence organisation run by Volunteers. The only reward the Bantry Volunteers got for their efforts was denunciation by the authorities for the raiding of the wagon and the removal of the case of rifles. The Bantry Volunteers rather ruefully turned elsewhere in search of arms.

Volunteer Ropes exchanged for R.I.C. Guns

On 26 September 1918 a Fianna scout named Jack O'Mahony reported that two R.I.C. constables had left Bantry on bicycles and were proceeding towards Ballylickey; one of the constables was armed with a .303 rifle, and the other with a revolver. Thereupon the Battalion Commander, Dan O'Mahony, decided to organise an attack on the constables with a view to disarming them. So with eight other Volunteers he selected a suitable ambush position at the bottom of Caher Hill near Donemark Bridge, and waited for the constables. The Volunteers had no guns, but each of them was supplied with two lengths of rope about four feet long. One of the party carried a blackthorn stick with a good stout knob on it. They waited inside a gap in the fence.

Dusk was falling by the time the constables were heard approaching, but there was still light enough to see them clearly as they unsuspectingly free-wheeled down the hill towards the scene of lurking danger. As the first constable came within striking distance, John Begley led the attack by stepping out quickly and striking him on the back of the head with the blackthorn stick and brought him and his bicycle tumbling to the ground. Begley had scarcely time to step out of the way of the second constable, but he succeeded in doing so, and at the same time got in his second stroke with lightning speed and threw the constable across the road. Immediately the other Volunteers pinned their victims down. One of the constables managed to get a grip on his revolver, and was with difficulty prevented from drawing it from its holster. He refused to release his grip, with the result that the blackthorn stick had to be brought into service again; after a sharp rap on the back of his hand the constable quickly released his hold. The other constable had his rifle strapped to his bicycle, and he showed no resistance. Swiftly and deftly the disarmed constables were now bound hands and feet with the four-foot lengths of rope. This done, the jubilant party of Volunteers, bearing the coveted prize of the rifle and the revolver, hastily withdrew from the scene.[1]

This successful ambush without the use of firearms put new life into the Volunteers in Bantry. True, the prize was small enough, but what gave special significance to the action was the fact that it was the first in which arms were captured from Crown forces in the Battalion area. It suggested further possibilities, and led to further actions and to a gradual acquisition of arms that eventually made the West Cork Brigade one of the best armed and equipped brigades in the country.

1. Those who took part in this ambush were: Daniel O'Mahony, Ralph Keyes, John Begley, Michael Walsh, Willie Brennan, Thomas Breen, Richard McCarthy, Cecil Keyes, and John O'Sullivan.

CHAPTER 6

THE SKIBBEREEN BATTALION

It is a historical fact that on a market-day held in the town of Skibbereen on 12 September 1847 there was not a single loaf of bread or a pound of meal in the town. When the Commissariat officer was approached by members of the Relief Committee, and asked to sell or lend some meal from the Government depot he refused, and said that his instructions prevented his doing so. An angry scene followed.[1] This was quite a common occurrence up and down the country during the tragic period of the famine when our people were decimated by starvation and emigration. But Skibbereen became a byword because of the weekly descriptions of famine conditions there which appeared in the weekly *Illustrated London News* in the winter of 1846 and the spring of 1847.[2]

In Skibbereen the famine was looked upon as the symbol of the exploitation of the Irish nation by its British oppressors, and the influence it exerted in moulding the nationalist spirit of the townspeople is incalculable. Already in 1856 we find Jeremiah O'Donovan Rossa gathering a group of revolutionary-minded young men about him in the town and forming the Phoenix Society. Two years later we find this being absorbed almost entirely into the revolutionary I.R.B. movement, when James Stephens visited Skibbereen, and won O'Donovan Rossa to his movement by promising American arms and men to aid in an insurrection in Ireland, if sufficient Irish recruits could be enrolled for the task.[3] This was an important event in the history of the Fenian movement in Skibbereen, and marked the beginning of a powerful revolutionary tradition that continued into the present century, and eventually became incarnated in the Skibbereen Battalion of the West Cork Brigade. The spirit of O'Donovan Rossa remained alive, and could perhaps be best seen in another 'unrepentant Fenian' who served the cause of freedom in the Volunteer movement so well.

Neilus Connolly joined the Volunteers in Skibbereen in 1913, and regularly attended parades and took part in secret drilling exercises by night in fields remote from the town. The instructor was an ex-British army man named Vallon. At the time of the split

1. See Cecil Woodham-Smith, *The Great Hunger. Ireland 1845-49* (London, 1962), p. 124.
2. Cf. *The Great Famine. Studies in Irish History 1845-52*, edited by R. Dudley Edwards and T. Desmond Williams (Dublin, 1954), p. 232.
3. See Desmond Ryan, *The Fenian Chief* (Dublin, 1967), pp. 93-94.

in the Volunteers caused by John Redmond's Woodenbridge speech, Connolly was one of the thirty Volunteers in Skibbereen who broke away from the Redmond-controlled body of two hundred and fifty strong. Then, towards the end of 1915 he was one of six Volunteers who were sworn into the I.R.B. movement by Gearóid O'Sullivan. The Easter Rising was followed in Skibbereen by wholesale arrests with the result that the Volunteers who evaded the police went underground for some months. Despite this handicap, numbers steadily increased and drill parades were held once a week on Sundays in constantly-changing venues.

On 25 August 1917 Michael Collins and Count Plunkett paid a visit to Skibbereen and were given a most enthusiastic reception. The Volunteers paraded publicly in the town square that day for the first time since the Rising. Contingents came from Bantry and Clonakilty to join the Skibbereen Volunteers' parade and brought the total strength between officers and men to two hundred. On 11 December de Valera paid a visit to the town, and at Christmas Gearóid O'Sullivan arrived from G.H.Q. and presented the Company with a rifle and ten rounds of ammunition. This was kept in the care of Neilus Connolly and was used to train the men in loading and taking aim.

The pattern of events in 1918 was similar to that in other parts of West Cork. As elsewhere, the conscription threat sent big numbers flocking temporarily to the ranks of the Volunteers; as in other districts, the effort to provide arms for the men resulted in raids on loyalist houses to secure whatever shotguns were to be found. But most of the loyalists anticipated this development, and handed in whatever arms they had to the local R.I.C. before Volunteers organised the raids. The reaction to the raids on the part of the enemy was immediate. It was reported that Connolly had a rifle and ammunition. Secretly one night he was followed home from a parade, and was watched while he hid the rifle in a box which he concealed in a fence near his home. Next morning a party of R.I.C. men called to his home and arrested him, while two of them went straight to the concealed box and secured the rifle. Connolly was brought to Cork and there, together with nine other young men from Galbally, County Limerick, he was charged with subversive activities and the illegal possession of firearms. He for his part denied the authority of the court, and demanded that the rifle, which he argued was his personal property, should be restored to him. As could have been expected, his demand was ignored, and he found himself sentenced to two years' imprisonment. In view of its interest as part of the jail resistance movement that figured so significantly in the struggle for independence, we shall give here Neilus Connolly's own account of his experience in what are substantially his own words :

We were sent to Belfast Jail on 1 August 1918. There were already two hundred political prisoners there when we arrived, and as they were on strike because they were refused the treatment accorded to political prisoners the ten of us newcomers joined them. After 15 August, when the Proclamation was read at public meetings throughout the country, and a great number of Volunteers were arrested, we were joined by another hundred political prisoners. The prison diet was bad at the best of times, but because of our action we were put on *restraint diet*. There was a war on, and you can imagine what sympathy the higher officials had for our type. With the ending of the war on 11 November the internees were released, but the sentenced prisonrs were made complete their sentences.

On 1 December the dreaded 'flu struck the prison, and within a week most of the Irish Volunteers were victims. Some were critical and the prison chaplain asked that the cell doors be left open so that the prisoners could help each other. Most of the warders were also on the sick-list, and there was a general relaxation. The doctor in attendance did all he could to change the diet. Luckily we had no casualties and most of us were on our feet for Christmas.

The latest arrival was a young man from County Down named John Doran who had been tried for the possession of arms and was awaiting sentence. It was taken for granted that he would be treated as a convict. A council of war was held and it was decided to include this man among our party in our planned revolt. Christmas Eve fell on a Sunday that year, and after Mass we brought John Doran along with us, held up the warder, and taking his keys we opened the workshop and took all kinds of tools from it. We were in a three-tier ward with stairs leading up, and you would be surprised what havoc the sledges worked in a matter of one hour. We used the scrap metal to barricade the doors leading into our quarters. When there was no more to wreck inside, we demolished the slates and glass roof over the corridor. Through the apertures we could see military on the walls all round fully armed with machine guns.

We improvised a band the next day by collecting a few tin cans, spoons and a tin whistle, and had a merry Christmas. The one mistake we made was to throw off the slates from the roof of our ward as the rain poured in on us during the next seven days. This could have been very serious, but for the fact that we kept a roaring fire going day and night from the timber we broke from the doors.

On New Year's Eve a parley was held with Larry O'Neill, Lord Mayor of Dublin, Fionán Lynch, and Austin Stack (the last two were prisoners with us) on our side and the Governor of Belfast Jail, the Lord Mayor of Belfast on behalf of the Government. It was agreed that we would be transferred to an internee camp in Oldcastle, Co. Meath. So on New Year's Day we removed the barricades, and were treated to a meal of bread and milk. When we had finished the meal, we were locked into cells in another wing of the prison, and were kept in them day and night until St. Patrick's Day, when Father McAuley succeeded in getting permission for us to attend Mass.

When returning from Mass we arranged to knock all the cell doors off their hinges by placing the Bibles distributed to us between the doors and the jambs and then swinging the doors as far back as possible. Within minutes two hundred doors crashed to the ground, and within seconds the police were rushed in on us. We were made go to our cells, each of us accompanied by a policeman, while about one hundred more police were in the yard outside. To give the warders their due, they never exceeded their duty, and several of them took risks on our behalf.

On 30 April ten of us, including Fionán Lynch and Austin Stack, were removed to Strangeways Jail in Manchester. We were handcuffed and each of us was guarded by two policemen as we made our way to the boat. When we were a few miles out to sea our handcuffs were removed, and we were allowed to talk to each other. The police offered us some of their rations, so there was no ill-feeling between us. On the following morning we landed at a fishing port called Fleetwood, about thirty or forty miles north of Manchester. We were handcuffed for about an hour before the boat berthed. From the boat we were transferred to a railway carriage with drawn blinds on the windows, and conveyed non-stop to Manchester. There as we crossed from the train to the jail wagon a tremendous cheer went up from the railway porters as soon as they recognised the policemen's uniforms. I dare say that as we were a desperate lot, without a shave or haircut since the previous Christmas, our clothes in tatters with vermin *go leor* (in abundance), the railway men could not have recognised us as Irish.

In our conversation during the night it was agreed that we would continue the strike, and indeed start a hunger-strike, if we were not treated as political prisoners. Once the jail wagon reached the prison yard, we were relieved of our handcuffs by the policemen. Then the police officer in charge of us handed a paper to the governor, and when he had signed it the officer disappeared.

A warder then called us to attention, but we paid no attention to him. It was at this point that Fionán Lynch told the governor that we were determined to continue the strike, even a hunger-strike, if our demands were refused. The governor made no reply, but a score of warders forced us into cells on the ground floor. As soon as the doors were locked, we broke the stools, and with the broken pieces we were able to break the glass in the windows of our cells as they were only about three feet off the floor. No sooner had we broken the windows than a crowd of warders rushed in and put us in handcuffs again. Then the governor came to Fionán Lynch's cell and told him that he could not grant concessions but that he would make known our demands to the Home Office. At seven o'clock that evening, Fionán was called to the governor's office and was informed that our demands had been granted; we were allowed out of our cells six hours per day; were permitted to receive letters and write one letter per week subject to censorship by the prison office; and also to receive parcels from home. We were then put in a separate part of the prison and had no contact with the other prisoners except on Sundays. We were given clean clothes, had a hair-cut and shave, and then looked like civilians again. Shortly afterwards we learned through correspondence that our ordeal in Belfast Jail had created a problem for our captors as the press gave it publicity.

We no sooner entered the exercise yard of the prison than we counted the bricks on the wall, and thereby calculated that it was thirty-six feet high, and we observed that there was only one door leading in and out of the prison. After a while we got liberty to play handball, and took Irish lessons from Fionán Lynch. Fionán had fought in Easter Week, and had been in and out of prison since his release from penal servitude in 1917. He had only a few months more of his prison sentence in Strangeways Jail to serve and was due to be released in September.

Michael Collins paid us a visit in June together with Arthur Griffith. The two had come over to England to see de Valera off to the United States. Of course, they came under assumed names as Collins was a much-wanted man then. Shortly afterwards we were joined by two new prisoners, namely Piaras Beaslai and D. P. Walsh, both of whom had been sentenced to long terms of imprisonment.

Fionán Lynch duly left us in September, and when he got back to Dublin began to arrange for our rescue. In the event this was delayed considerably because of the fact that one of our party was a heavy fat old man who would have been unable to climb the ladder. It was for this reason that we waited for his release before making the attempt.

The date chosen was 25 October, and the reason for the choice was that it was a Saturday. On other days of the week we had two warders to guard us, but on Saturday evenings only one. It was decided to stage the attempt at 5.00 p.m. Three blasts on a whistle would be given by the rescue party outside. Then one of our group would give three hearty cheers where we were playing handball, after which we were to go into action.

As soon as the signals were given two prisoners and I jumped on the warder, handcuffed him with his own handcuffs, tied his feet with a strip of torn sheet, and put a bandage around his mouth. We then carried him into one of the cells and locked him in. Beaslai put little pebbles into the keyholes so that keys could not work in them.

A barbed-wire entanglement faced us at the bottom of the wall we selected for scaling, but Austin Stack made a ladder of bed-boards and with this we were able to get over the entanglement and also over the live wire on top of it. When we got into position we were shocked to hear the leading line with a weight attached to it hitting the wall as the man outside failed to throw it over, but to our delight a young man suddenly appeared on top of the wall and threw the line down to us. It was none other than Peadar Clancy, Vice-

Commandant of the Dublin Brigade, who, we learned after-wards, had been sent over to take charge of the rescue bid. In a matter of minutes, the rope ladder attached to the line was drawn to us. This ladder was made of new hard rope, and as we had to keep a firm grip, it tore flesh off our hands. Once over the wall and down on the other side, Beaslai, Stack, and Walsh got away by car. With two others I was directed across a disused field to a laneway, and there a young man gave each of us a bicycle and told us that a guide was waiting at the other end of the street to take charge of us.

I was the first to reach the end of the street, but the guide there allowed me to pass as he was expecting to meet three cyclists. When the other two came along they were allowed to pass also. I soon found myself in the midst of traffic and lost sight of my two pals, but I kept going from street to street thinking I would see an Irish name on a shop-door. There was a great deal of traffic in the streets between tram-cars, hackney horses and people, so that I found it hard enough to keep going.

Two hours passed and I was still circling round the streets. Then I thought I heard the word 'Strangeways' being shouted by the news-boys. It was the stop-press usually published when anything unusual happens. The only word I under-stood was 'Strangeways'. I got off the bicycle, and asked a man going to, or coming from, work where the nearest chapel was. I knew that he was a working-man as he had his lunch in a red cloth on his forearm. He told me that he was going in the direction of the chapel, so I walked along with him. We both went into the chapel together, and I thought I would see an Irish name over one of the confession boxes, but I did not see either box or name as the confessions were heard in another part of the building. On leaving the chapel I asked the stranger where the presbytery was and he told me that the chapel, presbytery and school were combined in one building.[4] I asked him who the parish priest was and he replied that his name was Father Cassidy. 'And that's his door,' he said, pointing his hand in the direction of a house close by. I knocked, and the maid told me that Father Cassidy was hearing confessions, and that she would let him

4. The name of this chapel was St. Patrick's, Livesey Street.

know I had called. With that she left me in a room close by.

In a few minutes the door opened and a fine big, old priest appeared. When he saw the blood on my hands he knew what kind of character I was. He was a very old man, over seventy, and got a little excited. I explained that six of us had got out of Strangeways Jail. 'Impossible,' he said, 'I spent six years there as a chaplain ... stay where you are.' He went out. In a few minutes I heard a strong, firm step coming. The door opened a few inches, and a young priest peeped in. He saluted in Irish, 'Dia dhuit!' I answered, 'Dia's Muire dhuit-se.' He rushed in at the same time saying, 'How in the name of God did ye get out? Where are the other five?' I told him what I had done. Then he bandaged my hands, and told me that I would be safe down in the engine-room that was heating the whole building, but that the rats would worry me. He left, and in a few minutes was back with a *taoscán* [small quantity] from a bottle of wine. He led the way down, and showed me a safe place, and asked me for the love of God to keep awake, as he had to go back to hear confessions. He returned to the engine-room a little after ten o'clock with a mug of tea, bread and butter. Having had a long chat he told me that Father Cassidy got a fright when he saw the blood.

It was midnight when Father O'Sullivan left, and before leaving he said that he would be down again before six in the morning. The rats were there in dozens, ugly-looking things, as all the hair was burned off their backs from running under the hot pipes. They did not try to attack, but they did not seem afraid, as they would come near and stare with their green glassy eyes.

At six in the morning Father O'Sullivan came to see me as he dreaded the rats, if I went to sleep. He went to his early Mass, and was back again at seven. We went to Father O'Sullivan's room and had breakfast. After breakfast I saw a violin case on a shelf, and asked him to play a few tunes. Having played a few he handed the fiddle to me. I was playing when in walked Father Cassidy with a paper in his hand. It was the stop-press of the evening before. He looked at Father O'Sullivan and then looked at me. 'I cannot understand the youth of today,' he said, and added, 'Do either of you think of your position? Nero playing and Rome burning!' I replied that I was very sorry that I gave him such a fright the previous night. 'Have you seen this?,' he asked, handing me the stop-press. 'I'm glad ye used no violence on the warder. What do you intend to do now?' 'Get back to Skibbereen,' I said, 'if I can.' 'I could get you to America,' he said. 'No thank you, Father,' I said, 'I'll try Skibbereen.' He shook hands with me and said, 'Good luck, and God be with you.' At that he took his leave. Then Father O'Sullivan said, 'When my morning work is over, I'll go to the club and I might get some account of the other five. I dare not go to Paddy O'Donoghue's as his house is being watched today.' Paddy was another Kerryman. He was in charge in Manchester.

When Father O'Sullivan returned, he had a full account of the adventures of the others. They were all well, and the six of us were to meet at Paddy O'Meara's that night at seven o'clock. There we had a royal time till midnight. The O'Meara's were Tipperary people. It was at their house that I heard the tale of my two pals who got separated from me when we cycled away from the jail.

The two had cycled about the streets of Manchester very much as I had done. They were going everywhere and nowhere, and were almost in despair. One of them had a sister in the nuns in Manchester.[5] He had the address of the convent, but did not know where it was. It was almost nine o'clock when he said to his companion that he would ask the first person they met where the convent was. They had not long to wait when a lady came along cycling. When she was asked where the convent was, she said that it was at the other side of the city. 'Ye are two of the men that escaped,' she said. 'We are,' they replied. 'Lucky that we met. I'm Talty from County Clare, and I'll do all I can to help.'[6] She told them to get on their bicycles, and to follow her at a distance of ten or twelve yards. She led them to safety and reported to the club.

5. The name of this Volunteer was Paddy McCarthy of Meelin, Newmarket, a leading North Cork fighter who played an important part in the capture of Mallow Military Barracks. A short time afterwards he fell in action in a fight at Millstreet, County Cork. For an account of these actions, cf. Florence O'Donoghue, *No Other Law* (Dublin, 1954), pp. 99-100, 104. The Volunteer who accompanied Paddy McCarthy in Manchester was John Doran from County Down.

6. Miss Kathleen Talty, a retired teacher, died in Kilkee, October 1972. She was a close friend of de Valera whom she helped to escape from Lincoln Jail in 1919. She was a teacher in Manchester at the time.

With one of my companions I remained in Manchester for seventeen days, and was brought around a great deal of the city. We were shown the Fenian arch where the attack on the prison van took place in 1867. We even went to the pictures in the daytime. We had a grand time.

When we left Manchester, we went to Liverpool, and stayed there for five days before arrangements were made by Neil Kerr to get us to Dublin in the hold of a Guinness boat hidden among the empty barrels. When we arrived in Dublin, Joe O'Reilly was waiting for us with a car, and brought us to Batt O'Connor's house in Donnybrook where we met Mick Collins and lots of other men of our type.

I arrived in Cork with a note from Mick Collins addressed to a Miss O'Brien of the West Cork Bar in Parnell Place. I walked in, and called for a lemonade. There were about ten R.I.C. men drinking at the bar. I gave Miss O'Brien the note when I was paying for the lemonade. She read it and told me that my tea was ready, pointing to a room nearby. The Cork Sessions were on at the time and that was the reason for all the police being around.

Florrie O'Donoghue, Adjutant of the Cork Brigade, called at noon, and told me that he would have a bicycle for me at four o'clock, and that we would cycle to Waterfall to meet the train for Skibbereen. When we arrived there Florrie brought my bicycle into the station to have it sent in the luggage van to Skibbereen, and then got me a ticket. When the train came in, Florrie took a stroll around to see if everything was safe. Then he came back and told me that there were a dozen R.I.C. men in the back carriages. So I got into a front one, and travelled with a number of the cattle-buyers who were going to Bantry fair.

There was a change at Drimoleague for Skibbereen, and when I got on the Skibbereen platform there I saw one of my old pals with a bull-dog on a lead, and he talking to an R.I.C. men. He was very much under the influence of drink, and as I was getting into the train he saluted me by my Christian name. I felt very unhappy, and when the whistle blew as the train entered Madore station, I opened the door and jumped clear of the embankment to freedom.

* * * * * *

Such is the story of Neilus Connolly's part in the prison resistance campaign. While serving to illustrate an important aspect of the struggle for independence, it shows also the calibre of the men who belonged to the Skibbereen Battalion. As the work of reorganisation later developed among the Volunteers of West Cork, I had very close relations with the officers of the Skibbereen Battalion, particularly with those outstanding officers, Sam Kingston and Pat O'Driscoll, and had personal experience of their loyalty and courage at all times. The area in which they operated was a very difficult one. The Volunteers were constantly threatened by the presence of the King's Liverpool Regiment which had its headquarters in the town, and there was also the menace of the strong force of R.I.C. men garrisoned in the local barracks. Besides, apathy was a debilitating influence in the area, and vigorous opposition was another. This latter was given virulent expression in the columns of *The Skibbereen Eagle*. This weekly newspaper spared no efforts in denigrating the Volunteers, and in castigating them as 'Wild West Hooligans'. It hurled criticism after criticism at every activity of what was a national movement until in the end the Volunteers were provoked to take drastic action. Some members of the local Company seized the editor of the newspaper, and, within thirty yards of the R.I.C. barracks, tarred him. For this distinction he claimed damages, and in a British Court he was awarded five hundred pounds by his imperial masters. In spite of difficulties of this kind the Battalion played an outstanding role in the developing struggle not only in its own area, but throughout the Brigade area. This will be seen more clearly as our story unfolds.

CHAPTER 7

THE DUNMANWAY AND CLONAKILTY BATTALIONS

The Sam Maguire Cup is not merely the well-known trophy presented each year to the victors of the All-Ireland Football Final: it is a historic monument to a great Protestant patriot from the Dunmanway district and to the services he rendered to his country.[1]

Long before Sam Maguire was born at Mallabracka near Dunmanway, the Fenian tradition there was strong. Colonel Rickard O'Sullivan Burke, one of the outstanding pioneers of the Fenian movement and the organiser of the escape of Colonel Kelly and Captain Timothy Deasy from the jail van in Manchester in 1867, came from the district.[2] Then in 1889 seven young men from the parish of Dunmanway, Pat Aherne, Dan McCarthy, John O'Brien of Girlough, and four others, were sworn into the I.R.B., and worked to keep the revolutionary spirit alive in the area.

Even as a boy Sam Maguire gave evidence of that nationalist bent that was such a powerful force throughout his life. He first became connected with the G.A.A. as a schoolboy, became an outstanding footballer, and played for London G.A.A. in three All-Ireland Finals, namely in 1900, 1902 and 1903. On leaving school he qualified for a position in the British Civil Service and was appointed to the London Post Office. In London he was soon prominent in Irish circles, graduating through the G.A.A. and the Gaelic League to the ranks of the I.R.B. Some years later, he met Michael Collins who had followed in Sam's footsteps to a position in the London Post Office. There he recruited Collins into the I.R.B. movement, and communicated something of his own spirit to his young disciple. As the struggle for independence developed at home, Sam became Chief Intelligence Officer of the Volunteer

1. This large silver cup is wrought to the design of the Ardagh Chalice, and is an outstanding example of Irish craftsmanship. One of Sam Maguire's intimate friends, Jerome Hurley of Shanacrane East, who figured prominently in the vital years of 1919 and 1920 in the building up of the Dunmanway Battalion, suggested to a few I.R.B. friends in Dublin the idea of having a perpetual memorial of Sam Maguire. With the funds subscribed the cup was commissioned, and presented to the Central Council of the G.A.A. It was first at stake as the trophy for the All-Ireland Football Final in 1928, the year after Sam Maguire's death.

2. He was born in Kinneigh, near Dunmanway, in 1838. For an account of his life, see John Devoy, *Recollection of an Irish Rebel* (New York, 1929), pp. 347-52; *Devoy's Post Bag 1871-1928*, edited by William O'Brien and Desmond Ryan (Dublin, 1948), pp. 35-36.

movement in England, and controlled all the major Volunteer and
I.R.A. operations in the country. He was a born underground
resistance leader and, like Collins in Dublin, broke through all
barriers of the British Intelligence to obtain and transmit vital
information to the Volunteers in Ireland. Frequently he travelled
to Dublin for meetings with Collins. In the end British Intelligence
became suspicious, and inquiries began to circulate to all police
stations and intelligence centres in England to trace the mysterious
'S.M.' Sam was soon tipped off that Scotland Yard was hot on his
trail. Thereupon he abruptly took his leave of London and returned
to Ireland where he died in February 1927.[3]

In the Dunmanway district there were many young men in the
mould of Sam Maguire when the Volunteer movement began to
develop there in 1914. Units were formed in Dunmanway itself, at
Behagh and at Ballinacarriga.[4] As could be expected, the sons of
the Dunmanway men who took the Fenian oath in 1889 were to
the fore, and when the Dunmanway Battalion was formed we find
Con Aherne, son of the Fenian Pat Aherne, being elected Commandant, Michael McCarthy, son of the Fenian Dan McCarthy
(Cooper) as Vice-Commandant, and Paddy O'Brien, son of the
Fenian John O'Brien of Girlough, being elected Adjutant.

In the mobilisation orders for the 1916 Rising the three Companies of Dunmanway, Behagh, and Ballinacarriga were instructed
to join forces with the Company of Lyre (Clonakilty) and march to
Inchigeela on Easter Sunday. A short parade was conducted there
after which the Volunteers were ordered to return to their homes,
and to await further instructions. The Dunmanway Company
remained on the alert all during Easter Week until news of the
surrender in Dublin came on the Saturday. With that news came
the sad report of the death in action of a local Volunteer, Seán
Hurley of Maulagow.

The Companies of Dunmanway, Behagh, and Ballinacarriga
were very active during the reorganisation that took place in 1917,
and they prepared the way for the ten new Companies that were
soon to spring into life in the Battalion area.[5] The importance of

3. He was buried in the Church of Ireland cemetery in Dunmanway. A
Celtic cross was erected over his grave by the people of Dunmanway and
his numerous friends throughout Ireland and England in recognition of
his services to his country.

4. Also spelt: Ballynacarriga and Bealanacarriga.

5. These Companies were founded at Togher, Aultagh, Coppeen,
Kenneigh, Ballineen, Shanavagh, Enniskean, Clubhouse, Knockbue and
Kilbarry.

the Dunmanway Battalion in the developing struggle must be emphasised. Due to its central position in the West Cork region, due also to the mountainy nature of its terrain and the protection it offered against attacks, this Battalion area was obviously an ideal location for a headquarters to control Volunteer activities in West Cork. Indeed when the West Cork Brigade was later formed, its council meetings were almost invariably held in this area, and during the closing months of the war, the Brigade Headquarters was almost permanently quartered there. Again, as a safe retreat for men 'on the run' and for the wounded and for those who needed rest, the Dunmanway area was invaluable, and its officers and men, besides their outstanding service in the various military engagements of the war, never failed in their tasks of scouting, dispatch-riding, intelligence or guard duties. The role of the Battalion in the coming fight was truly a noble and generous one, and worthy of the strong Fenian tradition that had for long matured among the patriotic men of Dunmanway and its mountainy environs.

The Clonakilty Battalion

If to Dunmanway goes the merit of producing Sam Maguire, to Clonakilty redounds the glory of producing Michael Collins. Indeed, if Clonakilty made no other contribution to the War of Independence, its name would be forever illustrious in the pages of Irish history, I mean, by reason of its association with his name.[6]

But Clonakilty did more than provide one of the greatest leaders of our national struggle for independence : it also gave a strong and vigorous Battalion to the West Cork Brigade, and it can rightly lay claim to glory by this title also. It is with the rise and early growth of that Battalion that we are concerned here.

On Easter Sunday morning, 1916, a small party of Volunteers left a hamlet called Lyre, four miles north-east of Clonakilty *en route* for Inchigeela, a village on the river Lee over twenty miles away. It was the first Company of the Volunteers to be founded in the Clonakilty area—in 1914—and it was on its way to take part

6. For accounts of the life and work of Michael Collins, see Piaras Beaslai, *Michael Collins and the Making of a New Ireland* (Dublin, 1926); Batt O'Connor, *With Michael Collins in the Fight for Irish Freedom* (London, 1929); Frank O'Connor, *The Big Fellow* (London, 1937); Rex Taylor, *Michael Collins* (London, 1958); Eoin Neeson, *The Life and Death of Michael Collins* (Cork, 1968); Margery Forester, *Michael Collins—The Lost Leader* (London, 1971).

in the Rising. Uniting with units from Dunmanway, Behagh, and Ballinacarriga, it marched to Inchigeela only to be dismissed after a short parade, and ordered to return home.

The disappointment of this episode and the apparent failure of the Rising were followed in 1917 by a remarkable development which was in itself evidence that the Rising was not a failure after all. The revolutionary spirit revived and spread rapidly. It was aided very particularly by an event that roused nationalist feelings in an unwonted manner, namely, the demonstration of welcome organised in Clonakilty in honour of Con O'Donovan of Casheliskey on his release from captivity in June 1917. O'Donovan had fought in Dublin during Easter Week, and had been sentenced to a term of penal servitude. Now he had been released after one year's imprisonment and was returning as a hero.

The effect on young and old was tremendous. The town went wild with excitement, and nationalist spirit was roused to a peak of intensity. Volunteer units from outlying areas marched to the town, and paraded for the occasion. The Countess Markievicz spoke and made a profound impression. The Clonakilty Company was the largest unit to parade that day, and it continued to be so till the Truce. But it was not merely great in numbers; it was also outstanding for its spirit and for the quality of its Volunteers. It provided some of the finest fighters of the Brigade.

As the year 1917 progressed Volunteer Companies multiplied in the Clonakilty area and sprang up in Ahiohill, Ring, Shannonvale, Kilmeen, Reenascreena, Rosscarbery, Kilkernmore (Milltown), and Ardfield. Towards the end of the year, these, together with the Lyre and Clonakilty Companies, coalesced into the Clonakilty Battalion under the command of Big Jim Walsh. The usual drilling exercises were performed, but the usual dearth of arms and ammunition made target practice an impossibility. Thus, two rifles, half a dozen shotguns, and a few revolvers constituted the total armament of the Clonakilty Company during the year 1917.

When in 1918 the British Government threatened to enforce conscription in Ireland, the membership of the Companies of the Battalion witnessed an unprecedented increase. The Clonakilty Company, for example, increased from forty members to one hundred and fifty. But when the conscription threat passed the numbers fell to fifty. Several raids for arms were carried out, and yielded a number of shotguns. Then, a group of Volunteers were engaged in the manufacture of home-made bombs and buckshot at Clogheen.

The Clonakilty Battalion area was small by comparison with the others in the West Cork Brigade, and though the strength of the Clonakilty Company was particularly high, the total membership of the Battalion was low. Yet what it lacked in quantity, it made up for in quality, and its contribution to the overall achievements of the Brigade was inestimable.

CHAPTER 8

THE BRIGADE IS ORGANISED. ACTION AT RATHCLARIN

Reorganisation was the main preoccupation of the Volunteer leaders in Cork during the opening months of 1919. Up to this there was only one brigade in the whole of Cork County, including the city, but it had become obvious to Tomás MacCurtain, the Commanding Officer of the Brigade, and his staff that the Brigade area was geographically too extensive and difficult, and the Volunteer units too numerous to be effectively administered by one Brigade staff. A division of the Brigade was seen to be imperative and the matter was discussed at G.H.Q. between October and December 1918. It was then decided, in agreement with Tomás MacCurtain and his staff, to dissolve the original Cork Brigade, and in its stead to create three new ones; it was further decided to put this arrangement into effect early in the new year.

The areas allotted to the new brigades were as follows : Cork Number One, commanded by Tomás MacCurtain, was to embrace Cork City and Mid-Cork, i.e. a strip of territory enclosed approximately by the watershed of the river Lee and extending westwards to the Kerry mountains, and East Cork; Cork Number Two, under Liam Lynch, was to include North and North-East Cork; while Cork Number Three, under Tom Hales, was to extend from Innishannon in the East to the Beara Peninsula in the West. The precise boundaries of Cork Number Three Brigade were the Bandon river from the Old Head of Kinsale to a point one mile north of Kilgobbin Castle; then a line turning eastwards across the Bandon river and embracing the united parishes of Innishannon and Knockavilla to Begley's Forge, two miles south of Killumney, then continuing in a westward course on a high ridge one mile south of both Crookstown and Kilmichael to the southern exit of the Pass of Keimaneigh. Thereafter the line continued to the Kerry border along the Coomhola-Kilgarvan road and followed the border to its end between Lauragh and Ardgroom.

On 5 January 1919 a meeting of staff officers representing the six Battalions that then existed in West Cork was held at Kilnadur, near Dunmanway, to inaugurate the Third Cork Brigade. Michael Collins representing G.H.Q., Dublin, presided at the meeting, and Tomás MacCurtain with his Adjutant, Florence O'Donoghue, was also present. The six Battalions which formed the new Brigade were Bandon (First), Clonakilty (Second), Dunmanway (Third),

Skibbereen (Fourth), Bantry (Fifth), and Castletownbere (6th); and the Brigade Staff Officers elected were Tom Hales, O/C., Hugh Thornton, Vice-O/C., Michael McCarthy, Adjutant, Denis O'Shea, Quartermaster, and Denis O'Connell, Intelligence Officer. It was at this stage that the history of the Volunteer movement in West Cork became the history of the Third Cork Brigade or, as it was more-popularly called, the West Cork Brigade.

With the inauguration of the new Brigade in West Cork came a new wave of enthusiasm, and with it an urge to intensify recruit-ment, to improve the performance of the companies, to reorganise the system of communications and to promote intensive training. An immediate result was the decision to hold a meeting of the West Cork Brigade officers—the first since the inaugural meeting of 5 January—at Rossmore on Sunday, 2 March, and the venue chosen was the house of Mike O'Donoghue of Fearlehanes. As Seán Hales, O/C. of the Bandon Battalion, was unable to attend, I was appointed to represent him, and on the Sunday morning of the meeting set off by bicycle with Tom Hales, O/C. of the Brigade. We travelled by Ballinascarty to Knockea, where we were joined by Jim Walsh, O/C. of the Second (Clonakilty) Battalion, who was to guide us to the venue of the meeting. When we reached a point within a quarter of a mile from Rossmore village, we were stopped by Tim O'Donoghue, who was Captain of the Kilmeen Company, and told that information about our proposed meeting had been betrayed to the R.I.C. As a result, a number of police officers had taken up positions approaching the house where we were to meet, and were ready to take action as soon as Volunteer officers arriving for the meeting appeared. To avoid this eventuality Tim had posted scouts on all routes leading to the house to warn the Volun-teers from the other Battalions to avoid Mike O'Donoghue's home, and to meet at Ballinvard Castle near Rossmore instead. There the group assembled and thence were guided to Tim O'Donoghue's house half a mile away at Ballinvard. It was there that the Brigade meeting was held, while the R.I.C. remained stolidly on duty below at the other O'Donoghue's house all the day long.

The deliberations of that meeting were important. Here it was decided to review the system of communications, to investigate the numerical strength of the units that constituted the Brigade, and above all to intensify training.

The System of Communications

Basically, the system of communications that had been taking shape in the West Cork area during the years 1917 and 1918 was simple. Each Company appointed one or more dispatch-riders— the number depended on the strength of the Company—to carry messages to and fro between Companies, and between Companies and Battalion Headquarters. This enabled the Battalion Comman- der to keep himself informed of developments in each Company of his area, and to communicate instructions to it, his own, those of the Brigade Staff, and those coming from G.H.Q. In his turn, the Captain of each Company could communicate all instructions received to his men at the weekly or bi-weekly parades.

As the dispatch-riders were normally boys or young men earning their livelihood by working during the day, military messages which were not of a very urgent nature were always transmitted by night. Though the task of the dispatch-rider was no easy one—it involved the risk of arrest, and could frequently be made more onerous by the inclemency of the weather or the unreliability of the bicycle provided as the only alternative mode of transport to Shank's mare—it had considerable appeal for the dedicated Volunteer. In those days the possibility of travel for the average youth in West Cork was very limited. Rarely did he have the opportunity to travel outside his parish, and apart from the weekly visit to the local village church for Mass on Sundays, and an occasional visit to the next or second next townland, he normally had to stay in the vicinity of his homestead. As a dispatch-rider, on the other hand, he was taken into entirely new areas, into what was for him the unknown, and each successive trip brought him new acquain- tances and new adventures. Besides, as a regular dispatch-rider he was always sure of being provided with a bicycle, if he had none, and could always look forward to the hospitality which almost invariably awaited him at his journey's end. In all, the work of the dispatch-rider was an attractive one at the time, offering excite- ment, variety, and a certain element of danger, with a sense of doing something that was important for the progress of the nati- onal cause. These factors had their part to play in sustaining the enthusiasm of our dispatch-riders, and of ensuring among them a high standard of efficiency.

To put the decisions made at the previous Brigade meeting concerning the review of the communications system into effect, a carefully-elaborated network was gradualy evolved in 1919 and altered where necessary during the changing conditions of the subsequent years. The men responsible for laying the foundations were, the Brigade Vice-Commandant, Hugh Thornton, and three officers of the Bandon Battalion, namely, Denis Lordan, Vice-Commandant, Flor Begley, Quartermaster, and myself, Adjutant—all under the direction of the Brigade O/C, Tom Hales.

The framework we laid down was a simple one, but nevertheless, proved capable of being adapted to changing conditions, and of bearing the great strain that was later to be imposed on it as the war developed. Wherever a more or less direct line of Companies existed between an outpost and headquarters, say at Bandon, dispatches were made flow from Company to Company, each of which had the responsibility of carrying them to the next Company in the line till the message reached its destination. Thus in the Bandon Battalion area, messages coming from Company areas south of the river Bandon were brought from Barryroe to Timoleague, then to Clogagh, and finally to the town of Bandon. On the north side, messages flowed either from Newcestown to Mount Pleasant (Farnivane), and then to Bandon, or from Crosspound via Kilpatrick to the town. The remaining Companies of Kilbrittain, Ballinadee, Innishannon, and Bandon brought their messages directly to Battalion Headquarters and vice versa.

In the wider context of the Brigade area, the chief difficulty so far as communications was concerned was that of distance. At a time when the quickest means of transport normally available was a bicycle, and when roads were so badly surfaced as to make cycling a real hardship, the distances could be formidable. Thus between Innishannon on the east side of the Brigade area and Allihies in the west was a distance of eighty miles, while that between Battalion centres at Bandon and Castletownbere was more than sixty.

Another difficulty arose from the fact that the average Volunteer at the time had little or no knowledge of places outside the town centre or district in which he lived. For a person living in Bandon in those days Bantry or Skibbereen seemed very far away, and not many knew the way. As for Castletownbere, it could have been in a different county so few in Bandon knew anything about it.

Bandon had automatically become the new Brigade Headquarters when the Brigade was established, possibly because the Brigade O/C resided in the district, or because the town had long been regarded as 'the gateway to the West'. At any rate, as the Bandon district grew in importance Frank Hurley's of Laragh (three miles north of the town) became Brigade Headquarters and remained so until well into 1920.

To test the inter-Battalion system of communications, two officers of the Bandon Battalion, Denis Lordan and Flor Begley, were commissioned by the Brigade Commander to conduct a trial run to all six Battalions. The immediate object of the test was to investigate the manning of the routes of communication, to determine the call-houses, and to ensure that confidential dispatch-riders would be known to all Battalion H.Q. staffs. With these objectives in mind, the two Volunteer officers appointed decided in May to set out on their tour. Starting one evening from Bandon, they proceeded to Dunmanway (Third Battalion), and then continued via Drimoleague to Bantry (Fifth Battalion). From Bantry they went to Glengarriff, to Castletownbere (Sixth Battalion), and returned by steamer to Bantry. Next they cycled to Skibbereen (Fourth Battalion), visited Clonakilty (Second Battalion), and then returned to Bandon. The test proved satisfactory, and the whole journey was completed in approximately forty-eight hours.

The inter-Battalion lines of communication were now planned and put into operation as follows : Bandon to Clonakilty, Lyre and Skibbereen; Bandon to Dunmanway, Drimoleague and Bantry; Bantry to Castletownbere. Normally the main roads were used and negotiated by bicycle, but when the enemy became more active in 1920 and 1921 by-roads were used. Throughout the very active period of the struggle the principal line of communication passed from the First Battalion area at Newcestown through the Third to the Fifth Battalion at Kealkil via Coppeen, Aultagh, Togher, and Derrynacaheragh.[1] The journey from Bantry to Castletownbere was exceptional in that it was usually made by passenger steamer, and this because friendly members of the crew facilitated Volunteers in their activities. Nevertheless, road links via Glengarriff and Adrigole were also used.

Communications with G.H.Q. in Dublin involved special problems, and called for special methods. Road lines were out of the question both because of the long distance, and the risk of arrest. But the railways offered possibilities which were exploited to the full. Volunteers and others who sympathised with our cause among the railway personnel—guards, checkers, engine-drivers, and firemen—played an important role in keeping the lines of communi-

1. Communications along this line were so efficiently maintained that during the entire period of the war no message ever failed to reach its destination in time. Credit for this achievement redounds to the Third Battalion Staff. Seán Murphy, O/C, Sonny Dave Crowley, Vice-O/C, Paddy O'Brien, Adjutant, Mike O'Dwyer, Quartermaster, and the Company Captains, Jeremiah O'Mahony (Coppeen), and after his death Phil Chambers, Jim Crowley (Aultagh), Jim Burke (Togher), Tim Hurley (Derryna-caheragh), and John Wrynne (Kealkil).

cation between G.H.Q. and Cork City open, and also between Cork City and Bandon through the main railway line that passed through Bandon and continued on to Bantry and Baltimore.

Besides using the railways, we also had recourse to the postal service as a means of communication, particularly between G.H.Q. in Dublin and Brigade Headquarters at Bandon. To reduce risk in this case we employed what we knew as 'the covering-address system'. This involved having postal dispatches addressed to persons who were in no way suspected by the authorities. Thus, for example, the address of James O'Donovan, Mill Road, Bandon, was used throughout the struggle till the Truce and never came under suspicion. As a method of communication this 'covering-address system' proved very effective and safe.

Numerical Strength of Volunteer Units in the Brigade

Durng the course of the Brigade meeting held at Ballinvard near Rossmore, I had been commissioned to investigate the strength of each Volunteer unit in the Brigade area, and in the ensuing months I carried out this task. By the following July I had a report prepared, and although it was not entirely complete, it served to give a picture of the situation so far as the numerical strength of our units was concerned. Leaving aside details, and concentrating on the over-all figures for each Battalion, the following were the results : Bandon Battalion had 478 members on the rolls of whom 290 were active; Clonakilty had 265 with 145 active; Dunmanway had 276;[2] Skibbereen had 150 with 108 active; Bantry 154 with 107 active; and Beara had 261.[3] This gave a total roll membership of 1,584 for the Brigade, with approximately 1,000 who were considered active. It is interesting to compare these figures with those showing the numerical strength of the opposing enemy forces at the same period. These show approximately 1,000 British soldiers and 232 R.I.C. men stationed at various posts throughout the Brigade area.[4]

Action at Rathclarin

By 1919 the Company of Kilbrittain comprised a force of about eighty men, including officers, and had reached a high standard

2. The number of active members in the Dunmanway Battalion was not recorded, and neither were those of the Skibbereen and Beara Battalions.

3. Appendix A gives details of membership for each Battalion of the Brigade.

4. Appendix B gives details concerning the disposition of enemy personnel in the different areas of West Cork.

of organisation. Despite police vigilance, raids, and arrests, a training programme of twice-weekly parades had been maintained,
and a creditable state of efficiency reached in so far as this was
possible with the few available weapons. Raids on local loyalist
house for arms had yielded five miniature rifles, for which there was
no ammunition, three obsolete revolvers and about a dozen shotguns.

During the early months of 1919 timber was being felled on the
lands of Kilbrittain Castle, and was being exported from Burren
Pier in Courtmacsherry Bay about three miles away. Agrarian and
labour troubles developed, and some Volunteers employed by a
firm which had recently acquired the Castle and its lands were
dismissed. Thereafter a reduced export trade in timber was carried
on under police protection.

In May the local police force, housed in a strong isolated building in Kilbrittain village, was reinforced by a party of military,
sixty to eighty strong, billeted at the Castle about a thousand yards
from the police barracks and in telephonic communication with it.
With the police acting as guides, this military party became very
active. Cyclist squads patrolled the district in the daytime and
parties on foot moved about at night. They paid particular attention to the roads leading to, and in the vicinity of, the homes of
the most active Volunteers, all of whom were, of course, well known
to the police.

These movements were kept under close scrutiny by the Company of Volunteers, and soon it was noted that there was a regular
night patrol going to Burren Pier, usually leaving the post at
Kilbrittain Castle towards nightfall and returning to it at 3.00 or
4.00 a.m. The patrol normally consisted of five soldiers under an
N.C.O. and one policeman, the soldiers being armed with rifles and
the policeman with a revolver. It was decided to attempt the disarming of this patrol on its return from Burren Pier, and Rathclarin was the point selected for the operation.

The night of 16 June saw fourteen Volunteers leaving their
homes, and moving unobserved across the fields to the rendezvous
at Rathclarin. Only two of them were armed, one with a shotgun,
the other with a revolver. As the military patrol to be attacked
sometimes moved in extended order, the two armed Volunteers
were placed well out on either flank to prevent any member of the
patrol in the front or rear making his escape when the attack
began. In effect, what had been planned was an attack with their
bare hands by twelve men on six trained and alert armed oppon-
ents. It was a very dark night. Eight Volunteers waited silently in

the cover of the hedges at the point where a laneway providing a short cut to Kilbrittain joined the road. On the opposite side of the road, outside the fence, the remaining six were posted. None of the Volunteers had any cover from fire. They relied entirely on the element of surprise and the strength of their hands, but they well knew that the greatest risk of failure lay in the possibility that the patrol might be moving in extended order or that some member of the patrol might straggle behind the others. For the unarmed Volunteers a simultaneous attack on all six members of the patrol was essential to a quick success.

It was after midnight when the tensely-waiting Volunteers heard the footsteps of the approaching party. Within a few feet of them the leading members of it stopped, and the voice of the policeman was heard asking, 'Which way will we go? Will we take the short cut?' So far as could be seen in the darkness there were only four men in the group, but in the few seconds they took to decide on their route the two remaining soldiers who had fallen a little behind came along. And then the Volunteers pounced on them. In a short and fierce struggle the policeman and four of the soldiers were disarmed. The remaining soldier broke loose for a moment and struck a Volunteer named Mick O'Neill two vicious blows on the head with the butt of his rifle. But he too was soon overpowered by the injured O'Neill and disarmed. One soldier was slightly wounded. All of them were bound with ropes, and an armed Volunteer was placed on guard by them till the rest of the plans were put into operation.

Three things now remained to be done immediately. The captured arms, namely five rifles and one revolver with two hundred rounds of ammunition and equipment had to be taken to a place of safety without a moment's delay; the men participating in the ambush had to get back to their houses some three or four miles across country before the police and military started the inevitable raids on the homes of the Volunteers in the Kilbrittain area; and finally, Mick O'Neill, who had been seriously wounded, had to be taken to a place of safety for medical treatment immediately.

Jeremiah O'Neill of Maryborough, a brother of the wounded Volunteer, procured a horse and trap, and accompanied by Con Crowley, who acted as armed guard, and by his own sister, Maud, who was a member of Cumann na mBan,[5] brought the semi-

5. Cumann na mBan, literally Society of Women, was the women's auxiliary of the Volunteers which was founded in Dublin in April 1914.

conscious Mick to a house near Ballineen, fourteen miles away. There Dr Eugene Fehilly of Ballineen, one of the few medical men in the area who was trusted by the Volunteers, dressed Mick's wounds, and continued to attend him till he recovered completely. It was this same Dr Fehilly who in 1918 attended Michael Crowley after his being seriously wounded in the chest during the raid on the house of a well-known loyalist at Ahiohill in quest of arms.

The captured arms, ammunition and equipment were hurriedly taken to Burren schoolhouse, and concealed in a drain there. Immediately afterwards the Volunteers, with the exception, of course, of Mick O'Neill and Con Crowley, made for their homes as quickly as possible, and got into bed. Within a half hour of their return the police and military were on their doorsteps.

It transpired that one of the ambushed patrol had succeeded in freeing himself shortly after the armed Volunteer guard had left, and he released the others. When the patrol reached the police barracks they telephoned the military and raised the alarm. Immediately, both police and military were turned out to raid the houses of suspects in Kilbrittain. So closely had the R.I.C. kept the Kilbrittain Company under observation that they made a very shrewd guess as to the men likely to have carried out the ambush, and they made directly for their homes. Fortunately, all the Volunteers, other than Mick and Jeremiah O'Neill, and Con Crowley, were in their beds when the police and military raids took place, and every shred of incriminating evidence had been hidden. In every house visited the Volunteers were stripped and examined closely for wounds or injuries. Their clothing was minutely examined for blood stains. By good fortune, this latter examination had been anticipated, so that all blood-stained garments were hidden away, and other articles of clothing substituted for them before the Volunteers had gone to bed. Deprived of the slightest clue, the raiders were unable to make any arrests. Naturally O'Neill and Crowley had to remain on the run after the ambush. Endless

---

The movement was launched in Cork City on June 8 of the same year. During the course of 1916, Miss Daisy Walsh of Kilbrogan Hill, Bandon, whose brother Paddy took part in the Easter Rising, helped to organise the Cumann in the Bandon district. Branches soon spread through the Brigade area. It would be impossible to extol sufficiently the contribution made by this heroic body of women to the national cause.

searches were made for them by the R.I.C. and military, and in their searches they were always looking for a man with a scar.[6]

* * * * * *

To appreciate fully the significance of the Rathclarin ambush on 16 June 1919 the time and local circumstances must be borne in mind, as well as the general national situation as it affected the Volunteer organisation. At such an early date, the Volunteers were still in the process of consolidating their movement after the not-unexpected defection of many of those brought into the ranks merely because of the conscription scare. The Volunteers who remained formed a smaller but more steadfast and determined body of young men for whom the accepted duty of fighting for national freedom was a hard reality. They were realistic and practical : they saw clearly that after organisation, discipline, and training, their greatest need was arms, and that to acquire them no other source was available than the enemy forces of occupation.

The Executive of the Volunteers in Dublin at this time was directing a nation-wide organisation that was very uneven in its development and without a firm, corporate outlook on its task and purpose. It was understandably hesitant about committing its poorly-armed force to a conflict that seemed very likely to spell disaster. A view of the role of the Volunteer movement at the time which had considerable support even in the ranks was that it would be most effective as a threat, and that any attempt at fighting in its almost unarmed condition could lead only to defeat and to the destruction of the nation's last shield against foreign aggression. Because of the policy of the Volunteer Executive at the time, the Brigade Commander could not give official sanction to the proposed action of the Kilbrittain Company, but the men of that Company, in whose minds an idea for the development of the struggle was germinating, decided to seize the opportunity they saw of gaining possession of some modern arms.

At this time too a distinction was beginning to emerge between

6. The men engaged in the Rathclarin ambush were, James and John O'Mahony, Denis and Daniel Manning, Patrick and David O'Sullivan, Patrick and Con Crowley, Mick and Jackie O'Neill (five sets of brothers), John Fitzgerald, John O'Leary, Tim Holland, and Jeremiah O'Neill of Knockpogue—all from the parish of Kilbrittain. Denis (Sonny) Crowley of Kilbrittain, who did scout duty between his native village and Rathclarin, should also be mentioned.

the view taken of attacks made on R.I.C. men and those made on soldiers of the British army. Prior to June 1919 the attacks that had taken place were directed mainly against the R.I.C. Some of these had occurred in the West Cork area, for example at Eyeries and Donemark, and others had taken place outside Cork County, for example at Camp and Gortalea in Kerry, at Soloheadbeg in Co. Tipperary and especially at Knocklong in Co. Limerick. In contrast, attacks on British army personnel had been very rare, and it is this fact among others that gives a particular significance to Rathclarin. The ambush was a deliberately-planned effort—and one of the earliest at that—to disarm a party of British troops. Then, the fact that it was completely successful had an immense effect on morale and on the whole direction of the Volunteer military effort in West Cork. It was a model of good planning and resolute execution, and demonstrated in a most-convincing way the ability of guerilla forces of intelligence and courage to maintain the initiative even against armed troops. During the period between 1917 and mid-1919 the Volunteer movement was slowly emerging from a state of flux and uncertainty as to its function and method. Rathclarin indicated decisively the way to follow.

* * * * * *

Meanwhile at Battalion H.Q., elation at the success of Rathclarin was followed by concern for the fate of the gallant Mick O'Neill. We were anxious to know whether he would survive the blows of the rifle butt he received on the head, and if he survived, what his chances were of evading capture by the enemy. Two days passed and the only news we received was that Mick had been given medical treatment, and had been moved from Ballineen to Behagh, three miles north-east of Dunmanway. The Commanding Officer of the Brigade, Tom Hales, discussed the matter with his staff, and it was decided that Flor Begley and I should make inquiries.

The following day, Thursday, being the half-day in Bandon was a day when most of the workers moved out of town; and so it was possible for Flor and me to set off by bicycle in search of Mick O'Neill's whereabouts without rousing suspicion. To throw possible spies off our tracks we left the main Dunmanway road at Palace Anne, eight miles out from Bandon, and went to Castletown. Thereafter we lost our way among the hills for a time, but eventually found the home of the Behagh Company Captain, Tom

O'Donovan. There to our pleasant surprise we learned that Mick
was in the house next door. We were shown to the bedroom, and
found our hero with his head swathed in bandages sitting up in
bed. He was unable to speak but the laughing eyes of the man
spoke more eloquently to us than words. We felt that he was out of
danger so far as his wounds were concerned, and with the reliable
Con Crowley, who was remaining with him, we knew he was safe.
We remained until one o'clock the following morning, and then
left for Bandon. Both Flor and I were due back for work in the
town at eight o'clock, and it would have been dangerous not to
put in an appearance on time.

On the return journey we joined the main Dunmanway-Bandon
road at Manch, and continued on our way towards Bandon. As
day was dawning, we suddenly ran into a big convoy of military
lorries parked in the square in front of Bandon military barracks
with armed soldiers on guard. It was too late to retreat so we had
no option but to continue on our way and hope to be allowed pass
unchallenged. In the event we were permitted to pass. Later we
learned that the convoy was being organised to fine-comb the
Kilbrittain district with a view to finding the man we had left in
the safety of the mountains and in the care of his friends at Behagh.

CHAPTER 9

GLANDORE TRAINING CAMP

After the successful engagement at Rathclarin, the possibility of conducting guerilla warfare against the enemy on a more extensive scale suggested itself to our minds, and the need of a proper course of training in guerilla tactics with such a possibility in view then seemed to be urgent. This, of course, was not the first time that the question of training appeared as a pressing necessity. Already at the Brigade Council meeting held at Rossmore in March a decision was made to promote more-intensive training throughout the Brigade. Further attention had been focussed on the subject as a result of the trial organising tour undertaken by Denis Lordan and Flor Begley. These men had returned with the report that the matter of training was uppermost in the minds of all the responsible officers in the Brigade, and that the organisation of some kind of training course was to be recommended. It was pointed out that besides serving the immediate need of training, such a course would also serve to bring the most active Volunteers from the different districts together, enable them to become acquainted with each other, and to profit by a mutual exchange of ideas and experience. The upshot was that the Brigade Commandant put the matter before G.H.Q. towards the end of June 1919.

The response was rapid. G.H.Q. sent the Adjutant General, Gearóid O'Sullivan, and the Director of Organisation, Diarmuid O'Hegarty, to a special Brigade Council meeting which was held at Hurley's of Laragh, Bandon, on 13 July. At this meeting it was decided to organise a Brigade training course in a camp to be set up at Shorecliffe House, Glandore, in the following August. G.H.Q. offered the services of Dick McKee, then Director of Training at G.H.Q., and also Commandant of the Dublin Brigade. As there was no possibility of carrying our project through without the knowledge of the R.I.C. who would immediately break it up once they had information about it, it was decided to hold the Training Course concurrently with the annual Gaelic League Irish Course for National Teachers held in Shorecliffe House, and make this latter serve as a temporary cover for it.

On Saturday, 9 August, thirty-five Battalion and Company officers, and potential officers representing the six Battalions of the Brigade took to their bicycles, and headed for Glandore in order to be there for the opening of the week's course at 6.00 p.m. For almost all the men this was the first over-night venture from home, and it held an element of excitement and anticipation. They were young men whose ages ranged from sixteen to twenty-five, and they thought little of the long cycle ride—sixty-five miles in the case of Liam O'Dwyer who came from Eyeries—that was necessary to take them to the camp. Each man had been instructed to come prepared to spend the week under canvas, and to bring a ground-sheet, a blanket, and a change of shirt and socks.

For my part, I had been looking forward to the camp with great enthusiasm, and had arranged to take my annual week's leave during the week of the Training Course. So on the sunny afternoon of the opening day I set off in high spirits with my gay comrades from Bandon, Newcestown, and Crosspound to cover the twenty-five miles journey to Glandore. Waiting for us at Ballinscarthy were the officers from Kilbrittain and Clogagh; and at Curragh, two miles west of Clonakilty, were the two officers from Barryroe who completed the Bandon Battalion unit of eleven that had been selected for the course. We continued on our way in a joyful, care-free, holiday spirit, and the warm bright sunshine matched our mood. Soon we caught a glimpse of the sea to the south. Glandore and the week's excitement were near. Presently, we found ourselves at Shorecliffe House admiring its truly beautiful setting. There was the house in its own grounds fronted by a two-acre lawn that was adorned with clumps of rhododendron bushes of various sizes. Southwards from the house could be seen Glandore Harbour and beyond it the strikingly-picturesque coast that dips into the Atlantic. What a setting for an exciting holiday!

But we no sooner found ourselves on parade that evening at Glandore than we were quickly jolted into another mood. One glance at the stern military countenance and bearing of Dick McKee as he stood in front of our ranks was enough to dispel our holiday mood, and that even before he opened his mouth. A ten-minute introductory talk from him on the week's programme, on the necessity of punctuality, and on our duties sufficed to set the tone for serious work. 'Absorb the instructions you will get in all grades,' warned McKee, 'and be prepared to impart the information in your own way to your fellow students when called upon to do so during the week ahead.' This warning certainly polarised our attention, for we knew that McKee would put his words into effect, and that to avoid humiliation we would have to learn our lessons thoroughly. Then came half an hour's close order drill, interrupted many times by sprints at the double, and this vigorous exercise left us so exhausted that when it was over even our food ration was not as welcome to us—and we were hungry—as the rest that eased our aching muscles. After our evening meal, which consisted of the ration of bread we had brought with us for the day, and tea which was prepared in a large urn, we were subjected to another hour of close order drill. Finally, a brief talk in which the schedule for the next day, Sunday, was outlined brought the day's activities to a close. It was 10.30 p.m. and we were exhausted. We lay down on the ground in our billets, and knew no more till we were called at 7.30 the following morning.

Sunday was to prove even more exacting than the previous evening. It began in the early morning after breakfast with a parade in the grounds at nine o'clock and a two-mile trek to Leap for Sunday Mass. We marched there openly in formation, and as we approached the church we came under the observation of two local R.I.C. men, who hastily withdrew upon seeing us to report our presence at their barracks. When we emerged later from the church, we found that four members of the R.I.C. had taken up positions outside the gate, and they scrutinised us closely as we lined up in front of them. They were obviously trying to identify us, and judging by the expressions on their faces they were finding it difficult to do so. Of the thirty-five of us they could recognise only the three who belonged to the immediate neighbourhood. For our part, we formed a column without delay and marched off in the direction of Glandore Camp. It was then that the excitement really began among the policemen. The sergeant and a constable made haste to report us to the District Inspector at Skibbereen, eight miles away, and then conference after conference took place to discuss the action to take to scotch our unlawful enterprise.

Back in camp we were given an hour's instruction on tactics, and this was followed by practical exercises in extended order movements, first at the double and then while crawling. In the case of this latter form of the exercises we were obliged to traverse several fields to the north and east of the camp. They appeared small fields in area on the average, but the task of crawling through them on all fours, made them seem like endless prairies. A short break at midday brought a welcome rest and a much-needed meal. During the long, sunbaked afternoon we repeated the exercises of the morning and continued without a break until seven o'clock in the evening. Footsore and weary in every limb, we made our way to the seaside, and there enjoyed a refreshing swim and a well-earned rest as evening fell on the sea and on the lovely shores of the village of Union Hall on the opposite side of the bay.

Monday brought a change in the training-programme. Many of us were called upon in turn—as we had been warned we would—to apply the knowledge we had gained on the two preceding days by standing in front of our comrades, and putting them through the various training exercises. Though this would normally have been an exceedingly embarrassing task for any of us, as none of us knew more than his comrades at the time, in the circumstances of the camp it was a welcome change from the marathon activities of the previous day.

The next day, Tuesday, was devoted to lessons in signalling and scouting given by Leo Henderson, Assistant Director of Communications, and practical instructions in engineering given by Tom McMahon, Assistant Director of Engineering. Henderson and McMahon were, like Dick McKee, experienced officers who had been sent by G.H.Q. to help conduct the training course. It should be mentioned that Gearóid O'Sullivan was also present both to keep an eye on the course and to give a series of lectures on the Irish language to the teacher students in Shorecliffe House.

From the Sunday morning when we had come under the notice of the police in Leap, constabulary activity in the area had been more than usually intense. It reached its climax at 5.00 a.m. on Wednesday the 13th when the stern voice of the law disturbed our slumbers and roared, 'Wake up, dress and come outside. You are surrounded by His Majesty's forces.'

We were neither shocked nor surprised; indeed we had been prepared for such an eventuality. McKee, anticipating a raid of the kind, had instructed the leader of each Battalion unit to marshal the men under him according to whatever instructions the R.I.C. or military might give. He intimated that when the men were paraded on the lawn he would take over and speak on behalf of the entire body. By six o'clock we had emerged from our billets and slowly prepared to take our place, as we were instructed, on the lawn. To our surprise we found all the occupants of Shorecliffe House together with the G.H.Q. officers who were in residence there had already been made prisoners, and were obliged to parade on the lawn in front of the house. A glance sufficed to show that we were surrounded by a ring of steel : armed military and R.I.C. men held all the vantage points. Without delay a party of police directed by a Sergeant Mulhern, an efficient and ruthless intelligence officer of the R.I.C. barracks at Skibbereen, interrogated each prisoner and carried out a careful search of his person and belongings. It was slow work, and was still in progress three hours later when an unexpected diversion occurred that roused our flagging spirits.

A few soldiers had been prowling round the outskirts of the lawn when one of them suddenly shouted, 'Hi, Sarge, there's another bloke here,' and he pointed to a pair of hobnailed boots projecting from the cover of a rhododendron bush. Two soldiers grabbed the boots, and unceremoniously pulled their owner into the sunlight. The new prisoner was none other than the well-known writer and teacher of Irish, Pádraic Ó Conaire who had been sleeping peacefully under the bush during all the commotion.[1] He had arrived on foot the previous night with the intention of helping at the Irish Language Course. Evidently, he had wandered into the grounds of Shorecliffe House when all were sound asleep, and rather than disturb anyone either in the house or camp, he had settled down to sleep under the rhododendron bush. As soon as the comical, diminutive figure was extricated from the shrubbery he was recognised by his friends, and a loud cheer went up from them. Thereafter pandemonium reigned, and despite all Mulhern's efforts the hilarious confusion continued during the remaining two hours of the search. By 12.30 p.m. even Mulhern had enough of it and prepared to depart. Taking with them four prisoners on whose persons had been found either incriminating documents or some rounds of ammunition, the military and police withdrew in the direction of Leap. The prisoners taken were Gearóid O'Sullivan, Adjutant General, J. Barney O'Driscoll, a former O/C of Skibbereen Battalion, Seán Murphy, O/C of Dunmanway Battalion, and Denny O'Brien of the Newcestown Company. The four were subsequently sentenced to several months' imprisonment.

It was now close to 1.00 p.m. and we were still without breakfast. Worse still, the search party had roughly handled our cooking equipment and had put it out of commission, so that we were now without the resources necessary for preparing a meal. Fortunately, the teacher students who had been staying at guest-houses in and around Glandore had come as usual that morning to Shorecliffe House for their Irish classes, and they had been watching the morning drama from the other side of the ring of steel. They now quickly came to our rescue, and brought us in groups to the guest-

1. Pádraic was a native of Galway where he was born in 1881. To sleep in the open was a common enough occurrence with him during his travels. Indeed it may have been one of the causes of his early death. He died in Dublin in 1928.

houses in which they were staying, and had us served a very much appreciated meal. Subsequently, we learned that in many cases the teachers had generously deprived themselves of their own midday meal in order to supply our needs. Subsequently, too, we found that the friendships we formed that afternoon with a number of the student-teachers became very close and stood the test of time. In all, the enemy raid, despite its many inconveniences, had not been without its compensations.

It was late afternoon before Commandant McKee succeeded in assembling us again. He observed that the enemy raid had cost us an entire day's training, and explained the likelihood of another raid and further interruption of the training schedule if we remained in Shorecliffe House. It was necessary to move camp to another position, preferably to a site with a vacant house in its vicinity. Pat O'Driscoll of Myross, the only Volunteer present with an accurate knowledge of the locality, was consulted as to the possibilities. He knew of but one vacant house in the area, and that one was locally reputed to be haunted. McKee had no objection to the sinister repute of the house, and once he had satisfied himself as to its size and location decided that we should move into it under cover of darkness, sleep the night there on our ground sheets, and be prepared to follow the prearranged programme the next day.

Breakfast the following morning presented no problem, because two mechanically-minded Volunteers, Stephen O'Neill and John 'Flyer' Nyhan of Clonakilty, with the help of a local blacksmith, had repaired our cooking urn the evening before, and with it was made the necessary tea. Our training programme followed on time, and was continued through the day without interruption. Towards evening, however, news came to us that the R.I.C. at Leap had located our new site, and that they had reported it; military and police from Skibbereen had surveyed the immediate neighbourhood during the late afternoon, and all signs indicated that a raid on 'the haunted house' would very likely be made during the night.

Another rapid decision was made by our Commander, Dick McKee. He announced that we would move camp again that night, this time to a pre-selected point in Connonagh Wood a short distance away. The reason for the choice was that from this position dominating the main Skibbereen-Clonakilty road it would be possible to observe enemy movements on the road below without being seen. McKee informed us that there was one factor influencing his decision and that was his determination to complete the week's training programme, as far as possible, and to end the course at the time and date pre-arranged, namely 3.00 p.m. on Friday, 15 August. So, as darkness fell, we moved quietly through the fields to Connonagh Wood, leaving our bicycles and cooking equipment behind till the next day. Once among the trees, we took up a position about two hundred yards east from the Leap end of the wood. We were ordered not to smoke lest the lights should betray our position to the enemy. Then we were commanded to lie down on our ground sheets in a selected area and to sleep under our blanket or coat until we were called the following morning. The response was immediate. We had experienced two successive nights of disturbed rest, and all of us felt thoroughly exhausted.

But Dick McKee did not lie down. Instead he took up a standing position leaning against one of the fir trees, watching the road below, and remained thus throughout the night. I was sitting near him on a tuft of heather I had prepared as bedding for the night, and after some time I suggested that he should rest and get some sleep. Quietly he replied, 'No, I would prefer it this way,' and he remained as he was till dawn. I was profoundly affected by the example of this iron-willed man. Though he had been actively engaged for six days in conducting an intensive course of training in the most trying conditions, there he stood throughout the night with his back to a tree guarding his men. It was an incident I have never forgotten, and the memory of it served as an inspiration during many a difficult moment in the later campaign.

Friday was 15 August and a Holyday of Obligation. Early in the morning our Commander moved the camp back to Glandore. There we were ferried across the harbour in two rowing boats to Union Hall village for Mass, as there was no church in Glandore at the time. After Mass we returned by boat and assembled on a hill north of Glandore for a meal, and a final parade. Dick McKee made an eloquent address in which he summed up the week's work, and then dismissed us without further ceremony. Thereupon we collected our equipment and bicycles, cast a parting glance over the beauty of Glandore, heaved a half-nostalgic sigh, and headed in various directions for our homes.

* * * * * *

What was achieved at Glandore Camp? An incalculable amount every way. Indeed it was already possible to see some of the results of the course even before its end in the changed bearing of the men, in their spirit of discipline, and the quiet determination with which they performed the various exercises. They had learned a great deal in the lessons on drilling, scouting, signalling and the general tactics of guerilla warfare. Above all, they had acquired confidence in their own ability to lead and train others, they were fired with a new enthusiasm for their work as officers, and they gained a clearer consciousness of their responsibility in regard to their own Companies and Battalions. They were also made keenly aware of the fact that the coming struggle—that it was coming soon was now beyond all doubt in their minds—was not going to be an isolated and disorganised effort, as so many previous efforts had been. It was going to have behind it a nation-wide network of units well-trained and organised to launch the final offensive against the age-old enemy of our country. With reason we could regard ourselves as fortunate in having a man of Dick McKee's calibre to train us at this decisive juncture in the history of the West Cork Brigade, and we always felt that we owed a debt of gratitude to him and his colleagues for the herculean efforts they put forth at the Glandore Training Camp.

On the day after the camp was disbanded, a special Brigade Council meeting was convened at Caheragh, Drimoleague. Michael Collins presided and Dick McKee attended in order to give his report on the week's work at Glandore, and to make a number of recommendations. Then Michael Collins quickly drew up a comprehensive scheme for the reorganisation of personnel in the Brigade, and several new appointments were made. As I was not present at the meeting, I knew nothing about its transactions until the following day when Tom Hales informed me that I had been appointed Brigade Adjutant to replace Michael McCarthy who had been sent as Acting O/C to the Dunmanway Battalion.

I accepted my new appointment with mixed feelings. For a young man of twenty-three the post presented a big challenge, and I had no illusions about the difficulties that lay ahead for responsible Volunteer officers. I was indeed human enough to feel a little proud of the confidence placed in me by my superior officers, but I was not so sure that I would not serve the Volunteer cause better in the midst of comrades who had by this become as close to me as were my brothers. I doubted whether I could acquire the same degree of topographical knowledge, and form the same solid friendships in the wider area of the Brigade in the short time that I felt was left before the days of battle came. These doubts were uppermost in my mind during the weeks that followed. I could not shake them off or see my way clearly. Meanwhile I carried out all the administrative duties of my new post as best I could until 18 September when the enemy helped me to resolve my doubts and come to a clear decision.

CHAPTER 10

'ON THE RUN'

A clash with the R.I.C. and military in Bandon on 2 September put me on the wrong side of the law : a Volunteer parade in which I was conspicuous had been held in the town that day, and had marched with a display of arms despite the ban prohibiting it. A repetition of this kind of activity on the following Sunday under similar circumstances did nothing to improve my position in the eyes of the upholders of law and order in the land. Add to these incidents the fact that only a matter of weeks earlier I had been found by Sergeant Mulhern in the thick of the subversive activities of Glandore, and it is easy to visualise how imminent was my disappearance behind bars in Cork Jail or in some prison further removed from my native West Cork. Worse was to follow. On 16 September a party of R.I.C. raided the building in which I was working, and surprised me in the act of writing our instructions for one of the Battalions of the Brigade.

At this early period there was some sense of justice left in the upholders of the law. R.I.C. officers were obliged to prepare warrants and read them to supposed lawbreakers before taking them into custody. Fortunately for me, arrests were not necessarily part of the raids made by the R.I.C. They usually waited a few days before serving a warrant on the evidence obtained from a raid. Rather than risk what now seemed inevitable arrest I decided to go 'on the run' two days later, on 18 September 1919.

Life 'on the run' was considered very difficult and trying by many of my comrades, particularly those who had to flee in order to avoid arrest after the Rising of 1916. My own experience was not one of unrelieved difficulty and hardship. From the day I was forced to leave Bandon and my employment, I enjoyed the challenge of the life and the adventures it brought; I had extensive Volunteer organising work to do in the Brigade area, and this kept me fully occupied in activities which I found congenial.

The fact that I had lost my employment, and was without an income caused me no worries. Perhaps this was due to the fact that I was not the spending type and that I never had much money for spending in any case. My personal needs over and above food and clothing were few, and were supplied in some way or another by kind friends in the various districts I had occasion to visit to do my work. Thus, for example, I was rarely without a fill of tobacco for my pipe from the plug of some acquaintance, and even the bicycle I was now obliged to use more frequently and for longer distances than before, was kept in reasonably good repair by generous friends who supplied a tyre or tube whenever it became necessary. Normally I was not entirely penniless, because either my mother and one or two friends would slip half a crown into my pocket on the occasion of my cautious visits home. During the two years of my wanderings I was never flush, but neither was I ever hindered from getting through my programme of work for want of money

Nevertheless, life 'on the run' was not something that came naturally to me. I had not anticipated it, and had given no thought to the problems it entailed. In fact, it was only gradually that I became aware of the conditions involved in this way of life. First and foremost among the problems was that of 'asking' or perhaps, 'begging' would be a more appropriate word. I knew there was no need to beg at the houses of friends where one was known, and this was a factor that made it easier to be 'on the run' in one's own locality than in a strange district. But I could not remain in the vicinity of Bandon : my work as Brigade Adjutant required that I should range extensively over the whole Brigade area at least as far westwards as Glengarriff, and in that September of 1919 I was almost a complete stranger in a strange land once I crossed the boundaries of the Bandon Battalion area. However, my first week 'on the run' was spent among friends, so that I was only gradually introduced to the conditions of my new existence. I was considerably encouraged as a result and helped to face with equanimity the rigours of the long winter months that approached.

When I left Bandon, I made my way to the Clonakilty district in search of Tom Hales, Brigade O/C, who, I knew, was threshing corn somewhere west of the town. To avoid an undesired encounter with any urban members of the R.I.C. to whom I would be known, I made my way via Gaggin, Ballinascarty and Shannonvale, and joined Tom Hales and his threshing party on the main road at Lissavaird. They were moving to Rosscarbery, and I was there and then 'hired' as one of the helpers. During the ensuing days I spent my time happily on Tom's threshing machine as we moved to different farms in the area, and eventually returned to Rosscarbery. On the day following our return to the town my suspicions were roused by questions put to me in a particular house, and I decided to move further westwards that evening for safety.

At this stage I entered upon my duties as full-time Adjutant of the Brigade, and planned to go about by bicycle to visit the Commanders of the different Battalions. Together with them I would arrange staff-meetings to discuss ways and means of forming new Companies and strengthening the existing ones. So, leaving Rosscarbery I cycled to Glandore, Union Hall, and found accommodation for the night at Barnie O'Driscoll's place near Castlehaven. This house was unlikely to be visited by the R.I.C. since Barnie was one of the four Volunteers committed to jail after the raid on Glandore Training Camp the previous month. The following morning I broke entirely new ground. Passing through Bauravilla, Caheragh, Aghaville Cross, and Cullomane Cross to Big Dan O'Sullivan's house in Baurgorm, I spent five or six days visiting Companies of the Bantry Battalion in the company of its Commander, Ted O'Sullivan. The kindness of the O'Sullivans during my stay in Bantry was very heartening, and what I remember in particular was the genial, great-hearted hospitality and encouragement of Big Dan.

My First Visit to Dublin and G.H.Q.

Before I left Rosscarbery and the threshing party there, Tom Hales informed me that he had been summoned to a Volunteer meeting in G.H.Q., Dublin. However, he suggested that since I was now free to do so, I should go in his stead, as soon as I returned from a visit he wished me to make to the Bantry Battalion. I gladly assented and on the conclusion of my work in Bantry returned with my report to Brigade Headquarters at Hurley's of Laragh. Thereupon I cycled to Cork where I stayed the night with a Volunteer friend, Paddy O'Keeffe, who later became General Secretary of the G.A.A. Early the next morning, 14 October, I left my bicycle in the care of my friend, and took the train for Dublin.

Due to the fact that I was 'on the run', I had to exercise the greatest vigilance on the journey to avoid capture. This matter must have been uppermost in my mind at the time, but now in retrospect what I remember best is the excitement I experienced at the prospect of visiting Dublin for the first time and there meeting the almost-legendary figures of the G.H.Q. staff.

On my arrival at Vaughan's Hotel—now headquarters of the Workers' Union of Ireland—in Parnell Square, I met Michael Collins, Gearóid O'Sullivan, Seán Ó Muirthile, Peadar Clancy, Diarmuid O'Hegarty, and Dick McKee. Later in the evening many other officers arrived including Frank Thornton, Liam Tobin, and representatives of the Meath and North Tipperary Brigades. Every aspect of organisation was examined during the course of our discussions. It was particularly pleasant to meet Dick McKee again and to speak to him about developments that occurred in West Cork since he had left after the week in Glandore. I felt he was a friend, one for whom I had conceived a strange and lasting admiration.

My recollection of that first night in Vaughan's Hotel is of a very informal meeting where G.H.Q. staff were constantly coming and going, and it was a surprise to me to see how nonchalantly they seemed to accept the constant risk that was theirs. The ready comradeship which they so warmly extended to me was the source of great encouragement, and served to strengthen the bond that united me with the Volunteer cause, and helped to sustain me in my military endeavours during the long struggle that was soon to commence in real earnest.

On the following day, 15 October, I attended another Volunteer meeting at Lalor's on Upper Ormond Quay, and there met that very impressive personality, Cathal Brugha, the Minister of Defence, whose heroic courage during the fight of Easter Week was legendary. With him I also met the Chief of Staff, Dick Mulcahy; and Mick Collins was there to introduce me. Here the informality of the previous night was gone. In an atmosphere of military efficiency the discussion opened on Dick McKee's report dealing with the Glandore Camp. Then was emphasised the need for an immediate extension and development of the West Cork Brigade. It was clear that in the view of this meeting military efficiency was the target to be aimed at in all Volunteer units; and it was no less clear that the inculcation of the principles of guerilla warfare was to be an essential part of all training.

Naturally the question of arms and equipment was discussed, and in this context many suggestions were made and examined. It was quite evident to me that these men were anticipating an early development of hostilities on the part of the enemy, and that they were calmly making the necessary preparations to counter them. I was questioned about our potential in the West Cork Brigade, and how many guns we had and the quantity of ammunition that was available, and whether we could carry out attacks on enemy barracks in our area. In the end, authorisation was granted to conduct attacks on barracks in West Cork from the beginning of the coming year, that is, 1920. It was clearly understood that only such attacks as offered a reasonable hope of success were to be attempted, and loss of life was to be avoided, if at all possible. Hitherto G.H.Q. had not openly advocated attacks on enemy forces as a matter of general policy. For this reason the decision of this meeting to authorise attacks was specially significant, and it was to have immense consequences for the development of activities in our Brigade in the following year.

At this same meeting I was also informed that a decision had been made to hold a National Convention of the Volunteers in Dublin during the course of December, and that all Brigades throughout the country were to elect delegates to attend it. Finally, an important instruction to be issued by G.H.Q. was discussed. This called upon each Brigade Commander to convene a meeting in his area consisting of two delegates from each Company to put before it the Volunteer Executive's decision to transfer the Volunteer organisation—under the title of 'I.R.A.'—to the control of Dáil Éireann, and the terms of the oath of allegiance each Volunteer would be called upon to take.

On my return to West Cork I sought our Brigade O/C and eventually located him at Johnny Collins's of Woodfield. There I was given the warmest of welcomes by Johnny and his wife, and spent the night long discussing with Tom Hales the question of the National Convention of the Volunteers and the arrangements we ought to make for it. With a view to carrying out the instructions of G.H.Q. we decided to hold a Brigade Convention at Caheragh without delay. In the meantime I would begin an organising tour of our area, and endeavour to put into effect the directives that I received in Dublin for the expansion and development of our Brigade. So on 1 November I bade farewell to Johnny Collins and his wife, and set off on my travels. When I left that happy homestead at Woodfield, with its warm hospitality and Johnny's optimism and enthusiasm for the Volunteer cause, I felt lonely for a while, conscious that I had to rely now very much on my own resources in the accomplishment of a responsible mission fraught with many dangers.

During the weeks and months that followed I supervised the system of organisation in each of the Battalions, and gradually came to know intimately the different localities, and most of the individual Volunteers—at least the active ones—throughout the Brigade area. This extensive knowledge was built up piecemeal in many a long trek by bicycle and on foot, and it was to serve me in good stead later when the struggle was at its height. My constant wanderings on occasions involved real hardship. On many a long wintry wet day after a tiring journey I found myself towards evening without food since the morning, soaked to the skin, and still with a long distance to go before I could hope to have a meal to end my hunger and the warmth of a fire to dry my clothes. The feeling of loneliness on such occasions became acute, and it was difficult to cast aside the mood of dejection which it brought. Then the fear of capture was a constant companion. It was not the fear of being deliberately betrayed to the police—this risk was negligible—but rather the greater risk of provoking gossip that would make its way to the local barracks, and either bring immediate arrest or make the route unsafe for future travel. It was this risk as much as a kind of shyness that made it difficult for me, even when famished with the hunger, to go to strange houses and appeal for food. Would I be queried as to the cause of my plight? Then there was the possible danger that lurked at every important crossroads, the possibility of running suddenly into a party of the R.I.C. or military and of being questioned by them. These things inevitably caused a strain, and so also did the endless vigilance that had to be exercised to avoid attracting attention as one moved from district to district—all in order that the work of organisation could continue without interruption.

This does not mean that my experience while 'on the run' was one of unrelieved misery. Far from it. There was always the heart-warming hospitality of friends waiting somewhere along the road, the encouragement of the many sympathisers with our cause, and the generous co-operation of dedicated comrades. These more than compensated for the drudgery and fatigue of the long journeys. Besides, as the months passed the number of my contacts in all districts increased, so that I gradually came to have friends to call upon everywhere.

One of the most memorable experiences I can recall during the opening months of my organising tours of the Brigade occurred at Drinagh about seven miles south of Dunmanway. On 1 November I had gone to meet Sam Kingston, O/C of the Skibbereen Battalion, at Tureen with a view to visiting his area, and was given an unforgettable welcome by the whole Kingston household. Sam invited me to accompany him to Drinagh to see if the defunct Company there could be revived. A meeting of the Volunteers was arranged for 3 November and only four men put in an appearance on the appointed night. Such, however, was the spirit and enthusiasm of the quartet that the Company went from strength to strength, so that within the next twenty months it had over a hundred dedicated men on its roll.[1] The Company served a very useful function in protecting our lines of communication south of the town of Dunmanway, just as the Companies of Togher and Derrynacaheragh did on the north side, and the Company of Knockbue (Kilnahera East) between Drinagh and Togher. Indeed we attached so much importance to the local protection work of these and other Companies near the central lines of communication between Bantry and Bandon that we rarely thought of weakening them by taking Volunteers from them. This was in keeping with our general policy of keeping the local organisations at maximum efficiency.

The experience I had at Drinagh was not an isolated one by any means. It was indicative of the strong movement of revival and development that spread rapidly as the new plan of organisation got under way and gained momentum. The cumulative effect of Rathclarin and of the other Volunteer offensives elsewhere in the country, of Glandore Camp and the enthusiasm of the leaders trained there was now becoming very evident.

Charlie Hurley joins Bandon Battalion; A Campaign is Planned

The Brigade Convention to elect four delegates for the National Convention of Volunteers that was to be held in Dublin during December was held on 27 November at Caheragh, a village on the main road between Skibbereen and Bantry. The delegates elected at this meeting were Hugh Thornton, Seán O'Donovan and myself —Tom Hales as Commander of the Brigade was a *de jure* delegate. In due course we proceeded to Dublin, but on the night before the National Convention was to be held in the University College Dublin Grounds, Terenure, G.H.Q. acting on special information cancelled the meeting and ordered the delegates to return to their areas. This was the first intimation we received that the British Government had resolved on an intensive drive to arrest and imprison Volunteer leaders on a large scale.

After the meeting at Caheragh, I returned to Brigade Head-quarters at Frank Hurley's of Laragh, and there learned the welcome news that Charlie Hurley had been released from Mary-boro' Jail on ticket-of-leave. He had served one year of a five-year sentence for Volunteer activities, and with others had been unex-

1. The four men were Jim O'Donovan of Carrigbawn who was appointed Captain; Neilus McCarthy of Reavouler, First Lieutenant; Pat Hurley of Maulagow, whose brother Seán was killed in the fighting at Church Street, Dublin, in 1916; and Donal McCarthy of Carrigbawn.

pectedly released—why, we could never discover. By arrangement
we met a few days later at Fitzgerald's of Clashreagh close to
Ballinspittle. It was a happy reunion, and sitting by the open fire
we talked long into the night about the sequence of events that
had occurred since his arrest and imprisonment twelve months
earlier. Charlie's one ambition now was to return to Castletownbere
and resume there the Volunteer activities that his imprisonment
had interrupted. But as the night wore on he came to appreciate
the new situation that had developed during his absence. He
finally agreed that since the Bandon area would become the gateway to West Cork in the coming struggle, it was here that he
could best meet the challenge. Once this decision was made known
the Brigade O/C and staff were only too happy to offer him an
appointment as Vice-Commandant of the Bandon Battalion.[2]
Subsequent events were to prove the decisive importance of this
appointment.

Charlie Hurley was born in the Kilbrittain district in 1892, and
now at the age of twenty-seven his reputation as a soldier was
widespread not only in the district of West Cork, but throughout
the entire country. When he was arrested in Castletownbere a
year earlier he had been found in possession of documents out-
lining plans for the capture and destruction of every enemy post on
the Beara Peninsula. He was courtmarshalled in Cork on this
charge, and sentenced to five years' penal servitude. And here he
was back among us—on ticket-of-leave, it is true, but with no more
intention of complying with the conditions attached to this legalism
than he had of promising to comply with them even had he been
asked. We were indeed fortunate to have such a man at such a time
and in such a place : his experienced leadership, personal magne-
tism, indomitable courage, and initiative were so perfectly blended
as to make him the automatic choice when a post of higher
command fell vacant later on.

A short time after the happy reunion at Clashreagh, a Brigade
Council meeting was convened, and Charlie Hurley, in the absence
of the Bandon Battalion O/C, attended. Two matters were discussed at this meeting which were to have momentous consequences
in the development of the struggle during the following years,
namely, (a) the sanction given by G.H.Q. to attacks on barracks by
local Volunteer initiative, and (b) plans to carry out wide-scale

2. This post had been vacant since the previous September when Denis
Lordan temporarily resigned in order to move to the First Cork Brigade
area.

attacks on these barracks in our Brigade area. A general survey of all enemy positions was made, and it was decided to begin the offensive early in the New Year with attacks on the police barracks at Allihies, Mount Pleasant, and Timoleague, and to follow these up with attacks on the barracks at Ballineen, Baltimore, Durrus, and Ballydehob. Considering how poorly we were equipped with arms and ammunition at the time, this may appear as a very ambitious campaign, if not simply as a foolhardy one. But by this time we were seasoned in the belief that it was not a question of our waiting to be supplied with arms before attacking the enemy, but rather of attacking the enemy in order to become armed. We aimed at two things, namely, to make conditions so difficult for the enemy that he would be forced to withdraw from our area, and in the process to despoil him of his arms.

Meanwhile a plot was being hatched in Kilbrittain. Stationed there was a particularly dangerous and obnoxious member of the R.I.C. who was the leader of all the raids on Volunteer houses that were conducted in the district and was chief intelligence officer for the enemy. He was well aware of the wrath he was rousing among his countrymen, and had frequently been warned to moderate the zeal he was showing in the service of the national enemy, but unfortunately to no avail. Normally, he took precautions not to expose himself, and would appear in public only in the company of the military. But he permitted himself one exception to this rule : in the company of an R.I.C. sergeant he would cross the street at very irregular intervals for a drink in the local public house. For sixteen nights members of the Volunteer Company waited in the street to get him. Eventually on 15 December he appeared and was shot down.

CHAPTER 11

RAID ON A BRITISH NAVAL SLOOP AT BANTRY BAY

Early in November 1919 the Bantry Battalion staff with the co-operation of Ralph Keyes, Captain of the Bantry Company, conceived the idea of raiding one of two naval sloops which plied regularly between Bantry and Bere Island bringing mail and provisions from the mainland to the island. At the time, there was scarcely a single rifle in the possession of the Volunteers in the Bantry Battalion, and while the British authorities were anxious that this position should remain unchanged, the Volunteers were very anxious to change it, and so they thought of the raid. For the sloops were known to be well manned and well armed, and it was hoped that a raid on one of them would yield a quantity of much-needed rifles and ammunition. Knowing that the Volunteers were likely to think of making such a raid, and that they were desperate enough to think of putting it into effect, the local R.I.C. and military leaders strongly advised the captains of the sloops never to berth their ships by the piers at Bantry town.

A feeling of security must have gradually taken possession of the sloops' captains, because they abandoned their practice of casting anchor out in the bay, and began to bring their ships alongside the new pier about two hundred yards from the town square, known as Wolfe Tone Square, and tied them there. They probably felt safe in Bantry because the town was a well-protected British stronghold. To the south, and only three hundred yards from the square was a garrison of two hundred soldiers of the King's Liverpool Regiment billeted in Bantry Workhouse. In addition, the town had an R.I.C. garrison of fifteen men in a barracks situated on the south side of the square within sight of the new pier. Each night a strong patrol of military and R.I.C. paraded the town, and made any Volunteer activities there extremely perilous.

Through Volunteer McCarthy, who was employed as mate on the Bantry steamboat, *Princess Beara,* which plied between Bantry and Castletownbere, the Volunteer officers at Bantry were able to collect valuable information regarding the movements of the crew when the sloops were in port, the general lay-out of the vessels, and particularly the location of the armory. After careful study, plans were finalised and it was decided to raid the sloop which was likely to arrive during the weekend between 15 and 17 November. A boarding party of six was selected and included Maurice

Donegan, Vice-Commandant of the Battalion, Seán Cotter, Adjutant, Michael O'Callaghan, Quartermaster, and Ralph Keyes. Two Volunteers were appointed to stand guard on the pier, while four scouts were to take up positions between Wolfe Tone Square and the pier itself. A Volunteer was detailed to procure the key of the Bantry Boys' National School, and two others were to procure a ladder and have it in position at the school so that any arms captured could be stored away quickly over the ceiling of the school.

On Sunday, 16 November, at 7.00 p.m. a local Fianna scout reported that one of the sloops *M.L. 171*, had berthed at the new pier. Immediately all the Volunteers taking part in the projected raid were brought together and given final instructions. At 8.00 p.m. the four scouts went to their respective positions. The other eight men proceeded through Wolfe Tone Square towards the pier in pairs walking in a casual manner so as not to attract attention. As the first pair, Maurice Donegan and Ralph Keyes, arrived on the pier, they were amazed and delighted to observe the naval watchman on deck leaving his post, proceeding towards the forward hatchway and disappearing down the ladder. No time was lost. Without a moment's hesitation the two men jumped on board and rushed to the hatchway. As they did so the next pair was signalled to follow. After them came the rest of the boarding party including John Teahan, the blacksmith, carrying a heavy hatchet.

Donegan raced to the forward hatch and before closing it down warned the crew below that if they shouted for help a bomb would be thrown down on them. In point of fact the raiding party had no bombs, but the bluff worked and the crew kept quiet. While this was taking place another member of the party rushed to secure the stern hatch. This was a wise precaution as there could have been a passage between the forward and stern hatches. Meanwhile, John Teahan, the blacksmith, was breaking down the door of the armory with his hatchet. He made short work of it, and there in the room were found six Ross-Canadian rifles chained to a rack and also two heavy black boxes. Immediately the rifles and boxes were conveyed to the pier. Fifteen minutes had elapsed since the party boarded the sloop and they were now ready to depart with their prize. Before leaving Maurice Donegan opened the forward hatch again and warned the crew that they were not to call for help for another hour.

At this point, a fortunate accident occurred which diverted attention from the pier at a critical moment, and allowed the

Volunteers to slip away unnoticed. A Gaelic team from Dunman-way had played a match in Bantry in the afternoon and some of the team's followers went for a stroll in the bright moonlight towards the harbour. One man with 'one too many' took a step from the square into Bantry Bay and caused a certain amount of excitement and distraction in the square just when it was needed most. A crowd collected and was so preoccupied with the efforts to get the man out of the water that the frantic shouts of the crew on the naval sloop were not noticed, and valuable minutes were gained by the raiders as they retreated. Quickly they collected the rifles and the two boxes, and spirited them away along the strand over very rough ground to Cove Road, then on to Barrack Road, over a field and across the main Bantry-Glengarriff Road, across the field at Slip and on to the railway line at the crossing at Church Road. Following the railway the party came to the back of the National School where the booty was to be stored. There to their chagrin the party found that the ladder was too short to reach the attic hole in the ceiling where the rifles and boxes were to be stored. The situation was critical with the barracks of the military only one hundred yards away. At this juncture Ralph Keyes suggested the possibility of storing the booty over the ceiling of the sacristy in the local church. A messenger was sent to get the key. Soon the church sexton was on the scene, and with his co-operation the booty was quickly stored away in safety. While this was being done, the Volunteers could hear the bugler in the military barracks close by sounding the alarm. In a very short time army lorries were rushing past on their way to the pier.

When the two black boxes were opened, they were found to contain four .45 revolvers, two Verey pistols, a quantity of ammunition and a large supply of equipment. Together with the rifles this capture considerably improved the Volunteers' position in the Bantry Battalion and indeed in the West Cork Brigade generally. Not merely did the success of the raid greatly boost the morale of the men, but the arms were a welcome addition to the Brigade armament. Good use was made of them in many important engagements later in the war.

Two days after the raid on Bantry Pier, the following report appeared in the *Cork Constituton* :

According to a report from Bantry, a reckless raid was made on a Government launch on Sunday night between 10 and 11 o'clock. The launch was lying at the new pier, which is near the railway station and is readily accessible at all times and would seem to be a secure place for a launch or any larger boat to avoid being raided. The raiders must have carefully planned the affair and carried it out regardless of consequences. It is stated that they found six rifles and three revolvers, but it is not known what quantity of ammunition was taken. The robbers easily escaped, for the crew of the launch were overwhelmed before they could put up a fight. When the incident became known, military and police searched several houses in the town, but no arrests were made and no arms found. While these searches were being carried out motor cars and armoured cars of the military went along the road to Dunmanway with no result. The M.L. which was raided left the pier on Monday morning.

On Wednesday, 19 November, the following report appeared in the same *Cork Constitution* :

Notwithstanding the activities of the authorities to trace the rifles stolen from the Government's motor launch at Bantry, no trace of them, or any clue to the identification of the perpetrators have been discovered. It is thought that the stolen articles must have been dropped into a waiting boat alongside and conveyed to a place of safety along the coast.

A Joyful Interlude before the Battle—Christmas 1919

Dick Barrett was a schoolteacher at Gurranes National School near Crossbarry and a member of the Crosspound Company. Nevertheless, because of his position he was not permitted to parade. Unsuspected by the enemy of complicity with the Volunteer organisation, he was able to move about in all circles, and rendered very useful service from 1918 onwards. He was particularly valued as an adviser to the Brigade staff, and was in our full confidence.

As December advanced he invited Charlie Hurley and me to spend the Christmas with him at his home in Hollyhill, Ballineen, and we gladly accepted, knowing full well that our own homes would be surely raided during the Christmas period by the R.I.C. as they searched for us. Hollyhill at this time was considered a reasonably safe locality for a rest during the Christmas period, but even there the usual precautions were necessary to prevent any indiscreet gossip about 'strangers in the vicinity' reaching the ears of the police. So the day before Christmas Eve we left Crossbarry and stayed that night at Jerry O'Callaghan's of Laravoulta, Newcestown. There we spent a pleasant evening among very good friends whose hospitality knew no limits. Soon all thoughts of battle were forgotten as we relaxed a while in the gay atmosphere of a truly Irish home.

After midnight on Christmas Eve, Dick, Charlie and I crossed the Bandon river at Enniskean, and proceeded in high spirits to Hollyhill. To add to our jubilation we found that a number of the Kilbrittain Volunteers had arrived in the same townland for Christmas before us. They had been forced to abandon their homes as a result of the intensive raiding that took place after the shooting of the R.I.C. constable on 15 December.[1] And to crown our joy we found among them the wounded hero of the Rathclarin ambush, Mick O'Neill, now completely recovered, and as courageous as ever. We spent a very happy Christmas at Hollyhill, while Dick, together with his mother and sister did everything to make our stay a pleasant one. As we had to avoid appearing in public during the daylight hours, we were left with no option but to forgo the Masses on Christmas Day; it was indeed a strange experience for us to miss the Christmas ceremonies for the first time.

In the course of the subsequent days we had the opportunity to reflect on and talk about the serious side of our work, and the plans we had been forming for the immediate future. Good use was made of the time between Christmas and the beginning of the New Year, and we had Pat Harte, Brigade Quartermaster, along to discuss our plans. He was still living at Clonakilty at the time, and had been working hard to reorganise the Battalion in that area.

On New Year's Eve we parted company. Leaving Dick at home to finish his holiday, Charlie Hurley went with the Kilbrittain lads to the south side of the Bandon Battalion area, while I went to Brigade Headquarters at Laragh for a staff meeting with Tom Hales and Flor Begley. Flor was to come by arrangement to report on the situation in Bandon and to arrange for the two barrack attacks : Mount Pleasant and Timoleague in the Bandon Battalion area. The prospect that presented itself as the New Year dawned showed the promise of dramatic action and plenty of excitement. It did not betray its promise.

1. See above, p. 86.

CHAPTER 12

AN OFFENSIVE LAUNCHED AGAINST THE R.I.C.

You are requested to have a return prepared and furnished to this department showing the strength of Sinn Féin or Irish Volunteers. The G.A.A. : showing matches played; if attendance is increasing, and general information regarding the society. All fixtures of the G.A.A. to be attended by a sufficient number of constables to be able to mix freely with the crowd. The following points are to be noted : (a) tendency of the crowd politically; (b) are the officials Sinn Féiners or Revolutionaries; (c) are fixtures used for bringing local leaders in different parts of the country or adjoining counties together; (d) do officials mix with local leaders where they are not leaders themselves?

Such was the circular issued by the Special Crimes Department of Dublin Castle on 9 September 1916 and addressed to each County and District Inspector of the R.I.C.

The Royal Irish Constabulary was a force to be reckoned with in 1916, and even more so in 1920. It had thirty-two police barracks situated at key points throughout the Brigade area stretching from Innishannon to Allihies. The smaller barracks in outlying districts were usually manned by a sergeant and three constables. In the larger stations there was a District Inspector, Head Constable, two or three sergeants with from twelve to fifteen constables. The personnel of the force was recruited from all over Ireland, and for obvious reasons it was the practice that members would not be stationed in their native counties. All enemy military activity in our area depended largely on the assistance and co-operation of the R.I.C.; without this body the military could not hope for much success in the country or even in the towns for that matter. Physically and intellectually the R.I.C. was a highly-selective force, and one that presented a formidable challenge that had to be met before our campaign could get fully under way. But it must not be thought that all members of the Constabulary were equally hostile to the national movement. Far from it. Many of them, for example, resigned rather than be associated with the Black and Tan campaign that was to break out later, while others remained on in the force, and there proved very helpful in keeping us informed of raids and other matters of military intelligence.

Already in 1918 the first Volunteer attack on an R.I.C. barracks

in West Cork had taken place, and thereafter the enemy, realising
the vulnerability of the more isolated barracks began to evacuate
them. This was the first sign of retrenchment, the first chink in the
R.I.C. armour, and we were determined to push forward our
advantage in the New Year.

Attack on the R.I.C. Barracks at Allihies

Arms and ammunition captured in the Brigade area during the
previous two and a half years had made it possible at this juncture
to contemplate attacks on enemy barracks with a reasonable assurance of success. Besides the total of twenty-nine rifles and 3,000
rounds of .303, we had also at our disposal about thirty hundredweight of gun-cotton that had been captured on Bere Island in
June 1918, together with another ten hundredweight captured at
Mizen Head a year earlier by a unit of the Bantry Battalion led by
Ted O'Sullivan, Battalion O/C, and Maurice Donegan, Vice-O/C.
As a result, one of the first decisions put into effect early in 1920
was that concerning the attacks on R.I.C. barracks in our Brigade
area, and the Battalion to lead the way was that of the Beara
Peninsula.

For the attack Volunteers were drawn from the Companies of
Eyeries, Inches, Castletownbere, and Bere Island. It was planned
that about twenty men would take part in the actual attack, while
a number of others would be involved in scouting and outpost duty.
Besides a number of shotguns, the Volunteers had eight rifles, four
of which had been captured in the raid on Eyeries R.I.C. barracks,
and the other four captured from the British at Castletownbere.
The mine to be used in the attack was assembled by Corney
O'Sullivan of Inches, then a member of the engineering staff of
Cork Number One Brigade, and the explosive was supplied from
the gun-cotton captured by the Beara Volunteers in 1918.

On 12 February the attacking party assembled at Inches, about
one mile from Eyeries, at 8.00 p.m. Thence the party moved across
country to Allihies, a distance of about seven miles. When close to
their destination, they removed a wooden plank from a haybarn
as it was required in order to lay the charge of gun-cotton.

The Allihies barracks was an isolated building in the village.
There was a stone wall enclosing a yard in front of the building,
and a section of the Volunteers armed with shotguns took up positions behind the wall. The remainder of the attacking party, armed
with rifles and shotguns, were placed in various positions at the
front and rear of the barracks. While these sections were moving

into position, the gun-cotton slabs, which had been tied to the fourteen-foot wooden plank, were placed in position, and a detonator and fuse were fixed to the charge. The charge was then borne by Christy O'Connell and Corney O'Sullivan and placed at the base of the rear wall, underneath the only window in the wall. It was tamped with bags filled with earth. The fuses were then lit and the two men dashed for cover. They had barely reached a safe spot when there was a loud explosion, and a breach about fourteen feet wide and extending from the ground to the eaves of the roof was blown in the wall.

For a moment the Volunteers hesitated to rush the breach as they were taken aback by the extent of the damage caused by the explosion; besides, they assumed that any members alive inside the building would immediately surrender. When the dust cleared, the attackers found that two cross walls at either end of the breach were still standing and offered cover to the police within, so that there was no means of exposing them. At this point all sections of the attacking party opened heavy fire on the building and called upon the inmates to surrender. They refused to yield. For about two hours the Volunteers besieged the barracks, but eventually, when they realised that there was no hope of capturing it, they decided to withdraw.[1]

Following this attack the R.I.C. not merely withdrew altogether from Allihies, but also from nearly all the small barracks in the area; and shortly after their departure the evacuated barracks were destroyed by explosives and fire by members of the local Volunteer units. In consequence, a large part of the Beara Peninsula was cleared of enemy forces, and made available as a safe place for tending wounded Volunteers of the Brigade, as well as a haven for those 'on the run' and in need of a rest. That one Volunteer attack on the Allihies barracks, without the loss of arms and without casualties among the attackers, should have achieved so much was more than compensation for the disappointment caused by the failure to effect the immediate capture of the barracks in question.

1. Among those who took part in this operation were Peter O'Neill, Christy O'Connell, Corney O'Sullivan, Jeremiah McAuliffe, Denis O'Neill, Jack O'Sullivan (Shamrock), Mort McCarthy, Jim McCarthy, Mike Walsh, Neilus O'Neill, Mike O'Sullivan, David O'Connell—all from Eyeries and Inches Companies; Christy McGrath, William O'Neill, Ned Harrington, Dan O'Sullivan—all from the Castletownbere Company; Jim O'Sullivan, Florence O'Sullivan, Tim Harrington, Michael O'Sullivan—all from the Bere Island Company.

Attacks on Mount Pleasant and Timoleague R.I.C. Barracks

Early in February, Ted O'Sullivan, Commandant of the Bantry Battalion, brought a quantity of the gun-cotton captured in 1918 from the Royal Engineers on Bere Island from Trafrask, three miles east of Adrigole, to the Carbery shore at Gearhies—a most dangerous operation because Ted transported the explosive by boat while enemy destroyers swept the sea in the vicinity with their searchlights Having succeeded in landing his cargo, Ted transferred it to Johnny Sweeney's of Maughanaclea, near Kealkil, where I collected it and brought it by pony and common cart via Coosane Gap, Coppeen, and Newcestown to Brigade Headquarters at Laragh—a journey of over thirty miles. Next, the Brigade Commander, Tom Hales, took counsel with Ted O'Sullivan and the engineer of the Bandon Battalion, Pat O'Sullivan, to examine the possibility of constructing a mine from the gun-cotton for use in a proposed attack on Mount Pleasant R.I.C. Barracks.

Ted had worked in the barytes mines near Bantry where he had gained some experience of gelignite explosives. Pat, on the other hand, had but a general knowledge of gunpowder and gelignite explosives. The use of gun-cotton as an explosive was entirely foreign to all of us, though we knew that its potential was far greater than that of gelignite. With the limited knowledge they had, Ted and Pat set about assembling the mine, and when it was ready we planned the attack.

The R.I.C. barracks at Mount Pleasant was a large stone building standing in a farm yard. Originally it had been occupied by a farmer, but for some years it was rented by the R.I.C. from its owner, and at the time of our contemplated attack it was garrisoned by six policemen. A linny or farm shed extended the full length of the rear wall of the building, and formed part of it. Our plan was to enter the linny, and place our manufactured mine against the side of the barracks in the hope that the explosion would breach the walls for a storming party. To do this it was necessary to enter a gateway in the surrounding wall of the farm yard and to cross to the linny. Having decided on a plan of attack, the Brigade O/C mobilised approximately forty men from Companies north of the Bandon river and twelve from the Dunmanway Battalion, and arranged to carry out the operation at one o'clock in the morning of 27 February.

When the main body of Volunteers was in position with six picked men in readiness to rush the expected breach in the wall, Tom Hales, Ted O'Sullivan and I advanced to the gate. Ted was carrying the mine—indeed though it weighed nearly half a hundredweight, he had carried it together with some Mills bombs all the way from Laragh, a distance of nearly three miles. We opened the gate of the farmyard, and as we were about to enter a burst of fire came from the linny, and Ted was wounded in a finger of his left hand. It was only then we realised that the garrison had been alerted by the accidental discharge of a shotgun two fields' distance from the barracks, and this upset the whole plan of attack. Nevertheless, Ted, despite the wound he had received, put an alternative phase of the attack into operation. He threw six Mills bombs on to the roof of the main building hoping they would roll down on to the roof of the linny, explode there, and put the defenders out of action. Unfortunately, the bombs rolled from the roof of the linny, and exploded harmlessly on the ground. Meanwhile our men in front had opened fire with shotguns and the five service rifles we had with us for the operation. The R.I.C. continued firing and suddenly Verey lights rose from the building, transforming the inky darkness of the night into noonday brightness, and summoning help from Bandon five miles away. This was our first experience of Verey lights and it was a rather disturbing one. Thereupon we withdrew in order taking the mine with us, and all the outlying units posted for scouting and guarding were ordered to retire.

I set off across country with nine of the Crosspound Company. We were obliged to keep to the fields because a big bi-annual horse fair due to start in Bandon later in the morning meant that all roads leading to the town were likely to be dangerous. Travel through the fields—and we had to cover four miles—was made all the more difficult because of the darkness of the night and the hedges of blackthorn and whitethorn bushes through which we had to scramble. These difficulties naturally intensified the sense of failure and disappointment that followed our reverse at the barracks. The preparations had seemed well-nigh perfect, and the successful exploding of a mine made from gun-cotton a fortnight earlier had given us reason to hope for success at Mount Pleasant. I was fortunate that night in having Pat O'Sullivan as a companion. He refused to be depressed, and repeated that our organisation was now such that a reverse was only an incident which did not affect the overall picture.

As we passed through Ballinacurra and crossed the Brinny river, day was dawning, and we halted for a rest and a smoke by the roadside. The night had been fine but a heavy February dew had fallen, and though the grass was wet we stretched ourselves on the ground for the first respite in seven hours. It was not bright enough for me to see all my companions but I noticed that one of them, Jack Kelleher of Crowhill, was parading up and down as if on sentry duty. I was surprised to see him as I did not know he was one of the party. It was our practice not to mobilise more than one member from any given family for an engagement with the enemy, and that because of the risk of casualties, and I had thought that a younger brother, Tom, had been with us that night. Facing him I asked, 'Jack, why did you come tonight?' 'What do you mean?', he replied. 'Well, I presume Tom is with us, and one is enough from any family.' He looked at me with a very stern face as he terminated the interview, 'I am afraid you are misinformed; we left that young fellow at home.' In the campaign later I was to have many opportunities to value the great soldierly qualities of Jack Kelleher whose strong will-power mastered a disability of severe asthma and chest troubles that afflicted him through his life and up to his death in 1926. Incidentally his brother Tom was to be one of the greatest soldiers in the Brigade.

Although the attack on Mount Pleasant may be described as a failure, it was invaluable in giving our men their first experience of being under fire. Among my own personal memories of the event is precisely that of coming suddenly, and for the first time, under a hail of bullets at close range from a totally unexpected quarter as the R.I.C. opened fire on Tom Hales, Ted O'Sullivan, and me from the linny. The general reaction on the part of the Volunteers who took part in the engagement was good, and showed their eagerness to resume activities as soon as possible. No one grumbled at the failure. All were happy and eager to renew their efforts when the next opportunity presented itself.

On the same night as that of the attack on Mount Pleasant barracks, another party of approximately forty Volunteers drawn from Companies south of the Bandon with ten from Clonakilty Company, under the command of Seán Hales, Bandon Battalion O/C, attacked Timoleague barracks. The plan in this case differed from that of Mount Pleasant in that having no mine the attackers sought to burn down the building by igniting a load of hay that was pushed up to the barrack door. A group was in readiness to throw canisters of home-made bombs into the building as soon as the door had been burnt down. Here, too, the plan miscarried and there followed a heavy exchange of fire. When Verey lights were fired from the barracks to signal help from Clonakilty, the attackers withdrew without casualties.

The operations at Mount Pleasant and Timoleague, the first to be officially sanctioned by G.H.Q., while considered failures by us, must have had a very serious significance for the enemy; within a few weeks both stations were evacuated, and a wave of wide-spread arrests of Volunteer leaders followed.

The Black Month of March

A week after the attacks on Mount Pleasant and Timoleague barracks, I was staying at Hurley's of Laragh with Jim O'Mahony, Battalion Adjutant. We were sitting round the fire with Frank Hurley, Captain of Mount Pleasant Company, his sister, Anna, and their brother Dan, an Irish Christian Brother visiting his aged father who was seriously ill in a bedroom upstairs and not expected to recover. On the hearth we had spread a number of cartridges and detonators to have them dried by the fire, when, shortly after midnight, there was a hammering with rifle butts on the door and a peremptory order demanding admittance.

Quick as thought, Anna collected the cartridges and detonators and hid them so safely that they were not found in the ensuing search. Then she led her brother Dan, Jim O'Mahony, and me upstairs to her father's room. 'Under the bed, Liam!', she com-manded, 'there is no other place.' Jim and I crawled under the bed as directed while Brother Dan stood between the bed and the door. Meanwhile, Frank gained time fumbling with the door-bolt below in the kitchen. Eventually a party of soldiers from Bandon military barracks burst in, led by a friendly R.I.C. sergeant named Lorrigan, and the search began.

We could hear the party approaching the sick man's room. They entered, and we had a few breathless moments under the bed while Brother Dan explained that his father was dying and should not be disturbed. The sergeant turning to the military officer confirmed this fact, explained that the 'priest' was a son of the sick man, and suggested that the party withdraw. They did, and we began to breathe again.

When Anna descended to the kitchen, she found that her brother Frank had been arrested and handcuffed. Hurriedly he was escorted to a waiting tender and brought away into the night. Later we learned that he was brought to Cork Jail and shortly afterwards removed to Wormwood Scrubs Prison outside London.

The days that followed brought news of extensive military acti-vity throughout the Bandon Battalion area, and many officers and men were arrested and imprisoned. On the same night as that of the raid we experienced at Laragh, there was another raid at Newcestown that ended with the arrest of all the local Company leaders, namely, Jack Allen, Dan Canty, and John Lordan, together with the latter's brother, Jim. Then in Kilbrittain, Paddy and Denis Crowley and John O'Mahony were arrested.

Luckily, six other Kilbrittain Volunteers evaded arrest as they were absent from their homes when the raiders called in the hope of arresting them. Extensive raiding was also carried out at Timoleague, Barryroe, Clogagh, and Ballinadee. All this widespread raiding was part of the enemy's reaction to our attacks on the Mount Pleasant and Timoleague barracks, and was aimed at ending our activities by removing the leaders and active Volunteers from the area.

The arrest and imprisonment of so many of the most militant officers and men was a serious blow, and caused a major difficulty in our plans. At this time, when we were still in the process of building up a strong guerilla force, trained and courageous leaders were a prime necessity. Hence the removal of the Captain of Mount Pleasant Company, and so many officers of the very active Kilbrittain and Newcestown Companies constituted a grave reverse.

Fortunately, a meeting with the Battalion Vice-Commandant, Charlie Hurley, had been arranged for the day following the widespread raids and arrests. So the morning after our narrow escape at Laragh, Jim O'Mahony, the Battalion Adjutant, and I set out on a seven mile trek to the rendezvous at O'Mahony's of Belrose. On this journey we exercised more than ordinary caution as we anticipated that the enemy might still be actively engaged in their raiding expeditions. In due course we reached Belrose and the meeting began as soon as Charlie Hurley arrived.

The business principally discussed at our meeting was the crisis caused by the arrest of experienced officers at Kilbrittain, Newcestown and Mount Pleasant, and the two problems which this crisis raised, namely, the replacement of the captured officers, and the problem of restoring the morale of the people—and more especially of the Volunteers—after the set-back of the arrests.

So far as the first problem was concerned, we were faced with the responsibility of finding men with the potential to command among those who had not yet been trained or tested. Of the two Companies requiring replacements Newcestown created the more-difficult problem. The Mount Pleasant Company still had its First Lieutenant, and he was able to fill the vacancy left by the arrest of Frank Hurley. In the case of the Newcestown Company we took a chance and a big one. This Company was one of the largest and most active units in the Bandon Battalion, as well as a vital Brigade communications centre. A great deal, therefore, depended on its leader. Only a short time previously, a soldier named Dick Hurley had returned after some years of active service in the Australian Army during the First World War. He was now living at Newcestown with dedicated Volunteers named Sweeney who were cousins of his. When he became aware of the situation, he had offered his services on the eve of the attack in Mount Pleasant, and was one of the twelve from the Newcestown Company who took part in that engagement. As a result of his performance on that occasion, he was appointed Acting Captain of the Newcestown Company, and it must be said that he ably fulfilled his duties in this role until the return of the regular officers after their release from jail three months later.

In the case of the second problem, that concerning morale, we felt that it was of the utmost importance to prosecute the campaign against the R.I.C. with redoubled energy. In this way, we hoped to stimulate the men and rouse them from the discouragement into which a number of them had lapsed in face of our recent reverses, and particularly the capture of so many of our most outstanding fighters. Could we but take one or two R.I.C. barracks by storm and gain possession of the arms, we could more than undo all the damage caused by our recent setbacks. I had been instructed to investigate the possibility of attacking two R.I.C. barracks in the Skibbereen Battalion area, namely, Baltimore and Ballydehob, and also one in the Dunmanway area, Ballineen. This I now proceeded to do with all speed, and went first to the Skibbereen area. Meanwhile a plan was being prepared in the Bantry Battalion area to strike the enemy in a vital centre.

Durrus R.I.C. Barracks Attacked

Durrus barracks was strategically placed at the head of Dunmanus Bay. With Schull on Roaring Water Bay, it was one of two outposts of vital importance to the enemy intelligence, and was a constant menace to the Volunteers. For this reason, the question of attacking it had been for some time a matter of careful study and detailed planning on the part of the Bantry Battalion officers. A strongly-fortified stone building with the usual loopholes, with steel-shuttered windows slotted for rifle fire, and with extensive outer defences of barbed wire, the barracks could not be taken easily by assault. It was inaccessible from the front or rear. There was only one way by which it could be approached and that was from the house next door which adjoined it but was much lower than the barracks. Besides, the building was defended by twelve R.I.C. men armed with rifles, grenades, and revolvers. To make matters more difficult, Bantry was only six miles away to the north and had a strong garrison of R.I.C. together with two Companies of the King's Liverpool Regiment, while Skibbereen to the east was another strong centre of military and police from which reinforcements could be quickly drawn.

The first preoccupation was arms and ammunition. And indeed the supply available was meagre enough; six Ross-Canadian rifles that had been captured in the raid on the British M.L. sloop at Bantry Pier in the previous November, one carbine, one Martini single-loader rifle, and a number of shotguns. For explosives, a small quantity of gelignite was available, and with this home-made bombs were manufactured from metal down-pipes cut into suitable lengths and filled with scrap iron and mixed with plaster of Paris. A cylindrical hole was provided for a charge of gelignite. Metal plates were bolted to the ends of the pipe, and in one of them a small hole was made for the fuse. These bombs weighed from three to fourteen pounds.

To prevent relief parties arriving on the scene, the approaches from Bantry, Skibbereen, Ballydehob and Schull had to be blocked and guarded. Trees were knocked across the road at Durrus Road Station, two and a half miles from Bantry, and a shotgun party was posted there to ambush any reinforcements approaching from that quarter. Within a mile of Durrus village on the main road to Bantry the same procedure was adopted; and again on the main road from Durrus via Parkana, and on the road into Durrus from Ballydehob and Schull. The Caheragh Company took charge of the roads between Skibbereen and Durrus. Two of the eight rifles were given to the protection parties nearest the village of Durrus, one on either side, and the remaining six rifles were used at the barracks, three in front, together of course with shotguns, and at the rear. The main attacking force was to be drawn from the Bantry and Durrus Companies, the former to be responsible for transporting the arms, bombs, and quantities of petrol and paraffin to the Durrus area on the night of the attack.

The attack began in the early hours of the morning of 31 March. A section under the command of Maurice Donegan occupying the loft of a stable directly in front of the barracks and another section behind a fence at the rear opened fire while the storming party armed with revolvers, the home-made bombs, petrol and a sledge-hammer got into the house adjoining the barracks. There they broke through the ceiling and roof of the house and climbed out through the hole. Continuous fire from the rifles and shotguns was kept up while the Battalion Commander, Ted O'Sullivan, next climbed from the roof of the small house on to the roof of the barracks. There he succeeded in breaking a hole in the slates. Meanwhie, the Vice-Commandant of the Battalion, Seán Lehane, carried the bombs forward with the aid of the Battalion Adjutant, Seán Cotter, Tom Ward, Captain of Durrus Company, and John J. O'Sullivan. The bombs were handed to Ted O'Sullivan and all of them were dropped with their fuses lighted through the hole made in the barrack roof. Next, the roof was sprinkled with petrol, and some of it poured into the barracks. It was then set alight.

The fight went on for three hours, and the occupants of the barracks were called upon several times to surrender. However, they refused to do so, kept up a continuous rifle fire, and sent hundreds of Verey lights into the sky in an effort to bring reinforcements. The whole engagement took longer than had been anticipted, and day was beginning to dawn by the time the fire had a good hold of the building.

Time was running out for the attackers. The approach of day-light meant that the arrival of reinforcements was imminent, and whatever chance the poorly-equipped protection sections had of guarding the approaches under cover of darkness, they had no possibility in daylight of holding the enemy reinforcements long enough to allow the attacking party to get away safely. Besides, many of the attacking party were from the town of Bantry, and had to be home for work that morning or they were liable to incur suspicion. In the circumstances it was thought wisest to abandon the attack and allow the fire that had been started to complete the destruction of the barracks.

The fight was called off and the storming party escaped by breaking holes in the walls leading from one house to the next until they emerged safely without exposing themselves to enemy fire. Then the whole party retreated towards the south for a while, and then turned eastwards towards Shroneageeha where they dispersed. As the party moved up the hill towards Shroneageeha, the barracks was in a blaze and the fire could be seen for miles.

The capture of arms following the hoped-for surrender of the barracks had to be waived, and this was a disappointment, but the

Volunteers had at least the satisfaction of knowing that by their efforts another enemy outpost—and that an important one—had been destroyed. In the morning the barracks was evacuated and this left a whole peninsula free from enemy occupation. And the only casualty on the Volunteer side was John Denny O'Sullivan of Baurgorm, who was slightly wounded. On the other side, two R.I.C. men were reported wounded.[2]

* * * * * *

On the day following the attack on Durrus barracks, the Battalion Adjutant, Seán Cotter, was arrested and taken to Cork Jail. While a prisoner in enemy hands in Cork, he was taken as a hostage on several raids conducted by the British military. From Cork he was later transferred to Belfast, and thence to Wormwood Scrubs Prison outside London. There he met Flor Begley, Quartermaster of the Bandon Battalion, who had been arrested on 1 January 1920, Ralph Keyes, Captain of the Bantry Company, who had been captured on 31 January, Frank Hurley, Captain of the Mount Pleasant Company, and many other captured Volunteers from the West Cork and other Brigades. On 21 April these Volunteers staged a hunger-strike, with the result that the authorities were induced to release them during the course of the following month.

An Attack on Ballydehob R.I.C. Barracks is Planned

Of the seven R.I.C. barracks originally selected for assault three still remained to be attacked, namely, Baltimore and Ballydehob barracks in the Skibbereen Battalion area, and Ballineen barracks in that of Dunmanway. Of these three, it was decided to concentrate on the barracks at Baltimore. Accordingly, on 16 March I set off with Mick O'Callaghan, the Bantry Battalion Quartermaster, to make a careful survey of the location of the barracks and its structure, only to conclude that an attack would be impracticable. The barracks was isolated in an open area that would provide no cover for an attacking party, and the building itself was structurally too strong and well defended to allow its

2. Besides those already mentioned, the following took part in the assault: Cecil Keyes, Acting Captain of the Bantry Company, Daniel O'Mahony, Sonny Spillane, Denny O'Sullivan—all from the Bantry Company; and Denis O'Leary, Timothy McCarthy (Casey), Dan O'Mahony, Mick Daly, and Jim O'Leary—all from the Durrus Company.

being taken by assault with the limited munitions we had at our disposal. We abandoned the idea of attacking it, and turned our attention to Ballydehob.

On the night of 30 March, with Charlie Hurley, Vice-Commandant of the Bandon Battalion, and two Volunteers of the Skehanore Company, Tom Hickey, and Joe Kelly, I carried out an inspection of the R.I.C. station at Ballydehob, and with my companions came to the conclusion that this was the most vulnerable of all the barracks we had considered to date. Its capture, we felt, would be a relatively simple matter. With a mine we could blow in the front door and rush the building, and in the case of that failing we could use canister bombs prepared from gelignite.

Without delay we set to work, collected and examined the guns and ammunition that were to hand, and set about making a mine and a number of canister bombs. By night we stayed at Jack Tom O'Driscoll's of Kilkileen in the Aughadown area, and by day we worked in a primitive munition factory which for security reasons was set up a good distance away in the barn of a farmhouse. As it was of the utmost importance that we should not be seen in the locality in daylight, we rose at five o'clock in the morning and had breakfast at O'Driscoll's very early so that we could reach our munition factory before daybreak. There we remained until nightfall working on the mine and manufacturing canister bombs from metal pipes taken from the Baltimore Fishery School. At about 8.30 in the evening we returned under cover of darkness to our billets at O'Driscoll's and there had our first meal since breakfast.

Preparations for the attack were almost completed by 1 April, and we had a Battalion Council meeting that night which included the Battalion Commandant, Sam Kingston, the Vice-Commandant, Neilus Connolly, Pat Joe Hourihan, Captain of the Bredagh Company, and Con Crowley of Kilbrittain, as well as Charlie Hurley and me. That same night, to our great disappointment, we learned that Ballydehob barracks had been evacuated a few hours previously, and that its five policemen had been withdrawn to the larger and more secure R.I.C. bastion at Schull, five miles to the west. Once more our bid to capture R.I.C. arms by storming a barracks was foiled. Nevertheless, by inducing the police to retire from Ballydehob we were responsible for clearing yet another area of the enemy, enlarging the scope of our own activity, and making it that much easier to organise and train our men for more ambitious engagements later. About this time, too, the R.I.C. barracks at Adrigole and Eyeries in the Beara district were evacuated and later destroyed by the Volunteers. And the same occurred at Kenneigh in the Dunmanway area, Ballygurteen and Milltown in that of Clonakilty, and Ballinspittle in that of Bandon.

Ballineen barracks remained. But by the time we were free to devote our attention to it, its personnel had been increased—very likely as a measure to cope with anticipated attack by the Volunteers—and for a period the R.I.C. force there was replaced by two platoons of the Essex Regiment from Kinsale. This spelt the end of our hopes in that direction.

In fact, these Essex soldiers became very active from the moment of their arrival in Ballineen, and we had our first encounter with them on Easter Saturday night, 3 April, when we were returning from the Skibbereen Battalion area to Brigade Headquarters at Laragh. Charlie Hurley, Con Crowley, Con Lehane, and I were cycling along the road from Ballinacarriga to Ballineen on a bright moonlit night. Rounding a bend in the road near Hatter's Cross we suddenly ran into a party of Essex soldiers about twenty strong standing beside their bicycles. They must have been as surprised as we were, but the imminence of our danger gave us an edge over them, for we succeeded in turning our bicycles before they recovered from their surprise, and retreated as fast as we could along the road we had just been coming. In the flurry the chain came off Charlie Hurley's bicycle, and he had to jump on to the back of mine. How we managed to escape is a mystery to me. For some reason known only to themselves the Essex soldiers did not open fire, but kept running after us and calling on us to halt. We succeeded in making a getaway, and were soon in the protective surroundings of Shanavagh Company area. There we spent the night in a hayshed at Corran.

Next day, Easter Sunday, we reached Brigade Headquarters at Laragh, and there reviewed recent developments. During the previous two months we had been giving our best endeavours to a campaign directed against seven R.I.C. barracks, and we had not succeeded in capturing a single one of them. It is true that we had forced the enemy to evacuate five of the seven barracks in question, and caused him to withdraw from several others. It is true also that, apart from a few minor wounds, we had no casualties resulting from our campaign, and our exposure to enemy fire was a helpful experience. But we had hoped to capture arms and ammunition from the barracks, and had not acquired a single rifle or round of ammunition, though we expended a considerable quantity of the latter from our own limited store. And yet it was the acquisition of arms and ammunition from our enemy that was essential for the success of our struggle.

. We decided that the time had come to bend our efforts in another direction. For the time being we would give our attention to ambushing the enemy. Military and police patrols were still operating in the Brigade area, and we decided that these would be the next object of our attacks. By successfully ambushing them we would not merely restore morale, we would also increase our store of arms from the weapons and ammunition captured. It was understood that this campaign could be conducted only in areas such, for example, as Bandon, Bantry, and Beara Peninsula, that had a sufficient supply of arms to conduct an ambush. Next, we contacted Tom Hales, the Brigade Commander, and submitted our plans to him. He gave them full approval, and suggested that all Battalions of the Brigade, in the measure of their resources, be permitted to act according to them.

The Bandon Battalion had acquired a sufficient number of service rifles and shotguns, either by capture or purchase, during the years from 1917 to 1919 to initiate a series of ambushes in its area, and this is what it now proposed to do.

Ambushes in the Bandon Area

A three-pronged ambushing attack was planned for the Bandon area. Charlie Hurley was to go south of the river Bandon to find a target either in the Kilbrittain or Timoleague district. Jim O'Mahony was to stage an ambush in the vicinity of Innishannon in the east, and I was to attempt one in the Newcestown area in the west.

In the event, Charlie had an early success. With a party of eight men drawn from the Companies of Kilbrittain, Timoleague, and Barryroe, he ambushed an R.I.C. cycling patrol four-strong at Ahawadda on the Timoleague-Lislevane road. Two constables were killed in the engagement and the other two surrendered, with the result that four revolvers and some ammunition were captured. Similarly, Jim O'Mahony with five Volunteers from the Crosspound Company armed with two rifles and three shotguns attacked another R.I.C. cycling patrol coming from Innishannon at Highfort on the Upton road. Again, two policemen were killed and one wounded and their revolvers and ammunition captured.

For my part, I went to the Newcestown Company and mustered twenty Volunteers armed with shotguns and sticks. We lined both sides of the road at Killowen on the Bandon-Ballineen road anticipating a military cycling patrol of twenty men that had been passing that way at irregular intervals. We remained in position from 10.00 p.m. to 5 a.m. the following morning but the patrol did not appear, and we were compelled to withdraw before daybreak lest our position should be betrayed to the enemy by loyalists living in the neighbourhood. Our abortive attempt was, however, followed up a few days later by the Newcestown Company under its Acting Captain, Dick Hurley, when they ambushed a patrol of R.I.C. men at Mount Pleasant and wounded one of them.

A short time afterwards, I discovered that the elusive military patrol I had hoped to ambush at Killowen had been appearing frequently on the Ballineen-Clonakilty road. So I selected an ambush position at One-eye Bridge, two miles south of Ballineen, and lay in wait there for three successive nights without results. The patrol failed to appear.

Ambushing Activity in the Bantry Area

During the month of April 1920 a fortunate strike was made by the Bantry Battalion Quartermaster, Michael O'Callaghan. An R.I.C. escort was bringing a large quantity of gelignite and four thousand detonators from Cork to Bantry. By an oversight, when changing trains at the Drimoleague Junction, the policemen forgot the detonators, and the carriage containing them continued on to Baltimore. There they were discovered by the Battalion Quartermaster. This valuable find came at an opportune time not only for the Bantry Battalion, but also for the Brigade when land mines operated by electric exploders became such an effective means of destroying enemy transport in ambushes during the year ahead.

Ralph Keyes, Captain of the Bantry Company, and Seán Cotter, Battalion Adjutant, were released from Wormwood Scrubs prison in May after a hunger-strike lasting twenty-three days. They were transferred to different medical centres, and Ralph found himself in St James's Hospital, Balham. One night after nine days of convalescence he felt sufficiently recovered to slip away quietly from the hospital and go to stay with a family of his acquaintance named O'Sullivan living in St James's Street. Here he was given the warmest of welcomes for the head of the household, a native of Bantry who, when he emigrated to England, brought with him the best of Fenian traditions : his three sons became active members of the I.R.A.[3]

3. Another of John O'Sullivan's sons, Joe, was hanged in 1922 for his part in the execution of Sir Henry Wilson.

Under the motherly care of Mrs O'Sullivan, Ralph made a rapid recovery, and in the evening time he eagerly discussed the progress of the war in Ireland. In these discussions he constantly referred with regret to the lack of arms to prosecute the struggle until on a given night one of John O'Sullivan's sons, Paddy, a Vice-Commandant in the Volunteers, brought news of the possibility of securing arms if only they could be conveyed to Ireland. Ralph quickly suggested a solution. He urged that a trial consignment of arms be sent as a case of machinery and addressed to G. W. Biggs & Co.—the principal merchant in Bantry and a well-known loyalist to boot. In December the first case of arms, labelled 'machinery parts' arrived at Bantry Railway Station, and was safely diverted to its proper destination. In February 1921 a second case arrived and in March a third : in all nine rifles were thus added to the armoury of the Bantry Battalion.

The initiative displayed by Michael O'Callaghan in the case of the detonators and by Ralph Keyes in the case of the rifles was one of the remarkable features of the struggle for independence. Officers and men everywhere were ready to exploit every situation to the advantage of their Company or Battalion and this was something that was fully encouraged by Brigade Headquarters. Individual and local efforts to acquire arms and ammunition by every possible means, ingenuity in thwarting enemy movements and devising means of attacking him were wholeheartedly approved.

During the month of June the Bantry Volunteers carried out an ambush on a police patrol at Snave Bridge between Bantry and Glengarriff in which a constable was shot. And a week later, on 21 June, they ambushed another police patrol at Clonee on the Bantry-Durrus road, killing a constable and wounding a sergeant, and capturing three revolvers.

The Volunteers suffered no casualties in either of these two ambushes, but three days after the second one the R.I.C. took their revenge in Bantry town. The homes of suspected Volunteers were raided. However, information about the raids had been received by the Volunteer Intelligence Officer during the previous twenty-four hours, and the Volunteers had accordingly left their homes before the raids took place. Infuriated at their failure to capture the Volunteers they were seeking, the R.I.C. had recourse to foul atrocities. Thus, when they failed to find Michael Crowley in his home, the police became so enraged that they shot his invalid brother, Con, in bed in the presence of his sister. They set fire to the house of David O'Mahony by throwing incendiary bombs through the windows and the roof. Fortunately, David's wife, his seven children and two female relatives who were living in the house managed to escape uninjured. During the remainder of that terrible week armed sections of the Bantry Company under its Captain, Ralph Keyes, were on protection duty in the town.

CHAPTER 13

THE MOMENTOUS MONTH OF JULY 1920

A Brigade Council meeting was held at Paul Kingston's of Tureen, Skibbereen, late in May and the whole situation was reviewed in detail. In the absence of Tom Hales, Commander of the Brigade, I presided and representatives of the six Battalion staffs also attended. Favourable reports were made on progress in each of the Battalions. The Brigade organisation was maintained intact, and in face of the powerful forces opposing us the plan of guerilla warfare was proceeding satisfactorily. Enemy raids and arrests had become the order of the day, and from time to time important officers and men had been captured. Yet, replacements were somehow found and Battalion meetings had been held fortnightly, and Company parades weekly and even twice weekly in some places.

Our system of communications was bearing the strain imposed on it by the rapidly increasing and diversifying activities of the Brigade. Attention was given to the allied services of intelligence, engineering, signalling, and transport. In regard to this last service, plans had to be made to keep abreast of the growing needs of the organisation, to provide protection for the men going to and returning from engagements, such as barrack attacks and ambushes as well as seeing to the increasing number of Volunteers being forced 'on the run'.

Vital in the matter of communications were the river crossings, particularly those of the river Bandon. To ensure safe crossings for the Volunteers permanent local organisations had been set up to keep crossing points under constant surveillance. So important was this work considered that many of the men engaged in it were not allowed to attend Company parades lest they should rouse enemy suspicion. At this particular time, and also during the more testing time that soon followed, these men did Trojan work in saving the lives of many Volunteers. The crossings most frequently used were at Manch Bridge, Desert Bridge,[1] Baxter's Bridge, Innishannon Road Bridge, Colliers Quay, and Kilmacsimon Quay—these last two were tidal—and it is a tribute to the men watching them that not a single Volunteer was captured at any of these crossings during the war, though they were often held by enemy patrols.

Another service that merited review concerned the question of

1. Desert Bridge is also known as Murragh Bridge.

justice. Following on the collapse of the British system of law and order, instances were reported of irresponsible people taking advantage of the new freedom to perpetrate crime. To curb these elements and to maintain civilian peace it was necessary for the Volunteers to do a certain amount of police work. The ready co-operation of the people, of course, made this work far more congenial and effective than the efforts of the R.I.C. who were now completely ostracised. There was a memorable case involving three elderly bachelors living together on a small farm at Coolmoreen near Innishannon. It will serve as an illustration of the way in which justice was upheld at the time by the Volunteers.

The three bachelors lived a Spartan existence, and it was generally assumed that they had saved a considerable sum of money. On 29 May 1920 these three men went to the fair at Innishannon leaving their home empty. When they returned that evening they noticed that the house had been entered and that the loose earth underneath one of the beds had been disturbed and that a tin box containing their life savings had been taken. They reported the robbery to the local Volunteers who passed the news to Brigade Headquarters which at the time was at O'Mahony's of Belrose. As the sum involved was considerable, amounting to one hundred and ten gold sovereigns, we took a very serious view of the matter, all the more so in that this was the first serious robbery in the area since the war began.

In the company of Dick Barrett I made inquiries in the local Companies of Crosspound and Innishannon, and found that suspicion fell on two youths who had been seen in the neighbourhood of the robbery on the fair day when the money was taken. They were arrested and held prisoners in a vacant house convenient to Brigade Headquarters. Although they vehemently denied all knowledge of the robbery, we were convinced that they were the culprits. For three days we interrogated them separately. Eventually one of them broke down and confessed that with the other prisoner he had taken the money and had buried it in an old graveyard which was directly opposite the Innishannon police barracks.

To enter the graveyard in daylight was obviously impossible as it was surrounded by a very high wall, and if we were seen inside from the barracks escape would be very difficult. To find the exact spot in which the money had been hidden would have been impossible in the dark, so we had no option but to attempt to retrieve the money at twilight. With Dick Barrett and Dan O'Mahony we took one of the culprits along to the graveyard. He led us straight to the spot where he had buried the tin box. We quickly removed the earth, and to our joy found the box with the shining sovereigns intact. Later that night we handed the money over to the local parish priest, and he in turn restored it to the poor old men who had been desolate and inconsolable since the disappearance of their hard-earned fortune.[2]

The military activities of the Brigade during the previous month were made the matter of a prolonged discussion at our Brigade meeting. From this discussion it gradually became obvious that the officers present were unanimous in their conviction that the campaign should be intensified, and towards the close of the meeting their conviction began to take a practical and concrete form. For any large-scale attacks the arms we had were quite inadequate and the first necessity was to increase our supply of modern arms and equipment. Hitherto the three principal methods used to acquire arms and ammunition had been raids on loyalist houses, attacks on R.I.C. barracks, and ambushes of police and military patrols. The first had by this time been exhausted as a possibility, the second had so far been a failure, and the third met with a considerable degree of success. Eleven of the most vulnerable police barracks had been evacuated over the previous six months, and their garrisons had been sent to increase the strength of the larger stations which were now virtually blockhouses protected with barbed wire entanglements, sand bags and steel shutters. For any sustained attack on these positions we would need rifles with a large quantity of ammunition and suitable explosives. We had plenty of gun-cotton as a raw material for mines, but had not yet successfully mastered the technique for exploding them. Military and police cycling patrols were also tempting targets, and experience over the previous two months had shown that we could overpower them and capture their arms. But the uncertainty of their routes, and the disappointment caused by failure to meet them after long hours of waiting on successive nights, tended to undermine the morale of our men. For this reason it was decided that only on really reliable information of enemy patrol movements would ambushes be attempted.

Eventually the discussion came round to the coastguard stations that were scattered along the coast from the Old Head of Kinsale

---

2. An interesting reference to the administration of justice by the Volunteers appeared at this time in the *Irish Independent,* 26 May 1920 : 'Evildoers in Co. Cork and Kerry are becoming alarmed at the thorough manner in which the Volunteers are dispensing justice.'

to Kenmare River at Ballycrovane Pier. The occupants had only recently been equipped with arms—Ross-Canadian rifles—and some of their garrisons strengthened with armed marines. It was suggested that these should be made the objects of attack. Finally, towards the close of the meeting all battalion officers were urged to secure arms and ammunition from the enemy in whatever manner was found practicable, whether from cycling patrols, police barracks or coastguard stations. It is a historical fact that it was from the time of this Brigade meeting that our offensive entered upon a new phase. Within ten days the first coastguard station was attacked.

Clonakilty Battalion in Action; Ring Coastguard Station Attack

The attack on Ring Coastguard Station was planned by Dan Harte, Commandant of the Clonakilty Battalion, and was to be carried out by a party of Volunteers selected from the Companies of Clonakilty, Shannonvale and Ardfield. At midnight, the hour decided for the attack, it was found that the Ardfield contingent had not yet arrived; they were crossing Ring Bay by boat and had been delayed by a strong ebb-tide. Nevertheless, Dan Harte decided to go ahead with the attack as it had been planned. The buildings were surrounded at the appointed time and the order was given to open fire at the windows on the first floor. Under cover of this fire, Jim 'Spud' Murphy and John 'Flyer' Nyhan rushed the door and surprised two coastguards who were defending the station. These immediately surrendered their rifles. No other occupants of the station were encountered as the other coastguards were residing in the married quarters adjoining the main building, and they had their rifles with them. Before the married quarters could be attacked the alarm was raised and Verey lights sent up. Dan Harte knew that these would be seen in Clonakilty, only two miles away, and that since no road-blocks had been set up, military reinforcements would be on the scene in ten or fifteen minutes. He immediately gave the signal to withdraw.

A certain amount of confusion followed. Murphy and Nyhan had not yet emerged from the station. They were searching for ammunition until they found two boxes containing two thousand rounds of .303. Hastily collecting these and the guns, they left the building only to find that their companions had already departed. So each carrying two rifles and a box of ammunition made a bee-line across country for Shannonvale where their capture was safely dumped. By comparison with later events this attack at Ring may appear a rather insignificant one, but it was the first of its kind and as such was considered a successful operation.

The First Attack on Howes Strand Coastguard Station

Towards the end of June the Volunteers of Kilbrittain Company decided to attack the Howes Strand Coastguard Station, an isolated building on the coast of Courtmacsherry Bay, four miles south of Kilbrittain. Up to a short time previously it had been manned by six unarmed coastguards. Close observation by local scouts living in nearby houses revealed that the garrison had been augmented to ten and all were supplied with rifles. It was also observed that on a fixed day each week three or four members of the station would cross the three-mile stretch of the bay by boat to visit Courtmacsherry station and collect supplies. This was the day chosen for the attack.

At 3.00 p.m. a party of sixteen Volunteers led by Jack Fitzgerald, the Company Captain, and Charlie Hurley, Vice-Commandant of the Battalion, managed to crawl under cover of a low fence right up to the gate leading to the station. The sentry on duty observed nothing until Denis Manning jumped upon him and quickly overpowered him. The others rushed headlong into the building, held up and disarmed four coastguards whom they found on the ground floor. Two others on the first floor surrendered immediately on the advice of their disarmed comrades. Thereupon, ten rifles and almost five thousand rounds of .303 ammunition were collected and transferred to a prepared dump at Clonbouig, nearly three miles away. Within an hour the operation had been successfully completed and the Volunteer attacking party dismissed.

The Brade Fiasco a near Tragedy

Neilus Connolly, our hero of Strangeways Jail, observed that five or six constables came to Skibbereen from Leap station on the first day of each month to collect their pay. He suggested to the Brigade Commander, Tom Hales, that if the Skibbereen men were supplied with five or six rifles and some cartridges they could ambush the party of constables with a view to capturing their rifles. The Brigade Commander approved of the suggestion and arrangements were made to carry it out at the first opportunity that presented itself.

The first of July was the date chosen for the attack and the position selected was a good one on the main Leap-Skibbereen road at Brade. Sam Kingston, the Battalion Commandant, sent out dispatches to all nine Companies of the Battalion requesting them to send the best shots among the Company officers, the object being to enable all Company staffs in the Battalion to have some experience of being under fire. Twenty-seven men mustered for the ambush, together with Sam Kingston and Pat Harte, the Brigade Quartermaster. No rifles were available so the men had to depend on shotguns and slugged cartridges. Writing of the engagement many years later, Neilus Connolly describes it thus :

> We had slugged cartridges made from home-made black powder for conscription (resistance) in 1918. They had been stored in Madranna slate quarry for more than two years, with the result that the powder was damp and useless, and worse still, we could not extract the cartridges because they were swollen by the damp air underground. A few of the cartridges made some kind of splutter which was sufficient to give our position away to the R.I.C. and they had the time of their lives, the five of them, giving rapid fire until we got away in disorder through the wood, so that our first clash with the enemy was a hopeless failure.

Undoubtedly, this engagement was a big disappointment, and its ending could indeed have been tragic. But it had one good result. It gave all those concerned experience of being under fire and this stood them in good stead later in the relentless struggle that developed during the months that followed.

Two days later Charlie Hurley received a report that a patrol of four policemen had cycled from Bandon to Innishannon. This news encouraged him to collect a party of eight Volunteers from the Innishannon Company and to prepare an ambush at Downdaniel Railway Bridge for the return of the constables. Charlie had a rifle, the others had shotguns. Five men were positioned on the east side of the bridge, while Charlie, Con O'Sullivan, and Miah Deasy went to the Bandon side. No one was to open fire until Charlie began to shoot. The reason for this was that Charlie wanted to ensure that the four members of the patrol were in the ambush position before the attack began.

In due course, the four constables cycled towards the bridge, but, unfortunately, there was a considerable distance between the first and second pair, so that by the time those taking up the rear came into the desired position, the first pair had gone beyond it and escaped. The other two were ambushed. One of them was wounded and his rifle and ammunition were captured, but the other, a Black and Tan, made a dash for the railway track. Miah Deasy saw him approaching at a distance of one hundred and fifty yards, but since his shotgun would have been useless at that distance he called Charlie Hurley's attention to the Tan. However, it was too late. The Tan dodged down the slope at the other side of the railway and made his escape.

Later that night a party of Volunteers drawn from the Ballineen, Ballinacarriga, Kenneigh, Coppeen, Enniskean and Behagh Companies, under the command of Pat Harte, Brigade Quartermaster, endeavoured to ambush a military cycling patrol at Carrigmore on the Ballineen-Dunmanway road. But the elusive patrol did not put in an appearance, and at dawn the ambushing party withdrew. And on the following day Newcestown Company ambushed an R.I.C. patrol near Mount Pleasant station which ended without casualty after an exchange of fire.

The Second Attack on Howes Strand Coastguard Station

The immediate reaction of the enemy to the first attack on Howes Strand Coastguard Station was to fortify the building in the manner they had been fortifying the R.I.C. barracks, and to increase its personnel. The station was now surrounded by barbed wire entanglements; the windows on the ground floor were sand-bagged while those on the upper floor were provided with steel shutters. The only entrances were in front, and consisted of two doors that could be easily defended by rifle fire directed from well-positioned loopholes that could be commanded from the first floor. The only cover available for an attacking party was a low fence about thirty yards from the front of the building, and it was in the process of being removed when the second attack was being contemplated. Delay on the part of the attacking party would have meant the removal of the last vestige of protective cover for them, and for this reason the date arranged for the attack was anticipated by twenty-four hours.

As well as fortifying the station, the enemy increased its personnel by adding five marines to the original party of ten coastguards who manned it. And as a further defensive measure it was arranged that a British destroyer should patrol the bay in front of the station from eleven o'clock each night until dawn the following morning, and throw a powerful searchlight on the building at intervals of one hour. At dawn the destroyer slipped out to sea.

As on the occasion of the first attack, three weeks earlier, Kilbrittain Company took the initiative in organising this one also, though the force which took part was supplemented by fifteen men from Timoleague, Bandon, and Ballinadee Companies—all under the command of the Battalion Vice-Commandant, Charlie Hurley.

On the night of the attack in Mid-July, eighteen men armed with rifles and some revolvers constituting the main attacking party, together with twenty-four others, met at Clonbouig, three miles to the north. Of the twenty-four men who were to support the main attacking party, four were armed and posted on the main Kilbrittain-Ballinspittle road to delay possible reinforcements coming from Kinsale, Bandon, or Kilbrittain; others were posted as scouts at points leading to the station; and the remainder were detailed to take up positions behind the main attacking party. Charlie Hurley, Battalion Vice-Commandant, was in charge of the entire operation, and carefully explained the plan of attack to those present. Thereupon the party marched to within four hundred yards of the station and there they were given final instructions. From their position they had a full view of the station as well as the enemy destroyer quite close in the bay.

As dawn was breaking, about four o'clock in the morning, the destroyer moved out of the bay, and as soon as it was out of sight the attacking party moved towards the station under the dubious protection of the partly-demolished fence in front. On reaching the fence, two groups of three men were to detach themselves from the main force, advance over the open space between the fence and the station, dodging the barbed wire entanglements by following the paths, and make for the two doors.

Charlie Hurley, Jim Hodnett, and Denis Manning rushed to the first door; Jack Fitzgerald, Mick O'Neill and Con Lehane to the second. The first two of each group had a brace of revolvers and a Mills bomb each. Manning and Lehane carried fourteen-pound sledge-hammers and a loaded revolver each. Both groups reached the doors simultaneously, and the first sound of action came when the giant Denis Manning shattered the first door of the station with a few mighty blows of his sledge-hammer. Before the enemy were aware of what was happening, Hurley and Hodnett, followed by Manning, who replaced the sledge-hammer with a revolver, gained possession of the ground floor and staircase.

The second door was still intact despite the herculean efforts of the brave Lehane with his sledge-hammer, and within minutes the enemy were firing through the windows and the loopholes above the door. Fitzgerald, O'Neill, and Lehane found ricochetting bullets flying all around them. Fire was opened up by the Volunteers behind the fence thirty yards away, and this constituted a further danger for the three men at the second door. Caught between two fires, they could not withdraw and had no option but to continue the effort to break down the door at all cost and enter the building.

Meanwhile, Hurley, Hodnett, and Manning reached the upper landing just as two armed defenders were coming through a doorway to meet them. The advantage was with the attackers at this point. Charlie could have shot both guards at close range but, cool as was always his way in action, he covered both with his revolver and demanded their surrender. They yielded, were promptly disarmed by Hodnett and Manning, and then directed into the next room where seven of the garrison who were firing from the windows were completely taken by surprise from the rear. Turning they found themselves covered by three revolvers and saw the Mills bomb ready in Charlie's hand. Quickly they obeyed his quietly-spoken order, 'Hands up!'

Hastily disarming this group of seven defenders and leaving Manning and Hodnett in charge, Charlie dashed into the next room and there captured a marine in the act of firing from the window. He capitulated without resistance, and this brought the number captured to ten. Five others in different rooms were firing from the windows.

The pounding on the second door of the station could still be heard below. So Charlie instructed Hodnett to descend the staircase and call the three Volunteers at the second door and tell them to enter the door which was already opened. On his way to carry out this instruction Hodnett was shot at by a marine just as he reached the top of the stairs and the bullet grazed his eyebrow. Despite this he rushed down the stairs just as the second door collapsed in splinters under the force of Lehane's sledge-hammer. The three men rushed into the building and were directed by Hodnett to the centre of the fighting upstairs. They were a welcome addition to their three companions now guarding ten prisoners with five others of the enemy armed and active in adjoining rooms of the building.

The captured arms are now taken from the occupied room to the landing outside. Leaving two of their number to guard the ten prisoners, the other four now go to a part of the building they had not yet explored, and in the first two rooms they enter they capture and disarm four of the remaining defenders.

The last defender of the station was the commanding officer and he was yet to be found. Eventually he was located in a room at the extreme end of the building and was called upon to surrender. He refused to do so, even though he was threatened that his room would be bombed. As Charlie Hurley moved forward to cast the

Mills bomb he held into the room, one of the prisoners asked permission to reason with his senior officer. This was granted and capitulation by the last defender of the station quickly followed.

At this stage, a white flag was shown from one of the windows and when this appeared the firing from outside ceased. The unarmed section of the Volunteers lying in reserve near the fence was now brought into action, and the captured booty was quickly collected and conveyed to Clonbouig, where it was safely deposited in dumps previously prepared on the lands of John Barrett. Fifteen service rifles and almost ten thousand rounds of .303 ammunition were captured.

As a military operation against an enemy fortified position this second attack on Howes Strand Coastguard Station was undoubtedly the most daring and successful attack so far organised in the West Cork area. Its effect on the morale of the men was altogether exceptional.

* * * * * *

About ten days after the second attack on Howes Strand Coastguard Station, three actions took place simultaneously in the Brigade area. Two of these were attacks on coastguard stations. The third concerned the Chief Intelligence Officer of the R.I.C. in the West Riding of Cork, at the time attached to the County Inspector's office in Bandon.

The Beara Battalion in Action again: Ballycrovane Coatsguard Station Attacked, 25 July 1920

Perched on a cliff overlooking Coulagh Bay and the Atlantic to the west, Ballycrovane Coastguard Station commanded an ideal vantage point. The station was surrounded by a stone wall five feet high which formed an outer defence, and gave protection to the windows on the ground floor. Inside the surrounding wall was the station building itself, consisting of four terraced houses from the upper windows of which there was a clear view of open fields on three sides, while the windows on the fourth side looked out towards the cliff edge which was about thirty feet from the surrounding wall. It was a formidable enemy outpost and had a garrison of about twelve marines. Nevertheless, two intrepid officers of the Beara Battalion planned to attack this station in the hope of capturing badly-needed arms and ammunition. This was in July 1920.

The arms available for the attack were pitifully few—four carbine rifles captured in Eyeries R.I.C. barracks on 17 March 1918, one Lee-Enfield rifle captured when a rearguard convoy was disarmed at Bealnalappa on 28 September of the same year, a few shotguns and four revolvers. And there were no more than a few rounds of ammunition for each weapon. With such a limited quantity of arms and ammunition, any kind of frontal attack had to be ruled out as impossible. It was necessary to find chinks in the defences of the station, and in an effort to find them recourse was had to the local branch of Cumann na mBan. Some members of this branch were instructed to cultivate the wife of one of the officers of the coastguard station. This assignment was so well carried out that one of the members of the Cumann secured temporary employment in the station itself and thereafter it was a simple matter to build up an accurate picture of its internal defences. In the light of the new information now forthcoming, it became even more obvious than it had been before that a frontal attack was out of the question.

At this point the possibilities of conducting an attack from the cliff side were examined. The project had its hazards and would necessitate a daylight attack rather than one at night, for to climb the precipitous cliff face in darkness would have been suicidal. Another serious hazard arose from the presence in the station of a wire-haired fox-terrier. This animal was a general favourite among the marines, and spent most of the daylight hours playing on the lawn between the station and the outer wall on the cliff side. Here lay the greatest threat, for the animal was liable to bark and raise the alarm if it heard any unusual noise caused by the attackers as they climbed the cliff face or if it got their scent in the wind. These dangers were pointed out to the men beforehand, and the need of taking special precautions was impressed upon all.

Liam O'Dwyer and Christy O'Connell, the two officers in charge of the attack, contacted the Castletownbere Company officers and suggested that they should attack a coastguard station similar to that in Ballycrovane in their area. This they readily agreed to do, and it was arranged that the two attacks would take place simultaneously, that is at twelve noon on Sunday, 25 July.

Plans were finalised and the attacking party was selected from the Eyeries Company, with reinforcements from Ballycrovane, Inches, Ardgroom, and Kilcatherine Companies. The actual storming party consisted of fifteen men, four of whom were to be armed with heavy sledge-hammers with which to break down the four doors on the ground floor. All were then to rush the ground floor of the station and gain possession of it, and launch the main attack from there. If this failed to effect the surrender of the garrison overhead, it was planned to gain access to a paraffin oil store on the premises, and set fire to the building. Transport was carefully organised and a section was detailed to be under cover a short distance from the objective, and be ready to convey the captured booty to safety as soon as the station fell. It was also arranged to have a party of signallers deployed along the heights between Eyeries and Castletownbere to ensure communication between the two attacking groups. Telephone wires were to be cut at the exact moment the attack was due to begin.

On the morning of 25 July the Eyeries party assembled in a field about a mile and a half from the coastguard station. Soon all the men from the different Companies taking part arrived, and final instructions were given. The signalling section was sent off first to take up positions on the heights between Ballycrovane and Castletownbere. The transport section was then moved close to the scene of the attack. As zero hour approached the men constituting the main attacking force were divided into four sections. Three men under the command of Liam O'Dwyer were to deal with the officers' quarters, the last of the four terraced houses constituting the station. Christy O'Connell was to lead the other three sections each of which would concentrate on one of the three remaining houses. In view of the fantastically exaggerated reports published later by the enemy concerning the numbers of the attacking party and their arms, it is of more than usual interest to record that O'Dwyer's party of four, i.e. including himself, had but two shot-guns, one with two cartridges and the other with one; O'Dwyer himself was armed with a Colt revolver and five cartridges, while the fourth member of the party carried a heavy sledge-hammer. The three sections under Christy O'Connell had between them six rifles with four or five rounds for each, four shotguns, four revolvers, and three sledge-hammers.

As the first sound of the midday Angelus rang out from the parish church, the party of determined attackers moved off to their objective. Their route had been carefully chosen, and was screened from view. It led down to the beach at a point about four hundred yards from the enemy post. In single file the men moved silently forward under the shelter of the cliff until they reached a position directly underneath the station. From there they had to climb a goat path for sixty feet and then make their way to the top. The final part of the ascent required a sheer climb with insecure and precarious footholds, with not sufficient cover for a snipe. Silently, carefully, and expectantly the men climbed, always conscious that up above them the keen ears of the fox-terrier would register the faintest sound of a falling stone or that his nose would pick up their scent and set him barking the alarm. In the circumstances the men were in a desperate situation. If the alarm were raised either by the barking of the dog or by any of the enemy who observed what was afoot, the attackers would undoubtedly have been shot down like sitting ducks. However, in those critical moments the only thoughts in the minds of the Volunteers concerned the climb to the top and the attack which was to follow. They reached the top without incident. As one man followed the other, he moved with the calm assurance of a veteran into his appointed position around the wall which formed the outer defence of the station. Lying flat the men waited for the signal to scale the wall and make for the doors. Once over that wall there would be no retreat.

The party had just taken up their positions by the wall and were waiting for the signal when the peace of that bright Sunday afternoon was shattered by the frantic barking of the dog which had at last discovered the danger that threatened its masters. In a flash the men were over the wall and racing for the doors before the marines had time to open fire. As O'Dwyer raced towards the officers' quarters, he could see them through the window grabbing their guns and cartridge belts. One of O'Dwyer's men covering his approach to the door of the officers' quarters with his shotgun fired at an officer, but there was only a dull click of the hammer on a dud cartridge. He had no other. The man with the sledge-hammer broke down the door and Liam O'Dwyer was in the kitchen facing the screaming and hysterical wife of one of the officers, a man named Brown, who was second in command. This man now came rushing from the day room and was called upon to surrender. He refused to do so. His wife dashed between him and O'Dwyer and implored him not to fire. Ignoring her pleas he raised his revolver but Liam fired first over the wife's shoulder and Brown's revolver dropped to the floor. Though shot through the right shoulder, he pluckily tried to pick up his gun with his left hand.

At this point the commanding officer, a man named Snowen, passed outside the window, intending to make an attack from the rear. Leaving one of his men with a shotgun to take care of the situation in the kitchen, O'Dwyer rushed out to intercept Snowen, who immediately retreated into the day room. There Snowen began firing. Splintered glass spattered around O'Dwyer as he ducked and continued to fight from the shelter of the pillar dividing the two windows.

Suddenly there was a roar from the shotgun in the kitchen, and the wounded officer, Brown, rushed from there into the day room to join Snowen. The latter was shouting orders as he fired to left and right of the pillar. Chancing a quick look in order to see the positions of the officers in the room, O'Dwyer noticed Brown standing to the right of Snowen who was in a crouching position reloading his revolver. A bullet grazed his head as he ducked back to the shelter of the pillar, but as he did so he chanced a quick shot in the direction of the officers. With that he heard a thud followed by a groan. Then followed a shot to the right and another to the left of the pillar as Snowen was back in action. O'Dwyer, who had been firing from a crouched position, suddenly stood up straight and chanced another quick look into the room only to duck immediately as Snowen's bullet knocked a chip off the plaster where he appeared. Crouching again he chanced another shot, firing from the other side of the pillar. Again he heard the thud of a falling body. After a few tense seconds of silence he peered around again and saw the two officers lying dead on the floor. He had only one round left in his revolver.

Rushing back to the kitchen to investigate the shot he had heard, he found that the Volunteers he had left there had fired a warning shot as Brown was getting up from the floor with his revolver in his left hand. This shot brought down a large portion of the ceiling and evidently frightened or distracted Brown, for he retreated back to the day room to join Snowen. Mrs Brown was now sitting in a chair in a state of collapse, covered with white plaster from the ceiling.

Elsewhere the fight was raging fiercely. Christy O'Connell gained entry to the ground floor of the three houses which had been the objects of his attack. The marines above were blazing away from the upper windows at anything that appeared to be moving in the outlying fields. O'Connell was shouting to the garrison to surrender, and threatening to burn down the entire building if they refused to do so. O'Dwyer then came on the scene, and called out that the two officers in command had been shot. There was a brief pause after this announcement, and a few moments later white flags appeared at the windows. In a room at the eastern end of the building one marine refused to surrender and continued firing. O'Connell's ammunition was now exhausted, but he reloaded his revolver from some of the captured ammunition found in the building, and peppered the room of the resister with bullets. This spray of bullets convinced the enemy that his position was hopeless so throwing his rifle down the stairs, he surrendered. Thus ended the fight.

The Volunteers were naturally jubilant over their success, and set about locking the captured marines in one of the rooms, and collecting the arms and ammunition and equipment that were to be found in the buildings. A thorough search yielded a total of twelve rifles with seven thousand rounds of ammunition; six Webley revolvers with fifty rounds for each; bandoliers, clips, Sam Brown belts and holsters, and various other items, including Verey pistols and rockets and a large marine telescope.[3]

The transport section was now called into action. Quickly collecting the booty, this party marched off to the east, flanked on one side by the sea and on the other by a few riflemen supplied with plenty of ammunition from the captured haul. As the party moved off, a thick fog rolled in from the sea and reduced visibility to a minimum. At this one wag remarked, 'God helps those who help themselves.'

Next morning a British destroyer anchored off shore. Two boats were lowered and rowed towards Ballycrovane Pier. The garrison of the station and the remains of the two officers were removed and taken to Cobh, or Queenstown, as it was then called. The station was not reoccupied, and was burnt down by the Volunteers shortly afterwards.

To visit the scene of this daring attack today and to retrace the steps taken by the attacking party from the starting point near Eyeries to the beach and thence to the cliff face causes one to marvel at the audacity of the men who planned the entire operation, and to admire the bravery and determination of the men who put it into effect. It was the kind of operation for which commando forces were equipped and trained in World War Two, twenty years later. But it is doubtful whether such well-trained and equipped commandos would have achieved the success won at Ballycrovane by the Volunteers whose courage and daring counted for so much more than their arms.[4]

3. The only striking difference in the accounts of this attack on Bally-crovane Coastguard Station by the two surviving officers, Liam O'Dwyer and Christy O'Connell, is that the former claims that the number of rifles captured was nineteen, the latter twelve. The only reason for the choice of the lower figure is the desire to avoid the possibility of erring by excess.

4. This account was put together from information supplied in 1964 by the two surviving officers, Liam O'Dwyer and Christy O'Connell, on the occasion of a visit which I paid to Eyeries in the company of Florence O'Donoghue. We were conducted over the ground by the two officers who

The attack on the Castletownbere Coastguard Station was synchronised perfectly with that at Ballycrovane. A party of local Volunteers, under the command of Billy O'Neill, entered the station and captured the main part of the building at noon, a time when the garrison of six was at a minimum. The officer in charge of the station surrendered immediately and was left with one guard in the main room while the other Volunteers searched in the adjoining rooms for arms and ammunition. Dressed in civilian clothes, the officer was taken to be unarmed. He began to chat in friendly fashion with the Volunteer who was guarding him. When he saw his chance, he suddenly drew a revolver, held up his guard and fired on the returning searchers. These latter, believing reinforcements had come, made a dash for the rear exit, but not before four of their number were wounded. This unfortunate incident taught the lesson that any lapse of vigilance with the enemy would be costly.

Liquidation of Enemy Intelligence Agent

In general, the members of the R.I.C. force in Cork—as indeed elsewhere throughout the country—served their British masters well. They acted as the eyes and ears of the British Government in our area, reported all Volunteer activities that came to their notice, led frequent raids on private houses of real or suspected sympathisers with our cause, and did everything in their power to thwart our struggle for national independence. Yet, it must be mentioned that some members of the constabulary were exceptions in this regard and proved to be friendly towards us, and even went so far as to help us on many occasions.[5]

There were some R.I.C. men in Bantry, Bandon, Kilbrittain, and Skibbereen who went beyond the requirements of strict duty in their efforts to destroy our movement, but none did more in this regard than the Chief Intelligence Officer for all West Riding and

---

explained in detail what took place. The account was published in *Éire-Ireland. A Journal of Irish Studies* (1966), pp. 71-76, published by the Irish American Cultural Institute, St. Paul, Minnesota. My thanks are due to the two heroes of the story for their generous help.

5. Here, as examples, mention should be made of Sergeant Lonergan who was stationed successively at Kilbrittain and Bandon, and Sergeant Dan O'Sullivan, stationed at Innishannon during my early days in the Volunteer movement, then transferred to Union Hall and later to Durrus where he was wounded in our attack upon the barracks which he commanded in the village.

the districts of Macroom and Millstreet. He was stationed at Bandon, and was obnoxious to the Volunteers and the people generally in that he took pleasure in very rough tactics with prisoners, and was utterly ruthless in his work as the enemy's chief spy. We determined to end the activities of this arch-enemy once and for all.

Located as he was within the strongly-guarded enemy citadel of Bandon, this officer was not easily captured. To wait for him outside the barrack door until he appeared was a possibility but it would have meant certain death for the assailant. Indeed he was so well protected that there was very little opportunity of dealing with him with any assurance of success. In the end, it was decided that the only way to end his activities was the invidious one of ambushing him on his way to Mass on a Sunday morning. Even this was risky because he could be accompanied by colleagues.

However, on Sunday morning, 25 July, he was alone as he made his way to the eight o'clock Mass. Three Volunteers were waiting for him that morning as he entered the church grounds, mounted the steps and approached the porch. As he was about to put his hand on the handle of the door leading into the nave of the church the Volunteers stepped forward and shot him several times. The parish priest rushed to his side and anointed him. He was dead inside ten minutes.

The circumstances of this shooting created a local sensation and perhaps understandably met with the condemnation of the parish priest. Indeed the Minister for Defence, a religious man, was equally upset and was satisfied only when it was fully explained to him that the shooting was a vital necessity as a means of defending those who were striving to advance the cause of independence, and that no alternative method to that employed was possible in the circumstances.

Two days after the Intelligence Officer's death an obnoxious member of the R.I.C. stationed at Clonakilty, was to meet a similar fate. This man had fired on unarmed civilians a few days previously, and the local Volunteers decided to put an end to his activities. On 27 July he was followed by a party of four Volunteers. Two of them caught up with him as he was entering a greengrocer's shop in Rossa Street, and shot him through the head. He died in the early hours of the following morning.

A Second Ambush is planned to take place at Snave Bridge, Bantry

Towards the close of July the Commanding Officer and staff of the Bantry Battalion decided to ambush two military lorries at

Snave Bridge on their way to Bantry from Kenmare. For this purpose a land mine was made at Jerry Connolly's farm at Hollyhill, Glengarriff, and was brought from the farm to Snave Bridge by Jeremiah O'Driscoll, a local tailor, in his horse and cart. Meanwhile, the Battalion staff and the Captain of the Bantry Company with Volunteers drawn from Coomhola, Glengarriff, and Kealkil Companies proceeded to the locality chosen for the ambush. While the officers were selecting suitable positions for their men on both sides of the road, they were alarmed by the sound of rifle fire and the noise of the military lorries approaching unexpectedly from the Glengarriff direction. The lorries were still two miles away, and the soldiers could be heard firing wildly as they advanced. Seeing that there was no chance of getting the Volunteers into their positions in time, the officers ordered them to retire, leaving the horse and cart with the mine on the road.

The military must have had some knowledge of the presence of the Volunteers in the area, for instead of driving over Snave Bridge, they turned their lorries up the Coomhola Road. Indeed they would have trapped a number of our men were it not that the Volunteer officers opened fire on the enemy with Peter the Painter automatic revolvers. This fire distracted the military and prevented them from cutting off the retreat of the Volunteers. Unfortunately, Jeremiah O'Driscoll's horse and cart containing the land mine under a bale of straw were captured, though Jeremiah himself managed to escape. Another Volunteer, however, was less fortunate and was arrested.

There is an amusing sequel to the abortive ambush on the next day when Jeremiah O'Driscoll called to the military barracks at Bantry and asked to see the officer in charge. He was brought before Colonel Jones and his Intelligence Officer and closely questioned by them for over an hour. Jeremiah, acting the part of a fool, said that his horse and cart had been taken by armed men whom he did not know; it was only that morning he had heard where his horse and cart were and he came along to get them. The officers were not accepting such a simple tale as that, and Jeremiah was forthrightly ejected from the barracks.

Nothing daunted by his summary dismissal of the day before, Jeremiah showed up at the barracks again the following morning, and made a very strong and pathetic appeal for the return of 'his little mare'. He explained to Colonel Jones that he was a travelling tailor and that without transport he could not get around to do his work. The fact that he was lame lent credence to his account, though he did not think it necessary to add that his three brothers were active Volunteers. His final appeal was too much for Colonel Jones : 'Sir,' said Jeremiah, 'if you cannot give me back my little mare, give me one of the army mules instead.' He was given his horse and cart, minus the mine, of course, and arrived home a happy man.

About this time, I became aware that certain internal troubles were brewing among the Volunteers of the Togher Company. It happened that the district around Togher, north-west of Dunmanway, was a particularly important one for the Brigade. Covering the hilly country from Kilmichael to Coosane Gap, it had its importance for communications, but it was also all-important as an ideal centre for resting and training active units of the Volunteers, and for hiding and treating the wounded. Besides, the Togher Company was numerically a very strong one with one hundred and thirty men on its rolls. That the officers of such a Company should be divided in outlook not merely threatened unity among them, but had a very adverse effect on the men.

In an endeavour to remedy this situation, I invited Dick Barrett to accompany me on a visit to Togher during the month of July. We called a parade of the full Company and pointed out the importance of strict military discipline and unquestioning obedience to officers and section commanders. We also stressed the importance of the Company for the Brigade as a whole, and emphasised that any dissension in the ranks at the crucial stage we had reached in the struggle would be fatal. An hour's break followed our address during which there was a full and frank discussion between us and the officers of the Company and some of the section commanders also. From the discussion it soon became evident that one of the big difficulties was the size of the Company area and the consequent difficulty of maintaining unity of command. Personality clashes had also a part to play in the trouble, and indeed they had from time to time in other areas. Nevertheless, the good will of all concerned was evident from the efforts the men made to find a solution, and towards the close of our meeting a solution was found. It was decided to divide the Company in two, to be known in future as Togher and Derrynacaheragh Companies, and a staff was appointed to the new Company on the spot. So ended the trouble, and thereafter excellent service was rendered by both Companies in providing billets for our men and guarding them, and also guarding Brigade Headquarters during the period it was quartered in the area.

The July Brigade Council meeting was held at O'Donoghue's of Ballinvard, Rossmore, on the 25th of the month. Tom Hales presided and the full Brigade staff and representatives from all the Battalions were present. The activities of the preceding month were passed in review, and all officers were urged to intensify their offensive against the enemy. The Brigade Quartermaster reported that since the previous Brigade Council meeting in June, the rifles captured in the Brigade area totalled twenty-seven and that the ammunition taken amounted to close on seventeen thousand rounds.

It was felt at the meeting that the shooting of the Intelligence Officer which had occurred that morning was very likely to lead to reprisals being carried out by the R.I.C. in the Bandon area. To meet this danger it was decided that the Brigade staff should move into the district at a point close to Bandon town. There steps would be taken, with the aid of the four adjoining Companies of Mount Pleasant, Newcestown, Kilpatrick, and Bandon, to cope with whatever situation should present itself; we had no idea what form the enemy reprisals would take, but we had to be prepared for the worst. Before closing our meeting, it was arranged that Tom Hales, Pat Harte, Charlie Hurley and I should meet at Hurley's of Laragh on Tuesday, 27 July, around midday to organise resistance to whatever reprisals the enemy attempted.

After the Brigade Council meeting, Charlie Hurley and I proceeded to Shanavagh with a view to planning an ambush on the northern road from Ballineen to Dunmanway. We had heard reports that a military patrol went out at irregular intervals from an outpost in Ballineen in which soldiers of the Essex Regiment from Bandon were quartered, and we were determined to ambush them at the first opportunity.

On Tuesday morning, Charlie Hurley and I departed from Shanavagh *en route* for Hurley's of Laragh. Our way lay by Desert Bridge that crossed the Bandon river east of Enniskean. Just as we were approaching this bridge from the south we were warned by a local resident that it was being held by a party of Essex soldiers from Bandon. So taking up a position behind Desert Railway Station, we waited for two hours until the enemy departed, and then we crossed the bridge in safety. At John Lordan's of Coolinagh we rested and there, to our dismay, we heard the news that Tom Hales and Pat Harte had been captured as they were about to enter Frank Hurley's house at Laragh by soldiers of the Essex Regiment, and that they had been taken to the military barracks in Bandon.

At the same time we learned about the arrests, the burning of houses, and the rough handling given to prisoners taken since the Sunday morning on which the R.I.C. Intelligence Officer was shot. We knew that Tom Hales and Pat Harte would be recognised by the enemy as Volunteer leaders, and that they would certainly receive brutal treatment and be cruelly tortured. In point of fact, we learned later that the two men were so barbarously treated that they were hospital cases by the time the enemy had finished torturing them, and that the head injuries inflicted on Pat Harte were so severe that he never recovered from them.

Anticipating another raid by the Essex soldiers on Hurley's house later that night, we quickly mobilised a party of thirty men, and set out for Laragh. We took up a position at Tinkers Cross which commanded the approaches to Hurley's house, and there lay in wait to ambush any enemy raiding party that happened to come along. For three consecutive nights we lay there, but the enemy never appeared.

So ended the momentous month of July 1920. From the purely military point of view, it witnessed the most important phase of the war in West Cork. The spectacular successes at Howes Strand and Ballycrovane Coastguard Stations had a decisive effect on morale in the Brigade. They also brought a very important addition to our armament and made it possible for us to launch the larger offensives that were soon to feature in the war. Hitherto one of our chief concerns had been to evade arrest, but now that our men were becoming suitably armed and provided with modern equipment from captured hauls, they began to realise that at last it would be possible to meet the enemy on an equal, or nearly equal, footing. Thirty-nine rifles had been captured in the month of July and this brought the total up to eighty-eight. Then the capture of approximately twenty-four thousand rounds of ammunition brought the total to approximately twenty-seven thousand rounds.

In former times Irish military struggles against British power had been all too frequently sabotaged from their inception by spies and informers. Early in our struggle we were made aware of this danger, and took vigorous measures to counteract it. So well organised and effective was our intelligence that the enemy was deprived of essential information regarding our plans and our movements. Indeed large units of Volunteers were able to move freely from one district to another without fear of informers alerting the enemy as to our whereabouts. Due to the turn our activities were soon to take, this freedom of movement was to prove a priceless asset.

CHAPTER 14

AN IMPORTANT DECISION OF G.H.Q. AND ITS SEQUEL

Orders had been received from G.H.Q. in the course of July summoning the Commanders of the Brigades of South Munster, i.e. Cork, Kerry, West Waterford and West Limerick, to a meeting in Dublin. As Tom Hales, our Brigade Commander, had been captured, we hastily convened a meeting at O'Mahony's of Belrose. Those present at this meeting were Seán Hales, Dick Barrett, Flor Begley, and myself. To fill the vacancy caused by the arrest of Tom Hales, we automatically selected Charlie Hurley as his successor, and Dick Barrett was our choice to fill the post of Brigade Quartermaster made vacant by Pat Harte's arrest. At this meeting it was also decided that I should represent the Brigade at the meeting in Dublin and there submit our recommendations regarding Brigade Staff appointments for the approval of G.H.Q. Finally, since we were anxious to introduce Dick Barrett to G.H.Q. it was decided that he would travel to Dublin with me.

We cycled to Cork on Saturday morning, 31 July, and at Glanmire Station met Terence MacSwiney who, as representative of the First Cork Brigade, was travelling to Dublin to our meeting at G.H.Q. The train journey was uneventful, but at Kingsbridge[1] we took the precaution of leaving the station separately, and we met later at Vaughan's Hotel. Shortly after our arrival there we were visited by Gearóid O'Sullivan and Seán Ó Muirthuile, who gave us details about the meeting that was to be held on the following day, Sunday, at 35 Lower Gardiner Street. Later in the course of that same evening, Michael Collins, Peadar Clancy, and Dick McKee came along and, as could be expected, the subject of conversation was the progress of the war in Cork. Dick McKee made many inquiries about the officers he had met at the Training Camp at Glandore a year previously. Dick Mulcahy also called and took Terence MacSwiney away with him.

The next day we spent a very pleasant afternoon at an *Oireachtas*[2] in Jones's Road, now known as Croke Park, and when it was over, we made our way separately to the venue of the meeting in Gardiner Street. There we met the Minister of Defence, Cathal Brugha, who presided. Also present were, Dick Mulcahy,

1. This is now known as Heuston Station.
2. An annual cultural festival.

Chief of Staff, Michael Collins, Director of Intelligence, Gearóid O'Sullivan, Adjutant General, Seán McMahon, Quartermaster General, Rory O'Connor, Director of Engineering, and Diarmuid O'Hegarty, Director of Organisation. Cork Number 1 Brigade was represented by Terence MacSwiney, Cork Number 2 by Liam Lynch, Cork Number 3 by myself. Kerry Number 1 by Paddy Cahill, Kerry Number 2 by Dan O'Mahony, and Kerry Number 3 by Jeremiah O'Riordan; Waterford West by Pax Whelan, and the West Limerick Brigade was represented by Father Dick McCarthy, then curate at Ballyhahil, in the unavoidable absence of the Commander, Seán Finn. This was our first formal introduction as an organised body representing the Southern Army to G.H.Q. It was also the first formal occasion on which we were introduced to each other.

The Chief of Staff reviewed the general position throughout the country as a whole so far as our struggle was concerned. Then he concentrated on the south and described the situation as it appeared to G.H.Q. He was very generous in his praise of the Brigades, and was most complimentary in his references to the capture of arms and ammunition that had been effected. He encouraged those in charge of areas that had not been quite so successful to become self-reliant by conducting operations that had been proved successful elsewhere.

Following on this preamble, the Chief of Staff continued with an important directive dealing with the question of ambushing. It was to be the policy of G.H.Q., said Mulcahy, to authorise general ambushing as the principal form of attack against the enemy, but in all cases the enemy should be first of all called upon to surrender. Here Mulcahy was supported by Cathal Brugha, but the matter was not allowed to pass unchallenged. It was pointed out that up to this ambushing attacks had been concentrated mostly on cycling patrols; in such cases the policy of calling upon the enemy to surrender before shooting at him was indeed feasible, though it would necessarily increase the danger for the attackers. But it was pointed out that an entirely new development was now taking shape in enemy transport that would make the policy advocated by Mulcahy and Brugha suicidal. The enemy convoys that were now on the roads were most often protected by armoured cars, and the military lorries had mounted machine-guns. To call upon the enemy to surrender in such circumstances before attacking him would be disastrous. Besides, it was emphasised that this directive which Mulcahy was sponsoring would rob our attacks of the element of surprise, our greatest advantage and one so vital to our inexperienced and inadequately armed men now opposing an enemy hardened by experience in war and fully equipped with the most modern weapons and with unlimited supplies of ammunition and bombs. In the end the Minister of Defence and G.H.Q. gave full sanction to the plan of attack outlined by the Brigade Officers present, and so our programme for the coming offensive was formally authorised.

The occupation by British forces of strategically-important towns in areas of south Munster represented by those attending the meeting was next raised for discussion by the Chief of Staff. Of the towns mentioned, Macroom was considered the most important. Situated in the heart of a district that was ideal as a training ground for fighters, and as a centre from which columns could operate, Macroom offered advantages that were being off-set by the enemy's presence in the town. The need of containing the enemy there was felt to be a pressing one, and various plans to meet the need were discussed. The one suggested by the Chief of Staff consisted in containing or confining the enemy to their bases by setting up a series of circles around the centres they occupied, the first ring being two miles from the centre, the second four miles, and so on. The main objection to this plan was voiced by Terence MacSwiney in whose area, in Macroom, the Manchester Regiment was stationed. He said that he could provide the men to carry out the plan suggested but that he could not supply them with sufficient arms. Other officers from the country districts thought that ambushing and town sniping were the best forms of resistance we could offer for the time being. In the final summing up, it was made clear that the mode of attack employed was left to the discretion of the Brigade Commanders. So the meeting ended.

Later that night and during the next two days, we were all given the opportunity of meeting the different members of the G.H.Q. Staff and the directors of special services. This personal contact was most helpful and encouraging, and we availed ourselves of it to the full to set out our problems and profit by the advice and experience of the men who were so successfully directing the national campaign.

For us in West Cork, it was emphasised that our greatest need was a greater supply of arms and ammunition. It was scarcely necessary to emphasise this as we were very conscious of the need ourselves. We were assured that the matter was engaging the attention of G.H.Q. and that negotiations were afoot to purchase a shipment of arms. We were promised a generous quota if the scheme materialised. Our recommendations concerning the appointment of Charlie Hurley to the post of Commander of our Brigade and Dick Barrett to that of Brigade Quartermaster were submitted and were cordially approved. So we returned to our areas on Thursday feeling very well satisfied with the whole proceedings of our historic meeting at G.H.Q.

On my return to Brigade Headquarters at Belrose, Upton, I had the very great pleasure of informing Charlie Hurley that he was now my commanding officer. He received the news of his appointment with a good deal of embarrassment, but without more ado accepted the responsibility, and with characteristic energy pressed forward with renewed vigour in the heightening struggle with the common foe. On our part, we felt lucky indeed to have such an excellent commanding officer over us, and his subsequent record fully justified our trust and confidence.

While Dick Barrett and I were in Dublin, plans were being drawn up by Charlie Hurley for an attack on Innishannon R.I.C. barracks. This was a large, strongly-fortified, isolated building with a garrison of six policemen. The time chosen for the attack was midnight on Saturday, 7 August, and the plan was to lay a mine at the front door of the building, and when this blew the door in an assault party was to charge and engage the police in hand to hand fighting. A number of men were mobilised for the attack from the neighbouring Companies. About sixteen of them were armed with rifles, another group had shotguns, while those who were unarmed formed a scouting party.

When the men were taking up their positions on the night arranged for the attack, a rifle was accidentally discharged, and the noise immediately alerted the garrison. Robbed of the element of surprise and attack was foredoomed to failure, and Charlie Hurley reluctantly called it off, as he saw that now the only result an attack could have would be a waste of precious ammunition. To make a decision of this kind was a most difficult thing for a man of Charlie Hurley's courage and determination, but the fact that he did make it reflected his true worth as a responsible and discerning leader.

On the following day, Sunday, at a Brigade Staff meeting held at O'Mahony's of Belrose, our new Commander quickly outlined his plan of campaign for the month of August. He intended going to Skibbereen. Ted O'Sullivan was instructed to go to Bantry, and I was to go to Dunmanway. Then in our different locations we were to carry out three operations simultaneously to emphasise for the enemy's benefit our determination to extend the war.

Charlie Hurley concentrated his attention on the R.I.C. barracks at Leap, six miles east of Skibbereen. With the co-operation of an R.I.C. man who was sympathetic towards our cause it was arranged to attempt the capture of the station. The attempt was to be made on a day on which this policeman was on duty within the building. He was to open the door at a certain time, and the Volunteers were then to rush the building and take it by storm. Unfortunately for Charlie's scheme, the internal arrangements of the barracks were unexpectedly altered on the day fixed for the attack, and the policeman who was to open the door was appointed to patrol duty. Charlie had his men in readiness on the day and at the hour arranged, but when he saw the policeman who was to open the door emerge from the barracks as a member of a patrol, he knew that plans had gone awry, and that it would be best in the circumstances to abandon the attempt on the barracks for the time being.[3]

Ted O'Sullivan's efforts materialised in a successful ambush on an R.I.C. patrol at Snave Bridge near Bantry, and resulted in the capture of a Lee-Enfield rifle. The operation for which I was responsible was delayed until 8 September, but since an ambush was organised at Brinny before that date, I shall describe this first, and then give an account of the attack with which I was concerned.

Brinny Ambush, 20 August 1920

It was becoming evident about this time that our offensive against the R.I.C. was proving effective, and we noticed that police cycling patrols were being replaced by stronger military patrols. These had been operating occasionally during the month of August, and an ambush was laid for one of them at Brinny on the Crossbarry-Bandon Road on Sunday, 29 August.

The ambush party was under the command of the Commandant of the Bandon Battalion, Seán Hales, and the men were armed with rifles and shotguns. They were drawn from the companies at Crosspound, Mount Pleasant, Kilpatrick, Newcestown, Timoleague, Clogagh, Innishannon and Ballinadee and had been in an ambush position at Black Quarry, a mile west of Brinny, for the preceding two days. On Sunday they were moved to the point at which a stone bridge carried the road over the Brinny river which

3. Later a party of Volunteers from the Myross and Leap Companies successfully ambushed an R.I.C. patrol at Leap. The Volunteers on this occasion were commanded by Pat O'Driscoll, Captain of Myross Company.

joins the Bandon at Downdaniel. The road approaching the bridge was straight and dipped slightly before crossing the bridge, and then rose sharply to a bend fifty yards west of it. The party was divided into four sections. One was posted west of the bridge on the north side; a second east of the bridge and also on the north side. Sections three and four were placed west of the bridge on the south side, one being close to the bridge, and the other being further west than the section on the opposite side of the road. A few men were placed east of the bridge on the south side of the road, but the major attack was to be launched from the west side as the patrol approached the bridge.

The long summer day passed without incident until about 4.30 in the afternoon. Then a volley of rifle fire suddenly opened up on the rear of section one on the north side of the road and west of the bridge. It came from the fields to the north west where there was good cover, and clearly indicated that the ambush party was being attacked from the rear. The section under fire evacuated its position, and succeeded in getting across the road and over the fence on the south side. When the military advanced to follow up, they came under fire from section three of the attackers under the command of Frank Neville. In the exchange of fire at this point, Lieutenant Tim Fitzgerald of Mount Pleasant Company was killed.

Frank Neville dashed across the road from his position to the south to aid his comrades there, but found that they had pulled out in time and were retreating with the main party across the river. There were no further casualties and no prisoners were taken. It was discovered later that the military, obviously acting on information they had received, dismounted, and advanced under cover through the fields until they came upon the ambush party from the rear. Lieutenant Hotblack of the Essex Regiment, who was in charge of the military, was later killed in action at Crossbarry.

Credit for the successful withdrawal of our men from a position of imminent danger was undoubtedly due to Frank Neville's defensive action. We never learned whether the enemy had any casualties in the engagement, but the loss of such a promising young officer as Tim Fitzgerald—the first Volunteer in our Brigade to lose his life in action—added sorrow to the serious reverse we suffered on the occasion.

Action at Manch, 8 September 1920

My efforts were directed towards putting into effect the ambush of the military cycling patrol which I had planned with Charlie Hurley on 8 August. The available information was to the effect that a patrol of between fifteen and twenty soldiers of the Essex Regiment under the command of an officer passed between Ballineen and Dunmanway each day, and our main objective in the action was the capture of the arms which the soldiers carried. Success in the capture of the arms would give Dunmanway parity with the other Battalions in the Brigade so far as the possession of rifles was concerned, and it was our aim at the time to make each of the Battalions independent in the matter of serviceable weapons.

The position selected for the ambush extended from Idle Bridge on the west to Blackwater Bridge on the east—a distance of about four hundred yards. The road was straight and level for a considerable distance to the west; straight also through the ambush position, except for a sharp bend over Blackwater Bridge at the eastern extremity. A road leading north joined the main road at the western limit of the position, and this was the prearranged line of withdrawal. On the north side of the road there was a high wall, behind which the Blackwater tributary of the Bandon river flowed along the whole length of the position and it was backed by open rising ground. Only its eastern end at Blackwater Bridge was suitable as a post for our men on the north side of the road. On the southern side there was good cover. The railway line ran close to and parallel with the road. Two fields further south was the Bandon river, also roughly parallel with the road and railway line.

The ambush party comprised about thirty men from Coppeen, Toger, Aultagh, Behagh, Kenneigh, Ballineen, Derrynacaheragh, and Dunmanway Companies. Among the officers present were Seán Murphy, Commandant of Dunmanway Battalion, Michael McCarthy, Vice-Commandant, John Fitzgerald, Captain of Kilbrittain Company, Con Lehane, Captain of the Timoleague Company, and myself. These five officers were armed with rifles, the remainder of the party with shotguns. Of those engaged in the action only three had been under fire before—Fitzgerald, Lehane, and myself.

The party assembled at Connagh, two miles north of Manch, on the night of 7 September, and were in position at 8.30 on the following morning. One section under Michael McCarthy was posted north of the road at the eastern end where they commanded a view of the road to the east, and could cover with shotgun fire part of the ambush position to the west. The second section under my command was posted inside the fence on the southern side of the road, extending eastwards from Idle Bridge to the point covered by McCarthy's section on the opposite side. The ambush position was rather long, but this was necessary as cycle patrols moved in extended order; fifteen to twenty men could cover two hundred yards of the road.

It was intended to allow the patrol to come fully into the ambush position, then to call upon them to halt, dismount, drop their bicycles to which the rifles were attached, and make a right turn so that they would be facing the wall on the north side of the road. This was intended as a precaution against subsequent identification of members of the ambush party by the military. If the order was not obeyed promptly the signal for attack was a rifle shot fired by me. Two men were posted east of the position to fell a tree that ws partly cut just when the patrol had passed through. A runner kept contact between Ballineen and Michael McCarthy, and his messages were to be relayed orally to McCarthy and from him along the line of men to me.

At 9.30 a.m. a military lorry passed through the ambush position going east. This was not attacked, partly because no measures had been taken to stop a lorry, and partly because the available arms were insufficient for the purpose, but mainly because more arms would be obtained by a successful attack on the cycle patrol. The men remained quietly in position, and the long hours of waiting dragged on.

After seven hours of waiting, about 3.30 p.m. a verbal message from Michael McCarthy reached me to the effect that our runner had reported that the enemy in Ballineen were aware that the ambush party was in position and were preparing to come out and surround us. I had no reason to doubt the accuracy of the message, though it became clear subsequently that the message had been distorted as it passed from one man to the next. The original message was to the effect that the cycling patrol was getting ready to move out from Ballineen. Not knowing this at the time, and thinking we were about to be surrounded by the enemy, I gave order to the men to retire.

For the section south of the road the only route available for withdrawal was northwards along the by-road at the western end. To the south, beyond the railway line, were a few fields and then the river, which was wide and deep at this point. There was little room for maneuvring and the terrain would be difficult for the shotgun men if they were obliged to fight their way out of it. So I decided to have them retire across the main road and to the north.

Instructions to this effect were sent to Michael McCarthy at the eastern end. He was directed to hold his position until the western section had crossed the road and made their way into the road leading to the north. He was then to move away independently with his own section and meet the main party at Kenneigh.

All the men of my section were on the road moving towards the north-bound by-road when there was a shout, and on looking back they saw a military lorry coming from the east not more than a hundred yards away. I immediately gave the order to the men to take cover behind the fence they had left on the southern side of the road and behind the railway line. The lorry continued on past us and stopped just beyond Idle Bridge. As the military dismounted, I ordered the shotgun men to retire to the next fence behind the railway line. The four riflemen followed and took up a position from which to cover the withdrawal of the shotgun men. The military were now firing and moving towards us. We held our fire until they came into view and then we opened up and drove them back to their lorry. They took with them one Volunteer of the Behagh Company whom they captured, and then moved off in the direction of Dunmanway.

So ended our hope of capturing arms at Manch. The attempt was a disappointment, but it was part of the pattern of the war we were waging, and we refused to allow ourselves to be discouraged. There were no easy victories to be expected, and the hazards were always great. But though such actions as that at Manch were unsuccessful in their main objective, they had their effect on the enemy, and tended to undermine his morale.

The Arms Fund

As the pace of the war began to quicken, and as our attacks and ambushes multiplied, the enemy reacted with increasing vigour. Wholesale raids and arrests became the order of the day, with the result that more and more of our men were being forced out 'on the run' to avoid capture. We were keenly alive to our responsibility towards these men and the obligation incumbent on us of protecting and caring for them, and reducing as far as possible the hardship that was their lot. The generosity of the ordinary people in providing for our men's needs and the sacrifices they were prepared to make for them were truly admirable, but we were aware that the rapidly-increasing number of men being thrown on the generosity of these people, particularly those in the poorer districts, caused a heavy burden which we were anxious to lighten.

To cope with this problem, it was decided at the September meeting of the Brigade Council, which was held at Murphy's of Ardcahan, to launch a drive to raise funds to support our hunted comrades, to provide them with clothing and the ordinary amenities of life. It was to be known as The Arms Fund, and was to be organised by the Brigade Quartermaster, Dick Barrett, assisted by the Quartermaster of the Bandon Battalion, Tadhg O'Sullivan. A levy, to be decided by the commanding officer in each locality, was placed on all the farmers and professional and business people in the Brigade area, and it is due to the generous and willing support of most of these people that a sum amounting to seven thousand pounds was raised. In some cases, it is true, the levy was refused, and where this refusal was found to arise from lack of sympathy with the national cause the Volunteers seized cattle and sold them publicly at fairs in quiet areas to recoup the refused levy.

The total sum was a very considerable amount and it needed a man of ability and business acumen to arrange for its safe deposit in various centres and for its subsequent disposal. Tadhg O'Sullivan had been creamery manager in Timoleague and he proved to be the ideal man for this work. He lodged the money in different banks in the names of friendly businessmen.

One of our immediate needs was clothing for our men, so our first order was placed with Hearne and Company, Ltd, of Waterford for one hundred trench coats at a total cost of six hundred and fifty pounds. This was followed by the purchase of a consignment of boots and clothing. So carefully was the fund administered that there was a sizable credit balance on hands at the time of the Truce.

CHAPTER 15

TOM BARRY JOINS THE WEST CORK BRIGADE

In face of the rapidly-changing pattern of the war, towards the middle of 1920, a new need made itself felt, namely, that of forming fighting columns to provide mobile striking forces that would help us maintain the initiative in our campaign. Indeed Charlie Hurley and several other officers were of the opinion that the formation of a Brigade Column was something that should be tackled as quickly as possible, and that risks should be taken if necessary in order to do so. In this context the question arose of finding a suitable officer to train and lead the new force we were contemplating. Thereupon, Seán Buckley, the Brigade Intelligence Officer, mentioned a young ex-British army sergeant who had offered his services for this very purpose. His name was Tom Barry. After some discussion in which the danger of placing trust in British ex-service men was debated, it was decided that Charlie Hurley and Ted O'Sullivan should interview Tom Barry in Cork. The outcome of the interview was that Barry was invited to join the Brigade as training officer. This was early in September.

Towards the end of September Tom Barry was invited to attend a staff meeting at O'Mahony's of Belrose, and it was there that I first met him. I listened in silence while Charlie Hurley and Ted O'Sullivan put questions to him, and I observed his reactions closely. His answers were direct and clear. He was smart and military in his appearance, and gave the impression of being sharp, quick, and dynamic. He presented himself to me as a very likable person and won my complete confidence. Had I to compare him with any of the officers of the Brigade at the time, it would have been with Maurice Donegan, who had the same soldierly bearing and showed the same decisiveness in all his actions.

At any rate, Charlie Hurley, Dick Barrett, Ted O'Sullivan, Seán Buckley, and I were all favourably impressed by Barry at the Belrose meeting. We felt that he would have much to offer as a professional soldier who had seen active military service in the Middle East. His subsequent distinguished service in the national cause became an inspiration, and as a guerilla fighter his name became a household word throughout the country.

The first task assigned to Barry was that of conducting an intensive training course for our officers. This was a matter that had been frequently discussed, and now that Barry was appointed

officer in charge of training, we proceeded to organise a training
camp at Clonbouig, Kilbrittain, for the officers of the eight Companies of the Bandon Battalion that lay south of the Bandon river,
namely Bandon, Innishannon, Ballinadee Ballinspittle, Kilbrittain,
Timoleague, Barryroe, and Clogagh. The Brigade was represented
at the camp by Charlie Hurley and myself. The Commandant and
Quartermaster of the Bandon Battalion were also present, and two
officers each from the Clonakilty and Dunmanway Battalions.

The camp assembled at Clonbouig on Sunday evening, 26
September, and included a total of thirty-six officers. The next
morning training began. Perhaps the order of the day will give the
clearest illustration of the military discipline that was instilled into
our men during this intensive training course. All the men were on
parade at 8.00 a.m. and, apart from breaks for meals at the billets,
activities continued throughout the entire day. The camp lasted for
a week, and towards its close there were two surprise night parades
during which the men were tested to see how quickly they could
react to surprise. On Saturday evening, 2 October, the men were
dismissed in order that they could return to their homes for a
change of clothing. They were instructed to assemble on the following Monday night at Clonbouig to begin the second phase of the
training course. This was to include long night marches, and, if
possible, an actual ambush. The position chosen for the latter was
close to Dunmanway town, and the first stage of the circuitous
route deliberately selected for our march there was over thirty
miles.

On that Monday night the column left Clonbouig at 9.00 p.m.
and set off for Newcestown. As this was the first movement of a
large body of armed Volunteers outside their Battalion area, we
took great care in planning the route. Thus Bandon was given a
wide berth, and Kilbrittain was avoided by making a detour south
of the village and crossing the Bandon-Timoleague road at Scar-
done, five miles south of Bandon. Next, the route continued over
Knockbrown, and by Crossmahon and Gaggin, to the Bandon river
crossing at Baxter's Bridge, three and a half miles west of Bandon.
This bridge was the big danger point and special precautions were
taken along the last stretch of two miles leading to it. Two of the
most experienced officers in the party, Paddy Crowley and Jackie
O'Neill of Kilbrittain, acted as special scouts at this stage, and
approached the bridge with extreme caution until they made contact with the section of the Mount Pleasant Company under
Charlie O'Donoghue that had been on scouting duty at the bridge

from the late afternoon. The bridge and the approaches were clear of the enemy, so we crossed quickly, and made for Hurley's forge. It was 4.00 a.m. and the men needed a rest. They had been marching since we left Clonbouig seven hours earlier. So a brief halt was made behind the forge, and there the men relaxed and had a smoke. After this we continued on our journey till we arrived two hours later at the billets prepared for us at Newcestown.

The column moved off on Tuesday night, and reached the next billets at Cooleenagow, five miles north-east of Dunmanway, at 2.00 a.m. on Wednesday morning. While the column rested, Jackie O'Neill of Kilbrittain and Dan Santry of Barryroe were placed on duty with the local scouts. Shortly after daybreak I moved around to inspect the men on duty and came on Dan at one point. He looked thoroughly exhausted and woebegone after the night's vigil. To cheer him up I slapped him on the back and said cheerily, 'Well, Dan, what do you think of this country around here?' It was his first incursion into the hills, and with all the lowlander's contempt for such wild country, he replied, 'To tell you the truth, if I had twelve lives, I'd gladly give them all for my own fair parish at Barryroe, but I can see nothing here but rocks and rocks and rocks.' What he said was very true, but the criticism was certainly influenced by a long night's cold vigil. In the months that followed Dan, and many others like him, came to know and love those hills where he gave gallant service, and enjoyed the sure protection of the rocks and the hospitality of the generous warm-hearted people who held open house during those anxious days. The column rested all day on Wednesday, but towards nightfall we moved off to the selected ambush position at Fanlobbus on the Bandon-Dunmanway road. Here we were joined by Charlie Hurley and Tom Barry, who had already inspected and approved of the positions to be taken. At this point Tom Barry took command of the column.

From intelligence reports coming in we knew that a military convoy of two or three lorries passed each day from Dunmanway to Bandon, and returned with supplies for Ballineen and Dunmanway itself. It was this convoy that was to be the object of our attack. Our forces were now reinforced by men from the local Battalion staff and from the Behagh, Aultagh, Coppeen, and Kenneigh Companies so that in all sixty men were under orders; thirty of them were armed with rifles and the others were stationed at vantage points as scouts.

A mine was laid at the eastern end of the position for the purpose of stopping the lorries and trapping them in the ambush position which stretched along both sides of the road for a distance of four hundred yards. The main attacking party was stationed just inside the road fence at both sides with a covering party not more than twenty yards behind them. We remained in this position until nightfall, but for some unknown reason the convoy did not travel that day. For security reasons it was inadvisable to hold the same position for more than one day; British military forces in Dunmanway alone, and that was only two and a half miles away, had far superior strength than ours as well as fast transport. So the ambush party had to march.

It was decided to withdraw after nightfall to Ahakeera, five miles to the north, and from there the men were to march back to the Bandon Battalion area and be dismissed. Meanwhile another group of officers from the remaining Companies of the Bandon Battalion, i.e. those north of the Bandon river, would be mobilised for a training camp that was to be held at Newcestown in the following week. Charlie Hurley, Tom Barry and I left the party at Ahakeera, and went on to Brigade Headquarters at Belrose to make the necessary arrangements for the second training camp. The command of the column was handed over to Seán Hales, Commandant of the Bandon Battalion.

On Saturday, 9 October, Hales led the column to Newcestown where the arms were to be dumped. When they arrived at Coolinagh, half a mile from Newcestown, part of the column was dismissed, and the remaining fifteen men were billeted for the night in Lordan's of Coolinagh and Corcoran's of Bengour. Seán Hales with his Vice-O/C, Jim O'Mahony, had gone into the village to complete arrangements when a local scout rushed into Lordan's with the news that two Crossley tenders with Essex soldiers were in possession of the village. John Lordan, then Captain of the Newcestown Company and also a member of the column, immediately took charge, and together with the local unit of scouts who were armed with shotguns, he led the column at the double across two fields in the hope of engaging the enemy on the main Newcestown-Enniskean road, if not in the village itself. There was no time for planning or positioning : circumstances would have to be allowed dictate the details of the action.

Most of the unit had reached the main road when the blazing headlights of the Crossley tenders as they returned from Newcestown exposed our men to view. John Lordan, Dan Canty, Jim Hodnett, and Jackie O'Neill scrambled over the northern fence, while most of the others crossed the ditch on the south side of the road. As the first tender flashed past fire was opened, and the vehicle was brought to a halt twenty yards further on. As the second tender approached, it was fired on by Jack Fitzgerald, Mick O'Neill, Paddy Crowley, and Miah Deasy. It too pulled up and returned fire. The two tenders were about one hundred and fifty yards apart, and their lights were extinguished.

The soldiers dismounted and heavy firing followed, but in the pitch darkness of the night it was impossible to distinguish friend from foe. The fighting continued for about half an hour when the officer in charge of the first tender, Lieutenant Robertson, led his men over a fence in an effort to outflank or surround the column. He had taken up a position along a ditch running at right angles to the road and quite close to the column's position. In fact, he was so close to two members of the column, Jackie O'Neill and Jim Hodnett, that both were in imminent danger. Suddenly Hodnett heard the noise of bushes being dragged from a gap, and he immediately realised how close the enemy was to him. He turned towards the gap which was about five yards away and fired three rapid rounds in its direction. This was the turning point in the fight. There was a general lull for a few minutes, and then the two tenders started to life and raced away into the darkness. The column had no casualties. The fifteen rifles used by the Volunteers in the engagement were then safely dumped to await use at the next training camp.

A prisoner, Dan Corcoran, who had been arrested in Newcestown, jumped from one of the tenders when the firing began, and he succeeded in escaping. Among those who accompanied the column that night was J. J. Madden from North Tipperary, an organiser of the Dáil Loan, who had earlier arranged to hold a public meeting in Newcestown on the following day in aid of the Loan. He kept his appointment, and after Sunday Mass held a very successful meeting in the village, despite the general tension caused by the attack of the night before. On that same Sunday morning, the cap and brains of an officer, believed to be those either of Lieutenant Robertson or Richardson, were found close to the gap through which he endeavoured to lead his men against the column.

The usual reprisals followed during the ensuing week. The public house in Newcestown was burned down. An attempt was made to set fire to John Lordan's house, and a rick of straw at Pat Corcoran's was burned. Later the enemy gave the following account of the engagement :

> In October 1920 there was a more serious engagement. When leaving Newcestown one night, Major Percival was ambushed with a party of two officers and twelve men in two Crossley cars by forty Irish. Three men were wounded by a bomb thrown into the leading car, but the remainder sprang out into the road and drove off the assailants, suffering, however, the loss of two officers (Flight Lieutenant Richardson, R.A.F., of the wireless detachment at Bandon, and Lieutenant Robertson of the Essex). Half the men were recruits and the action was fought in pitch darkness, yet, they gallantly drove off the assailants and brought in the wounded without the loss of a rifle. The Irish loss was believed to be at least ten killed and mortally wounded. For this service the Battalion was congratulated by Divisional and Brigade commanders, whilst Major Percival was awarded the O.B.E. and C.S.M.; Benton the M.B.E. Private Wootten was given the Medal of the British Empire.[1]

When the report of the Newcestown engagement reached the Brigade Headquarters, we were naturally elated to learn that our men had had the experience of a real fight with the enemy, and that they had fought so bravely. Many of the Volunteers who took part in the action had never been under fire before, and yet after a short week's training they were already able to fight against an experienced enemy with success.

In order to secure greater safety for the second camp it was now decided to change the location from Greenhill, Newcestown, to Ballymurphy near Crossbarry. There the men would have a better chance of training without interruption So instructions were sent out notifying all concerned of the change of location, and arrangements were completed for the transfer of arms and ammunition to the new site. The time-table to be followed and the drill and manoeuvres to be conducted were similar to those of the earlier camp. Again, as in the case of the first camp, it was also arranged that this one should finish with an ambush, and the site chosen for it was on the main Cork-Bandon road at Coolcullitha, two miles east of Innishannon.

---

1 Cf. *The Essex Regiment (First Battalion)* (Ministry of Defence Library, Whitehall), p. 272. The Essex Regiment published a regimental magazine during the war years in Ireland. The complete file of this magazine is available at the Essex Regiment Museum at Eagle Way, Brentwood, Essex, England.

The camp closed early on Saturday morning, and the column was marched directly into the ambush position at 8.00 a.m. There it remained throughout the entire day, but again no enemy appeared, and as night fell we evacuated our position and dumped the arms we had with the local Company. Then the men were dismissed with orders to parade again on Monday night, 11 October, at Ballymurphy.

* * * * * *

At this point, we must take leave of the Bandon Battalion for the time being, and direct our attention to spectacular developments taking shape in another part of the Brigade area, namely, in the region of Schull.

CHAPTER 16

THE FORMATION OF THE SCHULL BATTALION

The Schull peninsula is one of the strips of land of West Cork stretching out deeply into the Atlantic and extending west of a line drawn from Bantry to Skibbereen. Volunteer units had existed in this area since 1918, and had been associated either with the Bantry Battalion on the one side or with the Skibbereen Battalion on the other, but the peninsula was too far from either Skibbereen or Bantry, and as a result it tended to be overlooked and its possibilities ignored. From the point of view of the Brigade Staff, however, this situation was unsatisfactory, and it was felt that the peninsula called for some kind of reorganisation.

On the side of a fence at Baurgorm, near Bantry, on a fine July day in 1920, this question of the reorganisation of the Schull peninsula was discussed by the Commandant of the Bantry Battalion, Ted O'Sullivan, and myself, and in the course of our discussion the name of Seán Lehane was mentioned.

Seán Lehane was a native of Scart, near Bantry, and was one of the many natural leaders which the War of Independence produced in West Cork. A young man of no more than twenty-one when we spoke about him in July 1920, he had been a second year student at St Patrick's Training College, Drumcondra, Dublin, where he was also an active Volunteer. During his summer holidays he had been detailed to organise the new Dáil Loan[1] in the Schull, Bantry, Skibbereen, and Castletownbere areas, but his interest in the activities of the Volunteers was greater than in the Loan. For our part we felt that Lehane was a man who had all that was required for a position of command in his native district. But with officers of the calibre of Ted O'Sullivan, Maurice Donegan, Ralph Keyes, Seán Cotter, and Mick O'Callaghan already holding positions of command in the Bantry and Skibbereen areas, there was no post of command up to the level of Seán Lehane's capabilities and merits vacant. We were in a dilemma until we thought of the Schull area. Why not have Lehane undertake the organisation of the Schull peninsula, form it into a Battalion, and become its commander?

It happened that Lehane's home was only two miles across country from where we were having our discussion. It was the

1. For an account of the Dáil Loans, see Dorothy Macardle, *The Irish Republic*, pp. 284-85, 203-03, and *passim*.

middle of the week, and as Seán's main organising work was done at the weekends, he was at home when we sent for him and told hm about the scheme we had in mind. Without hesitation he accepted the proposals, and said he was ready to start organising the new Battalion, which was to be the seventh of the Brigade, immediately. We instructed him on the formation of Companies, but left the selection of Company officers entirely to his own discretion. That very evening he left on a bicycle for the peninsula to begin the new work, and his only possession was a revolver and ten rounds of .45 ammunition. It was 10 July 1920.

Subsequently, Seán Lehane made contact with us at the July, August, and September Brigade Council meetings and reported favourably on the progress being made in his work of organisation. In these few months he had, with the assistance of Seán O'Driscoll, Jack McCarthy, Gibbs Ross, and other local men, established nine Companies, i.e. at Lissagriffin, Goleen, Dunmanus, Gloun, Schull, Leamcon, Dunbeacon, Ballydehob and Skehanore. Granted that there were already units in most of these districts, they were now established as regular and independent Companies of the Seventh Battalion. As such they were responsible to their Battalion Commandant for all future operations. For his Battalion Staff, Lehane selected Denis Murphy as Vice-Commandant, Gibbs Ross as Adjutant, and James Hayes as Quartermaster.

On actions against the enemy Lehane had at first little to report. Up to the time of his appointment the only military activities in the area had been two raids for gun-cotton on Brow Head and Mizen Head by a Bantry Battalion unit, and the reconnoitring of Ballydehob barracks with a view to attacking it. The latter was evacuated a few days later and its garrison withdrawn to Schull barracks. The same thing had happened in the case of Goleen barracks, while those of Durrus and Kilcrohane had also been evacuated.

The Capture of Schull R.I.C. Barracks, 4 October 1920

Schull R.I.C. barracks remained a thorn in our side. It was not only an enemy stronghold, but it was also a centre of enemy intelligence. As such it was an ever-present threat to our safety. When the garrison was reinforced, the R.I.C. took over a large stone building situated on rising ground in complete isolation and strongly fortified with sandbags, barbed wire entanglements, and with steel shutters on the windows. About four hundred yards away was a coastguard station occupied by a detachment of the

Royal Marines estimated by the local Battalion staff at the time as forty to fifty strong. Although the marines were never active against us, they had to be considered in any plan of attack.

At the Brigade meetings the question of the Schull R.I.C. barracks was constantly being discussed, and Lehane was assured that, when the time was ripe, a column would be moved in there to attack the barracks in co-operation with his local forces. All this time he was active visiting each of the Companies, drilling, training and perfecting them and moulding them into fighting units. For arms and ammunition he had his own revolver, a few other small arms, and the usual supply of shotguns that came, for the most part, from raids on local loyalist houses.

Convinced as he was of the importance of capturing Schull barracks, and realising what a major military operation would be involved in an endeavour to take it by frontal assault, Lehane concentrated on the intelligence reports that were made by the Schull Company. From these he learned that every night at 7.30 five of the garrison left the barracks and were absent for half an hour to collect mail and newspapers from the evening train that arrived at the local station from Skibbereen. Over a period of weeks this custom was observed, and was found to be invariable. Further observation revealed that this party gained admission through the back door of the barracks by giving a password. This password changed from day to day, and the problem was to find out in advance the one decided upon for a given day in order to carry out the attack. At this point contact was made with a member of the garrison, a young R.I.C. man named Daly who was not unsympathetic to our cause. At first, he was reluctant to give us the password, though he offered to resign from the force. He was prevailed upon not to resign, and efforts were made in other directions to secure the all-important password. In the meantime Seán Lehane selected a party of twelve men, and had them in readiness for the attack as soon as the password of a given day was discovered.

Eventually, the young R.I.C. constable who had been contacted in the barracks overcame his scruples, and on Monday, 4 October, informed the Captain of the Schull Company that the password for that day was 'Kilmallock'. The mobilisation order was sent out immediately and Lehane ordered his party to gather at Charlie Cotter's farm-house at Ardmanagh, nearly half a mile from the barracks.

The plan of attack was a simple one. The men moved across country to a laneway at Meenvane, which led to the rear of the barracks. On the way there, and by arrangement, they met the local curate, Father Denis Ahern, and when he was told what was afoot, he invited the men to kneel, and he gave them general absolution. Then they moved into position a short distance from the back door of the barracks, and there followed those few tense moments that invariably preceded zero hour in every such engagement. The success of the operation would depend upon split-second timing.

Lehane had to judge his time of approach to the barracks in such wise that no suspicion would be aroused inside, and yet give himself time to intercept the party of R.I.C. returning from the railway station having collected the mail and newspapers from the evening train. With his eye on the face of his watch he calmly waited for the right moment. Standing beside him was Charlie Cotter who stood six-feet-four in his stockinged feet, a powerful man famous as a weight-thrower. He was now armed with a fourteen-pound sledge-hammer to meet a contingency that could arise. The back door of the barracks was secured by both a lock and a chain. However, no one doubted that if in response to the password the door was merely unlocked, but not unchained, that Charlie would make short work of the chain with his sledge-hammer.

With a final glance around, Lehane gave a silent signal. Then, followed by his men, he firmly approached the barrack door. He knocked. When challenged he replied in a clear, steady voice, 'Kilmallock', and waited. The men stood rigid : so much depended on the next few seconds. Then they heard the welcome sound of the key being turned in the lock, followed immediately by the still more welcome sound of the chain being unhooked. As the door opened, Seán led a swift rush of men into the barrack day-room, and pointed his revolver at the startled enemy. In less time than it takes to tell, the police were dismayed to find themselves being lined up against the wall by a party of men armed with revolvers and shotguns. So unsuspicious and secure had the police felt that they did not raise their eyes from the table at which they sat playing cards when the password was given : one of the policemen sitting beside the door simply leaned back and still keeping his eyes on his cards, unlocked the door and unhooked the chain. Quickly the police were disarmed and locked into another room while Lehane and some of his party rushed out to meet the returning patrol.

Here again the element of timing and surprise was perfect. Feeling quite relaxed in sight of the barrack door, the police were suddenly jumped upon in the darkness of the laneway, quickly disarmed and marched into the barracks to join their captured comrades. Next, the building was searched for arms and yielded thirteen rifles, twenty-six revolvers, sixty bombs, thirteen hundred rounds of ammunition, over one hundred shotguns that had been taken up by the police from local people, some Verey lights and a miscellaneous quantity of equipment.

It was part of the original plan to lead the British to believe that the raid was the work of outsiders, and not that of local men. To lend colour to this, two cars were in readiness, one being the property of Duggan's Hotel, the other being the property of Lieutenant Patsy Collins of Ballydehob. On being signalled the drivers of the cars drove up to the barracks, and the booty was quickly transferred to the cars—with the exception of the shotguns and equipment, which were taken away by the men of the local Company. The cars were quickly driven away northwestwards to Durrus and then by the coast to Kilcrohane where the arms and ammunition were safely dumped. A few nights later they were transported by boat across the bay to Dunmanus Pier.

When the cars had left the barracks at Schull and the shotguns had been removed, the police and Tans were freed and allowed to collect their personal belongings. They were then marched under guard to Duggan's Hotel. To the proprietor's bewildered inquiry, 'What shall I do with these men?' Seán O'Driscoll suggested that he should keep them for the night, and that it was most probable that someone would collect them the next day.

While this was going on, the barracks was being set on fire, and within an hour it was reduced to grim, smoke-blackened walls. Later it was learned that the sergeant in charge of the barracks was courtmartialled on account of the capture of the garrison and was dismissed, but that he was subsequently retired on a constable's pension. In official circles, too, there was much adverse comment arising from the fact that the Royal Marines had taken no action in the crisis. Actually the whole operation had been carried out so quickly, quietly and efficiently that the marines knew nothing about it until the flames of the burning barracks lit up the sky.

The success of the attack on Schull R.I.C. barracks had immediate and far-reaching effects. Not only did it mean that the Schull Battalion had now an effective armoury, but also that part of its spoils could be sent on to Brigade Headquarters, and some of the rifles captured helped in the formation of the famous Flying Column of the West Cork Brigade which was soon to be formed.

They were used also in the action at Kilmichael six weeks later, and in many other successful engagements. Besides, the destruction of Schull barracks dealt the enemy a crippling blow so far as the peninsula was concerned. Now that it was destroyed, the area became a very necessary and welcome rest centre for those of our men who were in need of respite and medical care. It was true that the marines still occupied the coastguard station, but the garrison of this outpost never ventured out from the station, and with no outside connexions they were regarded as a non-aggressive force.

CHAPTER 17

THE FLYING COLUMN

Monday, 20 October, brought discouraging news. That day we learned to our dismay that we had lost the services of two of our bravest and most experienced officers, Jack Fitzgerald and Mick O'Neill of Kilbrittain : they had been captured during the weekend. These two men had led the Kilbrittain Company in the dramatic ambush at Rathclarin in June 1919; in the two successful attacks on Howes Strand Coastguard Station which had provided a considerable proportion of the rifles and ammunition with which the Brigade was now armed; and also in other fights, including the recent one at Newcestown. Both men were endowed with natural qualities of leadership so that the loss of either of them would have been a severe blow, but the capture of both at the same time constituted a grave military setback.

But apart from these considerations, the capture of the two officers presented us with a special problem in the circumstances. During the weekend we had decided to ambush a military convoy at Tureen, three miles east of Innishannon, and we were due to occupy the selected position on Tuesday morning, 21 October. Intelligence reports now brought the news that the two captured men were in custody in Bandon military barracks where there was no possibility of rescuing them. We knew, too, from experience that prisoners were not detained for long in Bandon before being removed by road to Cork. If we proceeded with our planned ambush on Tuesday, there was a serious possibility that we would find ourselves attacking the convoy that was conveying Fitzgerald and O'Neill to Cork. In such a case, we would very probably be responsible for the deaths of our two comrades either as a result of our fire or that of the enemy. We could not take this risk, and decided to postpone the ambush, and instead continue work at the training camp until we had more news from Bandon.

The delay in executing our plans gave us an opportunity to check the mine we intended using on the road for the ambush at Tureen. The failure of our mines to explode on previous occasions had been attributed principally to faulty detonators. Charlie Hurley had secured a box of new detonators, and had actually tested twelve of them and found them perfectly satisfactory. Hence we had every confidence that the mine on this occasion would not disappoint us. Then, on Thursday night we had a report from

Cumann na mBan in Bandon to the effect that Fitzgerald and O'Neill had been removed that day by road to Cork. We prepared to march next morning to Tureen.

The Ambush at Tureen, 24 October 1920

As we made ready to go to bed on that Thursday night at the home of the Murphy's of Ballycourneening, Killumney, our Quartermaster, Tadhg O'Sullivan, asked the woman of the house to call us at 2.30 a.m. Charlie Hurley, Tom Barry, and I could hear him making this request below in the kitchen. Next, we heard him mounting the stairs, halting for a moment, and as if by way of afterthought—influenced no doubt by the sight of the flitch of home-cured bacon hanging from the rafters—asking Mrs Murphy to cut a few thick rashers of bacon for our breakfast. The typically generous answer followed spontaneously : 'I will, of course. Sure, you can have all the bacon you want.' 'No, Ma'am,' said Tadhg, 'just two rashers for each of us.' He had just reached the top of the stairs when we heard a plaintive plea from our hostess : 'Oh, Tadhg, alanna, tomorrow will be Friday. I'll give you all I have here, but I couldn't cook meat on a Friday !' We went to bed, but Tadhg returned to the kitchen, and evidently in his own inimitable and persuasive way convinced the good woman that the breakfast would possibly be the only meal we would have next day, and she need have no scruples. The result was that when we were called at 2.30 a.m. there was a sizzling sound and a most fragrant aroma of frying bacon coming from the kitchen. We had an excellent breakfast that sustained us for the long, trying day that followed.

At four o'clock in the morning, long before dawn, we were on our way via Crossbarry and the Kinsale branch railway line to Tureen. The mine was laid in the road in front of the farm-house of the Roberts family after the inmates had been evacuated to safer quarters. Charlie Hurley and Jackie O'Neill took up their positions inside the wall in front of the house in order to explode the mine. It was hoped that when the leading lorry was blown up, any other lorries in the convoy would be dealt with by three sections of the column which manned the southern fences for about three hundred and fifty yards. We had twenty-seven riflemen and we had also scouts posted on both flanks. The section in the west was commanded by Tom Barry, I had the section on the east and Charlie Hurley had the centre section. We were thus ready to attack a convoy coming from either direction once the leading lorry was blown up. Orders were issued to the effect that the explosion of the mine was to be the signal for the general attack.

At 11.00 a.m., when we had been in the ambush position for about two hours, the sound of approaching lorries could be heard in the distance coming from the Bandon direction. The men stiffened. A deadly silence fell upon them. Each man glanced down the sights of his rifle and waited in suspense for the explosion of the mine that would signal the opening of the attack. With Paddy Crowley of Kilbrittain and Mick O'Riordan of Kilpatrick, I stood at the entrance of a laneway leading from the road. We had only a limited view to our left because of a bend in the road, but we waited confidently for the explosion that would galvanise us into action. No explosion came. Instead a lorry of troops came whizzing round the bend and hurtled towards us. We immediately dropped to the road and fired at the driver as the lorry raced up to us, and again as it flashed past, but with what results we never knew.

The sound of our rifle-fire had one good effect : it slowed down the second lorry which was coming along at about two hundred yards distance behind the first one. Immediately Charlie Hurley and Jackie O'Neill opened fire on the driver and the vehicle swerved into the ditch. Simultaneously with this action, Tom Barry, Mick Herlihy, Pat Deasy, and two others came on to the road and lying flat fired into the lorry. Within seconds four of the occupants were killed, including the officer, Captain Dixon, and four others were wounded. The fight was over.

Next, the soldiers were disarmed and removed from the lorry. This was immediately set on fire. The wounded were laid on the grassy verge of the road to be tended by their unwounded comrades. Then, collecting the arms captured, we withdrew to a field at the rear of Roberts's house. There the column was paraded and checked. We had no casualties, and the arms captured amounted to eight rifles, one revolver, and two hundred rounds of ammunition.

Originally we had planned to return to the area from which we had come after the ambush, and then move westwards to higher ground in the Newcestown area. This plan was devised on the assumption that we would be completely successful in our ambush, and that the enemy in Cork, Bandon, and Kinsale would have no word about the engagement, and so would make no effort to intercept us for at least two hours after our attack. Now the position was different. One lorry had escaped. It had not stopped or made any attempt to help the occupants of the second lorry, and we could be certain that enemy headquarters in Cork would be very quickly alerted, and would send reinforcements rushing to the scene to cut off our retreat to the Crossbarry road which was two miles across exposed terrain.

Because of these considerations we changed the route we had planned for our retreat, and decided to go southwards and to veer towards Skeugh Cross, Ballydonaghy Cross Roads, Leighmoney and Ballydaly Quay. There we would cross the tidal Bandon river, land at Corta and continue on to Ballinadee and Ballyvolane. As on so many other occasions, our local knowledge of the countryside stood us in good stead, and proved invaluable in the kind of guerilla warfare we were waging against vastly superior numbers of fully-armed troops provided with rapid transport.

There was just one difficulty in our plan. There would be no boats available on the east bank of the Bandon at Ballydaly. The salmon fishing season had ended two months earlier in August, and the fishing boats had been beached on the far side of the river for winter. Only at Kilmacsimon Quay were fishing boats still afloat because of the shipping activities that continued there all the year round. So we decided to send Tim Crowley and my brother Pat on bicycles to Kilmacsimon Quay six miles away. They were instructed to procure a boat and row back to Ballydaly, a mile down the river, and then ferry the column across to the other side.

The column marched to Ballydaly, partly by way of the open fields and partly by road, and took almost two hours to cover the five miles' journey. When the men arrived at the water's edge, the boat was waiting for them, and they were rowed to the other side in two trips. Just as the last member of the party stepped ashore at Corta, a convoy of military from Kinsale passed through Leighmoney in the direction of Innishannon while another, also from Kinsale, travelled to the actual scene of the ambush with the evident intention of encircling Tureen and containing us there.

We were now well outside the net being laid by the enemy, and we marched southwards through Ballinadee and continued on one mile further to Ballyvolane. We arrived there at 4.00 p.m. and were soon enjoying our first meal in fourteen hours. Tired and exhausted we rested there that night and during the whole of the following day. Intelligence reports from Bandon informed us of scenes of violence perpetrated by the enemy throughout the town on the night following the ambush at Tureen. Anticipating further reprisals the next night, and in order to be better prepared to cope with them, we decided to move the column closer to the town under cover of darkness. However, the military were confined to barracks that night and there were no incidents. Shortly before daybreak

we moved to Ratharoon, four miles away, and there the men were
dismissed. The arms were collected and put into safe dumps by the
Kilbrittain Company. Tom Barry proceeded to the Bantry Battalion
area for the third training camp.

So ended another phase of the war in West Cork. It was 27
October and for the previous four weeks we had been on contin-
uos service with two special weeks of intensive training, three
attempted ambushes, and two successful ones. Then, between
forced day and night marches we had covered over one hundred
and fifty miles. Granted that there had been two separate units in
the training camps, yet the Brigade and Battalion staffs were
constantly on duty, and took part in all the engagements. The
discipline of the men had been excellent, and this was an index
both of the spirit which brought them to the camp in the first
place, and the efficiency and tireless example of the training officer,
Tom Barry.

We were constantly gaining experience both from our successes
and our failures. For example, after the unfortunate episode at
Brinny in which we lost that excellent officer, Tim Fitzgerald, we
learned a very valuable lesson regarding guerilla warfare, namely,
that a fighting unit which cannot occupy and maintain a position
against an enemy vastly superior in men and equipment must not
merely depend on the element of surprise for its success, but must
never remain long enough in any given ambush position to allow
the enemy gain knowledge of its whereabouts and thus snatch the
element of surprise from its would-be attackers.[1] As a result of
experience gained in the weeks under review, our columns were
never allowed to remain in an ambush position for more than
twenty-four hours, and extreme care was taken that the men should
not remain longer than was absolutely necessary in billets in the
same area.

The Third Training Camp

On Sunday, 31 October, a Brigade Council meeting was held at
Coppeen. When routine matters had been disposed of there
followed a general review of Brigade activities. Reference was made
to the Battalion columns[2] that had been operating for some weeks

1. For three days before the ambush at Brinny we had occupied a position
less than a mile away, i.e. at the Black Quarries, near Kilpatrick.
2. To distinguish the Brigade Column or the Brigade Flying Column, as
it was sometimes called, from Battalion columns, the former will be written
with a capital C, the latter with a small c.

previously in connexion with the training camps. There was complete unanimity about the need for maintaining these columns, but it was felt that the time had come for an independent Brigade Column comprised of men who would volunteer from the ranks for such a special service. It was not envisaged that officers would normally enrol—except, perhaps, when they happened to be 'on the run' for the reason that the existing Company and Battalion structure would have to be maintained and would require the constant presence of the officers. It was stressed, of course, that Brigade, Battalion, and Company officers would at all times co-operate fully with the Column Commandant, even to the extent of taking a fully-active part in any engagement organised by the Column in their areas. Tom Barry was appointed Commander of the Brigade Flying Column, and on the occasion of the appointment, the Brigade Commander, Charlie Hurley, paid a tribute to the outstanding service which Barry had already rendered.

Subsequent events proved how momentous was the step taken at this meeting when it decided to form a Brigade Flying Column. Its effect on the subsequent development of the war in West Cork was decisive. The Column took part in practically every major engagement in the ensuing months. It ranged through five of the seven Battalion areas of the Brigade bringing help to weak districts, and everywhere raising the morale of the people. Gradually it achieved its main objective : it took the initiative from the enemy and became an attacking rather than a defensive force.

Once the suggestion to form the Brigade Flying Column was accepted—and it was accepted enthusiastically—the question of the base to be selected for the Column and its field of operation called for some discussion. Tom Barry favoured the Bandon area, and this was understandable considering how intimately he was associated with it and how well he knew its military potential. Ted O'Sullivan, on the other hand, was convinced that the mountainy terrain in a district such as Dunmanway lent itself better to guerilla warfare than did the pastoral land of the Bandon district. Furthermore, he hoped that the presence of the Column in the Dunmanway area would be of immense value for the further development of efficiency and morale in this centrally-situated Battalion area. The Brigade Commander and several other officers agreed with the views of Ted O'Sullivan, and there and then the Togher Company area, seven miles north-west of Dunmanway, was chosen as the base of the Column. It was decided that the Column would be mobilised on Sunday, 21 November.

Before the meeting closed, the Brigade Commander paid a tribute to Captain Michael O'Brien, Kilbrittain Company, who had died from pneumonia as a result of exposure on active service.

The next day, 1 November, the third training camp opened, this time at Kealkil, seven miles to the north of Bantry. As in the case of the other camps, Tom Barry was in charge of training and he again threw himself into the work with an enthusiasm and dynamism that were astonishing. Officers from the Skibbereen, Schull, Bantry, and Beara Battalions were mobilised and thirty men paraded, including the Brigade Vice-Commandant, Ted O'Sullivan. At the end of a week's intensive training the men were dismissed and returned to their areas without any arrangements being made for the usual engagement with the enemy that had marked the close of the two earlier training camps.

During the weeks which followed the Brigade Council meeting of 1 November, the Brigade Commander and his staff were kept busy visiting the different Battalions, and even some of the more important Company areas, emphasising the need for greater activity and perfecting the intelligence system. We were particularly concerned to put every obstacle possible in the way of the enemy. To do this maps were prepared with tactical points marked in where road blocks could be set up and trenches cut to the greatest advantage. The aim in all this was to obstruct enemy motor transport which was now becoming so dangerous. Lorries were being used in nightly raids on houses and also on bridges where the enemy suspected to find active Volunteers.

The bridges had been given careful attention by us for some time, and we had organised local Volunteers living near them to do night duty as scouts to warn our men whenever the enemy was around. The most dangerous bridges were confined to that portion of the Bandon river which lay in the central and eastern parts of the Brigade area. In all, there were eight bridges between Dunmanway and Innishannon, and there were also two points for ferry crossings on the tidal portion of the river, namely at Colliers Quay and at Kilmacsimon Quay. These were vital to us.

The First Mustering of the Brigade Column

About 14 November I sent an order to the Commander of the Beara Battalion instructing him to send a party of his best trained men, fully armed, to the Brigade Column that was to assemble in the Togher Company area on 21 November. I also asked him to send six extra rifles and ammunition for members of the Column who would have no arms.

As the journey was about forty miles, and the burden to be carried awkward, the seven Beara men selected to form the party set off on Saturday morning, 20 November, with Liam O'Dwyer, Battalion Vice-Commandant, in charge.[3] They marched over Ballaghscart to Adrigole, a distance of eighteen miles. There they picked up another Volunteer named Mícheál Óg O'Sullivan and, after a meal, travelled by side-cars to Glengarriff where they got one motor-car in the village and commandeered another at Roche's Hotel. With these they made their way to the Togher area, and then dismissed their transport. They billeted that night in an empty cottage, and on the following morning they moved about looking for the Volunteer who was to direct them to the assembly point of the Column. Not finding him, they spent some hours making inquiries in local houses, but failed to get any information.

Realising that it would be dangerous for them to stay much longer in strange territory, and fearing lest an encounter with the enemy would mean the loss of precious rifles captured earlier, they decided to return home with their valuable armaments. It must have been a bitter disappointment for them to have come so far bearing a heavy load only to find that their journey was in vain.[4]

Actually, the first group to reach Column headquarters at Tim Farrell's of Clogher were the Dunmanway men who arrived a few hours after the departure of the Beara contingent from Togher, two miles away.[5] When this first group arrived it was decided to raid the house of a local loyalist at Coolkelure, near Dunmanway, and demand blankets and sheets there in order to provide some bedding for the Column. The group returned with twenty blankets

---

3. Those forming the party, besides Liam O'Dwyer, were Christy O'Connell, Captain of Eyeries Company; Jim O'Sullivan, Captain of Bere Island Company; Jimmy O'Sullivan, Captain of Urhan Company; Jim O'Driscoll, Eyeries Company; 'Quinlan' O'Sullivan, Kilcatherine Company; and Tim O'Dwyer, Ballycrovane Company.

4. The above is Liam O'Dwyer's recollection of the incident; cf. Appendix I, n. 10. In fairness it should be pointed out that Tim Hurley, Captain of Derrynacaheragh Company, has a different account of what took place. He states that he met the Beara Volunteers on the morning of 21 November at Jerh Holland's cottage in Clogher, and asked them to wait there as it was the centre for the mobilisation of the Column. The other Volunteers of the Column were not expected until the afternoon.

5. For this account dealing with the first mustering of the Brigade Column I am indebted to Paddy O'Brien of Girlough, Ballinacarriga, Dunmanway, one of the officers present on the occasion; cf. Appendix I, n. 7.

and twenty sheets. With these and a plentiful supply of fresh straw the Column was bedded down comfortably in a vacant labourer's cottage.

In accordance with Brigade orders, the men who were to form the Column were to be chosen from those already 'on the run', and during the course of that Sunday evening representatives of five Battalions arrived in the camp. Tom Barry was in command, and he had the assistance of some Battalion and Company officers.

The Column Quartermaster was Mick O'Dwyer of the Dunmanway Battalion, and he was very successful in providing ample supplies of food, though the cooking was not of the best. Dick O'Mahony of Ballineen supplied the Column with meat and John O'Regan, also of Ballineen, supplied bread and butter, while the neighbours were most generous with supplies of milk and potatoes.

All was now set for an intensive training routine and the men prepared to put their best efforts into it. Little did they realise at the time that within one week of the opening of the camp at Clogher they would undergo a baptism of fire and snatch a resounding victory from the enemy.

* * * * * *

On that same Sunday that saw the first mustering of the Brigade Column, a Brigade Council meeting was held at Kelly's of Gloun, three miles from the camp at Clogher. One of the most heartening items discussed at this meeting was the extraordinary response to the Arms Fund collection. In less than three weeks almost £2,000 had been collected.[6]

It was at this meeting, too, that we heard the regrettable news of the capture of Maurice Donegan,[7] Commandant of the Bantry

6. It has always been a matter of regret to me that this fund—and it eventually amounted to a total of seven thousand pounds—was never recognised as a national debt, all the more so since every penny subscribed was spent on the fighting forces of West Cork. Even more glaring, I think, is the lack of recognition in regard to the small farmers and cottiers of West Cork and elsewhere who, throughout the entire campaign, sheltered and fed our fighting men, often at the price of great hardship and loss to themselves. And they never complained or asked for any compensation. At least, I welcome this opportunity to express my personal tribute of gratitude to those who subscribed so generously to our cause, and co-operated so unselfishly with us. Without them victory would not have been achieved.

7. Maurice Donegan succeeded Ted O'Sullivan as O/C of the Bantry Battalion in August 1920.

Battalion, with two of his staff, Seán Cotter, Adjutant, and Cornelius O'Sullivan, and also the Captain of the Bantry Company, Ralph Keyes. The capture of these outstanding officers represented a major victory for the enemy and was a very serious loss to us. These men had taken part in the raid on the naval M.L. sloop at Bantry Pier where they captured a valuable collection of arms; they were in the attack that forced the evacuation of Durrus barracks; and took an active part in the successful ambush at Clonee, as well as in the many engagements with the enemy that were fought on the Bantry-Glengarriff road. Due to the captured officers, the internal organisation of the Bantry Battalion was a model of efficiency : it was going to be a problem to find adequate replacements for them.

Although we did not know it then, this third Sunday in November was made a more memorable day in the War of Independence because of a startling event that occurred that day in Dublin. The day became known as Bloody Sunday : it witnessed the almost complete disruption of the British intelligence system in Dublin, and the subsequent attack with rifle and machine-gun fire on an unarmed crowd watching a football match at Croke Park. As a further brutal reprisal, Brigadier Dick McKee, Commandant Peadar Clancy, and Volunteer Conor Clune were murdered by the Crown forces that day while being held prisoners in Dublin Castle.

It was on this date also that we were to have our first introduction to the Auxiliaries. This force of ex-officers of the British army had come to Ireland in June 1920 as auxiliaries to the police, and the first company was quartered at Inistioge in County Kilkenny; the second, after a short stay at Carden Castle, Templemore, had taken up quarters in Macroom Castle in County Cork. Up to 21 November, the Macroom contingent was confined in its activities to Macroom and the immediate environs, but by one of the strange fortunes of war they made their third sortie into our area on the afternoon of Bloody Sunday, and were holding the Bantry Line road to Cork in the village of Coppeen, three miles east of Gloun where we were holding our Brigade meeting.

Our meeting ended around 5.00 p.m. and we then made leisurely arrangements for our departure. Ted O'Sullivan, accompanied by the new Commandant of the Bantry Battalion, Tom Ward, and the Commandant of the Castletownbere Battalion, Peter O'Neill, set off by car in the direction of their areas. Next, Seán Lehane, Commandant of the Schull Battalion, with Sam Kingston, Commandant of the Skibbereen Battalion, departed. Charlie Hurley and Dick Barrett left by car for Brigade Headquarters which was at Belrose, Upton. They were accompanied by Bridge O'Mahony, an active member of Cumann na mBan, who was carrying all the important documents from the meeting; as well as a sum of almost two thousand pounds, the first instalment of the Arms Fund. I was in the next car with Dan Harte, Commandant of the Clonakilty Battalion, Seán O'Donovan, Brigade Police Officr, and two active members of Cumann na mBan, Babe Crowley and Lizzie Harte. Behind us came Seán Hales, Commandant of the Bandon Battalion, Con Crowley, Brigade Communications Officer, John J. Mahony, Battalion Police Officer, and Volunteer Jim Lordan of Newcestown. They travelled in a horse-drawn trap.

It was quite dark by the time we reached the road junction at Coppeen. There Charlie Hurley's car was held up and surrounded by the Auxiliaries. The occupants of the car were ordered out on the road to be searched. With admirable presence of mind Dick Barrett saved the situation by pleading with the officer in charge not to disturb the lady in the rear seat as she was seriously ill and was being taken to hospital. The ruse worked, helped no doubt by the prevailing darkness, for Bridge O'Mahony in daylight looked anything but a likely hospital patient. The men were then given a very perfunctory search and allowed to proceed.

Before the engine of Charlie's car started, however, the car in which I was came on the scene. We were ordered out on the road, and our car was subjected to a very close examination. Nothing incriminating was found. Next, the male members of the party were searched in much the same manner as those in Charlie's car, and from the way in which the Auxiliaries were acting it was obvious that they had no information about us, and that they were not in any way suspicious about our identity. As a safeguard, we had an alibi prepared to the effect that we were returning from a wedding in Bantry in which Charlie Dullea of Clonakilty had been married to Miss O'Mahony of Kilcrohane. This piece of information was accepted so readily and seemed to satisfy our interrogators so completely that we were inwardly congratulating ourselves on our good fortune. At this point the horse-drawn trap carrying Seán Hales and his companions arrived on the scene.

Once more the order to halt was heard. Once more the travellers were ordered out on the road to be searched. But this time incriminating documents were found on two members of Hales's party, namely on Con Crowley and on John O'Mahony, and this immediately produced a hostile and suspicious reaction in the Auxiliaries in regard to the members of all three parties. The three cars were now minutely searched, though the 'sick lady' was not asked to leave the car—actually she was sitting on a box containing all the money. As there was no lady searcher with the party, Lizzie Harte and Babe Crowley escaped with all the documents that they were carrying with them.

We were lined up on the side of the road, and remembering the reports that had already come through in relation to the ruthlessness of the Auxiliaries, we were prepared for the worst. In the centre of the road was Colonel Crake, commanding officer of the Auxiliaries in Macroom. He was consulting two of his officers. Surrounded by about twenty Auxiliaries and without any arms, we saw no possibility of escape and our plight can be more easily imagined than described.

After a few moments' consultation, the colonel approached us and said that he was holding Crowley and O'Mahony, but that the rest of us could proceed. I shall always remember his tribute to Seán Hales who had given his name as John McCarthy, a farmer from Lakemount, Enniskean, and said that he was buying 'a few cattle' in the district. So simply and naturally did Seán tell his story that the Colonel was completely taken in and dismissed Seán with the words : 'I believe what you tell me. You have an honest face, and if all your countrymen were like you, there would be no need for us here.' With that we were permitted to depart, that is, all except Crowley and O'Mahony who were detained.

We were, of course, very much relieved at our good fortune in escaping arrest, but our sense of relief was tempered with regret and a feeling of anxiety for the two who had been taken prisoner.

The news of the Auxiliaries' incursions into our area from Macroom and of our providential escape spread rapidly during the following days, and was the deciding factor that influenced Tom Barry's next move. He was determined to attack the Auxiliaries. At this point, Barry showed a remarkable grasp of military psychology that enabled him to project himself into the minds of the enemy without giving them the slightest suspicion of his own plans. He made two assumptions, both of which proved to be correct : firstly, that the Auxiliaries would repeat their sortie to Coppeen, and, secondly, that they would do so on the following Sunday. He made his plans accordingly.

For my part, having eluded the Auxiliaries at Coppeen, I continued on my way to inspect units of the Clonakilty Battalion in the vicinity of Rossmore. By Wednesday afternoon my tour of

inspection was completed, and I then departed for Brigade Headquarters at Belrose. On my way I called to Lordan's at Coolinagh,
near Newcestown, and received an unconfirmed report there that
the new Brigade Column at Clogher had encountered some trouble
from the enemy. This induced me to change my plans immediately.
With Jim Lordan I headed for the Dunmanway area to mobilise
the local Companies in the hope that with whatever shotguns we
could muster we would be able to relieve enemy pressure on our
Brigade Column.

At Castletownkenneigh we called to the house of Mary Kate
Nyhan, a pub which was an important communications centre. My
object was to find out whether any further reports of enemy activity in the neighbourhood were available. Just as Jim Lordan and
I arrived in the kitchen of the house, a party of Auxiliaries rushed
in on us, the very same party under the same Colonel Crake which
held us up at Coppeen on the previous Sunday night. Backing us
up against the wall, the Auxiliaries immediately began to search
us, but found neither arms nor documents on our persons. Nevertheless, we still had to face the inevitable questioning, and there
was very little time for us to concoct a plausible explanation to
account for our presence in a pub at Castletownkenneigh on a
Wednesday night.

Quite obviously the story I used on the previous Sunday night :
that my name was Jim Holland, an assistant in Charlie Dullea's
drapery shop in Clonakilty, who had been best man at the latter's
wedding in Bantry, could not be repeated : it would have been
impossible to justify the presence of a draper's assistant from
Clonakilty in Castletownkenneigh, sixteen miles away on a Wednesday night. As I cudgelled my brain for a fictitious name, I realised
in a flash that I could not use any local name, such as Crowley,
Mahony, Nyhan or Lordan, for the simple reason that all these
names were certainly on the enemy's black list. On the other hand,
if I took an obviously loyalist name, such as Hosford, Shorten, or
Appleby, the likelihood was that I would be taken for identification
to a family of the name I had borrowed.

Such thoughts were racing through my mind when suddenly a
rifle butt was jabbed roughly into my ribs and the peremptory
question hurled at me, 'What's your name?' Without thinking I
blurted out, 'John McCarthy, Lakemount, Enniskean.' Then I
could have bitten my tongue, for this was the name and address
that Seán Hales had used so successfully on Sunday night at
Coppeen. And there was no chance of my passing for Seán : he

was a well-built man of at least fifteen stone weight, whereas at that time I was a lanky youth of less than eleven. There followed a few anxious moments during which the Auxiliary who had questioned me moved over to report to Colonel Crake. Across the kitchen Crake now stared at me long and hard and when he ordered Jim Lordan and me out to the road, I felt that the game was up.

Jim was questioned first, and as soon as his explanation was accepted, he was released. Meanwhile I was standing beside the lorry which had brought the Auxiliaries along, and was being entertained by the men guarding me with some nasty threats. Then Crake came across the road, stood in front of me apparently sizing me up, and then after a pause he said, 'Did I not see you on the Coppeen road on Sunday night?' I replied with what I hoped was a firm 'No.' There was little use in making any other reply. Crake continued, 'I am almost certain you were my prisoner on Sunday night.' To this I replied instantly, 'I was not there.' He continued to stare at me, and after a moment or two said, 'I could have sworn you were the man who was there, but I will accept your word, and you may go.' I walked off as casually as possible until I was out of sight of the Auxiliaries. It was not long until I was lost to them in the darkness of the night.

It was only then that I really realised what an extraordinary escape I had had. The incident has often come back to my mind over the years since, and always there comes with it a kind memory of the man who released me at a time when I thought my end had surely come. Crake was killed four days later at Kilmichael, and I felt for him then in a more kindly way than for the corps under his command that met their doom with him. To this day, thoughts of Kilmichael are always associated with the names of four men who died that day : Michael McCarthy, a very close friend of mine; Jim O'Sullivan whom I had only known for a few weeks; my youngest brother, Pat; and Colonel Crake. I include him, I suppose, on account of the soldierly humanity which he showed. It was so different from the mercenary depravity of the majority of the Auxiliaries.

Following on our lucky escape, Jim Lordan and I made some local contacts, and learned that the report regarding the Column's being in danger was unfounded. On the contrary, we were informed that it was then actually on its way to Ahilnane near Castletown-kenneigh to complete the week's training and to make final preparations for the planned operation at its close.

Next, I resumed my journey to Brigade Headquarters near Cross-barry, and having dealt with routine matters there consulted with Dick Barrett and the Acting Brigade Adjutant, Flor Begley, on the best way of carrying out the orders of the Brigade Council concerning the organisation of diversionary activities in the various Battalion areas. My immediate assignment was to organise a column from the Companies of the Bandon Battalion area north of the Bandon river. The Battalion Commandant, Seán Hales, had a similar order for the area south of the Bandon, while Charlie Hurley was organising along similar lines in the Clonakilty area.

* * * * * *

Meanwhile, Tom Barry's scheme to ambush the Auxiliaries who were making incursions into our Brigade area from Macroom had been maturing, and as the week between 21 and 28 November wore on, he began to finalise his plans.

CHAPTER 18

THE AMBUSH AT KILMICHAEL

On Wednesday, 24 November, Tom Barry decided to move the Brigade Column from Clogher to a point closer to Ballineen, and this for security reasons: he did not wish to risk an unexpected encounter with the enemy before his scheme to ambush the Auxiliaries from Macroom had materialised. So on the evening of that Wednesday the men collected their blankets and sheets, and marched eastwards to Ahilnane, and there they were billeted in a large disused farmhouse on the property of Jack O'Sullivan. Shortly after their arrival news reached them that the Commandant of the Schull Battalion, Seán Lehane, was sending seven rifles from his Battalion in charge of Paddy McCarthy. The weapons were to be conveyed in the West Cork Bottling Company's lorry driven by a man named Stephen Griffin.

On Friday, Tom Barry with Michael McCarthy, Vice-Commandant of the Dunmanway Battalion, and Sonny Dave Crowley set off to find a suitable ambush position on the Macroom-Dunmanway road. When the trio returned, a council of war was held, and during this Barry intimated that he was not satisfied with the position they had surveyed, and that they would return next day to seek a better location. They did so, and this time they were more satisfied with the positions they selected.

Paddy O'Brien, Adjutant of the Dunmanway Battalion, at this stage felt the need of reinforcements, and pointed out that there were only twenty-eight men in the camp. He suggested that he would be able to round up a few more in his native Ballinacarriga. Besides, he knew that the Rural District Council—of which he was a member—would hold a meeting that Saturday night in Behagh school. There he could meet Tom Donovan, Captain of the Behagh Company, and inform him about the plans for the following day. As the Column was to retire from the scene of the ambush to Granure, through Behagh, Donovan could be instructed to mobilise his Company, and have his area scouted as far as Manch Bridge. Barry approved of these suggestions, and O'Brien put them into effect without delay. Besides enlisting the aid of the Behagh Company for scouting duties, O'Brien recruited four men from Ballinacarriga for the ambush. These men armed themselves with double-barrel shotguns and a supply of cartridges, and returned with him to Ahilnane.

Tom Barry sent for the parish priest of Enniskean, Father
O'Connell, and when he arrived it was explained to him that the
Column would very likely go into action next day, and that the
men would like to go to Confession. Before leaving the camp,
Father O'Connell gave a general absolution to all, and the men
retired to their billets. As a result of the intensive week's training,
and due also to the anticipation of going into action against a
crack force of the enemy on the morrow, some of the men were
feeling the strain and did not sleep. It must be appreciated that
while a number of the men in the camp had taken part in
attempted ambushes, not more than a dozen had previous experience of being under fire.

* * * * * *

At this point, I shall let one of the eye-witnesses, Paddy O'Brien,
give his first-hand account of the events that occurred on the day
of the actual fight :

We paraded at 5.00 a.m. on Sunday morning, and after a
breakfast of tea, bread and butter we set out on the five mile
march to Kilmichael. It was raining heavily and was so dark
that you could not see the man in front of you. When we
reached Gloun Cross it was still very dark, and we were
soaked through. We met people going to Mass, and they were
ordered to return home for their own safety—and for ours
also.

It was just coming daylight when we reached Kilmichael,
and without more ado, Tom Barry divided the Column into
two sections, taking charge of one section himself, and
placing the other section under the command of Michael
McCarthy. Positions selected on the previous evening were
taken up, and I was given orders to maintain contact with
the different units while immediate preparations were being
made. I went first to help Michael McCarthy. We rolled
down stones to within two yards of the verge of the road and
built a low barricade there and camouflaged it with furze
bushes. Thereupon McCarthy posted some of his men behind
it. Ned Young was placed south west of the road and
Michael Con O'Driscoll was stationed at the most northerly
point from which he had a clear view of the road and could
give a timely signal of the approach of the enemy.

Having completed my round I returned to the first position
inside the low fence where John Aherne and Battie Coughlan

were stationed. In the adjoining laneway stood Tom Barry, Sonny Dave Crowley, Jim 'Spud' Murphy, Mick Herlihy, ad John 'Flyer' Nyhan. Higher up, and overlooking this position, were Tim O'Connell, Jerh Cotter, Mick O'Donovan and some others. Shortly afterwards I crossed the road to the spot where Stephen O'Neill and Jack Hegarty were lying directly opposite the first position. Further on I met Paddy McCarthy and Jack O'Sullivan who were on a higher point overlooking the second position. We had two official scouts from the locality, namely, Tim O'Sullian and Jack Kelly of Johnstown—the brother of the former was busy during the day bringing buckets of tea to the men, and how very welcome they were too as the long hours dragged on!

Time seemed to move slowly. Yet in spite of the tense air of expectancy spirits were still high, though here and there a pale face glimpsed through the shifting mist reflected the inner fears of a youth facing the ordeal of battle for the first time, and the possibility of death. The early winter night was beginning to fall and light to fade when the signal from Michael Con O'Driscoll was given. The enemy was coming.

All weariness vanished, the quiet talk ceased, safety catches were released, rifle bolts were drawn and a bullet filled the breach ... In these last moments before the battle there was an extraordinary distraction : along the road from Gloun came a pony and trap with four armed men right into the middle of the ambush position. This was enough to upset the whole plan, and even bring disaster in its wake. The problem of removing the untimely intruders gave rise to a crisis. Never on the dramatic stage was a transformation scene carried out with such dispatch nor indeed with such efficiency. A sharp order directed the new arrivals to gallop the pony and trap up the lane to Murray's yard. Even as it reached the lane, the first Crossley tender appeared in view. Tom Barry had placed a stone on the road, and had ordered that when the tender reached it fire was to be opened.

The opening fusillade killed the driver instantaneously, and the tender came to a halt. Barry appeared on the road and threw a hand grenade into the back of the tender, and all was over so far as that one was concerned. When Stephen O'Neill and I came out on to the road from the opposite side, we found 'Flyer' and 'Spud' were at the first tender; all the occupants had been killed.

Meanwhile, the second tender was about one hundred and fifty yards behind, and had become stuck at the side of the road where the driver had tried unsuccessfully to turn it. The Auxiliaries had jumped out, threw themselves on the road and were firing from the cover of the tender. We then opened fire from their rear and when they realised that they were caught between two fires, they knew they were doomed.

It was then realised that three of our men had been killed in Michael McCarthy's section; he himself had been shot through the head, Jim O'Sullivan through the jaw, and Pat Deasy had two bullet wounds through the body. Two others had been wounded, Jack Hennessy and John Lordan, but though they had lost a great deal of blood, their wounds were not serious. It had been a short but grim fight. Of the eighteen Auxiliaries involved, one escaped and fled across country only to be captured and shot later, and another who was taken for dead survived for a while but never recovered from his wounds. The remaining sixteen had been killed outright.

The fight over, we proceeded to collect the arms left by the enemy, seventeen rifles and revolvers, together with ammunition and equipment. The two tenders were then set on fire, and the Volunteers prepared to withdraw as soon as they had laid the dead Auxiliaries by the roadside. The spoils were divided out among the men, and as darkness fell we left Kilmichael and set out on our long march of fourteen miles to Granure.

My brother, Pat, was clearly dying. To remove him, a door was requisitioned from a nearby house. He was carried on it to Buttimer's of Gortroe about half a mile away, and he died there at 10.00 p.m. It was only some time later that I heard this sad news.

The Column marched south under cover of the gathering darkness and headed for Manch Bridge. One man, Dan Hourihane, went ahead in order to make final arrangements for billeting the men. He made good time, and when the main body arrived at Granure he had everything in order. It was then 11.00 p.m. and the men were wet, tired, and exhausted after a trying day and a grim experience of the harsh realities of war. So worn out were they that as soon as they had eaten the meal prepared by some members of the Cumann na mBan, Nean O'Driscoll, Cissie Cronin, and Molly O'Riordan, they lay down on the straw in their wet clothes just as they were, and were instantly asleep.

Charlie Hurley left the Clonakilty area after the Kilmichael ambush, and made his way to Granure to join the Column there. He met the men in their billets and stayed with the guards and scouts who were protecting them that Sunday night after the fight. On the following day, when Tom Barry paraded his men, Charlie addressed them in simple terms, congratulated them on their wonderful victory, and explained what it would mean to the success of the war not only in West Cork, but throughout the whole country. He paid tribute to the three men who had fallen in the fight, and spoke with praise of the military spirit in which the whole operation had been carried out. Finally, he went round to each individual member of the Column, and in his own humble, quiet way encouraged him, thanked him for the honour he had brought to the Brigade, and communicated to him something of his own indomitable spirit of optimism and certitude about the final victory that would crown our efforts at last.

On Tuesday, 30 November, Charlie Hurley returned to Brigade Headquarters near Crossbarry. I met him there and was given a full report of the ambush at Kilmichael. I shall always remember his comradeship and his warm sympathy as he told me of my brother's death in action. I took him to my brother, Miah, who was a member of the Battalion column, and was in a billet nearby. Charlie broke the news to him, and then suggested that I should leave immediately with Dick Barrett to break the news to my father and mother. We left that night, crossed the Bandon at Colliers Quay, and arrived at my home at Kilmacsimon Quay at 10.00 p.m.

It was a sad duty that was mine to break the news to my parents that their youngest son had been killed on the previous Sunday. My father broke down completely, for Pat was his favourite boy, but my mother's reaction was a great help. She shed no tears, though her heart must have been well-nigh breaking. She accepted the cross as the mothers of Ireland have traditionally accepted it when they lost sons and husbands in the cause of Irish freedom. Pádraig Pearse immortalised this role of Irish mothers in one of his poems when he wrote, 'They suffer in our coming and in our going.' In the long and lonely reaches of the night they bear their sorrows, and are doubtless consoled by the thought of our faith which is essentially founded on the Cross itself.

Dick Barrett and I had to return to our Battalion column that night, and it was a sorrow for me to have to leave my home and my parents at such a time. But I had no option, and so with my companion I travelled through the night, and arrived back at the

column headquarters at O'Sullivan's of Raheen in the early hours
of Wednesday morning. There we remained on the alert for a
report from our scouts on enemy movements. This we considered
a more prudent thing to do than to lie in ambush for an enemy
that might or might not pass that way; the families in the area
could not all be counted upon, and if we were noticed in ambush
positions for successive days we would certainly have been reported
to the enemy.

CHAPTER 19

THE PROJECTED LANDING OF ARMS
AT SQUINCE STRAND

The townland of Clashinimud near Brinny is on the Crossbarry-Bandon road which was one of the two routes most frequently used by military lorries travelling between Cork City and British posts in West Cork, the other route being the main road via Innishannon. For more than a week I had been planning an ambush on this road, and had mustered about thirty men from six Companies of the Bandon Battalion north of the river with a few from Innishannon, Ballinadee and Kilbrittain. We assembled at Raheen, two miles north of the position selected for the ambush.

On Thursday morning, 2 December, our scouts reported that three lorries had passed on the way to Cork from the Bandon direction. Anticipating the return of the convoy in the late evening, we took up our positions at Clashinimud towards midday, and prepared to await the return of the lorries. Our position extended for about two hundred yards on a straight stretch of the road that was approached by a bend to the right at the eastern end, and a more pronounced sweep to the left at the western end. Quinn's farmyard with its high wall extended for about forty yards along the roadside, midway in the position and on the south side.

The ambush party were armed with fifteen rifles and twenty shotguns. They were posted in three sections, one at the bend on the eastern side, one in the farmyard, and the third at the western end where there was a clear view of the whole location of the ambush. I took up position with three companions inside the farmyard gate. Trees had been partly cut, ready for felling, at a road junction, a mile to the east and also at a point some distance to the west.

It was almost dusk when the lorries were heard coming from the east, and as the first lorry rounded the bend, I pulled the pin out of a Mills bomb, and prepared to throw it into the lorry. Fortunately, in our training we had been taught to retain the pin from the ring on the little finger of the left hand, for as I was about to hurl the bomb from some three or four yards' range, I saw that there were civilians as well as soldiers in the lorry. Fearing that the former were prisoners or hostages, I did not throw the bomb, but held the spring, and replaced the pin later. At the same time I ordered my companions to hold fire.

There were only two lorries in the convoy, and they quickly passed the point at which I was stationed. At the other end of the ambush position, about two hundred yards further on, our men opened fire as they were directly facing the lorry and could not see the occupants behind the driver. After their first burst of fire, however, the lorry drew abreast of them and when they saw the civilians they allowed the vehicle to escape.

In the discussion which followed this abortive ambush, we all felt regret that we had been forced to sacrifice the opportunity to ambush the enemy—the easiest for us to date—that had come our way. We were, however, very relieved that there had been no major casualties among the civilian passengers. We naturally thought that they were prisoners, but we learned later that they were Crown witnesses being conveyed back to Rosscarbery from Cork where they had given evidence in the Assize Court that was still being held in the city. Later, it was stated in an enemy report of the attack that a woman had received a bullet wound in the knee, and that two R.I.C. men had also been wounded. That night the ambush column was disbanded, and the men returned to the six Company areas from which they had been drawn.

The wisdom of the Brigade order concerning the formation of Battalion columns as well as the Brigade Column was soon in evidence after the abortive ambush at Clashinimud. It puzzled and alarmed the enemy to find that such an action could be attempted so soon after the Kilmichael success a few days previously. Knowing, as they surely did by this time, that the Brigade Column which attacked at Kilmichael was twenty miles away to the south of the river, in the Lyre district, they must have been very disturbed to find another full-scale ambush organised in an entirely different locality so soon after the Kilmichael engagement.

I left Raheen by bicycle later that evening after the attempted ambush, and arrived at Castletownkenneigh at about 10.00 p.m. All the arrangements had been made for the funeral of the three men killed at Kilmichael. Coffins had been supplied from Inchigeela, and taken to the bog where the remains had been hidden since the Sunday night. The three coffins were placed on a common cart and covered with the tricolour. Then the funeral party set out for the cemetry at Castletownkenneigh five miles away. It arrived there shortly after 11.00 p.m. and was met by the local parish priest, Father O'Connell of Enniskean. A party of local Volunteers were digging a common grave when we arrived, and the burial had been arranged for midnight. However, an unforeseen difficulty arose when the digging party encountered some rock and this delayed the interment for two hours.

At 2.00 a.m. on a clear, starry night the coffins were lowered into the grave.[1] Comrades of the fallen paid their last tribute in a volley of rifle fire, and Father O'Connell read the burial service. Besides the Volunteers, many of the local people who heard of the funeral were present, and all remained until the last sod had been placed on the grave. Then Father O'Connell addressed those present in moving terms, and paid his tribute to the dead and to the Brigade which was carrying on such a glorious fight for freedom. His concluding words made such an impression that they were soon being repeated all over the district; they gave a message of hope and encouragement as well as consolation. He said that whether as soldiers or civilians the future destiny of our country was in our hands, and must be regarded as a sacred trust by all. He reminded us that every man had but one life and if the freedom of his country demanded it, then he must be prepared to sacrifice it willingly.

From this sad scene I returned to Brigade Headquarters and there learned the shocking details of the capture and shooting of three Volunteer officers just outside Bandon town on the night of 2 December. Some weeks previously two soldiers of the Essex regiment had been captured and were being held prisoners in the Clonakilty Battalion area. They were subjected to a prolonged and systematic questioning in the course of which a daring plan was conceived, a plan whose realisation would achieve the most spectacular success of the war, at least in West Cork.

One of the prisoners had a brother in the military barracks at Bandon. He was a sergeant and would be prepared—at least so his captured brother affirmed—to co-operate with the plan if he were given a very substantial sum of money. Our prisoner agreed to write to this sergeant and ask him to meet some of our men outside Bandon town to discuss the proposition of his co-operating in the seizure of Bandon military barracks. The letter was written at the dictation, and under the supervision, of Tom Barry, and the meeting was arranged for 8.30 p.m. on 2 December, at the top of the Laurel Walk, a short distance out from Bandon on the Dunmanway road.

On our side it was arranged that the Brigade Column Commander Tom Barry, and three officers of the Bandon Company, Captain

1. Within three months this grave was extended to receive the remains of the local Captain, Jeremiah O'Mahony, who was killed accidentally. He was an outstanding Captain and fought his last fight at Kilmichael.

John Galvin, Lieutenant Jim O'Donoghue, and Section Commander Joe Begley, should be present at this meeting. On the actual
evening of the meeting as he was about to set out for the rendezvous at the top of the Laurel Walk, Tom Barry had a serious heart
attack and collapsed unconscious as he was actually stepping into
the car that was to take him close to the meeting point. This upset
the whole plan. Charlie Hurley had to have the sick man conveyed
immediately from Ahiohill, where he was, to McCarthy's of
Kilmoylerane where Dr Eugene Fehily and Nurse O'Neill of
Shanavagh treated him and fought for his life for some days.
Next, he was removed to O'Neill's of Shanavagh. When the crisis
eased Barry, accompanied by Nurse Baby Lordan, who was a
member of Cumann na mBan and Brigade Nurse, was brought to
the Mercy Home in Cork City, and there he made a rapid recovery.

Meanwhile back in Bandon the three Volunteer officers who
were to attend the meeting with the army sergeant were unaware
of Barry's plight. On the night appointed these men, together with
the brother of one of them, Miah Galvin, went to the arms dump
at Clancool to collect the small arms that were there. They found
three revolvers, and arming themselves with these the three officers
set off for their appointment without Miah Galvin : since there
was no revolver available for him, it was not considered prudent
that he should go. The three men avoided the direct route to the
Laurel Walk, and instead mounted Convent Hill and descended
through the fields towards the Dunmanway road about a mile from
the town. Just as they emerged from the fields on to the road they
were immediately surrounded by a large force of the Essex regiment
that had been lying in wait along the roadway. They were seized,
ill-treated, and then shot dead. When the bodies were found next
morning each had a bullet hole in the centre of the forehead.

The Projected Landing of Arms at Squince Strand

On the day after the Bandon tragedy which deprived us of three
invaluable officers, we received a verbal message from G.H.Q. in
Dublin that a shipload of arms was being purchased on the Con-
tinent, and that it had been decided to land it on the West Cork
coast at the point that was considered most suitable by us. This
welcome news precipitated a meeting of the Brigade Staff at which
it was decided that the coastline in the Skibbereen area would offer
most advantages for the project in view. Two reasons in particular
led us to this conclusion, the first being the distance that separated
this region from the heavy enemy concentrations at Cork, Kinsale

and Bandon and the second being the presence along the coast of sandy shores on which the ship conveying the arms could be beached, and so quickly and safely unloaded. There were no satisfactory ports in the area at which a ship could be berthed without attracting public attention before it could be unloaded, and it was for this reason that we considered a sandy shore the best alternative.

Accordingly, I was sent to the Skibbereen area to consult the Battalion Commandant, Sam Kingston. When the project was explained to him, Sam maintained that Squince Strand inside Rabbit Island in the Myross Company area would be the most suitable spot for the operation. An added advantage of this particular place was the presence in it of a very active and efficient Company of Volunteers who would help with the unloading and transport of the arms. Pat O'Driscoll, the local Company Captain, knew the coast intimately, and strongly approved of Squince Strand for the purpose we had in mind. He explained that a ship could sail in through the channel that separates Rabbit Island from the mainland, and would then be concealed from view on the seaward side by the island. We inspected the beach and the channel, and both Kingston and I agreed with O'Driscoll that this was the very best place for the landing.

That evening I returned to Brigade Headquarters, and the next morning, Saturday, 18 December, I left for Dublin to submit our recommendations to G.H.Q. I stayed the night at Dan Delaney's of Mylane, and early in the morning I set out by bicycle for Cork to catch the 8.00 a.m. train to Dublin. As I rode down Patrick Street in the mid-winter dawn I saw the burnt-out portion of the city was still smouldering; smoke was still rising from the ruins caused by the fire that was set alight on the night of 11-12 December.

By previous arrangement, I met Florrie O'Donoghue at Glanmire Station, and we both travelled together to Dublin in an empty carriage. The company was indeed very welcome, and we both availed ourselves of the opportunity to discuss in minute detail the progress of the war in our respective areas. In regard to the business that was taking us to Dublin, Florrie informed me that the Commander of Cork Number One Brigade had been consulted about the projected landing of arms in West Cork, and that he had agreed to release the Commandant of the Fourth Battalion, Mick Leahy, to pilot the ship because of his expert knowledge of the coastline.

The journey passed without incident, though military and police were on duty at most of the stations we passed. We were unarmed, and had names and alibis if we were questioned. We were reasonably well-dressed, and felt confident that we could meet any emergency. Before arriving at Kingsbridge Station we decided to separate at the terminus and to meet later at Barry's Hotel as we had been instructed. On the platform there was the usual company of military and plain-clothes men who scrutinised all the passengers as they left the train. I passed through without being questioned, but I noticed that a little further along the platform Florrie was being held up and questioned and then searched. Fortunately, his alibi was accepted, and we met later as arranged.

Having reported our arrival at G.H.Q. we were called to a special meeting at Barry's Hotel that evening at 5.00 p.m. Those present were : Cathal Brugha, Michael Collins, Seán McMahon, Liam Mellows, and Joe Vyse. There our suggestion for the landing of the arms at Squince Strand was discussed and accepted. We were then informed that the consignment of arms and ammunition had been purchased in Genoa and that a ship had been chartered to bring it to Ireland. The question of a pilot was dealt with by Florrie who reported on the choice of Mick Leahy. Florrie was then instructed to send this officer to Dublin immediately. Next, plans for the distribution of the arms were discussed. This operation was entrusted to our Brigade. We were to see to the unloading of the ship and the delivery of most of the cargo to Cork Number One Brigade in the Inchigeela-Ballyvourney district. The Volunteers there were to pass on allotted consignments to Kerry via Ballyvourney, to north Cork via Carriganimma and Kilcorney and thence through the country. Limerick was to have a special portion of the cargo sent there through north Cork. Briefly, our job was to bear responsibility for the choice of a suitable landing spot for the ship, for the transport of the arms, for the preparation of safe dumps and for the eventual handing over to units of our own and to other Brigade areas of the guns and ammunition landed.

Before the meeting ended, it was decided that the staffs of the three Cork Brigades should arrange to meet three weeks later to co-ordinate plans for the distribution of the arms. I remember that when the meeting closed Collins informed us that the Archbishop of Perth, Australia, had intervened to bring about an end to the fighting in Ireland, and that a truce had almost been agreed to when Sir Neville Macready, G.O.C. of British Forces in Ireland, on being approached by Lloyd George, the British Premier, denounced the idea and asked for just three months more; that was all he would require 'to clear up the mess'.

When I returned from the Dublin meeting I met our regular

contact in Cork City, Seán McCarthy. Seán was then teaching in a school at Brooklodge, and was a regular visitor to our Brigade Headquarters near Crossbarry. On the eve of the Tureen ambush he arrived at Ballymurphy where the Volunteers were waiting to take up their positions on the Cork-Bandon road, and he immediately volunteered to take his place in our ranks. But he was too valuable to us as a contact in Cork City, particularly in relation to Cork Jail, and also as Chairman of the County Board of the G.A.A. In this latter capacity he had connexions all over the County. The Brigade Staff considered that his services in Cork were of greater value that his part in a local ambush, and we refused him permission to join us in the fighting. On the many occasions on which I had to travel to Cork or Dublin, Seán was always available, and both he and another very good friend in need, Paddy O'Keeffe, must be remembered for their unfailing hospitality and help. On this particular occasion when I was returning from the meeting at G.H.Q., Seán had the very disappointing news that Paddy O'Keeffe had been captured a few nights previously when he was on his way to an operation in the city.

With Seán I went along to the Mercy Home to pay a visit to Tom Barry who was convalescing there when I arrived. I was delighted to find him so much improved. We scarcely noticed the time passing there was so much to relate, but the hour for the departure of the last train to Dunkettle approached and we prepared to leave As Seán and I were leaving, Tom invited me to stay and share his room with him for the night, as we still had a great deal to discuss. Seán departed and we were settling down for our chat when suddenly the door opened and in came the Reverend Mother. It was a most unexpected visit, but apparently the reverend lady was making a spot check of the Home. She expressed her surprise that I should still be in the room considering how close it was to curfew time. Barry explained that he had invited me to stay the night, and endeavoured to elicit her consent. It was all in vain; she refused point-blank, and told me that I would have to leave immediately. As there was no point in arguing further, I rushed out of the home and ran most of the way to Glanmire Station, which was a mile distant. I was very fortunate to be able to board the train just as it was leaving the platform. Then on arriving at Dunkettle I was able to rejoin a very surprised Seán McCarthy and spend the night with him in his digs at Brooklodge.

On the following day I returned to Brigade Headquarters, and gave a full report of all that had taken place in Dublin, with particular reference to the proposed landing of arms at Squince Strand, and also to my experiences in the Mercy Home. Indeed I innocently prefaced my report with an account of my visit to Tom Barry and of my being ordered out of the Home by the Reverend Mother almost on curfew time. Charlie at this could not resist making one of the sallies for which he was famous, 'You should have understood that the Reverend Mother had to protect her flock, and you must admit that you looked like one that was safer outside the convent than in it!'

In connexion with the arms' landing, we planned the routes and aternative routes to the Cork border, and made arrangements for the preparation of one hundred dumps to receive the arms when they arrived.

CHAPTER 20

CHRISTMAS INTERLUDE

After Tom Barry's collapse at Ahiohill on 3 December, Charlie Hurley sent for Seán Lehane, Commandant of the Schull Battalion, and asked him to take command of the Brigade Column until Barry returned. Lehane willingly agreed, and filled the post until the demobilisation of the Column for the Christmas period a short while later.

At this stage the Column was reinforced by the addition of twelve men who were armed with rifles captured at Kilmichael, and was moved away from Ahiohill towards the east. A few days later, on 8 December, it was decided to ambush a party of Essex soldiers that travelled regularly by lorry between Clonakilty and Bandon. On the appointed day, some time before dawn, the Column advanced to take up positions on the main Clonakilty-Bandon road near Gaggin. As the Column men made their way through the fields under cover of darkness, Lieutenant Michael McLeane of Lowertown, near Schull, fell into a drain and injured his arm. At this, Charlie Hurley replaced the injured man's rifle with a Webley revolver, and sent him to a nearby loyalist house to warn the occupants to remain indoors until the signal for withdrawal was heard. The rest of the men were in the ambush position when the military lorry came along the road. However, owing to an unfortunate misunderstanding of the orders given to him, one of the section commanders allowed the lorry to pass his position without opening fire as he had been directed. This lapse caused the failure of the entire plan. A few belated shots were fired, but none of the enemy was hit.

The lorry continued on its way for about half a mile and then halted. The soldiers dismounted, and made their way back through the fields to the point at which they had been attacked. As they advanced they captured Michael McLeane in the loyalist house, and having tortured him mercilessly riddled him with bullets in view of a sixteen-year-old lad who witnessed the atrocity from a nearby cottage. Next the soldiers caught the Column unawares on its flank as it was retiring from the scene of the ambush. A confused skirmish followed, and some of the Volunteers panicked. However, the enemy was surprised by the number of Volunteers involved in the engagement, and hurriedly withdrew to their lorry after firing a few volleys. That same day an attack was made on some military in

Bandon by the local Company, but there were no casualties on either side.

After five weeks' continuous service in atrocious weather conditions, Charlie Hurley felt that the Column was well-nigh exhausted, and that it would be wise to demobilise it for the Christmas period in order to provide the men with an opportunity for a complete rest to restore them physically and raise their morale. When Seán Lehane was informed of this decision he paraded the Column on 21 December at Kildea, Rossmore, where it had been billeted for the previous few days. He addressed the men briefly, and having instructed them to report back on 18 January, he dismissed them.

The local Kilmeen Company then took over all arms, ammunition, mines, equipment and even the new trench coats that had recently been issued to the Column. All was removed to Mick Larry O'Sullivan's at Lisnabrinna, about one mile from Kildea, and there a great fire was lit to dry out all the kit. The work took an entire night. Before daybreak the Company removed everything to a large dump that had been prepared on O'Hara's farm at Kilmeen. Finally, on the following night the thirty-five rifles were taken by the Company to a house in the farmyard of Mrs Collins of Rossmore and were cleaned, dried, and oiled, and made ready for further action in the New Year.

On Christmas Eve the Brigade Staff dispersed, and I set off for home with Charlie Hurley. We had a pony and trap to take us as far as Colliers Quay, and from there we were ferried across the Bandon river by Dan O'Riordan and Bill Hogan. We covered the remaining part of the journey on foot, and reached my home at Kilmacsimon Quay about 5.00 p.m. that Christmas Eve.

The joy caused by our visit at such a time and on such a day can easily be imagined. It brought consolation to my father and mother in their sorrow after my brother Pat's death at Kilmichael. That very morning my brother Jack also arrived home, and with other local Volunteers acted as scouts while we were in the house. While we were enjoying a meal in the warmth of our kitchen, Miah, another brother, told us an interesting tale.

On the same morning, at about eleven o'clock, two British soldiers were noticed in the locality, and had called to our house for food and cigarettes. My good mother supplied them with both, but as soon as they left the house they were arrested by local Volunteers and questioned. They said they were deserters from their regiment, the Cameron Highlanders, in Cobh—then known as Queenstown—and because they were cold and hungry they had asked for help. Miah, Bill Hales, and Con Flynn, who had arrested them, took them to a safe place of captivity at Knockpogue in the Kilbrittain area where they were being detained.

Making a mental note of these interesting facts, we gave ourselves for the moment to the joy of this Christmas homecoming; it was a reunion which circumstances made for ever memorable. Because our house was in an exposed position we could not remain too long, and we prepared to leave around seven o'clock. My mother's parting gift to us as we left was her blessing accompanied with a liberal sprinkling of Holy Water. Such a gesture was typical of Irish homesteads everywhere, but it seemed to have an added significance for us on that holy and blessed night of Christmas.

For the sake of greater security we made our way to an isolated farmhouse about a mile away to put up for the night. There we were given a warm welcome by the family of Mike Good and enjoyed its hospitality until the following morning. We left at a very early hour and proceeded to Kilbrittain and then to Knockpogue where the two deserters were being held under guard. They were brought before us for questioning, and they repeated in substance the story that we had heard from my brother Miah on the previous day.

What struck us from the outset as being most extraordinary about the two men was the fact that they seemed to have so little in common. The spokesman, who gave his name as Peter Monahan, was quite evidently a well-educated man, and far above the standard of the ordinary British Tommy. His companion, on the other hand, was a nondescript type. He gave his name as Tommy Clarke, and seemed to have had no higher ambition than to get away from a life that was entirely distasteful to him. There was something so implausible about the association of these two men that we were highly suspicious, and subjected the pair to a long and severe examination.

Monahan was a man of medium size, and presented a good appearance even in the rough uniform of a British Army private which he wore. His complexion was sallow, his hair fair, his eyes bright, penetrating, and intelligent. Speaking in the cultured accent of a well-educated Scotsman, he explained that he and his companion were members of the Cameron Regiment then stationed at Queenstown (Cobh), and that they were both disgusted with the trend of events in Ireland. In consequence they had decided to desert, and to offer their services to the Volunteer movement in West Cork. Three days previously they had left Ringaskiddy and had travelled across country in an effort to locate our forces. Asked about his previous history, Monahan said that he had been a mining engineer in Scotland; had joined the Royal Engineers at the outbreak of the World War and had attained the rank of Captain. When he was demobilised, he returned to Scotland, but on finding his home life wrecked joined the Camerons as a private under the assumed name of Peter Monahan.

Normally, I suppose, a story of this kind would, in the circumstances, be scarcely credited, and the two men would have been courtmartialled as spies, but we were intrigued by Monahan's claim to have been a mining engineer. The man's evident sincerity also impressed us; so we adjourned to discuss the case. After talking it over with us, Charlie made a typical decision. Hitherto our efforts to manufacture mines had met with little success for want of knowledge and experience. Here was a man who could possibly have something to offer us in this respect, and we could avail ourselves of his services to have a mine manufactured from gun-cotton or tonite for a contemplated attack on Kilbrittain R.I.C. barracks. Monahan had a job.

The Attack on Kilbrittain R.I.C. Barracks

The R.I.C. barracks at Kilbrittain was by this time in late December 1920 mainly occupied by the Black and Tans. It had always been a great menace to us, and a constant thorn in our side. From the start it had been an objective marked for destruction in our planning, and the local Volunteers sighed for the day when they could annihilate it. It was now the only remaining enemy outpost in the area, and it was thought that, perhaps, the time had come to make the long-desired assault on it. Two months earlier, an attempt had been made to capture the barracks with help from inside, but the friendly R.I.C. sergeant—a newcomer—whose help was solicited, refused to co-operate in so drastic an undertaking, and the plan fell through. A direct attack was the only hope.

The barracks stood in the centre of the village, about twenty feet in from the roadway. It was an isolated building and very strongly fortified with barred windows protected by heavy loopholed steel shutters, and had portholes in each wall for releasing bombs. A strongly-built porch protected the main entrance, while barbed-wire entanglements covered the area in front and around the sides.

Explosives were our first preoccupation. Under the supervision of the Brigade Engineer, Mick Crowley, Monahan began work on two mines that were intended for the attack. They were made with powerful charges of tonite that were packed in strongly-constructed wooden boxes. These in turn were affixed by means of strong hinges to the ends of two ten-foot lengths of timber. Each charge was primed and wired and made ready to be set off by a plunger.

The six roads leading to Kilbrittain were to be blocked by fallen trees, and for this part of the operation sixty men were mobilised from the Kilbrittain and neighbouring Companies. In the darkness of the night the trees were quickly felled by experienced men who then remained on guard with a dispatch-rider to send news of any enemy activity in the locality.

At twelve o'clock midnight, 31 December, the assault began. The mines had been brought to the area in a common cart and were now carried through the village on the way to the barracks by five tall men from Kilbrittain and three others from outside. The main attacking party now moved into position in and around the village. The mining party were accompanied by Peter Monahan carrying the wires, and Mick Crowley bringing the plunger. In their stockinged feet they penetrated to the outskirts of the barbed-wire entanglements, and then threw the planks bearing the mines upright against the front wall of the barracks, one on either side of the porch. The covering party of three armed men and those who carried the charges then retired, leaving Monahan and Crowley under the shelter of the gable end ready to work the plunger.

Occupying the houses immediately opposite the barracks were eight men with rifles who covered the front of the barracks while a similar party was in position covering the rear. Close by in reserve was a party of twelve men ready to charge the position once the wall was breached.

When everything was ready, Mick Crowley worked the plunger. But no explosion came. He tried repeatedly but in vain; he could not set off the charge. The enemy were now alerted and were aware of the attack being attempted. Immediately the crack of rifle fire was heard from the barrack windows in front and was returned by our men from the houses across the street. Shots were also fired at the mines in an effort to explode them, but without success. Eventually the attacking party was ordered to withdraw. Continuous rifle fire rained from all points of the barracks as the attackers withdrew to safety; several of them narrowly escaped being shot.

The failure to take the barracks at Kilbrittain was a great disappointment. Everything depended on the mine, for without first breaching the doors or walls of this strongly-protected fortress, its

capture was out of the question. Though disappointed the men
were not disheartened, and within a matter of weeks they will be
found before the barracks again in another effort to reduce it.

*　*　*　*　*　*

As the year 1920 drew to its close, we naturally reviewed the
general situation in our Brigade area, so far as the war was concerned. We noted first of all the disposition of enemy troops and
their quality, the positions that were abandoned and those that
were strengthened. In Kinsale, for example, outside the Brigade
area but at our doorstep, the infamous Essex Regiment still had its
headquarters with outposts in Bandon, Clonakilty, and Ballineen.
At their comparatively secure base at Kinsale, where Volunteer
activity was negligible, they could give protection and shelter to
weary troops from the outlying posts. Bantry town was strongly
held by the King's Liverpools, who also maintained an outpost at
Skibbereen. Bere Island was the headquarters for the King's Own
Yorkshire Light Infantry and they too had an outpost at Furious
Pier and also at Eyeries.

By this time strong units of Auxiliaries held posts at Glengarriff,
Dunmanway, and Macroom, and though the latter was outside our
area, we were subjected to frequent raids and sorties from it along
our communications routes from Newcestown to Kealkil. These
Auxiliaries engaged in terrorist activities of the most brutal kind,
particularly after the Kilmichael ambush, and constituted a grave
threat to our movements and even to our survival. The area most
seriously threatened was that between Manch Bridge and Kilmichael, and it was felt that special efforts would have to be made
by the Brigade Staff in that area to counteract the demoralising
effect of the intensified campaign of aggression waged by the
Auxiliaries. Towards the end of December, it was decided at a
Brigade Council meeting that Tom Barry, who had recently
returned from hospital, and I should visit the Companies of the
Dunmanway Battalion north of Manch Bridge to rouse the morale
of the Volunteers in the area, and to maintain the organisation
intact in face of the raids and savage attacks of the Auxiliaries.

The R.I.C. still occupied barracks at Innishannon, Bantry, Glengarriff, Drimoleague, and Dunmanway, and all these stations were
now reinforced by the villainous Black and Tans. Either by attack
or threat, we had forced the evacuation of the R.I.C. from fifteen
stations, namely Mount Pleasant, Ballinspittle, Timoleague, Balti-

more, Castletownsend, Union Hall, Ballydehob, Goleen, Kilcrohane, Schull, Durrus, Adrigole, Allihies, Eyeries, and Ballineen.
This indeed represented a very substantial list of victories, but we
were not satisfied with it. Somehow we did not at this time, or at
any later period, consider the military, or the Auxiliaries, or even
the notorious Black and Tans such formidable foes as the R.I.C.,
for to our way of thinking, they were the eyes and ears of the enemy
forces in Ireland. They knew the people intimately, the topography
of the various districts in which they operated, and the local history
of each one of us. It was for this reason that we were convinced
that our task of clearing the enemy from the area, and indeed from
the country as a whole, would be made much easier if the R.I.C.
could be removed altogether from the scene. On our border, the
First Cork Brigade had by this time cleared Inchigeela, Kilmurry
and Farran R.I.C. barracks, and this made inter-brigade communications more direct and safer.

We had no accurate estimate of the strength of the enemy units
that opposed us or any clear idea of their armaments. All that we
were certain about was that the enemy was numerically far stronger
than we were, and that they were vastly superior to us in arms.
Yet, as we reviewed the year that was ending, a year during which
we faced the old enemy in actual warfare, albeit guerilla warfare,
we had every reason to feel that at long last victory was no longer
the tantalising rainbow which wo many generations of our forbears
had bravely but unsuccessfully followed. We began the year with
twenty-nine rifles, a collection of shotguns—better suited to farmers
and others who wished to enjoy a day shooting game than soldiers
engaged in real warfare—a few revolvers, and a very limited supply
of ammunition. We ended the year with one hundred and twenty
rifles, sixty revolvers, a supply of Mills bombs and home-made
bombs, over a ton of gun-cotton, and about thirty thousand rounds
of ammunition.

The organisation of the Brigade witnessed considerable development during the course of the year under review. Despite the losses
sustained either through the death or capture of key officers and
men, the Brigade units were functioning exceptionally well. At the
beginning of the year, the organisation in several areas was weak
and many Companies were in danger of disintegration due to lack
of military activities. But the actions that were planned and put
into effect against the enemy from the opening of the year had a
stimulating effect generally, and the different units that constituted
the Brigade all showed progressive improvement as the months

passed and the *tempo* of the war quickened.

The special services had been given a good deal of attention, and in almost all cases showed marked improvement. But it was in the domain of communications that the greatest improvement was noticeable. There was now a daily service operating between Brigade Headquarters and six of the seven Battalions. Communication with the Beara Battalion was understandably less frequent on account of the great distance separating it from Headquarters at a time when motor transport was a rarity, and also on account of the occupation of Glengarriff by the Auxiliaries.

Numerically, too, the Brigade had improved. At the end of 1919 it consisted of six Battalions with sixty Companies, and a census taken in July 1919 showed a total of approximately two thousand nominal members, of whom about a thousand were listed as active. During the course of 1920 some new Companies were formed in the then existing Battalions, and an entirely new Battalion was formed in the Schull peninsula with nine Companies. This brought the total strength in the Brigade at the end of 1920 to seventy Companies and almost 3,500 members, almost all of whom were now active in some capacity or other, for example, as scouts, dispatch-riders, road-cutters and so forth.

The auxiliary organisation of Cumann na mBan was very active, particularly in the towns and neighbouring districts of Bandon, Clonakilty, Dunmanway, Skibbereen, Bantry, Ballydehob, and Castletownbere. In all these vital areas the members of the Cumann were performing work in the sphere of intelligence that was invaluable. They had access to sources of information that were often closed to the Volunteers, and they exploited all the possibilities open to them to the advantage of our cause. Besides the countless services they rendered to men 'on the run', to the wounded, and those captured and imprisoned, they kept headquarters informed of the daily—and sometimes hourly—movements of the enemy in and about his headquarters and at his various posts. Many a life was saved and many a Volunteer protected from arrest by the painstaking and patient labour of these dedicated girls.

The overall picture was truly a very encouraging one. The spirit of military discipline was everywhere in evidence, and could be seen even in the manner in which routine duties were carried out, such as the setting up of road blocks or the cutting of roads. It could be remarked also in the work of scouting, intelligence, communications, billeting—all these activities were now carried out with a military efficiency that was exceptional. The spirit of devotion to the national cause and the spirit of sacrifice in face of the great demands required by our struggle were perhaps the most encouraging features that could be observed at the time. Small wonder that we looked forward to the New Year with a greater optimism than ever.

CHAPTER 21

THE YEAR OF VICTORY DAWNS AT LAST

New Year's Day 1921 was a particularly memorable day for me, and that for a number of reasons. For one thing, it was the first occasion in several months on which I could venture to Mass. The danger of being captured in church on Sundays was a formidable one and, in fact, several of our men were arrested when the church in which they were attending Mass was unexpectedly surrounded by the military. But on New Year's Eve, Tom Barry and I were near Enniskean, and we thought it would be reasonably safe to assist at Mass in the local church on the following morning. And we could not think of a better way of beginning the New Year than by assisting at Mass and receiving Our Blessed Lord in Holy Communion.

The celebrant at the Mass was none other than Father O'Connell, the parish priest of Enniskean, who had officiated at the burial of my brother Pat and his two fallen comrades a month earlier. After the Gospel he preached a most encouraging sermon in which he reminded the people that they had arrived at a critical stage of the war, a time when they must face the enemy with faith and courage, remembering that they had but one life to offer, and that if necessary they ought to offer it willingly for the sake of their country.

While distributing Holy Communion, Father O'Connell recognised Tom Barry and me at the rails, as we were both well known to him. When he returned to the altar, he called one of the servers to summon the sacristan, and he whispered a word to him before he continued his Mass. As we left the church afterwards, the sacristan approached us in the porch, and told us that the parish priest requested us to come to the presbytery for breakfast. We were very pleased indeed to accept this invitation and joined him at his hospitable table.

We made a point of thanking the good priest for his courageous sermon; indeed we thought it was really heroic considering that Father O'Connell's neighbouring parish priest, Canon Magner, had been murdered by the Auxiliaries just two weeks previously. Father O'Connell turned the conversation to the progress of the war and showed the keenest interest in every detail of our activity. He was most complimentary in his references to our own contribution to the national effort, and encouraged us to persevere in the patriotic task to which we were committed. A few hours slipped by unnoticed, and as midday approached we were suddenly inter‧ rupted in our discussion. A Volunteer had arrived on a bicycle at the front door of the presbytery with the news that the house in which we had spent the night had been surrounded by a party of Auxiliaries just ten minutes after we had left it to attend Mass.

Looking back now in the evening of life at this particular escape, it stands out in my memory as a reminder of God's kind providence which ever rules out destinies and guides our ways. There were ten tenders of Auxiliaries in the district during the remainder of the day; houses were raided and ransacked from top to bottom; the people were searched and closely questioned; tenders were crossing and recrossing the bridges so frequently that they were impassable for us. So we remained all day with our kind host in the presbytery, and did not venture to leave until the scouts reported that the enemy had withdrawn.

As we bade farewell to Father O'Connell that New Year's night we thanked him warmly for his kind hospitality and encourage‧ ment. He is a man whom I have always remembered with affection not merely for his enthusiastic support, but for his priestly and fatherly services on many occasions. In particular, his memory will be revered for the services he rendered at Castletownkenneigh when he waited in the graveyard through the long hours of a cold night to conduct the funeral service for the casualties of the Kilmichael ambush. He never made any secret about his disapproval of the pastoral of Dr Coholan, Bishop of Cork, condemning our activities, and in this he shared the feeling shown privately by many other priests in the diocese.

When we left the presbytery, we crossed the Enniskean bridge, called to O'Neill's of Shanavagh where we met Paddy Crowley and Paddy O'Brien who accompanied us on our way to O'Donoghue's of Rossmore. There we contacted Charlie Hurley and held an official meeting of the Clonakilty Battalion staff. In contrast to the restful, though very informative and heartening day we spent at the presbytery, our comrades had had a very disturbing and hazardous time. It had been the heaviest day of raiding ever experienced in this area south of Ballineen, and many valuable men had narrow escapes. The local Volunteers numbered up to two hundred, and there were besides many others in the locality who were 'on the run'. Yet most of these men managed to evade the net which was case widely to ensnare them. Later we discovered the reason for the concentrated enemy activity in the area : the fact that the

Column had been disbanded before Christmas became known, and also the fact that the arms had been dumped in the district south of Ballineen. Hence the frantic raids and searchings and questionings. Yet, despite all the endeavours, and despite the questioning of prisoners taken who knew the whereabouts of the dumps, no information was released, and the enemy failed to find a single dump or even a single gun.

The meeting of the Clonakilty Battalion staff continued late into the night. The newly-appointed Commandant of the Battalion, Jim Hurley, although not yet twenty, was an excellent officer and he subsequently gave distinguished service in many engagements both inside and outside his own Battalion area. We had great confidence in this Battalion and found that its internal organisation and administration were exceptional. Much of the credit for this high standard must be ascribed to the Adjutant, Batt Murphy, who was then the longest-serving member of the Battalion staff.

On the morning after the Battalion meeting at Rossmore, Charlie Hurley and I left for the special inter-brigade meeting that we had been instructed by G.H.Q. to convene for the three Cork Brigades in order to complete plans for the distribution of the arms that were to be landed at Squince Strand. The venue decided on for this meeting was Goulding's of Donoughmore in the First Cork Brigade area, about forty miles from where we were, so we set off on foot in very severe winter conditions that entailed considerable hardship. The officers present at the meeting were Seán O'Hegarty and Florrie O'Donoghue representing the First Cork Brigade, Liam Lynch, and George Power representing the Second, and Charlie Hurley and I representing the Third.

The general plan of the landing was first discussed with a view to carrying out the intentions of G.H.Q. As the actual landing of the arms was to take place in our Brigade area, we submitted plans which we had drawn up for the immediate handling of the cargo as well as plans for its disposal in the case of all foreseeable emergencies. Following a lengthy discussion of the proposed routes for transporting the arms, it was agreed that we should hand over the major part to the First Cork Brigade at Inchigeela. The Kerry Brigades were to receive their portion at Ballyvourney.

Before the meeting concluded, a general review was made of the achievements of the three Cork Brigades. We were naturally very interested to know how the other two Brigades were faring and to hear about their experiences. We were agreeably surprised to find that the pattern of development was very similar to our own. The other two Brigades had evidently been increasing in military strength, in experience resulting from frequent encounters with the enemy, and in the acquisition of arms in very much the same proportion as ours had been. There was the same picture of all-round improvement in all sectors of organisation, in the spirit of the men, in military achievement, and in confidence regarding the ultimate outcome of the struggle.

An interesting feature of our discussion centred round the information which Michael Collins had given us in G.H.Q. of the first peace feelers that had been set in motion, first of all through an American journalist, and later through the offices of Archbishop Clune of Perth in Australia. Our attitude was very sceptical in regard to these moves. Suggestions that the British Cabinet was anxious for a truce to end hostilities were indeed interesting, but we were not in the least enthusiastic about them. Neither were we in any way perturbed by them, nor did we accept them as an indication of a weakening on the part of the enemy in the field. We faced the future with a confidence that we felt was fully justified by our achievements to date.

The Second Attack on Kilbrittain R.I.C. Barracks

On the day following our first attack on Kilbrittain R.I.C. barracks, the enemy became very active in the area. They invaded the village in force, cut away the barbed wire in front of the barrack building to remove the explosives we had placed there, and brought them to the military barracks in Bandon. Next, they re-set the wire entanglements in a much more effective manner than before so that half the width of the roadway, together with the barrack square, was now included in a network of barbed wire four feet high. The barbed wire protecting the walls was also strengthened, and a large tree at the rear was cut down in order to remove cover for would-be attackers.

Despite this strengthening of the outer defences of the barracks, the Kilbrittain officers, under Captain Jackie O'Neill, decided to make plans for another onslaught on the building and the date chosen was 15 January. The plan of attack was similar to that used on the first occasion, and the full Kilbrittain Company with support from Ballinadee, Ballinspittle and Timoleague again took part, and was deployed in much the same manner. The form of the explosive, though, was different, and consisted of a mobile charge of tonite placed in a wooden box provided with a hand-grip that enabled it to be carried by one man.

The man who carried the explosive was Denis Manning, and he was covered by Mick Crowley, who was armed with a revolver. Both men silently approached the barracks in stockinged feet, and when Manning had made his way through a portion of the barbed wire, he cast the explosive towards the barrack wall. He then lit the fuse and immediately rushed with Crowley for cover. The two men had scarcely got clear when Verey lights went up from the barracks and rifle fire blazed from the windows. The fire was returned by the Volunteers in the nearby position, and all waited hopefully for the explosion. Again it failed to come, and once more the attacking party found itself obliged to retreat over an exposed area for one hundred and fifty yards under a hail of rifle fire. Fortunately, the men escaped without casualties.

On the morning after the second ill-fated attack on Kilbrittain R.I.C. barracks, i.e. on 16 January, a unit of fourteen Volunteers of the Bandon Battalion under the command of their Commandant, Seán Hales, marched off to Rossmore to join the Brigade Column that was to be mobilised there on 18 January. At Quarry's Cross, seven miles north of Bandon, the unit was surprised by an enemy raiding party consisting of Essex soldiers, and a skirmish ensued. Fire was exchanged, but the unit carried out a successful rearguard action, and got safely away. It duly covered the fifteen-mile journey and arrived at its destination well on time.

When the Column reassembled and paraded for inspection at Rossmore, some of the 1920 members were missing, but in their stead many new members appeared, and brought the numbers up to forty again. Changes in the personnel of the Column were considered desirable by us and we welcomed them. We knew that not many men could endure for long the appalling mid-winter conditions that were prevailing at the time and that replacements in the Column would in consequence be necessary. Some weeks later, four new Volunteers were introduced by Michael Crowley, Brigade Engineer. They had been attending University College, Cork, where they were active members of the College Company. Three of them decided to interrupt their studies in order to give themselves whole-time to the national struggle, and they had requested to be transferred to the Flying Column of the West Cork Brigade. They were Pete Kearney, Eugene Callanan, later Dr Eugene Callanan, known to his friends as 'Nudge',[1] and Jerh McCarthy. The fourth,

1. Eugene Callanan had also offered his services at an earlier date, and took part in the attempted ambush at Clashinimud on 2 December 1920.

Connie Lucey, was well known to us as a prominent hurler who had won an All-Ireland Championship with the Cork team against Dublin in 1919. He had trained as a National School teacher, but subsequently took up the study of medicine and qualified in 1920.

The introduction of these four men, and other young men from the Brigade area, at this time was like a blood-transfusion, and caused general elation.[2] It was most heartening to see how readily the recruits were accepted and warmly welcomed by those who had been carrying on the fight for so long against such heavy odds. The ages of the men in the Column now ranged roughly from eighteen to thirty. Their numbers tended to vary for the demands of guerilla fighting were so testing and exacting that a steady stream of replacements was always necessary. The constant strain, vigilance without respite, hardships without number, marching for days in wet clothing with only brief rests and hurried meals—all these things tested the stamina of the men in the Column to the utmost. What is surprising is that so many endured the strain and danger of the war years unflinchingly, with a courage and generosity that were astonishing, and even with an unconquerable, unforgettable good-humoured optimism.

Without formality, but with the emphasis on military discipline, the Column was paraded, the roll was called, arms and equipment were issued, and then as night fell the men marched off to Shanavagh two miles away where billets had been prepared for them. Shortly after the Column left Rossmore, two other Volunteers arrived, Connie O'Leary, Captain of the Ardfield Company, and John L. O'Sullivan from Milltown. For some reason or other the two men had been delayed on their way to the remobilisation and by the time they reached Rossmore the Column was settling down for the night at Shanavagh. They met the Captain of the Kilmeen Company, Jim O'Hara, who knew them both, but since he had been given instructions not to tell anyone where the Column was to spend the night, he refused to answer the late-comers' query about the location of the Column, and allowed them to return to their own areas to await instructions. A small point, perhaps, but one that speaks well for the military discipline that prevailed. O'Sullivan was captured shortly after this episode, and spent the

2. Prior to this two other students from University College, Cork, returned and rendered valuable service both in the Column and in local duties during the remaining six months of the war. They were Pat Murphy and Jack Buttimer of Ardcahan, Dunmanway. Both were present at Fanlobbus and Gloundaw.

remainder of the war months as a prisoner on Spike Island. O'Leary, for his part, succeeded in rejoining the Column. A few months later he was captured, but acted the fool so successfully in the barracks to which he was taken that he was kicked out as being more of a nuisance than a danger. He continued as an active fighting man, and his record ranks with the best among those of his comrades.

On 19 January Charlie Hurley and I contacted the Column at Shanavagh, and I can still vividly recall the joy I felt on meeting old comrades again. For me the month since the men had been disbanded had been a period of continual strain and anxiety and also, at times, of loneliness. I had been constantly on the move from one point to another. In the company of the men of the Column, however, I experienced an exhilarating feeling of *camaraderie* and confidence. I felt that the mobilisation of the Column would bring a sense of protection and encouragement to all the Brigade area particularly to those that had been so cruelly harassed by the enemy since the ambush at Kilmichael. I remember feeling that if it were a matter of choice for me I should have opted to remain permanently with the Column, but I knew that my duties as Brigade Adjutant demanded a round of organising tours that could only rarely be made synchronise with the movements of the Column.

The reign of terror which began in mid-December with the arrival of the Auxiliaries in Dunmanway had continued into the New Year, but now that the Column was in the field again under the inspiring leadership of Tom Barry, we felt that the Auxiliaries' worst efforts could be successfully countered, and that we could strike again and again with devastating effect as had already been done at Kilmichael. Soon the indiscriminate raids and nocturnal visits organised by the Auxiliaries ceased almost entirely, and they rarely moved out of barracks except in full strength, in convoys of five and six lorries or tenders. Even then they had to exert great caution and were constantly being restricted in their movements by our planned road-cutting and by the fear of being ambushed. The Column, for its part, moved constantly from one area to another, a mobile striking force always on the alert, always on the watch for an opportunity to deal a lethal blow when it was least expected.

When Charlie Hurley and I joined the Column at Shanavagh, we set out with Tom Barry and Mick Crowley to survey the Bandon-Ballineen road for a possible ambush position, and selected one at

Mawbeg. The Column moved into position at 8.00 a.m. next morning and remained there all day, but neither the Auxiliaries from Dunmanway nor the Essex Regiment from Bandon appeared.

At nightfall, when the Column was actually withdrawing from the scene, a man appeared on the road walking from the Bandon direction. He was immediately arrested and taken for questioning. From our appearance, dressed as we were in trench coats and carrying arms, he evidently concluded that we were Auxiliaries, and straight away told us that he had just come from Bandon military barracks where he had informed the authorities of all those who were active against them in the Newcestown and Castletown-kenneigh districts. To us he was a self-confessed spy, worse still an informer, and when he was being courtmartialled later he further acknowledged his guilt. He was an ex-soldier, and well known to some members of the Column. He was sentenced to death and a priest was sent for. The Column then marched with their prisoner through the night to a new position on the Bandon-Newcestown road at Mallowgaton near Laragh. There he was executed, and his body was left lying on the side of the road, four miles from Bandon.

Next morning, the Column took up a favourable ambush position nearer to Bandon. It was a Saturday morning, and market-day in Bandon, so there was a number of farmers passing on their way to the town. We hoped that some of them would report the presence of the corpse on the roadside to the police or military, and in fact we stopped one supporter of ours who happened to pass, and took him into our confidence. He was asked to mention the news that he had seen a corpse on the roadside when he got into town. It was suggested that he should do so in some houses from which the information would most likely flow to the military in the barracks. In spite of these efforts to lure them from their stronghold, neither police nor military made an appearance on the Bandon-Newcestown road while we were there. In accordance with our usual custom, we retired before nightfall, crossed the Bandon at Baxter's Bridge, and marched during the night into the Gaggin-Clogagh area, where we set up headquarters at Con Donovan's of Cashel.

Later we learned that about fifteen minutes after our departure from the ambush position two lorries of Black and Tans from Bandon approached from the Newcestown side. They had moved out of Bandon by the main Macroom road in the direction of Old Park where they crossed westwards to the Newcestown-Bandon road There they picked up the informer's body, and returned with it to Bandon.

The capture of the informer and the confession he made of having given the names of prominent Volunteers to the military in Bandon alarmed us to the danger that could arise from other spies and informers in the same area. From a number of incidents in which the enemy could have acted as they did with knowledge supplied beforehand, we suspected that information was passing from this area to the enemy. Suspicion pointed to a local farmer, and we decided to investigate the matter immediately after our withdrawal from Mallowgaton.

Posing as Auxiliaries, Peter Monahan and two other officers called to the suspected farmer's house at night. Peter's strong Scotch accent and his gentlemanly bearing immediately convinced the farmer that he was being visited by the Auxiliaries, and his first greeting was, 'I thought you would never come.' Thereupon he quickly named many of our men who were active in his area. In particular, he mentioned one officer from Newcestown who was in the Column, and who was actually waiting outside the door during the interview. When the farmer had finally and definitely committed himself, the officer was called in to face the accuser, and it was only then that he realised that the game was up. He was immediately taken prisoner, courtmartialled later that night, and executed.

These two incidents convinced us beyond all possible doubt that information was being supplied to the enemy in this area. We also discovered an organisation which called itself the Anti-Sinn Féin Society in the area of the Bandon valley. This organisation was responsible for the raiding in Breaghna, Ahiohill, and the shooting of two brothers of the Coffey family there. The cold-blooded shooting of these two boys in their beds met with a sharp reaction from our side. Two members of the gang were arrested, court-martialled and shot without delay. Another member of the party took flight from the district altogether. This vigorous action put an end to espionage in this valley and nipped in the bud an organisation that could have developed into a real menace.

At the same time, it must be emphasised that in cases involving spies and informers, the accused were invariably given every opportunity to defend themselves, and sentence was passed only when the evidence against them was conclusive. A case to illustrate this point occurred a few months after the incidents recorded above, and involved a farmer who was arrested in Drimoleague area on the suspicion that he had given away the location of some dumps, and the name of a Volunteer who was arrested, to the enemy. He was tried by the local Battalion staff and sentenced to death. As the sentence could not be carried out without Brigade sanction, and as the evidence of the prisoner's guilt, though strong, was not conclusive, the Brigade opened an appeal court. As there was still some doubt after the second trial, the prisoner was acquitted and set free.

One of the notable features of the war of independence was the collapse during it of the enemy espionage system. This was due mainly, I should think, to the prompt and effective action always taken against espionage by our G.H.Q. and the fact that its example in this regard was closely followed right down through the various levels of the organisation. Rigorous and stern action was for us a strict duty in dealing with spies and informers on all occasions. That it was an unpleasant duty is obvious; that it was a necessary duty becomes evident when one thinks of the many noble efforts made down the ages to secure our freedom that were defeated by English gold and Irish greed.

Attacks within the Enemy Stronghold of Bandon Town

In view of the failure of the two attempts to ambush the enemy, namely, at Mawbeg and Mallowgaton, we decided to challenge the enemy where we knew he definitely was to be found, i.e. within his stronghold in Bandon town. Plans were immediately drawn up for a simultaneous three-pronged attack on the military barracks and on the two R.I.C. barracks with the object of enticing the enemy to come out to challenge us to open combat. Sunday night, 23 January, was the day chosen for this ambitious engagement. That night we left Con Donovan's of Cashel and allowed ourselves two hours to get into the town and to take up our positions for the threefold attack arranged to begin at midnight.

Our route lay along the old Clonakilty road by Crossmahon to Old Chapel where Charlie Hurley led his section of eighteen across Castle Bernard Park and over Lord Bandon's private foot-bridge to the north side of the river. They then took up positions in front of the military barracks. Tom Barry circled the town on the south side and brought his section of sixteen to positions at the Foxe's Street and Boyle Street corner which gave him command of Shannon Street, and which led to a little bridge crossing a tributary of the river. Finally, I took my section of twelve into the town by the back of Saint Patrick's Church, and continued along Market Street to Main Street where I was to open the attack on one of the R.I.C. barracks.

Before the attack began, Miah O'Neill of Knockpogue, who was a member of the Kilbrittain Company, carried an explosive charge through barbed-wire entanglements, and laid it at the gateway of the military barracks in such wise that the opening of the gate would set off the charge. The general intention in the planning of the attack was to induce the enemy to come out on the streets at the sound of our fire and expose themselves to the ambush parties we had lying in wait to deal with them.

On the first stroke of midnight, fire was opened by all three sections and continued intermittently for two hours. The enemy replied, but refused to sally forth from their fortresses as we had hoped. The gate of the barracks was not opened so the mine laid there did not explode. When the order for withdrawal was given, the same Miah O'Neill who carried the mine to the gateway, went forward again, this time under fire, and courageously retrieved it before the Column retired. We lost one man, Dan O'Reilly of Kibrittain, in the fire from the military barracks.

Naturally, disappointment was keen at our failure to entice the enemy into the open. Nevertheless, we considered we had won a moral victory inasmuch as the military and the Black and Tans with their armoured cars and superior equipment of every kind, refused to venture forth to meet us.

According to the plan previously made, Charlie Hurley's section retired to the Kilpatrick area. Tom Barry's section and mine met by arrangement at Ballymodan cemetery south of the town, and retired to O'Driscoll's, Kildarra House, in the Ballinadee area. On the following night we crossed the Bandon by boats at Colliers Quay and joined forces with Charlie at Crosspound. Fresh plans were immediately drawn up for an attack to be launched on Innishannon R.I.C. barracks on the following night, Tuesday, 25 January.

The Second Attack on Innishannon R.I.C. Barracks

Almost six months after he had led the first attempt on Innishannon barracks, Charlie Hurley took part in a second attack on the fortress. The plan devised for the attack of August 1920 depended on the successful exploding of a mine placed at the front door after which an assault party was to charge in and take the barracks by storm. The accidental firing of a rifle spelt failure for this attack even before it began. The plan on this second occasion was substantially the same as that used on the first; we knew that the building was so well fortified that only the successful explosion of a mine laid at the front door would give us any hope of capturing it. So our plan once more included a mine, and this time, at least, we hoped it would not fail us. One development of the plan on this second occasion as compared with the first was our design to ambush the reinforcements that we hoped would be sent from Bandon when the attack began. For this reason, Ted O'Sullivan with a strong party of eighteen riflemen took up positions at the neighbouring school wall enfilading the bridge and covering the main road from Bandon. Charlie Hurley had another strong section commanding the Kilpatrick road to Innishannon at Brinny. A third and final section of twenty-two men, to which Tom Barry and I were attached, was deployed on three sides of the barracks.

When zero hour approached, three of us in stockinged feet carried the mine towards the barracks and placed it at the front door. This done we retired round the corner of the building where Peter Monahan was waiting to drive home the plunger. To our utter disappointment, the mine failed yet again. There was no explosion, but the order was nevertheless, given to open fire on the barracks. We kept up an intermittent fire for about two hours during which time the garrison replied with continuous fire, and repeatedly sent Verey lights into the sky. But no reinforcements were sent out from Bandon, and when we were convinced that none would be sent, we withdrew the main force leaving a covering party to protect our rear. We assembled at Brinny, and from there marched through the night towards Newcestown. Dawn was breaking as we approached our destination. After a hurried meal, Charlie and I returned to Brigade Headquarters.

I spent the night at Headquarters, and on the following day set out to keep an appointment with the officers of the Schull Battalion who had taken part in recent actions with the Column. I was to catch the evening train from Cork at Kinsale Junction, and meet the Schull Battalion men at Desert railway station when the train arrived. In due course I boarded the train and found myself in a carriage with five other people. One of them was very well known to me as an active officer of the Volunteers, but being unaware of the identity of the others, we remained aloof.

As the train steamed into Bandon station I was alarmed to notice a party of twenty armed Auxiliaries on the platform. This was so unusual that I could only conclude that they were going to search the train, and my first thoughts turned to some way of escape. The Auxiliaries had seldom been known to travel by train in our area, but now to my further astonishment, I saw the party boarding the train in the two carriages next to mine and behaving very much like ordinary passengers. The train pulled out of the station leaving me with a new and major problem. It was the most anxious and uncomfortable journey I ever made, and as the train steamed into Desert station my state of tension increased almost to breaking point. For there on the exposed platform stood the three Volunteer officers in a group apart, Seán Lehane, Gibbs Ross, and Seán O'Driscoll, all dressed in the accepted uniform of the Volunteers at the time, that is, leggings and belted trench coats. They stood there nonchalantly smoking and waiting for me to appear. How they escaped the attention of the Auxiliaries is still a mystery to me.

As my travelling companions had all left the carriage in which I was at the previous station, I quickly beckoned to the officers from the door which I was holding open for them, and invited them to enter. As they piled into the carriage, I told them of our fellow travellers in the next two compartments, and as the train continued on its way we discussed ways and means to meet the emergency which we felt would certainly occur at the next station. To expect that our identity would continue to escape recognition was to hope for too much, and we were prepared for the worst. As the train drew to a stop at Dunmanway Station, we saw the Auxiliaries, to our amazement and immense relief, jumping out on the platform, and we could have cheered them as they marched from the station.

At Knockbue Halt, four miles further on, we left the train, and continued the twenty-mile journey by horse and trap via Caheragh and Barnagaoite to Dunbeacon. We reached this latter point in the early morning, and intended to continue on our journey that same day. However, our plans were thwarted by an unusual raid, and indeed the biggest one ever carried out in the district. Twelve tenders of Auxiliaries poured into the area from Glengarriff on that morning of 29 January, and carried out an intensive and systematic campaign of raiding and searching throughout the day. The raiding began on the Schull side of the peninsula and we were in some danger. But the Captain of the Gloun Company, Ned O'Sullivan, came across the shoulder of Mount Gabriel to warn us. At that we retreated to higher ground and with grim forebodings watched the Auxiliaries as they advanced. They were no more than half a mile from where we were, and we could see them making their way to raid houses of well-known officers and men of the local Companies. In fact, from our vantage point we could observe them raiding the house in which we had billeted that morning.

Reports continued to reach us throughout the day, and it became evident from the selective nature of the raiding and the capture of prominent officers that the Auxiliaries were acting on information that had been supplied to them. Among those captured were the Captains of the Schull and Goleen Companies, Gerry McCarthy, and Ricky Collins, but the Captain of Dunbeacon Company who was with us escaped. In the late evening the Auxiliaries withdrew, and we hiked to the Goleen and Lissagriffin areas, and stayed the night in the home of the local schoolteacher, Connie Lehane. In spite of the stress and anxiety of the day, the night brought a very welcome respite.

There was an old Irish custom in the parish in which we were staying according to which a special celebration occurs on the four Saturdays after Christmas in order that the Christmas season be commemorated in its entirety. These Saturday celebrations were held in different houses and the neighbours gathered to them for a night of conviviality. Whether by chance or design, when we arrived at the house of Connie Lehane, we found that a crowd of people was arriving there to hold one of these special Christmas celebrations. After the suspense of the day we were in a mood to relax and make the most of the festivities. Perhaps nowhere could the volatility of the Irish character have been so evident as in the house of this Irish teacher that night. It is possible that the presence of well-known members of the Brigade Column, and the fine ringing voice of Seán Lehane, added to the general hilarity. At any rate, the welcome we received from everybody was so heart-warming that it would never be forgotten; it was a true reflection of the spirit of the people of the Schull Peninsula during the war years.

The next day, Sunday, was spent in reorganising the Companies of the Schull Battalion that had been hit by the previous day's raiding, and in finding replacements for the captured officers. The very rapidity with which this was done was in itself a clear indication to the Volunteers and the people of the vitality and resilience of our organisation. It could surmount all reverses, adapt itself to changing conditions without a moment's delay, and continue to prosecute the war with renewed energy. Late that night, after an exhausting day spent visiting the different Company areas, Seán Lehane and I planned a trip to Squince Strand at Myross, which was about thirty miles away. I was anxious to inspect the locality personally and to complete all arrangements, down to the least detail, for the proposed landing of arms on our coast.

The itinerary from Dunbeacon, where we were, to Myross had to be carefully planned in order to avoid the danger zone of Skibbereen. After some thought, Seán Lehane and I mapped out a route by Ballydehob, Skehanore, and Lisheen, and set off the next day. On our way we halted in the Company areas of Skehanore, Lisheen, Baltimore, and Castlehaven where we made a point of meeting the officers and some section commanders, and praised them for the progress that we remarked to have taken place since my last visit. As soon as we arrived at Buckley's of Gortbrack— one of our unfailing havens of hospitality—we stayed there for the night, and on the following morning contacted Pat O'Driscoll, the Vice-Commandant of the Skibbereen Battalion. He was the man who had been put in charge of the landing operations and the dumping of the arms.

In a motor-boat provided by the O'Driscolls of Rabbit Island, we moved out into the channel between the mainland and the island. We made soundings at various points to ensure that there would be sufficient draught in the channel to allow the arms ship to approach the strand. It was a beautiful sunny morning after a wild and stormy night, and the channel was perfectly calm. But once we rounded the island we encountered a heavy swell that seemed to get worse as we moved out into the open sea. Never a good sailor I was soon a victim of that most demoralizing of afflictions, sea-sickness, and as I leaned over the side of the boat in distress I parted with a set of dentures that had been fitted during my recent visit to Dublin. But I was in no mood to regret them as they sank into the depths of the Atlantic. Indeed I felt so badly at the time that I should not have cared if I followed them. However, two hours later when I found myself at O'Driscoll's island home, all unpleasant thoughts of the voyage were forgotten and I was able to enjoy a hearty meal.

Back on the mainland, Pat O'Driscoll and the new Captain of the Myross Company, Pat Sheehy, assured us that they had made arrangements to have a hundred dumps ready to take the arms as soon as they arrived. Having satisfied myself that we had prepared for all foreseeable eventualities I departed for Rossmore to attend a Brigade Council meeting there. Two days later the meeting was held and the landing arrangements were discussed and approved. All that was necessary now was to await news telling us when the arms ship was to arrive and the machinery for landing and distributing the cargo would be put into operation.

CHAPTER 22

DARKNESS BEFORE DAWN

At the Brigade Council meeting of 6-7 February held at Ballinvard, Rossmore, I heard a complete report on the Brigade Column's activities during the preceding week. During my travels from the Schull peninsula to Squince Strand and back to Ballinvard, varying accounts of enemy activities had been filtering through to me, many of them grossly exaggerated and quite alarming, but at the Council meeting I was given an account of the facts.

The Column had moved from its billets at Newcestown and had crossed the Bandon river into the Clonakilty Battalion area in order to attack Rosscarbery R.I.C. barracks. It spent the night of Monday, 31 January, in Ahiohill, and on Tuesday occupied Burgatia House, the residence of a loyalist family, situated within a mile's distance of the barracks. There the Column was to remain during the following day to manufacture explosives for the attack and to make final preparations.

On Wednesday morning a postman from Rosscarbery, an ex-serviceman of the British army, called with letters to Burgatia House. He was promptly arrested and brought before the Column O/C. Thereupon he promised on his word of honour and swore by all he held sacred that he would not divulge any information about the presence of the Column to anyone. After this he was dismissed and allowed deliver the letters he had for the district. However, as was later discovered, he did not keep his word, and soon had the R.I.C. at Rosscarbery informed of the situation at Burgatia.

Towards 4.00 o'clock on Wednesday afternoon the sentries reported that a strong force of R.I.C. and Black and Tans were attempting to surround Burgatia House. Within a few minutes the Column O/C detailed various sections of the Column to such positions as would prevent the enemy from closing in on the house. Then, a section under Jim 'Spud' Murphy was instructed to remove the explosives to a place of safety, and to hold a line between the sea and Burgatia House in the direction of Owenahincha bridge; it was to cross the main Clonakilty-Rosscarbery road and attack the enemy on the left flank and rear.

Meanwhile, the enemy had opened fire from the roadway smashing the windows in the front of the house. Presently a pony and trap containing the local Protestant clergyman and his driver were seen coming up the drive. When the trap arrived at the house, the

occupants were ordered to alight and enter the building for protection, and it was then seen that the approach of the clergyman in
his vehicle was used by the R.I.C. as a ruse to enable them get as
close as possible to the house without being observed.

Heavy fire was now directed by the R.I.C. and the Tans on the
Column's position, but the Column O/C had instructed his men
to reserve their fire except when the enemy exposed himself. 'Spud'
Murphy's section was unable to cross the road from Owenahincha
bridge because of the presence there of enemy forces, and proceeded instead eastwards from Owenahincha. Then, on reaching
the high ground beyond, it opened fire on the enemy flank. Taken
completely by surprise and fearing that they were on the point of
being trapped in an encircling movement, the R.I.C. and Tans
retreated, and in doing so opened the way for the Column to withdraw. Withdrawal was considered advisable in view of the fact
that strong reinforcements of British military were available in
Clonakilty, approximately six miles away, and as Burgatia House
was situated on a peninsula, it could be easily surrounded by a
force of vastly superior numbers in such a way as to make the
retreat of the Column impossible. So the entire Column retired
eastwards in perfect order, and made its way towards McCarthy's
of Kilbree where it was later joined by Jim 'Spud' Murphy and his
section. The successful withdrawal of the men from Burgatia House
on this occasion added greatly to the prestige of the Column and
enhanced the daring ingenuity of the Column Commander, Tom
Barry. The only casualty was Volunteer Bob Brennan of Castle
Donovan who was wounded in the leg.[1]

Late in the night of that same day, Tom Barry with Jim Hodnett,
Jim Hurley, and Con O'Leary returned to Burgatia House and
having carefully encircled the building entered it, piled up the
furniture and bedding, and set the place on fire. This done the four
men moved quickly into the village of Rosscarbery and opened fire
on the R.I.C. barracks. The police refused to venture forth, and
the attackers withdrew. Meanwhile the Column rested at Kilbree,
and on the following night moved to the Kippagh area, thence to
the Mohona district and so to the west bank of the Illen river
between Skibbereen and Caheragh where they rested over the
weekend before carrying out intended attacks on Skibbereen and
Drimoleague.

1. I am indebted to Jim 'Spud' Murphy for information used in the
above account of the fight at Burgatia House. See Appendix I.

Following on this report on the Column's activities came the news of the death of Lieutenant Paddy Crowley, a Kilbrittain Volunteer who was shot while trying to fight his way out of a round-up on the previous Friday, 4 February. In an all-out endeavour to wipe out the Volunteers from the very active Kilbrittain area, an exceptionally strong force of military, Black and Tans, and R.I.C. from Bandon converged on the townland of Maryborough between Kilbrittain and Timoleague. In an encircling movement taking in small portions of the adjoining areas of Bandon, Ballinadee, Ballinspittle, Timoleague, and Clogagh, the enemy gradually closed in on the Kilbrittain area where every house, with the exception of a few in isolated positions by the sea, was raided. All the men from sixteen to sixty were arrested and brought to Kilbrittain village. They were closely scrutinised by the R.I.C. men from local and outside areas, and the unwanted among them were forced, under the observation of the Black and Tans, to help demolish two houses which had been burned by the Auxiliaries on the night of 14 January. Fourteen others, including two Volunteers, were taken into custody in Bandon military barracks. In the course of the ensuing three weeks, all except the two Volunteers, Denis (Sonny) Crowley, the outstanding Intelligence Officer of the Kilbrittain Company and a brother of the deceased Paddy, and Daniel O'Neill, were released. They were both sentenced to three months' imprisonment on the charge of giving false names.

But Paddy Crowley's death was a bitter blow to us all. From 1917 he had been a most active Volunteer and an outstanding leader. In April 1918 he organised a defensive training camp in Kilbrittain to resist conscription. In the following year he was the chief architect of the daring Rathclarin ambush in which a valuable collection of arms and ammunition was captured. Thereafter he was involved in the two successful attacks on Howes Strand Coastguard Station, the Newcestown and Tureen ambushes, the two attacks on Kilbrittain Barracks, and in many other engagements as well.

While Paddy's death spread gloom and sadness, there was no one who felt the loss more keenly than the Brigade Commander, Charlie Hurley. He and Paddy Crowley had grown up together, had been comrades on the playing field with the Kilbrittain Hurling Club, and had been closely associated ever since Charlie's release from prison in 1919. It was small wonder that, despite great personal danger, Charlie decided to attend the funeral at Clogagh. As he stood by the graveside of his fallen comrade, the Brigade Commander paid his last tribute in a short panegyric and then, alone,

fired the last salute with his revolver. We often wondered afterwards whether Charlie had any premonition of the future as he
fired that salute. At any rate, he could scarcely have thought that
in six weeks' time his own remains would be brought to that lonely
graveside of Clogagh and be laid to rest only a few yards from the
spot where he left his comrade in his last sleep.

Such in substance were the reports on events which occurred
during my absence that were made at this Brigade Council meeting
of 6-7 February. In fact, besides these, a detailed review of all our
Brigade activities since the previous meeting at Ballinacarriga on
29 December was also made, and many urgent matters were
discussed.

One matter that had been giving us grave concern was raised by
the Brigade Commander for discussion. It was the question of spies
and informers. It had become evident that information was being
supplied to the enemy in several different localities. In the preceding month a number of informers had been tracked down, tried,
and executed. The Brigade Commander felt that the time had
now come to give extended powers to Battalion Commandants to
meet the danger. In this connexion, Seán Hales, Commandant of
the Bandon Battalion, instanced a case which had been dealt with
during the preceding week. Thanks to the efficiency of our intelligence agent in the Bandon post-office, a letter addressed to the
commanding officer of Bandon Barracks was intercepted and for-
warded to Battalion headquarters. The letter bore the address of a
local farmhouse, and was signed by a girl of seventeen who lived
there. In the letter she revealed the names of sixteen officers and
men of the local Companies. As soon as the Battalion staff made
this discovery, three of the officers called to the girl's home and in
searching her room found the blotting paper she had used when
writing the letter. The markings on the blotting paper showed
convincingly that the girl's guilt was beyond doubt. When questioned she admitted writing and posting the letter, but in her
defence she said she had acted as she did because a local Volunteer,
whose bicycle had broken down while he was on dispatch duty,
had commandeered hers to complete his mission and left her his
broken one. She resented this action so much that she had written
the letter to take revenge. In the circumstances the officers felt
that drastic action should not be taken, but instead they ordered
the girl and her family to leave the country within twenty-four
hours. This sentence was considered to be suitable punishment,
and a necessary protective action.

The Brigade Intelligence Officer next reported that the enemy had recently been travelling in larger convoys and increasing his activities in the Brigade area. To meet this challenge, the Battalion Commanders were instructed to intensify the work of road-cutting in their areas, and to re-open trenches that had been filled in by the enemy.

My report dealt mainly with the proposed landing of arms at Squince Strand. I informed the Council that I had inspected the area and was satisfied with the dumps which had been prepared and also the proposed routes for the transport of the arms. The appointment of Pat O'Driscoll as officer in charge of the landing and immediate handling of the arms was also confirmed. In this connexion the Column Commander was instructed to have the Column available to protect the men engaged in the landing operations, and the Battalion Commanders were likewise instructed to have all available forces on the alert to cover key points on the routes selected for transporting the arms.

One of the most encouraging items discussed at this meeting was the report on the success of the Arms Fund : it had now reached the figure of almost five thousand pounds, and had already provided a much-needed supply of clothing, overcoats, boots and leggings. In the course of the report it was mentioned that difficulties had arisen in some areas where the levy was refused, and to meet this contingency Battalion Commanders were instructed to seize cattle or other goods in lieu of the levy. However, it should be mentioned that lack of co-operation in this matter was very rare, and in many cases even those who differed from us in their political views readily subscribed.

Before the conclusion of the meeting, the Brigade Commander referred to the losses we had sustained, and mentioned the death in action of Paddy Crowley, and the capture of John 'Flyer' Nyhan, Stephen O'Neill, Denis (Sonny) Crowley, Miah Deasy, and others. Despite these losses—and they were serious—the Commander was quite confident from his personal observation and from information received that more and more young men were coming into the ranks, and that our armed units were everywhere becoming more active.

This was an indication of the answer which was being given to the latest act of coercive martial law that was enforced, that, namely, which compelled all householders to put a list of the occupants at the back of the door. Finally, the appointment of two new Battalion Commanders was made, namely Jim Hurley for the

Clonakilty Battalion to replace Dan Harte whose health had broken down, and Neilus Connolly for the Skibbereen Battalion to replace Sam Kingston who was promoted to the post of Brigade Police Officer. The resignation on the grounds of ill-health of Pete O'Neill as O/C of the Beara Battalion was accepted. The Vice-O/C of the Brigade was instructed to visit the Beara Battalion area and to appoint a successor to O'Neill. In the event, the man appointed to the post was Liam O'Dwyer, formerly Vice-O/C of the Battalion. So ended the longest Brigade Council meeting we ever had.

It was now 5.00 a.m. on Monday, and many of the twenty-four officers gathered for the meeting were showing signs of weariness after such a long uninterrupted meeting. And the armed guard of thirty men of the Kilmeen Company outside must have felt the strain also. However, a warm breakfast was soon provided by Mrs O'Donoghue of Ballinvard, and this roused the drooping spirits of both officers and men. Meals during the day and night of the meeting were supplied from the neighbouring houses of the O'Donoghues and the O'Mahonys. Catering for such a large body of men would perhaps appear to us today to require a catering company, but in those far-off days it was something that was accomplished frequently in many areas by the local families, and that with a generosity and cheerfulness which added to the pleasure of the meals that were served.

*   *   *   *   *   *

As we parted at the end of our all-night meeting from O'Donoghue's of Ballinvard on the morning of 7 February, we all realised that we were very much in 'the thick of it', and none could say with any assurances that we would ever meet again. Our good fortune had held out so far, but we could not forget that many who started with us were now missing either through death or capture.

My own thoughts went back to the previous Brigade Council meeting held five weeks earlier at Ballinacarriga and to Paddy Crowley's gaiety and optimism then. He had been the life of the party. Now he slept in the old graveyard at Clogagh and we would never hear the loved voice of that hero of many battles again. My thoughts turned also to the many other pioneers who were with us no more—Michael McCarthy, Jim O'Sullivan, Jim O'Donoghue, John Galvin, Joe Begley, Tim Fitzgerald, Dan O'Reilly, John Connolly, and my brother Pat who lay in their graves, and to the many others who were prisoners in enemy hands. I had ample time for reminiscing as I travelled on horseback with Tom Barry and

Seán Lehane through Ballygurteen, Kippagh, Derryclough, and Madore to Mohona, two miles north-west of Skibbereen. Our intention was to force a major engagement on the enemy in the town of Skibbereen and to make this serve as the opening of an offensive concentrated at various points in the outlying districts as far as Bantry. The reason for choosing Skibbereen as the focus of our activities at this time was that the town had been unusually inactive so far as the national struggle was concerned, and we felt that if the Brigade was to operate uniformly as a whole, Skibbereen would have to become more involved and be induced to play its part. Volunteers were active in the town but they were very few in number and were not widely supported by the populace. Indeed considering how little encouragement they were given, their spirit and achievement were all the more remarkable.

The first news that reached us when we joined the Column at Mohona was bad. A local Volunteer named Pat O'Driscoll had been killed accidentally over the weekend while on protective duty, and we arrived in time to make arrangements for the obsequies. This duty done we turned our attention to the offensive we had in mind. On the night of 8 February, towards 10.00 p.m., we entered the town of Skibbereen at the junction of the Caheragh and Bally- dehob roads at the railway station. Probing parties moved into the centre of the town, but no enemy was in sight other than two privates of the King's Liverpool Regiment who were off duty at the time and unarmed. These were arrested and kept in custody as a precaution until the following morning. On account of the great respect we had for the commanding officer of the Liverpools in Skibbereen, Colonel Hudson, an upright and humane man, we were particularly kind to these two privates of his regiment and treated them with all the hospitality we could afford. We brought them to Caheragh where we shared our meal with them, and later provided a horse and trap to take them back to their unit. Incidentally, Colonel Hudson later paid a laudatory tribute to the manner in which his men were treated on that occasion.

Failing to draw the King's Liverpools from their barracks, we retired with the Column to Caheragh in the early hours of 9 February. Thence we moved across the southern slope of Mount Kid to Barnagaoite and then to McCarthy's of Derryvahalla near Durrus road station. There we rested for two days while the engineering group in the Column were engaged in the preparation of a mine that we hoped to use in an attack on Drimoleague R.I.C. barracks.

It was the most powerful mine we had yet prepared, and it was also the longest. In deciding its length we were influenced by two considerations. In the first place, we were under the impression that explosives made from gun-cotton to be effective had to touch the objective at the moment of the explosion. In the second place, the walls of Drimoleague barracks were known to be covered with barbed wire almost up to the roof of the building. So two eighteen-foot beams, five by five inches, were provided and the charge of gun-cotton was lashed to the end of one to ensure contact with the wall above the barbed wire.

The plan of attack next took shape and was determined in understanding with the Captain of the Drimoleague Company, Dan O'Driscoll. It was decided that the Column would be divided into two unequal sections, the larger section constituting the attacking party was to be three times more numerous than the smaller one, and would proceed to the outskirts of Drimoleague where the local officers would be waiting to lead it to the barracks. The other section would hold the main road at Aughaville to prevent reinforcements arriving from Bantry. The main point of withdrawal after the attack would be Castle Donovan, four miles due north of Drimoleague where both units would reunite.

The distance between the headquarters at Derryvahalla and Drimoleague was eight miles as the crow flies, but by the route we had chosen via Murdering Glen and Inchingearig approximately twelve. All of this distance would have to be travelled on foot. Each man would have to carry full equipment, while a horse and cart would transport the mine, the plunger and the fuse. Four hours were allowed to make the journey.

Shortly after 7.00 p.m. on Friday, 11 February, the Column moved off in the direction of Drimoleague. The total number of men including additions from the Bantry Battalion and also scouts amounted roughly to seventy. At Dromore eighteen armed men and a number of local scouts under the command of Ted O'Sullivan, Brigade Vice-Commandant, remained to hold the main road at a point selected by Ted between Dromore and Aughaville.

The main section of the Column continued on its way towards Drimoleague, and arrived at the appointed rendezvous with the officers of the local Company shortly after 11.00 p.m. As the attack was not due to begin until midnight there was some time in which the men could rest by the roadside within five hundred yards of the objective.

As zero hour approached, three units of the attacking party took up positions surrounding the barracks to prevent any of the occupants escaping either through the front or rear doors. A smaller section of six men moved close to the barracks in order to form part of the charging party as soon as the mine had blown a breach in the wall of the building.

To place the mine against the wall of the barracks without the enemy's knowledge required the co-operation of four tall men in stockinged feet. They would have to carry the load on their shoulders to the foot of the barbed-wire entanglement, raise it on one end and guide the other end with the gun-cotton charge towards the upper part of the wall above the barbed wire. For this kind of operation Column officers were automatically chosen, and if they were not available in sufficient number, others were asked to volunteer. Invariably on such occasions requests for volunteers met with a hundred per cent response. In order to make doubly sure that the mine would explode this time, a fuse was used as well as the electrical plunger. This meant that two sets of long cables had to be kept in position from the starting point thirty yards away.

Everything was in readiness at the stroke of midnight. The fuse of the mine was lit, and began to emit a fizzling sound. Four of us, John Jack O'Sullivan, John Denny O'Sullivan of Bantry, Jack Corkery of Ballinadee, and I took up the eighteen-foot mine casing and made towards the barrack wall. Peter Monahan, the enigmatic British deserter who had joined our ranks six weeks earlier, came behind us carrying the fuse and the electrical cable. With him came Mick Crowley, Brigade Engineer, and the Column Commander, Tom Barry. All seven of us were in stockinged feet.

When we reached the edge of the barbed-wire entanglement, we raised the eighteen-foot beam aloft, rested one end on the ground and tilted the other end with the charge towards the barrack wall. Stepping on a low outer wall we guided the beam and pressed it against the barbed wire. We hoped that the weight of the mine together with our own weight would suffice to ensure contact between the mine and the wall above the height of the barbed wire. The position selected was directly in front of the guard-room window. As soon as the mine casing pressed against the barbed wire and the wall, the guard inside was alerted and came to the loophole of the window and watched our movements. For some reason or other he did not fire, though we presented him with a very easy target, as we were no more than ten feet away.

Having placed the mine in position, we dashed for cover. A violent explosion shattered the midnight silence, and we immediately rushed back to enter the barracks. Unfortunately, the mine failed to blow the expected breach in the wall, and, as we learned later, caused more damage to other houses nearby than to our objective. To make some further show of attack was now imperative, so we opened fire on the barracks and kept it up for approximately half an hour. We were, however, very careful, as was our custom in such circumstances, to limit the wastage of ammuntion as much as possible.

Eventually we withdrew northwards to Castle Donovan, and rested there till daybreak. Then we set off to cross the western shoulder of Nowen Hill on our way to Kealkil. But we had not gone far when we observed four lorries of Auxiliaries from the Dunmanway district approaching. We immediately took up positions to meet them, but they refused to advance against us, though they saw our positions clearly. Instead they left the area, and we continued our march up the mountain road, over the pass between Mullaghmesha and Derreennacrinnig, and down into the Mealagh valley at Barnagowlane to Mickey Owen O'Sullivan's where we had food and the possibility of resting for the day. Towards nightfall we continued our march to headquarters at Keohane's of Ardrah and billeted in various houses in the neighbourhood.

When the men were paraded at Ardrah that Saturday night it was found that one of the members of the Column was missing. He was none other than the British army deserter, Peter Monahan. No one had seen him since early morning, and no one could account for his absence. Some thought he had returned to his old allegiance; others felt he had been careless and had been taken prisoner. However, on the following day, Sunday, at five o'clock in the evening Peter walked into Column headquarters and gave an account of his absence.

On the ascent from Castle Donovan on the previous morning, he came upon a wayside house, and caught the odour of poteen as he passed by. Being more than partial to strong spirit, he was attracted to the door, and soon found himself by the fireside drinking the health of the occupants in a spirit that was unwontedly devastating in its effects. Sunday morning came before Peter recovered, and then he set off to find the Column. It baffled us at the time to know how he·succeeded in tracking us down, and it baffles me still. How a soldier with a strong Scottish accent could have succeeded in getting directions leading to our whereabouts over the six miles of rough country that separated him from us is still a mystery to me. Scarcely anyone on the route knew where we were, and even if they did, they would be most unlikely to give the information to a stranger with Peter's foreign accent. Good soldier that he was he took his punishment of extra duty like a man, and then resumed his place in the ranks with the same enthusiasm as before.

After two nights at Ardrah we moved to Ahildotia[2] on the north side of Kealkil village. By this time the temporary reinforcements and the scouts we had recruited for the attack on Drimoleague barracks had returned to their units, and the Column was back to its normal strength of forty. We remained in billets in the Ahildotia district until Tuesday morning, 15 February, when we marched to a position on the Bantry-Glengarriff road near Snave Bridge. Here it was intended to ambush a convoy of British military or Auxiliaries travelling either to or from Glengarriff. Having spent some hours in this ambush position without encountering the enemy, we returned to the Kealkil area and rested there for the rest of the day. Towards nightfall information concerning the movements of British troops in the district reached us, and we decided to march through the Pass of Keimaneigh to Gougane Barra.

It was our normal practice when staying overnight in an area to divide the Column into sections of about ten and to have each section billeted in a separate house. In many cases, even ten men would put a strain on the resources of the house in which we billeted, but the widespread practice among housewives in West Cork of always having a half sack of flour in the house invariably saved the situation. Not infrequently the woman of the house would spend the night baking for the meals of the next day, drying out our wet clothes, and maybe darning our socks while we of the Column slept. No words could adequately praise those wonderful people who opened their doors so generously to us during the long period of struggle, and that at the risk of having their husbands or other members of their family shot. The fact that we were frequently in need of billeting on householders in districts that suffered great economic strain meant that the sacrifice demanded of them was all the greater.

Gougane Barra was special in that the entire Column was put up in Cronin's Hotel there. How Mrs Cronin succeeded, without prior notice, in providing forty of us with three meals, during the off-season period is a question I have never been able to answer.

2. Referred to locally as Ahil.

Many years after the event I put the question to her, but she pushed it aside with the remark, 'God has always been good to me.'

From Gougane Barra we travelled on the following night to Derrynacaheragh and set up headquarters at another great homestead, Timothy Seamus Hurley's, Shanacrane East. Like Cronin's of Gougane Barra, Hurley's had risen splendidly to the demands of hospitality during the previous eighteen months, and invariably gave us the warmest of welcomes. There were many other good patriotic homes in this district among the mountains and they never failed us.

Tom Barry, who had left the Column for a few days after the attack on Drimoleague barracks, now returned and took over the command of the Column once more, and led it away to the Coppeen area. Meanwhile I left Shanacrane and headed for Brigade Headquarters at Ballymurphy, Upton.

CHAPTER 23

THE TRAGIC AMBUSH AT UPTON RAILWAY STATION

In our struggle to gain national freedom by waging guerilla warfare on the British forces of occupation we were keenly conscious of our dependence on the goodwill and support of the people. Without their generous co-operation nothing could be achieved. With their co-operation we felt we must eventually triumph. Appreciating these facts, we made it a standard practice to avoid, as far as at all possible, exposing the civilian population to danger. In fact, quite a number of planned attacks were abandoned where a serious loss of civilian lives seemed probable if the attacks were carried out.

British armed forces took advantage of regular passenger train services extensively as a means of transport, and this was something we could not tolerate. The refusal of railwaymen to operate trains on which armed military were to travel was part of the effort to deny British forces the use of ordinary civilian rail transport. But we felt that something else was needed. We considered that where possible, ordinary passenger trains carrying military ought to be ambushed and that the consequent risk to civilians had to be accepted. We had a very good precedent.

On 11 February a very successful ambush had been carried out by the Millstreet Battalion on the Mallow-Tralee train at Drishanebeg in the Second Cork Brigade without civilian casualties. A party of troops travelling on the train had been attacked and defeated with a loss of one enemy killed and several wounded. The attacking party had no casualties and had succeeded in capturing fifteen rifles and several hundred rounds of ammunition.[1]

Cork Number One Brigade, through its Intelligence Officer, Florence O'Donoghue, was sometimes able to get advance information on the movements of British troops. Where this concerned other areas it was normal practice to pass the information to the Brigade concerned, if there was a possibility that it could be utilised there. It happened that two or three days after the successful train ambush at Drishanebeg, the intelligence of the First Cork Brigade informed our headquarters that a small party of British troops, probably twelve to fifteen in number, would leave Cork for Bantry on the 9.30 a.m. train on 15 February. An arrangement was made to send a coded message by telephone to Bandon on the morning of the 15th to confirm the departure of the troops and to give

1. Cf. Florence O'Donoghue, *No Other Law* (Dublin, 1954), pp. 131-32.

their numbers and their location in the train.

The Brigade Commander, Charlie Hurley, considered that the risk to the civilians in the train, in the event of an ambush, would not be abnormal, and indeed that it would be limited by the fact that the carriages occupied by the troops would be known in advance. There appeared to be every reason why an ambush on this train should be as successful as that of Drishanebeg a few days before. So the ambush was decided upon, and the location chosen was Upton station, four miles east of Bandon. As there was no time available in which to mobilise a Battalion column for the operation, Charlie quickly collected a party of local Volunteers together with the Acting Brigade Adjutant, Flor Begley, and the General Staff Officer, Seán Phelan, and with them finalised his plans.

The passenger platform of Upton station was on the north side of the railway line. On it were the usual buildings, station-master's house, ticket-booking office, waiting-room, and toilets. Extending west from the buildings as far as the signal cabin was a timber paling with a wicket exit. On the opposite side of the rail a goods store occupied the eastern end of the station and the goods bank to the west was bounded by a low wall to the south. At the southern extremity there was a two-storey public house.

Arriving at the station a few minutes before the train was due to arrive—to ensure the element of surprise the station could not be taken over earlier—Charlie Hurley quickly put the attacking party in position. Pat O'Sullivan and John Butler were stationed at the toilets, the former armed with two .45 revolvers, the latter with a rifle. Flor Begley and Seán Phelan, both with Colt automatics, were in the waiting-room. Paddy O'Leary took up his position at the wicket gate, and Seán Hartnett at the gable-end of the signal cabin, both armed with rifles. Charlie himself took up a position on the footbridge that spanned the line at the western end of the platforms, and was armed with a Peter the Painter with stock.

On the opposite side of the station Batt Falvey and Neilus Begley were posted at the goods store; Denis Desmond and Dan O'Mahony behind the low wall, and Paddy Coakley at a window upstairs in the public house. Finally, Tom Kelleher and Denis Doolan held positions behind a wall at the entrance to the goods yard. These seven men were armed with rifles. All was now in readiness : an attacking party of fourteen men within the station, and a party of local Volunteers for scouting and protection duties posted outside in the neighbourhood of the station. The scene was set. Presently the noise of the approaching train was heard.

Unfortunately, there had been an unforeseen development. Between Cork and Upton there was a railway junction known as Kinsale Junction where British troops from Kinsale could join the Cork-Bantry train, and this is precisely what occurred that morning. A party of close on fifty soldiers from Kinsale Barracks boarded the train at the junction, and mixed among the civilian passengers. Seeing what was happening at the junction, a valiant effort was made to warn the ambush party by Bill Hartnett, a brother of Seán who was waiting to attack the train at Upton station. Realising the danger he jumped on a bicycle and rode as fast as he could in the hope of reaching Upton before the train. Unfortunately, he arrived a minute or two too late.

As the train pulled into the station the attackers opened fire. This was immediately returned by the soldiers as they poured out on to the platform. When Charlie Hurley from his vantage position on the bridge saw what was happening and that the enemy force greatly outnumbered his own small group, he gave the order for withdrawal, shouting to those on the south side to fall back towards the level crossing and gate house to the west of the station. His own gun jammed after the first shot, and as he jumped down from the bridge, he received a bullet wound in the face from ear to ear, and also sprained his ankle.

Among the six on the north side casualties were heavy. Pat O'Sullivan was mortally wounded and Seán Phelan was killed as he tried to escape through the waiting-room window. Flor Begley, Paddy O'Leary, John Butler, and Seán Hartnett succeeded in getting clear under fire, though the latter was wounded. On the southern side Batt Falvey was shot through the head and died instantly. The others fell back to the level crossing, helped by the protecting fire of Tom Kelleher and Denis Doolan. When Doolan joined his companions he found that Dan O'Mahony had been wounded, and he carried him on his back for almost a mile to Tim Cronin's of Clashinimud. Later Dan was taken to Ballinphellig and from there was conveyed by Willie Cotter to the South Infirmary, Cork. Although he recovered under treatment, he died a few years later as a result of his wounds.

Tom Kelleher went to the assistance of Charlie Hurley who was so seriously wounded and lamed that he had no chance of escaping on his own. However, Kelleher practically carried him from the scene and conducted him by a strategic circuitous route in the direction of Kilmore. Mile after mile the pair struggled on, Hurley repeatedly begging his rescuer to leave him and make his own escape. Kelleher with indomitable courage and unflagging determination insisted on bringing his wounded companion to safety. Eventually, in the late afternoon, the pair reached the comparative security of Patsy Sheehan's of Kilmore. Here they rested while Charlie's face and ankle were bandaged. Then they continued their journey to Tim O'Sullivan's of Cloughduv where professional treatment was soon available. For several days Charlie recuperated at Coughduv, and during that time he was ably nursed by Mrs O'Sullivan. Security reasons demanded his transfer, first to Healy's of Farran, and then, to Brigade Headquarters at Denny Ford's of Ballymurphy.

Pat O'Sullivan, shot through the stomach and bleeding seriously, managed to escape from his position on the station platform and, under the protection of a deep trench, dragged himself out of the danger zone and continued for almost a mile to Tim Cronin's of Clashinimud. He was completely exhausted when he finally crawled into the house. Only a short time earlier Doolan had arrived with his wounded companion, Dan O'Mahony, and as soon as Mrs Cronin put a temporary dressing on Dan's wound, the two set off again. The good woman now did what she could for Pat O'Sullivan, and then had her son Batty take him in a horse and trap to Healy's of Farran before the military cordon had sealed off the area. On the following day Jack Kenefick of the First Cork Brigade conveyed O'Sullivan to the North Infirmary. It was too late. O'Sullivan died shortly after his arrival there.

The bodies of Seán Phelan and Batt Falvey were taken to Cork, but were later handed over to their relatives, and then, together with the remains of Pat O'Sullivan, were honourably buried in the Republican Plot at St Finbarr's Cemetery, Cork. The fate of Seán Phelan was a particularly sad one. The only son of Liverpool-Irish parents, he had come to Ireland a short time previously to offer his services in the national struggle and the ambush at Upton was his first experience of being in action. In addition to the casualties among the Volunteers, some soldiers were wounded. Unfortunately, there was a heavy toll among the civilian passengers. Six lost their lives and five others were wounded.

This engagement at Upton was undoubtedly the most serious reverse suffered in the Brigade, and what was particularly unfortunate about it was the loss it entailed of so many civilian lives as well as the loss of three outstanding Volunteers. Pat O'Sullivan had been Battalion Engineer and was not easily replaced; Batt Falvey had been active in many engagements throughout the Battalion area, while Seán Phelan, a primary school teacher who qualified in England, was a most promising Volunteer, and showed remarkable aptitude for military administration. Finally, the wounding of the Brigade Commander proved in its consequence to be the major calamity of the engagement.

Though the depressing effects which followed the Upton fight were very real, it must be said that the fighting spirit of the Volunteers in no way faltered, and their activities continued with the same intensity as before. Pressure was maintained on enemy posts, and sniping attacks on the R.I.C. barracks in Bandon, Kilbrittain and Innishannon, the only remaining police stations now in the Bandon Battalion area continued. Local actions to impede enemy transport went on as usual throughout the month of February, and all main roads and several intersecting by-roads in the Kilbrittain area were trenched. This work was invariably carried out under the protection of strong armed guards.

On 15 February the drawbridge over the Bandon river, three miles above Kinsale, was blockaded by the Ballinadee and Ballinspittle Companies. About the same time a bridge on the main Bandon-Kilbrittain road was demolished, and the back road between Bandon and Kilbrittain was trenched at Maulnaskimlihane. At the scene of these two last-mentioned operations a party of Volunteers lay in ambush positions to attack any enemy that chanced to approach.

Tragedy again struck on 16 February. Two squads of Kilbrittain Volunteers were digging trenches on intersecting roads within a few hundred yards of Crushnalanive Cross. Silently, unknown even to the armed guard and the scouts, the squads were surrounded by one of several enemy road patrols on duty in the Kilbrittain-Bandon-Ballinadee areas that night. Suddenly fire was opened on the Volunteers and four of them, Jerh O'Neill of Knockpogue, Timothy Connolly, Jack McGrath, and Con McCarthy fell mortally wounded.

The shock caused by these deaths to the people of the Kilbrittain area was exceptionally severe. Parents, relatives and friends were deeply affected by what was considered the biggest calamity that had befallen the district within living memory. Within four weeks a total of six men from the small parish had lost their lives in the struggle. This was indeed something to undermine the morale of the people, and to induce them to persuade their sons to withdraw from the fight or at least to ease the pressure on the enemy. But the people of Kilbrittain remained steadfast behind the Volunteers so that far from relaxing their efforts, they intensified them during the critical months that followed. To such a race of people freedom could not in the end be denied.

* * * * * *

All in all, the month of February 1921 can be recorded as Cork's Black Month, and West Cork had no monopoly of the reverses and disappointments that were a feature of the period. As January moved into February anxieties and reverses did indeed mount in our Brigade, and at the same time depressing reports began to filter through from the other two Cork Brigades. Thus, on 27 January a column of the Donoughmore Battalion in the centre of Cork Number One Brigade area was surprised at Dripsey, and of its members five were captured, four of whom were subsequently executed and the fifth died of wounds in prison. In the same Brigade the full column of the Midleton Battalion was practically wiped out at Clonmult on 20 February, five being killed in action, seven shot having surrendered, and two later executed. In the Second Cork Brigade the Mallow Battalion column was defeated at Mourneabbey on 15 February, with five killed in action and two others captured and later executed.

In our own Brigade area, on 5 February, we suffered the loss of one of our best officers, Paddy Crowley, during the general round-up at Cloondereen,[2] Maryborough, near Kilbrittain. Ten days later, in the engagement at Upton railway station, three Volunteers were killed and three wounded, including the Brigade Commander, Charlie Hurley. Finally, on 16 February we were shocked by the reverse at Crushnalanive in which we lost four experienced Volunteers.

Then the Column, though it had been under arms and continuously in the field for several weeks, had had only four engagements with the enemy and none of them had been decisive. A number of ambushes had been attempted, but apart from the experience gained from them they were without result and tended to produce discouragement and to sap morale. It is true that except for two days spent in a futile attack on Innishannon and Bandon barracks, the Column had been seeking encounters with the enemy in districts west of Bandon, such as Clonakilty, Dunmanway, Skibbereen, and

2. Also written Cloundereen.

Bantry, but in these districts, so favourable to guerilla warfare, the enemy was not appearing. On the few occasions when the enemy did venture out it was in extended formation and in such large numbers that engagements were not practicable. These were indeed dark days for the Brigade and the Column. Perhaps now, with hindsight, one can see in them the effect of the boast made in December 1920 by General Macready, Commander-in-Chief of the British Forces in Ireland, with reference to the War of Independence, that given another three months, he would 'smash the murder machine in Ireland and clean up the mess.'

Besides the loss of valuable men killed in action, we had also sustained the loss of others through capture. The frightful brutality shown to these latter by the enemy became known to us in various ways, and was a matter of the gravest concern to us. We were aware of the fiendish torture inflicted by a ruthless enemy on those of our men who had the misfortune to fall into his hands and the efforts made to force them to betray their comrades. These considerations added to the discouragement which February brought us.[3]

And yet this fearful brutality was met with a calm courage that proved to be invincible. Instead of terrifying the people into submission it seemed to cement them into a new unity and to inspire them with a new determination. The victories of our armed forces had their part to play in all this, but so also had the unflinching perseverance of the men in face of defeats and reverses, and the sacrifices they were prepared to make as an organised body, as part of a nation-wide movement. All these things conspired to produce the conviction that we were no longer to be hunted as individuals, and that as a united body we were now, for the first time, ready to meet the enemy on any terms that he might dictate.

Strangely enough, the heroic resistance being made by our army and our people to the enemy was winning recognition in the councils of the world, in the consciences of free people who knew and valued the precious right to freedom. The name of Terence MacSwiney was regarded with a reverence comparable to that shown for the Spartan heroes of ancient Greece. At last our ancient struggle was being recognised for what it was, namely, a nation's struggle for freedom, that inalienable and God-given right, that

3. As illustrations of the brutal treatment meted out to Volunteers captured by the enemy in our Brigade area, two sworn statements taken in the prison camp on Bere Island and witnessed by the late Right Reverend Monsignor Alfred O'Rahilly, who at the time was himself a prisoner on Bere Island, are given in Appendix D.

had been too long denied us. Not only abroad, but even in England itself, a new and more humane public opinion was spreading in regard to the Irish question. It was a consciousness of the disgrace which the atrocities perpetrated by the British forces in Ireland was bringing on England in the eyes of the free world. Commenting on the refusal of the British Government to publish the official report of the burning of Cork City submitted by their G.O.C., Major-General Sir E. P. Strickland, the London *Daily News* of 19 January 1921 said, 'The report is so damning that public opinion would demand the removal of Sir Hamar Greenwood.' Sir John Simon speaking at Sunderland on 29 January said, 'A system of vengeance had been established in Ireland, and after what had happened there, I beg to hear no more about what the Germans did in Belgium.' On the same day *The London Times* reported, 'Deeds have unquestionably been done in Ireland which have lastingly disgraced the name of Britain in that country.' Speaking at Euston Theatre on 19 February Mr H. H. Asquith said, 'I say deliberately that never in the lifetime of the oldest amongst us has Britain sunk so low in the moral scale of nations ... things are being done in Ireland which would disgrace the blackest annals of the lowest despotism in Europe.' Other well-known figures, such as Lord Robert Cecil, Commander Kenworthy, and Brigadier General Seely expressed themselves publicly in similar terms, and were joined by the whole British press with the single exception of *The Morning Post,* the last sponsor of hatred and bigotry. The opinions quoted represented a cross section of British political opinion, Conservative, Liberal, and Labour. But imperialism dies hard and the end was not yet in sight. The unmistakable swing of public opinion in our favour was indeed very heartening, but for us at the time what remained before our mental vision was the immediate duty of prosecuting the war with all the energy and determination of which we were capable.

* * * * * *

On 17 February I handed the Column over to Tom Barry at Shanacrane, and left for Brigade Headquarters at Ballymurphy near Crossbarry. Arriving there on the following day, I met Seán Buckley and Flor Begley, and was given details about the Upton Station reverse. The reports concerning our dead and wounded that had filtered through to me earlier were now confirmed, and I was informed that Charlie Hurley's condition was improving.

We then dealt with dispatches that had come from G.H.Q., from Cork Number One Intelligence, as well as with local dispatches and various other routine matters.

I left Brigade Headquarters about 22 February and cycled via Cork City to a meeting of Staff Officers from the South Tipperary, East Limerick, West Waterford, and the three Cork Brigades that was to be held at Tubbereenmire near Watergrasshill. The meeting was really a continuation of an earlier one held at Glanworth nearly two months before at which our Brigade had been represented by Charlie Hurley and Dick Barrett.[4] At that earlier meeting suggestions had been made, and subsequently sent, to G.H.Q. urging more active participation in the struggle by those counties which had been hitherto apathetic. At this resumed meeting which I was attending a great deal of time was devoted to the proposed landing of arms at Squince Strand and their distribution. What was specially significant about this and the earlier meeting at Glanworth was that they helped to bring about closer relations between the Brigades involved, encouraged them to develop concerted action in the prosecution of the war, and prepared the way for the formation of the First Southern Division that took place in the course of the following months.

When the Tubbereenmire meeting ended, I returned by bicycle to Cork with Florrie O'Donoghue who, with Seán O'Hegarty, had been representing the First Cork Brigade at the meeting. We reached the city without mishap, but then found that the police and military were staging a general hold-up on Patrick Street close to the Grand Parade. Everyone who happened to pass was searched and questioned. Florrie and I had no desire at that time to meet any of the British agents, but we were badly in need of something to eat. So parking our bicycles in a side street, we adjourned to a restaurant where we had a meal. Afterwards, finding the streets cleared of the enemy, we parted company, and I returned to headquarters at Ballymurphy.

Meanwhile the Column had not been idle. Led by Tom Barry, it marched from Shanacrane and made its way to Farnivane, five miles north of Bandon. It arrived there in the early hours of 22 February. A decision was then made to advance into the town of Bandon that night and to shoot any British forces that came in sight. Two sections were formed for this attack, one under the command of Tom Barry was to enter the town from the north by

4. Cf. Florence O'Donoghue, *No Other Law,* pp. 153-54.

the Street named Cork Road, and the other, under the command of Vice-Commandant John Lordan, was to approach as closely as possible to the British military by the Dunmanway Road.

On Tuesday night, 22 February, the two sections left Farnivane as arranged and moved towards Bandon. On reaching the junction of Cork Road with Kilbrogan Cross, Tom Barry decided to proceed into the town with Mick Crowley ahead of his section. He put the latter under the command of Denis Lordan with instructions to follow him into the town ten minutes after he and Crowley entered it. Lordan did as he was instructed, and when he led the section to the point where the Cork Road crosses the Bandon river, they suddenly encountered a party of three Black and Tans, and opened fire on them immediately. Two of the three were killed outright. The third made a dash up North Main Street where he was intercepted and shot by the Commander of the Column. A few moments later the Column Commander rejoined his section at the bottom of the Cork Road, and ordered it to withdraw.

In its turn, the second section under John Lordan approached the town from the Dunmanway direction. They shot two British soldiers a short distance from their barracks and captured a British Naval Wireless Operator. This man was later released.[5]

After the successful engagement with the British in Bandon, the two sections withdrew to Newcestown where they were joined by the other sections of the Column that had marched to Farnivane. There Barry decided to dismiss the Column until 12 March, but before doing so he gave the officer in charge of each section orders for his Battalion O/C instructing him to send a specified quantity of ammunition with the section officer when he was returning to the Column in March. This was in view of plans which Barry and I had tentatively discussed at Shanacrane about a week earlier, and which we hoped to put into operation when the Column remobilised in March.

The respite for the Column was indeed welcome for all concerned. After six weeks of hardship involving the fatigue and monotony of constant marching in mid-winter conditions, or lying in ambush positions for hours on end, and sometimes for a whole day at a time, in wet clothes and with irregular meals, the men needed a break to renew their energies and to restore their morale. In returning to their districts, they had the opportunity to see their

5. I am grateful to Denis Lordan and Michael Crowley for their personal accounts of the above incidents relating to the night attack in Bandon.

parents and relatives, to get a complete change of clothing, and above all the chance to get a well-earned rest.

On the day following the dismissal of the Column, 23 February, Tom Barry made his way to O'Mahony's of Belrose to attend a Brigade meeting, and I met him there with Ted O'Sullivan and Dick Barrett. Our main concern at this meeting was to review the situation in which we found ourselves and to plan our next move, particularly the action we would take when the Column reassembled in March. One conclusion very quickly emerged from our discussion, and met with unanimous agreement. It was that to give the Column a reasonable chance of meeting the enemy, it would have to relinquish the district west of Bandon that was so favourable for guerilla warfare, and operate instead east of the town, either on the Cork-Bandon Road or on the Bandon-Kinsale Road. Of the two the latter appeared to offer the better opportunities, and the portion of the road that seemed best for our purpose was the three mile stretch between Colliers Quay and Dunderrow. We were not anxious to operate south of this latter village, which marked the southern boundary of our Brigade area, because neither the people nor the terrain there were very familiar to us, and because it approximated too closely to the enemy stronghold at Kinsale.

Kinsale was the headquarters of the Essex regiment, and traffic between it and Bandon was more regular than between enemy Divisional Headquarters in Cork City and Bandon. But before we could make any plans for an engagement with the enemy between Kinsale and Bandon, there was one matter of crucial importance that had to be considered carefully, a matter that was essential in the kind of guerilla warfare in which we were engaged. It was freedom of movement, especially freedom to withdraw from an engagement if we were taken by surprise or unexpectedly confronted by vastly superior forces. The Kinsale-Bandon area was difficult in this respect because the Bandon river, being tidal all the way from Innishannon to Kinsale sealed off any safe retreat to the west. Then the presence of the enemy stronghold at Kinsale eliminated the possibility of retreat to the south, while the north could easily be cut off by an enemy force holding the main Cork-Bandon Road. This left only one way of escape, namely, an opening on a narrow sector to the east leading into the First Cork Brigade area at Ballymartle and Ballinhassig. Here we knew the Volunteers were well organised, and, all things considered, this outlet appeared to us to be the only possible escape route should the enemy attempt to form a ring around us.

Having decided on the location of our projected ambush in a general way, we had to take steps to cater for special difficulties to which it might give rise. As the forces to be met were likely to be greater than any hitherto encountered, it would be necessary to build up the Column beyond its normal strength of approximately forty men to a hundred, and as the engagement might last for several hours, it would be necessary to increase the number of rounds per rifle from the forty to fifty rounds hitherto considered for an engagement to at least a hundred rounds. Fortunately, our store of ammunition had been progressively built up over the previous two years, and particularly since the successful actions at Howes Strand, Ballycrovane, Schull, Tureen, and Kilmichael so that we were in a position to meet the demands so far as ammunition was concerned. Besides, while the question of ammunition was being discussed Ted O'Sullivan brightened the outlook yet further by mentioning a personal contact in Cork City from whom he hoped to collect at least a thousand rounds of .303. And in fact, within a few days an innocent looking consignment of 'hardware' arrived at a local station addressed to Willie Barrett of Killeady and safely made its way into Volunteer hands for use in our next action.

The question of reinforcements received a great deal of attention in our discussions. It had been arranged that Christy O'Connell would march to Castletownbere and bring fourteen fully-armed riflemen with an additional eight hundred rounds of reserve ammunition. Mick O'Driscoll and Mick Lucey of the Bantry Battalion were to accompany O'Connell. But the chief reinforcements of men and rifles would be drawn from such districts as Newcestown, Mount Pleasant, Quarry Cross, Kilpatrick, Crosspound, and Innishannon for the reason that they lay on the route to the location selected for the ambush.

Such was the substance of our deliberations at the Brigade Staff meeting held on 23 February. They envisaged a major attack on the enemy somewhere on the Bandon-Kinsale Road between Innishannon and Dunderrow. After this they made some provision for an attack on the R.I.C. barracks at Rosscarbery. Before we dispersed Tom Barry and I arranged to meet at Crosspound on Saturday, 12 March, in order to carry out a survey of the Shippool area with a view to selecting the precise ambush position that would be best suited for our attack. Naturally we hoped that the month of March would be more auspicious to our endeavours than the month of February had been.

CHAPTER 24

THE TRIUMPH OF CROSSBARRY

By a curious coincidence the first site chosen provisionally by Tom Barry and me for the ambush we planned to stage somewhere between Innishannon and Kinsale was—as we learned later—historic ground. It was at Ballinamona, and the area is now marked by a plaque. Here on 3 December 1601 Red Hugh O'Donnell and Hugh O'Neill led an Irish army to attack the English under Mountjoy who were besieging Kinsale. Unfortunately, owing to treachery or the ignorance of the guides, Mountjoy's force was expecting them, and the Irish were forced back over the ground we were surveying in search of a base of attack against the old enemy.

It was on 13 March that Barry and I conducted our search, and passed through Ballinamona. Later in our tour that day we found a place that better suited our purpose at Shippool, directly opposite the old castle of Dun-na-long and extending for a quarter of a mile on the Innishannon side. Its exact location was two miles from Innishannon and seven from Kinsale. Making a mental picture of the area, we withdrew and in the gathering dusk returned to our starting-point at Skeugh Cross. There we learned that it had been a day of intense enemy activity. Soldiers of the Essex regiment had arrived in considerable numbers and carried out the most extensive raids yet experienced. In the light of the information we received that night, it seemed that we had led charmed lives throughout the day. The raiding parties of soldiers had come from and returned to Kinsale along routes we had been travelling for four hours in a pony and trap. It seemed incredible that we did not fall into their hands, but as we pieced the information together the reason for our escape became clear. We had left Skeugh by the eastern road and had returned by the western or main road, whereas the enemy had travelled the same roads, but had started on the western road and returned by the eastern one. The fortunes of war were with us that day.

That night we set off to join the Column which by this time had reassembled and moved to Behagh over thirty miles from where we were. We travelled in a horse-drawn trap through the darkness of the night and discussed the plan of our projected ambush. Shippool was to be the place, and Thursday, St Patrick's Day, was to be the date. Next we discussed the route to take in marching the Column to the location of the ambush. This was a matter of capital importance. The column that was being mobilised for this engagement was the largest one with which we had to deal, and for this reason special precautions had to be taken to ensure strictest security while it marched to its destination. The first halt would be at Lisnagat, Newcestown, the second at Rearour, and the third at the ambush position beside Shippool. So starting on Monday night, 14 March, the Column would reach Shippool before dawn on the following Thursday morning, 17 March. Such were our plans : it remained to put them into effect.

Barry and I arrived in Behagh after an all-night drive, and met the men of the Column there on Monday morning. While Barry remained with the men, I set out to arrange for the reception of the Column at the two points along the route which we had chosen. Scouts were detailed, extra men for the Column were alerted, all spare ammunition was collected, and preparations were made for a major attack.

On Tuesday, I continued on to Brigade Headquarters, and was delighted to meet Charlie Hurley there. He had just come from Healy's of Farran. He was limping badly and was using a stick in his endeavour to walk. The reverse at Upton and the loss of three of his men still weighed heavily on his mind. No doubt his own wounds were partly responsible for his depression, and nothing I could say would console him. Flor Begley who had fought at Upton was with him now, and later Dick Barrett, Seán Buckley, and Tom Kelleher arrived. From the latter I got a very clear picture of the Upton train ambush and from it I came to the conclusion that it was due the conspicuous bravery of Charlie and Kelleher that the others had been saved against very heavy odds.

When Charlie heard of our plans for the Shippool ambush, he had only one comment : 'I am going too.' Faced, however, with the unanimous opposition of us all, he eventually consented to remain behind, and we promised that when we returned from Shippool we would willingly have him accompany the Column for the next engagement at Rosscarbery. It was sad to see a man of his courageous and habitually cheerful disposition plunged in such gloom. As we discussed the prospects of the fight that was due in two days' time, St Patrick's Day, I suggested to Flor Begley that he should bring his war pipes along on the eve of the battle. The suggestion was made on the spur of the moment, but, unfortunately, it had a disastrous effect on Charlie. Flor had been his constant companion all during the planning of Upton and for long before that. Now he saw himself as an invalid, unable to take his part, and it was too much for him. He broke down completely, and the parting with him affected us all. It would seem that he had some premonition of the tragedy that was impending.

On the following evening we met Charlie again. We had gone to visit the Column at Rearour, and while we were there learned that Charlie was following us to visit the Column also. He managed to limp as far as Crosspound, and we went back to see him there. It was our last meeting with him, and I can still remember our farewells as we parted on the roadside in the darkness of that night. We never saw him again, but his memory remained to influence us, and the recollection of his fighting spirit continued to inspire all those of us who had the privilege of serving under him.

At midnight on Wednesday, 16 March, one hundred and two Volunteers including four Brigade officers left Rearour and marched in the direction of Shippool. It was the largest armed Column yet mobilised in our Brigade area. The night march was without incident, and we reached Shippool before dawn. Then we moved into our positions and began the long wait. Naturally in guerilla warfare one must be prepared to accept all kinds of discomforts, but I have no hesitation in saying that this day was the most trying of all we experienced, and we had been through many bad ones indeed. We were lying there in cramped positions throughout the endless day, while continuous showers of cold sleet not only soaked our clothes, but sent the piercing cold to the marrow of our bones. Our position was so isolated that the nearest houses were half a mile away. Yet, thanks to the generosity of the Hurley and O'Leary families and their neighbours, buckets of tea and a supply of bread and butter were sent down to us at intervals during that weary day. The help and kindness of these good friends can never be forgotten.

As the day wore on and the hope of encountering the enemy faded, the hardship increased. It was, to say the least, most unusual that a convoy of Essex soldiers did not travel that day. Years later we learned that the enemy were observing St Patrick's Day as a 'peace day'. Perhaps this was true, but the Essex military had given so little evidence of anything bordering on chivalry that we found it difficult to credit them with honouring St Patrick's Day. As that cold winter's evening closed the signal for withdrawal was given, and a thoroughly disappointed and dispirited company of men marched to Skeugh a mile away. The warm welcome and hospitality we received in the homes of the people there and of others at Derrynagasha, Clogheen, and Slievegullane soon restored our spirits and good humour. With the Innishannon Company on guard, we could relax, and the resilience of our Irish character allowed us to make the night merry in the best traditions of the National Festival.

In complete contrast with the previous day, Friday, 18 March, dawned bright and clear. Tom Barry, Tadhg O'Sullivan, Con Lucey, and I were staying at Arthur O'Leary's of Slievegullane, and when we woke to the bright rays of the winter sun shining through the window, our spirits rose. After breakfast we sat around the fire to discuss the situation. Naturally we were disappointed with the results of the previous day. After weeks of planning for a major engagement with the enemy, we had now no option but to arrange a speedy withdrawal since news of our presence would quickly spread. Our chief worry was the effect of the previous day's disappointment on the morale of the men. They needed action and there was no immediate prospect now of carrying out an attack on the enemy. Various suggestions were made, discussed and discarded until a piece of information gleaned at Brigade headquarters two days previously offered a possible solution. 'We are near Crossbarry,' I said, 'we should occupy a position there tomorrow and it may give us the opportunity we so badly need. Five lorries passed that way on Monday. We may be lucky this time.'

There was no time for an exploratory trip such as we had made in preparation for our planned ambush at Shippool, and to Barry's question regarding the terrain, I recommended the western end of the road at Harold's and Beasley's houses. Tom Kelleher, Captain of the local Company, was sent for, and when he heard of the suggestion that Crossbarry should be chosen for an ambush, he confirmed the opinion that it was an excellent position for the purpose intended. That settled it. The decision was made immediately to occupy Crossbarry next day, 19 March. As things turned out this was to be the most momentous decision in the whole campaign in West Cork.

That evening at seven o'clock the Column marched from Skeugh Cross and proceeded towards Crossbarry. Tom Kelleher, as the leader with expert local knowledge, was in charge of the advance guard, and he took special precautions at Barna Cross Roads on the main Cork-Bandon road. We reached Crossbarry safely towards 8.30 p.m., set up headquarters at Paddy O'Leary's of Ballyhandle, and billeted our men to the north and south of the ambush position. Thereupon Barry and I went immediately to examine the position. It stretched from Harold's house on the west to within one hundred yards of Crossbarry Bridge on the east. The western end of the position was perfect, but the eastern end did not appear so suitable.

The stretch from Beasley's house to Crossbarry Bridge was devoid of all cover and had the further disadvantage that the ground rose from the roadway and offered nothing more than a shallow fence for protection. As we surveyed the setting in the clear light of a bright new moon, we came to the conclusion that the advantages outweighed the disadvantages, and agreed to go ahead with our project. Section positions were chosen, and final plans were completed by 10.00 p.m.

Barry and I were on the point of returning to O'Leary's when a figure approached us clearly visible in the moonlight. It was John Lordan of Newcestown, a hero of the Kilmichael ambush and many other engagements. He was now a section leader in the Column, and his men were billeted close to Crossbarry Bridge. In his usual breezy style he greeted us : 'Well, what do ye think of tomorrow?' Tom Barry replied in an equally light-hearted manner : 'This fellow Deasy is responsible for our being here, and if there is going to be any retreating I hope he knows where he should be.' The conversation continued in this inconsequential fashion, and then Lordan with typical generosity said he had a few bob left and offered to stand us a drink in the local pub. Neither Barry nor I had any money at all. We crossed the bridge to Mrs Cronin's where we were joined by Dan Canty of Newcestown and Mícheál Óg O'Sullivan of Adrigole.

Mrs Cronin's pub that night may not have been as dramatic a setting as the mess tent on Flanders' field immortalised by Davis in the *Battle Eve of the Brigade,* and our toast was less elegant :

God prosper old Ireland—you'd think them afraid,
So pale grew the chiefs of the Irish Brigade.

Yet between those in the two settings there was in common the fierce determination of men who saw a chance to repay their country's wrongs and were resolved to do so till the last breath. On the field of Fontenoy the Wild Geese repaid the age-old enemy with interest. John Lordan had no such ambitious hopes when, as host, he raised his glass to the toast : 'Good luck for tomorrow, boys!' But neither he nor any of us could have foreseen that in these simple words he was toasting to the greatest fight of all to be fought by the West Cork Brigade.

At 11.00 p.m. we parted company and made for our billets. Barry and I had a ten minute walk to O'Leary's, and when we arrived there Tadhg O'Sullivan was waiting to report that he had inspected the detail of local Volunteers who were doing guard duty in the area for the night. At 2.30 a.m. we were alerted by Mick Crowley and Tom Kelleher. Together with some scouts they had been moving around for a few hours and from a high vantage point they had seen bright headlights about three miles away near Kilpatrick in the Bandon district. In the still morning air they could also hear the faint noise of the slowly-moving vehicles. This was the first warning we had that the enemy were active in the district and all billets were immediately alerted. The full Column assembled in the field at the back of Beasley's house in accordance with instructions issued the night before to all section commanders.

At 5.00 p.m. the mining party went into action. They cut a hole in the road at the last turn before Crossbarry Bridge, and placed a large mine of gun-cotton there. Peter Monahan was in charge of this. Another mine was placed at the western end at Harold's Lane with Dan Holland in charge. Bill Desmond, Captain of the Newcestown Company, was instructed to go to Denny Forde's, a mile and a half distant, to inform Charlie Hurley of our new plan and to help him to join us at Crossbarry. On the way Desmond was surprised and captured by the enemy and so the information we sent failed to reach the Brigade Commander. By 6.30 a.m. all seven sections were in position, five along the road from Harold's house on the west to Crossbarry Bridge on the east and two others placed well back to cover our flanks and rear. Each section prepared earth works where the fences did not give the necessary cover. Breastworks with loopholes were constructed in particularly-exposed sections and then camouflaged with shrubs and grass. The positions were as follows :

Section 1   Laneway and Harold's house : Seán Hales in command.

Section 2   Beasley's house : John Lordan in command.

Section 3   Beasley's garden. Mick Crowley in command.

Section 4   Field fence from Beasley's garden to mine position : Peter Kearney in command.

Section 5   Between mine position and Crossbarry Bridge : Denis Lordan in command.

Section 6   Protecting rear of the Column near Ballyhandle Castle and covering left flank : Tom Kelleher in command.

Section 7   Right flank covering Bandon road : Christy O'Connell in command.

Both Kelleher and O'Connell had specific instructions to guard our rear and flanks. In the event Kelleher's section held the key position in meeting the enemy as he advanced in extended formation from the east. O'Connell's section covered a boreen running at right angles to the road. This was later used as our withdrawal route. It was now almost four hours since we were alerted to the fact that the enemy were coming in our direction from Bandon. The only development reported since was the raiding of a farmhouse to the west of our position, and it began to appear that enemy movements would be confined to the western area.

Daybreak was followed by a beautiful sunrise that ushered in the finest day we had in a long time, sunny, calm and clear. Tom Barry and I had inspected the different sections and had met at the Fifth Section close to Crossbarry Bridge at the eastern end of the ambush position. Nearby one of the two mines had been laid in the road with Peter Monahan in charge. Here it was hoped that the engagement would commence. It was assumed that the enemy would travel from Bandon in the west to Cork as was their custom when travelling via Crossbarry. However, lest they should come from the Cork side, a second mine with Dan Holland in charge had been placed near Harold's Lane at the western end. It was planned to allow the convoy to come into the ambush position and to start .the attack as soon as the mine exploded under the leading lorry. As the ambush position extended for six hundred yards a convoy of anything from three to six lorries could be catered for. In this plan the obvious place for headquarters was the Fifth Section under Denis Lordan. The cover provided there was very poor, and the same was true of Section Four, but we were agreed that nothing could be done about it. The range was very short—no more than three yards—and this would ensure for us the element of surprise. This would enable us to fire the first salvo, and we considered this to be more important than adequate protection from enemy fire.

Daylight was now well advanced. We chatted and exchanged views with Denis Lordan and voiced our determination to wait for the enemy all day, if necessary, and to withdraw only with nightfall. We did not feel inclined to dwell on the possibility of a repetition of the two previous days' futile wait at Shippool, as we knew that another frustrating day of inaction would put a great strain on the morale of the men. It has to be appreciated that of the hundred men under arms that morning fewer than half that number had been under direct fire before, though most of the others were seasoned soldiers. All had received some training and were well disciplined. Yet for many of them the prospect of another withdrawal without encountering the enemy would have been more than disappointing.

About 7.15 a.m. we were suddenly alerted by an outbreak of revolver and rifle fire coming from our rear and about a mile distant. While not close enough to cause us immediate alarm, it indicated that the enemy had not retired from the area. All sections were now at the ready. From the direction of the firing it seemed to me that it was coming from Denny Forde's farm where Charlie Hurley was convalescing. The shots were the first intimation we had of enemy activity in the north east. Enemy activity in the west had been reported earlier and we now had to consider the possibility that the enemy was planning an encircling movement in which case we would have to change our plans from attack to a break through. However, this possibility did not worry us unduly at that moment. Charlie Hurley was evidently fighting a lone battle and we would have to go to help him immediately.

If our forces had consisted of only one or two sections of men, it would have been a relatively simple matter to rush to Charlie's aid, but with a hundred men as well as a party of scouts to consider it was necessary to hold an immediate council of war to deal with the matter. Once again, as in all guerilla warfare, local knowledge of the terrain was of the first importance. Acting on such knowledge I suggested that we should move the entire Column through the fields at the rear to Ballyhandle Quarry a mile away. From the high ground there we could look across on Denny Forde's house at Ballymurphy and then decide our next move in the light of the situation that presented itself. This was agreed, and Tom Barry immediately proceeded to lead the eastern sections commanded by Kearney, Denis Lordan and Kelleher to the quarry rendezvous, while I was to lead the western ones commanded by Hales, Crowley, John Lordan and O'Connell. I had scarcely gone twenty yards when I heard the unmistakable sound of lorries approaching towards us from the Bandon direction. These must surely be the military lorries, I thought, and immediately I shouted back to Barry, 'Do you hear the lorries?' I do not think he heard the question for at the same instant shots rang out from our Sections One and Two on the right of the ambush position. The battle had begun. It was about 7.30 a.m.

The attack did not open, as we had planned, with the explosion of the mine near Crossbarry Bridge. Indeed the first lorry of the convoy did not even reach the mine position before the opening shots were fired. Subsequently we learned the reason for the miscarriage of our plans. As three lorries came into view, one over-enthusiastic Volunteer poked his head out of a window in a house which we had occupied. He was observed by the military in the first lorry, and the driver braked immediately. John Lordan saw in a flash what had happened and on his own initiative ordered his section to attack. To this officer and his section must go the credit of gaining for us the vitally necessary element of surprise, and thereby of preventing the enemy from securing any advantage at this initial stage of the fight. Many of the soldiers in the three lorries were killed in the first burst of rifle fire. A few who jumped from the lorries and attempted to get into position to return the fire of the Column were 'picked off' by six Volunteers on the opposite side of the road. This part of the action lasted scarcely twenty minutes.

By a stroke of good fortune it happened that with John Lordan's section was the Brigade Acting Adjutant, Flor Begley. He had followed my suggestion made a few nights previously that he should bring along his war pipes in honour of St Patrick's Day. He had the pipes with him now, and as soon as the shooting started he began to play rousing war tunes which could be clearly heard during pauses in the rifle fire. The stirring marching airs brought life and encouragement to the Volunteers in their grim struggle. This was Begley's finest hour and one on account of which he will be ever remembered as 'The Piper of Crossbarry'.

A young Volunteer named Ned White of Newcestown, whom the British troops had taken prisoner in the early morning as they passed through Kilpatrick, was being conveyed in the first lorry as a hostage. At this period it was usual practice on the part of the British to force some local people into their lorries and to take them along as hostages. In case of attack these hostages were sometimes shot by their captors. However, in the present instance, almost every British soldier in the first lorry was killed in the first burst of fire, so White jumped from the lorry and ran headlong towards the farmyard gate that was close to him. Though heavy rifle fire was pouring from this position at the time, not a single bullet hit the lad and he was brought to safety unscathed.

As the fight was concentrated on Sections One and Two and on our western flank, Barry and I naturally rushed towards these sections. Even before we reached Section Three under Crowley we could see disorganised enemy soldiers racing away from the fighting area and heading south for the railway line some two hundred yards from the road. Assuming that they meant to take up positions there to engage our western sections, we crossed the road and followed them firing as we ran. Barry, Kearney, Denis Lordan, 'Whistler' McCarthy, and Tim Allen were spread out on either side of me as we advanced in pursuit of the enemy. We succeeded in preventing them from taking up a position, if indeed they ever intended to do so. As we chased the fleeing soldiers, Barry took Kearney's gun to fire on them, but Peter quickly rearmed himself with a dead Tommy's rifle and continued the pursuit until all the enemy had either been shot down or escaped over the railway embankment.

As the field south of Beasley's house was now cleared, I went back to the front line where heavy fighting was continuing. Using the low fence for cover for about fifty yards, I then crossed the road and was in the act of scaling the opposite fence to join Crowley's section when I had the narrowest escape of my life. Fortunately for me I had come to a spot held by two seasoned fighters, Denny O'Brien of Newcestown and John O'Donovan of Aultagh. They both fired as my cap appeared over the fence, but recognising me before firing again they helped me over and I shall always remember the greeting from one of them, 'We are very sorry.' I thanked heaven for my good fortune, for the fault was entirely mine.

Firing was still continuing around Section Two. The three lorries had been close together when the engagement opened, and one of our men threw a Mills bomb in the direction of one of them. However, it struck the branch of a tree overhead and dropped on our side of the fence. Without hesitation Paddy O'Sullivan Cromane picked it up and threw it out on the road where it exploded near one of the lorries.

As the first phase of this battle ended, a new burst of rifle fire opened on our left rear. It was immediately clear that an attack was being made on Section Six which was under the command of Tom Kelleher and lay about four hundred yards to our rear. This attack was a serious matter, and very much more so than the road fight which was now almost over. If it succeeded our withdrawal route to the north by Skeenahaine[1] to Raheen Hill would be endangered, and this route had, at all costs, to be kept open. To judge by the noise of the rifle fire, the enemy were approaching from Ballymurphy, and were no more than four to five hundred yards from Skeenahaine. And the volume of the fire gave a clear indication that the enemy was a strong force whose weight of numbers alone might compel Kelleher to fall back before them.

As I discussed the situation with Mick Crowley, 'Spud' Murphy

1. Another form of the name is Skeheenahaine.

who was attached to Pete Kearney's section, appeared on the scene. He had his right arm in a sling as a result of a wound received a week earlier in the attack on the police at Rosscarbery. He was accompanied by 'Nudge' Callanan, and those two great veterans, Paddy O'Sullivan of Kilbrittain and Denny O'Callaghan of Newcestown. I told 'Spud' to pick four additional men and to go at once with his party to reinforce Tom Kelleher's section. I emphasised the seriousness of the situation and the danger that the enemy might succeed in securing the all-important Skeenahaine height. I impressed upon 'Spud' that since his right hand was out of action he should not attempt to fight himself, but that his duty was to see that the young Volunteers in the section held their ground and fired straight at the enemy. The group was soon selected and 'Spud' and 'Nudge' left immediately. In my opinion this reinforcement placed under Kelleher's leadership was a very important factor in helping to arrest the enemy advance towards Skeenahaine and to keep it clear for our subsequent withdrawal. It was the key fight of the whole action, and for this reason must be described in some detail later.

Back at the scene of the road ambush, I joined John Lordan's section. In his own simple, almost casual, way John described what had been taking place, and with a laugh that was typical of this cool daring soldier concluded, 'We have them well in hand now.' Presently we were joined by Tom Barry who, because of the noise of gunfire where he was, could not have heard the shooting that had begun on our left rear flank. I explained what was occurring there, and then we discussed our next tactics. He agreed with my suggestion that I should take Sections One, Two, Three, and Seven, while he would take Sections Four, Five, and Six out of their positions and fall back to Skeenahaine where we would meet and plan our subsequent movements. As far as we could see, the south and east were free of the enemy, but the strong attack coming from the north-east now sugested that the enemy was engaged in a pincer movement and, in consequence, we felt that no time should be lost in getting the Column intact to Skeenahaine. Next, we collected all the enemy arms available, including a Lewis gun with ten pans of ammunition, twelve rifles and a quantity of .303 ammunition which, as we learned later, just about balanced the amount expended by the Column in the entire engagement at Crossbarry. Subsequently, too, we discovered that there were at least six other lorries in the convoy which for some unaccountable reason did not come into action.

At 8.15 a.m. Sections One, Two, and Three were quickly with-drawn up an old laneway or boreen leading into the fields beyond Harold's house. There they were joined by Section Seven and set off at the double for Skeenahaine, which they reached and occupied without incident. From this vantage point we had a panoramic view of the country to the south and east. Leaving the men to keep watch behind the shelter of a high fence, I looked for Tom Barry who had not yet appeared with his three sections. Directly in front of us to the east was the position of Tom Kelleher's section, but apart from sporadic firing there was no sign of our men or the enemy anywhere in that area. Of greater concern, however, was the area covered by Section Five and part of Section Four near Crossbarry Bridge. From there could be heard constant and heavy firing. There was also a new threat visible towards the east where a party of from twenty to thirty soldiers in extended formation could be seen moving at the double with the evident intention of cutting off the two sections near the bridge. To me at the time the situation appeared to be becoming critical.

Between our position at Skeenahaine and the detachment of the enemy coming from the east there was a deep valley through which the Aughnaboy river[2] flows, and the road runs from Crossbarry to Begley's forge and Killumney. The detachment was making for this road through two fields at Killeen, and if it achieved its objective the result would have been fatal for our beleagured sections. To avert this danger sixty men were ordered to line the fence and to fire, independently, three rounds each at nine hundred yards' range on the advancing enemy. At such a range it was impossible to see the results on individuals, but one thing could be clearly seen, namely, the hasty retreat of the enemy detachment to the houses at Killeen's from which they had come. Checking our range subse-quently it was found to be much too short, and would have been more correct at a thousand, two hundred yards. However, the fusillade brought our sections near the bridge a vital relief. In his report, Denis Lordan stated later that his section, i.e. Five, was being attacked from the south and east as well as from Killeen's. Then he heard our firing from Skeenahaine after which the attack from Killeen's ceased. He was, however, still under heavy fire from Dunkereen road and Crossbarry Bridge,[3] and his position was so exposed that it was impossible for him to retire. Two of his men

2. The name of this river is given locally as Owenabee.
3. It was learned later that Major Percival was in charge at this point.

had been killed, Jeremiah O'Leary and Con Daly, and Peter Monahan was mortally wounded and was writhing in agony beside him.

Realising that if he remained where he was, it would be only a matter of time before he was completely surrounded, Lordan prepared to break out from his position. As he thought of this another of his men was wounded, Dan Corcoran, and he ordered Mick Kearney to look after his removal as soon as the signal to withdraw was given. At the critical moment a lucky accident occurred which caused a diversion when it was most needed and helped Lordan in his bid to escape the enemy encirclement. It happened that when Peter Monahan had been shot, he rolled in agony on the ground and wound the wires attached to the mine around his body. So he had died. Just before attempting to evacuate his position, Lordan thought of detaching the electric wires from the exploder and bringing the latter with him. However, in moving Monahan's body, his arm accidentally made contact with the plunger and detonated the mine. A terrific explosion followed and sent a huge cloud of earth and dust high into the air. In the moments of surprise and confusion that followed, Lordan succeeded in getting his men out of the trap in which they were and leading them into the safety of Beasley's garden. Thence, with their wounded companion, Lordan and his men followed the route we had taken and arrived at Skeenahaine a short time after Barry and Kelleher.

It was indeed fortunate for us that it was Tom Kelleher who had been put in command of the section that was to guard our rear and left flank. He was the local Company Captain and was familiar with every detail of the terrain from his childhood. An experienced officer and an expert tactician, he was the ideal man for the situation that confronted him at Crossbarry. Soon after the engagement had begun, he observed a platoon of soldiers[4] in extended order approaching him from the direction of O'Driscoll's house at Ballyhandle, and evidently making for Skeenahaine Hill. No one in the section knew better than he that if this position were held by the enemy the whole Column would be trapped and quite possibly annihilated. On the other hand, realising that he was outnumbered, he knew that he could not meet and repulse a frontal attack. So

---

4. Tom Kelleher estimated that the enemy in front of his section numbered from 150 to 200. Jim 'Spud' Murphy puts the number at between 40 to 50. I agree with the latter estimate.

he simply opened fire to delay the advance of the enemy and to gain time to develop a rapidly-conceived plan.

Selecting two seasoned officers, Denis Meighan, Captain of the Bandon Company, and Con Lehane, Captain of the Timoleague Company—both of whom had been sent by Denis Lordan on his own initiative to help Kelleher as soon as his section was engaged by the enemy—Kelleher sent them to occupy the ruins of Bally-handle Castle on his left. He ordered them to hold their fire until the enemy were quite close to the castle, and then 'to pick off' the commanding officer leading the advance. Meanwhile, Kelleher with his section engaged the main body of the detachment whose advance guard was being led by the officer towards the castle. The main body was moving across the valley with the obvious intention of supporting the party that advanced towards the castle. The arrival of 'Spud' Murphy with his detail of eight seasoned fighters materially improved Kelleher's position, and enemy were now finding it more difficult to advance. Urged on by their officer, however, they continued to move forward, and were allowed approach to within twenty yards of the castle before Meighan and Lehane opened fire. The officer in front was shot dead, others were wounded, and the whole party then retreated in disorder.[5] This success altered the whole position as the enemy did not renew the attack, and Kelleher's section was able to withdraw in safety.

In the course of the fight at Kelleher's section, Jim Crowley of Ballinadee was badly wounded, evidently with a dum-dum bullet, as there was a gaping wound above his knee.[6] Even as he collapsed, John O'Leary of Kilbrittain picked him up and carried him on his back through the thick of the fighting, and brought him to the safety of Skeenahaine. There Dr Con Lucey had set up a temporary dressing station and, assisted by 'Nudge' Callanan, attended Crowley and the others who had been wounded. Two doors were requisitioned and made serve as stretchers for the two serious casualties in the party.

Although we had repulsed the enemy on three fronts, the only line that was open to us now was due north, and to consolidate our position it was of extreme importance that we should get to a higher and safer vantage point than that which we occupied.

5. The officer leading the enemy attacking party was Captain Hotblack, one of a ruthless group of Percival's officers with whom we had to contend in the Bandon area.

6. Jim Crowley was invalided as a result of this wound for the rest of his life. He died in 1970.

Our immediate objective, therefore, was now Raheen Hill, an eminence two miles to the north and the highest point in the locality. After a quick consultation, it was decided that I should take the main body by the shortest route to Raheen Hill and hold it if attacked. So far there was no sign of the enemy in this district, but we had an uneasy feeling that he was not far away. From the fact that attacks had been breaking out in so many different sectors we now concluded that the entire district was completely surrounded by enemy forces. In fact, as we learnt later, there were as many as thirty-four lorries of enemy troops brought into the area. Allowing for a maximum of twelve men per lorry, the total number of enemy in the field was between four and five hundred.[7] It was obvious to us at the time that what we had to contend with was no mere chance operation, but a well-prepared plan of action. Its immediate objective could not have been to capture the Column, because our decision to lay an ambush at Crossbarry was reached only fifteen or sixteen hours previously, and the enemy could not have known this. It was possible that they learned about our presence in Shippool, and came out in force with the hope of tracking us down in the area.

I set off at 9.30 a.m. for Raheen Hill with the main body of the Column, while Tom Barry led the rearguard. I was to take my party, which numbered about seventy men, by a direct route to the Hill, and this meant travelling by the road. There were three road junctions to be traversed on the journey, and as these could have been held by the enemy, the direct route was not without its hazards. However, for the sake of gaining Raheen Hill in the shortest possible time we were prepared to take risks. In the event our efforts were not in vain, and we succeeded in occupying the Hill twenty-five minutes before the Auxiliaries from Macroom arrived there. It was rumoured later that they had been delayed owing to a mistake in interpreting their orders : for Crossbarry they understood Kilbarry near Dunmanway.

Tom Barry had the difficult task of leading a rearguard of twenty-five men, together with four wounded—two of them seriously so—to Raheen Hill. In choosing the route to be taken he was greatly helped by Tom Kelleher whose intimate knowledge of the locality was a great asset. By taking a circuitous route along boreens

7. During the week following the Crossbarry ambush, Flor Begley conducted a careful investigation into the number of enemy lorries in the surrounding district on the morning of the ambush. The total was thirty-four lorries.

whose bordering fences offered cover from the enemy, Barry succeeded in bringing his men safely to the Hill about a quarter of an
hour after our arrival there.

By this time all the sections of the Column had reuinted, and the
men fell out for a brief rest before continuing on their way to a
place that we hoped would be outside the ring of enemy activity.
As we were much too close to the danger zone where we were, we
could not think of seeking a meal yet, and instead decided to move
on to Knockawaddra in the Aherla district where we could hope to
get food and rest. This meant a further march of over three miles
and the sooner we covered it the better. It was obviously vital for
us to get clear of the enemy ring, the size of which no one could
estimate, as soon as possible. As we scoured the country around
with our glasses, we could see no enemy in sight, though we could
clearly see that there was a fire at Forde's of Ballymurphy, two
miles away. Flor Begley, who knew the house and haggard well,
guessed correctly that it was a reek of straw that had been set
alight. There were two Mills bombs concealed in one end of it, but
despite the vigilance of the enemy, Miss Forde recovered them
before the heat of the fire could cause them to explode.

Just as the Column was about to move off the Auxiliaries
appeared to the north and east of our position at the Crowhill end
of Raheen lane. We had no idea how numerous they were. But in
any case, we had no desire for a prolonged engagement with them
at this stage. It was now close to midday, and many of the men
had neither food nor adequate rest since 6.00 p.m. on the previous
evening. So Barry ordered Mick Crowley, Pete Kearney, and Jim
Doyle to engage the Auxiliaries, and then to follow the Column to
Rearour Bridge and Knockawaddra. This detail took up positions
behind a ditch, waited until the Auxiliaries entered Jagoe's field,
and then opened fire on them. The officer in charge and his second
in command were killed in the first volley. At that the others turned
and ran. There was no sign of their returning, and our detail
caught up with the main body before Rearour or Tuough Bridge.

While the Column was resting at Crowhill, the wounded men
were again given medical attention and received fresh dressings in
the home of Mrs Drew. Dan Corcoran had been bleeding profusely,
and by the time his wound had been dressed again, the kitchen
floor was liberally spattered with his blood. Shortly after we had
left the house, and when Mrs Drew and her daughters were preparing to wash out the kitchen floor, three Auxiliaries came into the
yard with the intention of searching the house. From a corner of

the yard came a magnificent turkey-cock in full regalia, his scarlet comb a-quiver, his tail spread fanwise, and his wings drooped for battle. Thus formidably displayed, the bird faced the intruders with his challenging and guttural war cry. The vision seems to have intimidated the Auxiliaries for they hurriedly withdrew from the yard, and so the house was saved. All the other houses in the immediate neighbourhood were raided that day.[8]

When we crossed the Brinny river at Tuough bridge, we passed through Rearour, and continued on our way to Pat and Jerry O'Leary's of Knockawaddra and to Larry O'Leary's of Kilbonane, a mile from the village of Aherla. There Tadhg O'Sullivan, the Column Quartermaster, took steps to have a much-needed meal prepared for the men. Going to the different houses, he asked the housewife in each to put the largest pot she had available on the fire and to fill it with all the home-cured bacon it could hold. He sent men to collect bread, butter and eggs, and as a result ample supplies of food, including a surplus quantity of loaves left at Aherla by a Cork City bakery, were rushed to the cooking centres. By 3.30 p.m. everything was ready, and the men set to with voracious appetites after their long fast. The meal was a most satisfying one, and worthy of the generosity of the O'Learys and the other good families that worked so hard to prepare it. Fortified by the rest and the meal, the men were soon in shape to face the next stage of their march.

We had anticipated that the enemy would soon be on our trail with reinforcements, anxious to retrieve the prestige that they had lost in the defeat at Crossbarry. It was, therefore, necessary to take the Column to a place of safety without delay. After some discussion, it was decided that Gurranereagh, twenty miles to the west, offered greatest protection, and we prepared to march there after nightfall. As we were about to begin the march, Tom Barry felt unwell, and decided to go for a rest to Ted Ryder's of Carrigeen. I then took command of the Column. Batt Foley of Rathfilane, a member of Quarry's Cross Company whose local knowlede would enable him to plan the best route was sent for, and with him as guide we made our way to the main Bandon-Crookstown road, followed this for a short distance, and then took the mountain road to Bealnablath. There we took the Cork-Bantry road, and continued on our journey till we reached our objective

8. This account was given to the author by Mrs Drew's son, Tadhg, who got it from his mother.

at 2.30 on Sunday morning.[9]

One of the most vivid memories that remains with me of the last phase of our journey that night is that of the Column marching from Bealnablath to Gurranereagh. Practically half of the men were marching either in stockinged feet or barefoot, with boots or shoes tied across their shoulders. They were weary and well-nigh exhausted, but there was no word of complaint from them, and their discipline was better than could be expected from any company of professional soldiers.

On our arrival at Gurranereagh, we set up headquarters at Joe O'Sullivan's, and on my first morning there, after breakfast, I took a solitary walk through the fields of O'Sullivan's farm. I could not help thinking of the previous day's victory at Crossbarry, and what it meant to us. We had encountered a better trained, more numerous and far better armed force than our own, and had acquitted ourselves remarkably well. It is true that we left the enemy in possession of Crossbarry Bridge, but we had beaten them off in the road fight and subsequently when they tried with superior forces to surround us at Ballyhandle and Raheen. My thoughts

9. Details of the route from Kilbonane to Gurranereagh which was taken by the Column were kindly supplied by the late Batt Foley. They are as follows : Leaving Kilbonane the Column marched to Rathculen via Parkmore Cross. Thence it continued to Rathfilane. At that point scouts reported that the Auxiliaries from Macroom were at Foley's Cross, Carrigeen, on the main Macroom-Bandon road, a mile further west along the road the Column was to travel. On hearing this news, the Column abandoned the direct route, turned to the left into Rathfilane lane where it took up positions, and waited until it was reported that the enemy had gone back to Macroom via Crookstown. Then it continued to Ballinguilla and Kilbrennan, turned right at Strawhall Cross, and kept on the old road to Crookstown for about a hundred yards, when it turned left on to Halloran's boreen, Carrigeen, and continued to the main Bandon-Macroom road, the route taken by the enemy about an hour earlier. The Column kept to this road for about half a mile before turning left over Hickey's bridge and continuing westwards along the by-road. This road, which was about half a mile south of Crookstown village, brought the Column to the main Crookstown-Quarry's Cross road. at Belmount, where it turned left, and proceeded for a quarter of a mile in a southerly direction towards Quarry's Cross. The next turn taken was to the right, and this led along a cart track through the Commons mountain district via Ardra, and out on the main Bealnablath-Mossgrove road at the top of Murray's hill. It then headed for Bealnablath on the Cork-Bantry road where it turned left for Pullerick, Horn Hill and Bengour. Taking the right turn at this juncture it made directly for Gurranereagh. The entire march from Kilbonane took approximately eight hours.

went back over the previous two years, and I found myself contrasting the position at the beginning of that period with the present one. Two years—indeed even one year—earlier we could not have put up anything like the fight at Crossbarry, and the main reason for the change was the acquisition of arms. It was due to the herculean efforts of the pioneers who had captured arms and ammunition from the enemy at Eyeries, Rathclarin, Bantry Pier, Howes Strand, Ballycrovane, and Schull, Tureen, and Kilmichael that we were able to stand up to the enemy as we did on the previous day. The Crossbarry fight, in a sense, was not the most important one in the campaign, but rather those earlier ones that prepared the way, and wrested from the enemy the armament that made the Crossbarry victory possible.

Tom Barry's presence, too, was a major factor in the change that had made Crossbarry possible. He had proved himself an ideal Column Commander. At the three camps organised by him he had trained the officers well, and in the many engagements in which he fought he had won the confidence and respect of everyone who served under him. He was a strict disciplinarian and a good strategist, but he was something greater still : he was a leader of unsurpassed bravery, who was in the thick of every fight, and so oblivious of personal risk that his men felt it an honour to be able to follow him.

The Death of the Brigade Commandant, Charlie Hurley

My Sunday morning walk at Gurranereagh was interrupted towards noon by the arrival of Dick Barrett, Brigade Quartermaster. He brought a mixture of good and bad news. The good news referred to Crossbarry and showed our success there to have been all the greater in view of the strength of the enemy forces we now knew to have been in the locality at the time of the ambush, and the extent of the damage we had inflicted on them. The bad news brought confirmation of our suspicions regarding the fate of Charlie Hurley. The story Dick had to tell in this latter connexion was a sad one.

A Volunteer prisoner held by the enemy in Cork Barracks had broken down under pressure, and divulged the fact that our Brigade Headquarters was based at Forde's of Ballymurphy, and that Charlie Hurley frequently stayed there. Our officer in Cork, Seán McCarthy, got some inkling of what was happening in Cork Barracks and made it his business to come to our area on 18 March to alert the Brigade Staff. That night he met Charlie Hurley, Dick

Barrett, and Seán Buckley at O'Mahony's of Belrose, and warned them of the danger that could arise from a leakage of information about the location of Brigade headquarters to the enemy in Cork. For some reason or other, Charlie did not think that there was any immediate danger, and retired for the night as usual to Forde's of Ballymurphy. Barrett and McCarthy felt ill at east, and spent the greater part of the night in the open. Neither Charlie nor his companions were aware how close to them the Column was that night. And neither they nor the men of the Column were aware that enemy troops from Cork, Ballincollig, Kinsale, and Bandon, as well as Auxiliaries from Macroom, were to carry out on the following day an operation that had been planned two or three weeks previously. Local intelligence estimated that about four hundred British troops were engaged in the encirclement of Forde's of Ballymurphy on the following day. Our Column of one hundred and two men and twelve scouts happened to be close to the centre of it.

At about seven o'clock on the morning of the Crossbarry ambush, a party of military approached Denny Forde's house at Bally-murphy. The officer in charge of the party, Major Hallinan, knocked on the door. Charlie, partly dressed, was coming down the stairs when the door that faced the stairs was forced open and the military rushed in. Hurley attempted to fight his way through, shot two soldiers, knocked another and reached the back door. He had just gone through this door when he came under the fire of the soldiers outside, and he fell mortally wounded. His death must have been instantaneous. The body was taken to Bandon military barracks, and later was placed in the Workhouse mortuary.

Such in substance was the account of Charlie Hurley's death at Ballymurphy. It was the kind of death he had strangely anticipated and even desired : strangely anticipated, inasmuch as he had pro-phesied that when the time of his death came, he would fall fighting alone; even desired, inasmuch as he had intimated that death in action fighting against the foe in the cause of Ireland's freedom was the end he would most willingly choose. Perhaps the tribute made by Seán Buckley, Brigade Intelligence Officer, a com-rade who had soldiered with him to the last, will best serve to show the kind of man he was :

Charlie Hurley was one of the finest types of revolutionary patriots I have known. Selfless, tireless, fearless, relentless where the cause of Irish freedom was concerned, he had the candour of a child and a lovable personality which won him the loyalty of his colleagues in a manner I have only seen equalled in the case of two other leaders. There was something in his singleness of purpose and in his burning zeal which thrilled you when you got glimpses of it. Of him could be said, too, what Pearse said of Rossa, that 'he was of the Gael and thought in a Gaelic way'.

Besides the sad news of Charlie Hurley's death in action, Dick Barrett informed me that the bodies of Jeremiah O'Leary of Leap, Con Daly of Ballinascarthy, and Peter Monahan had been taken to the military barracks at Bandon. We spoke briefly of the dead men and had a special word to say about Peter Monahan, the enigmatic soldier who had joined the Column in such unusual circumstances nearly three months earlier. We never really penetrated the mystery that surrounded him, and never even got to know his real name. Nevertheless, from the time we first made his acquaintance till his death at Crossbarry he had proved himself to be among the bravest of the brave. Only once did he shed any light on his Irish background, and that was after the first attack on Kilbrittain R.I.C. barracks. While resting with his comrades after the withdrawal from the attack, he mentioned that his mother had come from Fermoy and that his real name was similar to that of one of the party he operated with that night. Beyond this he gave no further information, and his silence was always respected by his companions. At Crossbarry he performed a last invaluable service to the Column by preparing and laying the mine the explosion of which at a crucial moment made possible the withdrawal of his trapped comrades from an encircling ring of enemy forces. With the remains of Jeremiah O'Leary and Con Daly he was laid to rest in the Republican Plot in Bandon cemetery, and his headstone bears the pseudonym, 'Peter Monahan'. But he will be better remembered in West Cork as 'The Unknown Soldier', and he will always hold his place in the roll of honour of those who died for Ireland.

Dick Barrett and I discussed the situation created by the death of Charlie Hurley at great length. It was decided that Dick should contact the Cumann na mBan in Bandon and have some of the members seek Charlie's body from the military barracks in order to prepare it for burial in Clogagh cemetery. It was there with his family that Charlie had wished to be buried.

Next, we had to consider the question of finding someone to fill the post of Commandant of the Brigade. In this matter we were of the opinion that Charlie's successor should be elected rather than appointed, and that this opinion should be put before G.H.Q. in Dublin. Later we discussed the question with Flor Begley, Acting Brigade Adjutant, and Tadhg O'Sullivan, Bandon Battalion Quartermaster, and on the following day with Tom Barry when he returned from a short rest at Ted Ryder's of Carrigeen. All were agreed, as indeed was Ted O'Sullivan, Brigade Vice-Commandant, when we subsequently contacted him, that the method of election was desirable rather than that of appointment to fill the vacant post. Further, this point was seen to be of such importance that it was considered advisable to send an officer who was well known at G.H.Q. to explain our views to the General Staff. I was deputed to undertake this task.

Dick Barrett decided to return to his school at Gurranes on the following day, Monday, and to continue his teaching there. This seemed inadvisable in the circumstances, but Dick was confident that he would be able to talk his way out of any situation likely to be created by the enemy. And it must be admitted that his success in evading arrest up to this time warranted his confidence. But his luck did not hold, and two days after his return he was taken into custody and held as a prisoner, first in Cork military barracks, and then in Spike Island.

Barrett's arrest meant another serious loss to us. He had laboured unceasingly to build up the Brigade step by step until it attained an organisational and financial stability that made it a serious force to be reckoned with by the enemy. It is true that he will not be remembered for any spectacular feats in battle, because circumstances precluded any such possibilities in his case, but as Brigade Quartermaster, and indeed very often as Acting Brigade O/C, he excelled, and it can be said with truth that during the trying years of the War no one did more to develop and consolidate the West Cork Brigade than the schoolmaster of Gurranes National School.

The entire Column rested at Gurranereagh on Sunday and Monday and we were able to relax for a while after the strenuous activities of the preceding week. The unfailing kindness and unbounded generosity of all the people of this townland where we were billeted helped to make our stay all the more pleasant, and we considered ourselves fortunate to have chosen such a locality for the break we needed so much. The extra men who had been mobilised for the projected ambush at Shippool were dismissed on Monday and returned to their own areas, thus leaving the Column under the command of Tom Barry at its normal strength of approximately forty men.

On that same Monday, 21 March, enemy reports on the Crossbarry ambush began to appear in the newspapers. *The Daily Mail* that day stated that the Crown forces had heard that an ambush was being prepared at Crossbarry and that a large force left Bandon to sweep an extensive part of the county. It mentioned that the party which took the road towards Cork consisted of a patrol of the Essex Regiment and a few policemen and travelled in eight motor lorries and Crossley tenders. The account went on to say that the fighting was on an unusual scale and that in the first volley seven soldiers and one policeman were killed and several others wounded. The report continued :

The attackers were concealed in groves surrounding two farmhouses. Several of the other lorries dashed off for reinforcements while the remaining members of the ambushed party took cover beside their burning lorries and replied to the attackers' fire. When reinforcements about a hundred strong arrived from the Hampshire Regiment they found the first party almost all killed or wounded. They quickly engaged the attackers in a running fight through the furze and over the gorse-covered hills. The Crown forces endeavoured to carry out an encircling movement. At one time it looked as though seventy or a hundred rebels would be trapped, but they were saved by their intimate knowledge of the country and their skilful use of cover ... The fight lasted for four hours and covered a large area. Crown forces took possession of all roads and stopped traffic and in the afternoon fires were seen at several farm-houses in the neighbourhood.[10]

On Monday night the Column marched from Gurraneregh to Ahiohill, and on Tuesday night from Ahiohill to Clogagh to attend the funeral of Charlie Hurley and to ensure that his remains would be interred with full military honours. The funeral procession left Clogagh church in the early hours of Wednesday morning, 23 March, and was led by the local curate to the family burial place. The Column acted as guard of honour and Flor Begley who had played warlike tunes at Crossbarry a few days previously, now played the Dead March.

It was a scene never to be forgotten by those present—the flickering lights of swaying lanterns, the slow tramp of the Column, the sobbing of bereaved relatives, and the sad notes of the war pipes—all in the dark chilly hours before the dawn of a morning in

10. Other press reports of this ambush at Crossbarry are to be found in Appendix E.

March. When the lonely graveyard was reached, the last prayers were recited and the soldiers' last honours were paid to one of Ireland's most faithful and bravest sons.

Slowly and sadly we laid him down
From the field of his fame fresh and gory;
We carved not a line and we raised not a stone,
But we left him alone in his glory. (Wolfe)

CHAPTER 25

DESTRUCTION OF ROSSCARBERY R.I.C. BARRACKS

After Charlie Hurley's funeral I prepared to set out for G.H.Q., Dublin. Initially the main object of the visit was to discuss the question of Charlie's successor with the General Staff. But now that news of Dick Barrett's arrest reached us, it was necessary to consider the appointment of a new Brigade Quartermaster as well. Tadhg O'Sullivan was the obvious choice for this post, and as I thought it desirable to introduce him personally to the Staff at G.H.Q., I made arrangements to meet him at Crosspound—eighteen miles away—and have him accompany me on the journey to Dublin.

I set out at dawn, after the funeral, to keep my appointment with Tadhg, and reached O'Donoghue's at Rathrout about midday. There I was given a very warm reception. It was some months since I had previously enjoyed the open hospitality of this great family. Mrs O'Donoghue, who made me welcome, was one of those heroic Irish mothers whose intense nationalist spirit communicated itself to her five sons and two daughters, and inspired them to give of their best in the service of the movement. Her hospitality to me on this occasion was such that evening was falling by the time I resumed my journey.

I continued on my way to Kildarra and Knockroe, and at the foot of Dromkeen Hill took the river road to Innishannon. About a quarter of a mile from Innishannon Bridge I heard someone approaching, and immediately took cover behind the adjacent fence. It was a clear moonlit night and I could recognise Tom Lane, a local farmer and an old friend of mine, coming along the road. 'Good night, Tom!', I hailed as I bounded on to the road to meet him. He reacted in a startled manner and exclaimed, 'Good God, is it yourself or your ghost that's in it?' and, holding up the beads that he held in his hand, he added, 'I was saying the Rosary for your soul!' In a few words he explained the reason for his surprise. In the morning newspaper it had been reported that six Volunteers had been shot at Ballycurreen, near Cork City, and my name had been listed among the casualties. Our meeting, though brief, was pleasant, and as we parted I thanked him for his kindly and prayerful interest.

At Crosspound I met Tadhg O'Sullivan, and we set out together for Glanmire station in Cork to catch the eight o'clock train for

Dublin on Saturday morning, 26 March. We had no problems
getting tickets, and in due course found ourselves on the way to
the capital. Though military were posted on all station platforms
where the train stopped, they caused us no difficulty. But our trip
was not uneventful for all that, and we met an interesting travelling
companion. A man happened to walk along the corridor outside
our compartment, and glanced in at us with curiosity as he passed.
A few minutes later he came by again, and this time, agreeing to
believe his eyes, decided to enter the compartment which Tadhg
and I had to ourselves. He was Billy O'Driscoll of Kildarra,
Bandon, a farmer and horse dealer who was well known to us as a
friend and sympathiser. Indeed only two months earlier, after the
January attack on Bandon, about thirty-five of us stayed in his
house for a night and a day. On the present occasion he was on his
way to Dublin to see one of his two-year-olds running at the
Phoenix Park races. For the rest of the journey we were so agreeably entertained by this man's pleasant conversation that we
seemed to reach Kingsbridge station before the scheduled time.
There we parted company, but only to meet unexpectedly again
later.

On leaving Kingsbridge station Tadhg and I drove in a hackney-
car to Devlin's of Parnell Street where the Adjutant General,
Gearóid O'Sullivan, a brother of Tadhg's, was awaiting us. While
we were having something to eat, Mick Collins arrived and having
welcomed us to the capital in his usual breezy manner, turned to
Gearóid and told him to fetch a taxi to take the 'guests' for a
drive. As all four of us drove off from Devlin's, neither Tadhg nor
I had the faintest idea where we were going until we found, to our
astonishment and dismay, that we were being taken to the Phoenix
Park races. As this began to dawn on Tadhg he turned to me and
asked, 'Where are we?' 'I think this is the Phoenix Park racecourse,'
I replied. 'Good God,' he said, 'these fellas are mad, boy!'

Collins looked back smilingly from the front. Then jumping out
of the taxi, he led us into the racecourse. Nothing would do him
now but to bring us into the reserved stand where we stood shoulder to shoulder with many of the enemy. We placed some very
modest bets on the horses of our fancy, but the puckish good
fortune that preserved us unscathed on the field of battle deserted
us on the racecourse. In the interval after the third race, we again
met our travelling companion of that morning, Billy O'Driscoll.
He looked even more dumbfounded than when he saw us on the
train, and could only murmur incredulously, 'Ye're clean mad!' to

which sentiment Tadhg gave wholehearted endorsement. Finally, when the last race was over and the carefree crowd poured out from the course, we mingled with it and then made our way back to Devlin's.

Here we met Piaras Beaslai who was busy preparing the next issue of *An t-Oglac*h, the official organ of the Volunteers. Collins, who had left us on one of his many missions, returned at 8.30 p.m. to tell us that he was due to meet somebody in Vaughan's Hotel, situated on the western side of Parnell Square. He invited me to accompany him, which I did. When we got there the manager of the hotel, Mr Maguire, was standing in the vestibule, and realising what a short time it was to curfew exclaimed, 'Mick, Mick, you've only ten minutes to curfew!' To this Collins replied with a laugh, 'To hell with curfew! We must do our business.' He kept his appointment in an upstairs room, and did not come down until 9.30 p.m. Together we then went into the empty square, and as we returned to Devlin's we could hear the lorries rumbling down the far side of the square on their nightly curfew patrols. The daring Collins showed that night may perhaps seem to have been fool-hary, but perhaps it showed, too, that dauntless courage which in various forms was the life and soul of the movement that he inspired.

On Easter Sunday after breakfast, Collins asked me to go with him to meet a detective named Jim McNamara, one of his chief men in Dublin Castle. We took the side streets till we got to Liffey Street. Then we crossed over the Halfpenny Bridge and met McNamara outside Jury's Hotel in Dame Street. Having listened to McNamara's report on the information he had gleaned in the Castle since the previous day, Collins brought me across Dame Street and through a tangle of side streets till we arrived at 27 Harcourt Street where he had one of his offices. There he spent half an hour going through reports and documents, after which we hiked back to Devlin's at a smart four miles an hour pace. During this journey to and from Harcourt Street I was questioned by Collins on our position in West Cork, and I gave him what I thought was a full report. After this I was subjected to a fusillade of questions regarding details of the situation and the possibilities for further development. Collins's immediate grasp of military detail, as was evidenced by his relevant and piercing questions, was astonishing and impressed me in a singular way.

Back at Devlin's Gearóid, Tadhg, and Seán McCarthy were waiting for us. Lunch had been arranged in Rathgar at the house of a Mrs O'Donovan who was a distant relative of Tadhg and Gearóid O'Sullivan. Hailing a taxi at the Parnell Monument we drove across the city. Just as we were passing Rathmines Church at 12.40 p.m. when the congregation was coming out after the last Mass, we ran into a military and police hold-up. We were ordered out of the taxi, and I felt that this was surely the end. It is true that we had alibis, and I, for instance, was Bernie Flynn from Shanbally attending a teachers' congress in Dublin that Easter. But when I saw one of the plain-clothes policemen approach Collins and run his hand through his hair to have a good look at him, I felt that it would need something more than an alibi to save me from imprisonment and something worse. I held my breath, and waited for the inevitable. It is more than possible that the policeman did not recognise his man, but not less likely that he realised that Collins's arrest would be equivalent to the signing of his own death warrant. Whatever the reason, he allowed us all to pass.

Subsequently during lunch, Mick, who was in the most exuberant of moods, constantly referred to Tadhg's remark of the previous day, 'Good God, these fellas are mad, boy!', teased him about his timidity and the sense of inferiority countrymen betray in the city. It was all in very good fun because Collins came from what was practically the same locality as Tadhg in West Cork. When lunch was over, Mick sent Gearóid to hire a hackney-car in order—as he said—'To show these bloody country fellows what a grand place Dublin really is!' The five of us mounted the car, two on either side and one at the back, and so we drove off to Lamb Doyle's, a pub in Sandyford about six miles south of Dublin on the lower slopes of the Three Rock Mountain. In the bar we became part of an animated crowd discussing the weather and the war which was then at its worst in the country. This lively crowd quickened by occasional songs and stories reflected the spirit of a people that refused to be intimidated or crushed by the terror and ruthlessness of a powerful foe.

We returned to the city on the same hackney-car, and adjourned to a house in Palmerston Park owned by an Irish American named O'Sullivan who had recently taken up residence there. That night the house was the venue for a meeting of ten delegates of the South Munster I.R.B. at which Collins presided. The agenda dealt mainly with the need on the part of the I.R.B. to organise more extensive activities in the areas represented by the delegates. To this end it was immediately agreed that membership of the organisation should be extended and that more proved Volunteers should be enlisted. As our host had thoughtfully arranged accommodation for all those attending the meeting, we were in no hurry to depart and our discussions continued far into the night.

Next day I attended a meeting with Mick Collins, Dick Mulcahy and Diarmuid O'Hegarty at G.H.Q. where I reported the death of Charlie Hurley. Tereupon, to my embarrassment, the Chief of Staff, Dick Mulcahy, offered me the vacant post of Brigade Commandant. In this Mulcahy was following the customary procedure which insisted on having appointments made by G.H.Q. rather than by election, but I asked that this procedure be waived in the present case. I explained that our Brigade area was very extensive, and that each of its seven battalions was particularly active. I pointed out how important it was that the Brigade Commandant should have the complete confidence and support of all his officers and men. At that time we had in our seven battalions almost five thousand Volunteers and an active Cumann na mBan membership of over five hundred. Our location was so distant from G.H.Q. in Dublin that the Brigade Commander would always be forced to make decisions on his own responsibility. Finally, I explained, there were so many tried and proved officers commanding the various battalions as well as those of the Brigade Staff that I considered it imperative for all concerned to have a voice in the selection of their commanding officer. In support of this opinion I suggested to the Chief of Staff that he invite Tadhg O'Sullivan to the meeting at this stage and listen to his views. This was done and Tadhg confirmed what I had said. After further discussion it was agreed to depart from the normal procedure so far as the vacancy caused by Charlie Hurley's death was concerned, and to accept the Brigade Council's choice of a successor to fill the vacant post.

Later in the meeting we were told that our Brigade would eventually be expected to send out columns to serve in areas that were less active than ours, and this met with our whole-hearted approval. Finally, the question of the formation of a Southern Division comprising the Brigades of Cork, Kerry, West Limerick, and West Waterford was discussed. It was intimated that Liam Lynch who was both Commandant of the Second Cork Brigade and Divisional Centre for South Munster of the I.R.B. would be Commander of this Division, and on this note the meeting ended.

Tadhg and I remained on in Dublin for another few days. They were busy days, but they offered a welcome change from the constant marching in wintry weather through the hills of West Cork, and the general hardship of life 'on the run'. Yet, strange as it may seem, we looked forward to returning to the active life of the Volunteers of West Cork, and our eagerness to return was increased when on Thursday evening of that week we read in the newspapers the account of the successful attack on Rosscarbery Barracks.

Rosscarbery R.I.C. Barracks is Attacked and Destroyed

At the time we were planning an engagement with the enemy east of Bandon, that in the event materialised at Crossbarry, we intended to follow it up with an attack on the R.I.C. barracks at Rosscarbery. This station was a powerful bastion of the enemy, one, in fact, which they boasted could not be taken. It was, moreover, situated in an important area, and was such a constant source of danger to us that we were particularly anxious to obliterate it.

The Column had moved to the Ahiohill district on the night following the funeral of Charlie Hurley. Thence it made a series of zig-zag approach marches towards Rosscarbery, the purpose of which was to keep the enemy in ignorance of its next objective. When the Column arrived in the Kilmeen Company area, Tom Barry instructed Tim O'Donoghue, Vice-Commandant of the Clonakilty Battalion, to prepare a mine and some bombs with the assistance of Dan Holland, Quartermaster of the Bandon Battalion. In fact, the mine was made by Captain McCarthy, a British Army Engineering Officer who had returned on leave from India two weeks previously. When he saw the conditions that prevailed in Ireland, he had offered his services to the Brigade.

By Tuesday night, 24 March, the Column reached a district some miles to the west of Rosscarbery, and by this time a substantial mine containing approximately one hundredweight of explosives, collected in haste from Bantry and Crosspound, had been prepared. A number of crude grenades had also been manufactured. These latter were made by inserting a stick of gelignite, together with a detonator and time fuse, into coffee tins which were then packed with scrap metal and clay. Besides the explosives, there were also prepared short lengths of sticks like abbreviated broom handles around which pieces of sacking were wound. It was intended to saturate these with paraffin oil or petrol, set them alight, and throw them into the breach made in the barrack wall. In this way it was hoped to set the barracks on fire, if the storming party was unable to enter the building through the breach. Finally, orders were issued to the various Companies in the areas surrounding Rosscarbery to have all roads leading towards the town completely blocked by felling trees and cutting trenches in the roads on the

Wednesday evening.

As soon as darkness fell on the night of 30 March, the Column moved from its billet area towards Rosscarbery. On the outskirts of the town the main body of the Column was placed in position to hold the roads leading from Skibbereen, .Dunmanway and Clonakilty, the nearest points from which British reinforcements could be expected. A specially-selected party then prepared to advance on the barracks. They were ordered to remove their boots and leggings and to secure any loose equipment they carried so as to prevent its rattling and making noise. Each man was armed with a rifle and a hundred rounds of ammunition, and also a revolver and ammunition for it, as well as a number of home-made grenades and some torches.

The land mine, which was made up in a coffin-like box was carried on the shoulders of four men in turns. When it was brought to a point about twenty yards from the barracks, the mine was plced on the shoulders of the four men who had volunteered to carry it to the door of the building and place it in position. There were two detonators and two time fuses fitted to the mine. When all was ready the latter were lit, and as soon as they began to splutter the four men moved forward led by Tom Barry, Mick Crowley, and Tim O'Donoghue. On reaching the gate leading to the barrack yard, Barry raised the latch and opened the way for the four men carrying the mine. These brought it to the door and placed it against the porch and propped it up into position with a few stones.

The mine party ran back about thirty yards, lay flat on the roadway, put the palms of their hands to their ears and waited breathlessly for the explosion. It came after what seemed an eternity. Judging by the noise produced the mine seemed to have caused a devastating explosion, and the storming party rushed forward as prearranged, but all they could see was a dull glare and clouds of dust and smoke. It soon became apparent that a substantial breach had been blown in the barrack wall, but owing to the amount of debris that was now piled up in front of the building and because of the haze of smoke, the men were unable to rush the breach.

At this point a voice was heard shouting from the barracks, 'We surrender, we surrender,' and the Column Commander replied, 'Come out with your hands up.' Immediately another voice was heard clamouring, 'Hold the . . . barracks!' and this shout was accompanied with a Mills bomb. The bomb burst just a few feet from the storming party, but as it fell among the loose debris in front of the building it fortunately did no harm. The Column O/C then ordered the men to open fire, and the attacking party that had been placed in the houses opposite the barracks now opened heavy fire on the breach made in the wall, as well as on the windows from which the steel shutters had been blown by the explosion. A hail of rifle fire kept pouring from the building and a number of grenades were thrown at the attackers.

Tom Barry, noticing that no progress was being made in the attack, ordered some of his men to fetch buckets of paraffin oil from the local shops. The order was instantly obeyed, and then Barry and his men approached to within yards of the barracks, under heavy fire and the bursting of Mills bombs, and threw the buckets of oil into the building. Lighted torches were then hurled through the breach, followed by some home-made grenades. In a short time flames could be seen spreading rapidly inside the breach, and soon the entire building was threatening to become a raging inferno.

The attacking party waited outside hoping that the garrison would come out and surrender, but without their knowledge the occupants had already succeeded in withdrawing from the rear of the building and making good their escape into the local convent grounds and later to Clonakilty. When the whole building had become a mass of flames, and when it was seen that nothing further could be done, the Column Commander ordered the men to withdraw. The attacking party then withdrew to a point where they made contact with the main body of the Column and all moved rapidly from the Rosscarbery district. The need for haste was obvious, as day was beginning to break, and the noise of the explosion of the land mine, the heavy rifle and grenade firing, and the glare of the burning barracks were bound to give warning to the surrounding enemy strongholds. Strong reinforcements could be expected to be rushed to the scene of the attack without delay.

The Column suffered no casualties and succeeded in marnhing away to billets five miles to the north of Rosscarbery town. There the men rested for the day before continuing their march to the Newcestown area, and later to Bealnablath. There on 3 April the Column was divided into small units composed of men from the same Battalion areas. It was decided to have the men return to their respective Battalion areas and carry on armed activities there until such time as the Brigade Column would be again mobilised.[1]

1. In am indebted to Denis Lordan, who was a member of the storming party in the attack on Rosscarbery barracks, for the substance of the above account.

CHAPTER 26

AN ANSWER TO THE TERROR CAMPAIGN

Orders convening a Brigade Council meeting on Saturday, 9 April, were issued immediately after Tadhg O'Sullivan and I returned from G.H.Q., Dublin. The meeting was held at Foley's of Maulnadruck, near Newcestown, and was presided over by the Brigade Vice-O/C, Ted O'Sullivan, and besides the Brigade Staff was attended by the Commandants of all seven Battalions of the Brigade. At this meeting I was unanimously elected Brigade O/C in succession to Charlie Hurley, and the appointment of Tadhg O'Sullivan as Brigade Quartermaster in succession to Dick Barrett was unanimously accepted. Later in the meeting Gibbs Ross, Adjutant of the Schull Battalion, was appointed Brigade Adjutant.

This necessary reorganisation to fill vacancies had inevitable undertones of grief and evoked memories of those of our comrades who had recently fallen in battle or had been captured by the enemy. The loss of such men as Charlie Hurley, Paddy Crowley, and Pat O'Sullivan in addition to many others was keenly felt. Among those captured, besides Dick Barrett, Con O'Sullivan, Captain of the Innishannon Company, was particularly missed. He was an excellent leader and had maintained constant pressure on the enemy in the vital Innishannon area from the beginning of the War. To replace him Dick Russell, Signals Officer of the Bandon Battalion, was put in command. Under his leadership, and with the effective assistance of the local blacksmith, 'Poundy' O'Connell, the Company of Innishannon continued its activities against the enemy stronghold in the village.

I gave a report on the meetings I attended in G.H.Q. and the decisions that had been made at them. There was real enthusiasm for the plan to send active columns into inactive areas. Then, the plan to organise the Brigades of south and west Munster into a divisional unit was also acclaimed as a timely military development, though we were less able to envisage the results likely to accrue from it than in the case of the first project.

As our Council meeting continued a general feeling of optimism gradually asserted itself. We could cast our minds back to the previous full meeting of the Brigade Council we had held in Lyon's vacant farmhouse at Ballinvard, Rossmore, on 6 February, and we could not but feel that the situation had greatly changed for the better since then. In the February meeting we felt that we were on the brink of a crisis, and the events which followed bore out our intuition not only so far as our Brigade area was concerned, but also the rest of the County Cork and the country as a whole. Fortunately, the dark night had passed and the reports and discussions on the Crossbarry and Rosscarbery engagements clearly indicated that the tide of battle was definitely turning in our favour. Most of the men present at our meeting had taken part in either or both of these fights, and one could detect an air of quiet confidence in the way in which they were discussing the lessons to be drawn from them. Thus, for example, the vital necessity of rearguard action both as a means of extricating our forces from an encircling enemy, but also as a means of attacking the enemy while in retreat was seen to emerge as a clear lesson from both the Crossbarry and Rosscarbery actions. We felt that the situation was now well in hand and though the end was by no means in sight yet, we did feel that since we had succeeded in weathering the worst onslaughts the enemy could raise against us, we were in a position to intensify our offensive in the ensuing months, and that despite enemy superiority in armaments and trained fighting forces. We would continue our campaign of guerilla warfare, but as we were now facing the long bright days of summer, we would have to curtail the duration of individual engagements with the enemy, and conserve our supplies of ammunition for the winter offensive.

Before the meeting ended there was a lengthy and important discussion on the question of reprisals. The official execution of Volunteers who were captured with arms in their possession was now a settled policy in the enemy's terror campaign. During the preceding months there had been ample evidence of this policy in other areas, though our area had not yet been affected by it. We did, nevertheless, suffer much as a result of the *unofficial* execution by the enemy of many of our comrades who had the misfortune to be captured. In the circumstances we felt that it was our responsibility to counteract the enemy's policy of executions by a policy of reprisals. Accordingly it was decided : (a) that the enemy G.O.C. in Cork be informed that we would strike back should his dastardly execution policy continue; (b) that if our threat was ignored, we would carry out an attack on all armed forces appearing in our Brigade area.

Besides these measures taken to counteract the enemy's execution policy, we also discussed ways to deal with another kind of terrorist activity carried on by the enemy. This consisted in burning down the houses of those who were suspected of being our supporters.

Thus after the Crossbarry engagement the enemy had burned the houses of two good friends of ours. In retaliation we had burned the houses of two British supporters, and the officers at our Council meeting not merely approved of this action, but expressed the desire that the policy be continued as long as houses of enemy supporters remained standing. During the following week the Essex Regiment stationed in Bandon burned down three houses in the Crossbarry area, and in retaliation a special Brigade order was issued leading to the burning of six loyalist houses in the adjoining area of Innishannon. It is worthy of note that, unknown to us at the time, the two other Cork Brigades were putting a policy similar to ours into effect in their areas. Partisans of the enemy throughout County Cork were soon thoroughly alarmed, and held a meeting in the Royal Hotel, Mallow, to discuss their predicament. From that meeting a telegram was sent to Lloyd George, the British Prime Minister, appealing to him to put an end to the policy of burning nationalists' houses as otherwise there would be no loyalists left in southern Ireland. The effect was immediate, and the enemy policy of burning houses virtually ceased.

The meeting at Maulnadruck ended after several hours with a recommendation to set up Brigade Headquarters in constantly-changing venues during the ensuing months in order to give encouragement by close proximity in as many parts of the Brigade area as possible.[1] The meeting had been typical of the Brigade Council meetings that had become, during the two years since the formation of the West Cork Brigade, such an important factor in our organisation. Here the progress of the War was kept under continual review, new tactics were evolved in the light of the experience gained in encounters with the enemy, new objectives for attack were selected and discussed with a view to continuing and extending our offensive, and the invariable effect was that cohesion and direction and a constantly-renewed enthusiasm were given to the efforts of the individual Battalions and to the Brigade as a whole.

1. Between April and July, Brigade headquarters was changed to nine different localities, namely, John Maurice Buttimer's of Ahakeera; Walsh's, Barrett's and Delaney's of Coppeen; Farrell's of Clogher (Togher); Manning's of Shanacrane, Derrynacaheragh; Nugent's of Dunbeacon; McCarthy's of Caheragh; Hurley's of Coomhola, Bantry; Crowley's of Trinamaddree, Bantry; and Sweeney's of Maughanaclea. It must be appreciated that this constant changing of headquarters entailed a considerable amount of staff work. In order to maintain necessary daily contact with the various Battalions, these had to be advised of each new change of address.

Shortly after my appointment as Brigade O/C I was visited at Headquarters by a National School teacher named John Barry from Connonagh, Leap. He explained that his house had been burnt by the enemy nine months earlier as a reprisal for the Leap ambush of July 1920 and that subsequently he had been relentlessly harassed by the enemy in his locality. He was obviously a quiet, respectable man and having no official connexion with the Volunteers, it was difficult to account for the continued persecution to which he was so persistently subjected. At any rate, things had gone to such a pass that the local doctor, our good friend Dr Collins, had advised him to leave the district altogether as it appeared that his life was in danger. He had followed this advice and went to live in Cork City. There he made contact with a good friend of ours in Sundays Well, and this resulted in his meeting with me. It was a meeting which, I believe, did good to both of us. For me certainly this man symbolised the spirit of a people that refused to be crushed and was prepared to make any sacrifice in the hope of achieving victory. 'I am not a soldier,' said John Barry, 'I would be more of a liability than an asset to you in the ranks. Still, I have saved a tidy sum of money, and I have come today to give it so that it may help to win the fight.' I thanked the man for his gesture; and what a generous gesture it was to offer his life's savings in this way. While turning down Barry's offer, I assured him of my gratitude and my deep respect. Without doubt there were at that time many thousands of John Barrys up and down the country. But my encounter that morning with such a high-souled man gave me strength in my beliefs and steeled my resolve to allow nothing deflect me from the course I had chosen.

The First Southern Division is Formed

About 12 April I received a dispatch from G.H.Q. summoning me to a meeting at Lynch's of Kippagh, near Millstreet, in the Second Cork Brigade area. The purpose of the meeting was the formation of the First Southern Division, and I was instructed to bring along Tom Barry, the Brigade Column leader. At a meeting held in G.H.Q. on 28 March the idea was discussed of sending experienced officers and men from the more militant areas into weaker fighting ones and steps were now about to be taken to put this idea into operation. Liam Lynch, O/C of the Second Cork Brigade, and Ernie O'Malley, Staff Officer from G.H.Q., who had not previously met Tom Barry. were anxious to do so with the idea of having him train a Divisional Unit and to lead it in action in outside areas with the hope of easing some of the pressure exerted by the enemy in the extreme south.

Tom Barry and I set off for Kippagh on 22 April with the intention of arriving at our destination on the 24th. At Ballymakeera we met Seán O'Hegarty, O/C of the First Cork Brigade, and Florrie O'Donoghue, his Adjutant, both on their way to the meeting. From Ballymakeera we continued our journey over the mountainy country west of Carriganima, and were careful to avoid the dangerous road between Macroom and Millstreet. Both of these towns were held by units of the Auxiliaries, and the road between them was often held by one or other of the units.

On our journey we called to a house for a drink of milk and there met Father Joe Breen, a curate from Millstreet who had been forced to go 'on the run'. We had indeed heard of Father Breen's plight, but this was our first meeting with him. We knew that he was a native of Killarney, that he had been active in the Volunteer movement in Tralee in 1916, and that as a result he was on the enemy list. When enemy activities developed in Millstreet area in 1920 Father Breen was one of a number forced to leave the town and go into hiding in order to avoid death or imprisonment.

On the afternoon of 24 April, shortly after our arrival at Kippagh, the meeting began. It was presided over by Ernie O'Malley representing G.H.Q. and was attended by representatives of several Brigades of south and west Munster.[2] The main business of the meeting was the formation of the First Southern Division from nine Brigades, namely, the three Cork Brigades, the three Kerry ones, the two Waterford ones, and that of West Limerick. General agreement with the decision of G.H.Q. to form the Southern Division was expressed at the meeting, and Liam Lynch, O/C of the Second Cork Brigade, was appointed Divisional Commandant, and Florrie O'Donoghue, Divisional Adjutant. There were no other appointments made that day. Considerable enthusiasm was shown for the plan to send experienced officers and men in columns to weaker areas in order to extend the range of our military activity. Such an extension, it was believed, would have the effect of relieving pressure on the more active areas by forcing the enemy to move troops to meet the offensive in the new centres of fighting. At this time in the spring of 1921 we knew quite well that there

2. For accounts of this meeting see Ernie O'Malley, *On Another Man's Wound* (Dublin, 1936), pp. 291-306; Florence O'Donoghue, *No Other Law* (Dublin, 1954), pp. 154-58; Tom Barry, *Guerilla Days in Ireland* (Tralee, 1962), pp. 142-52.

was a growing anxiety among the people of England about the image that their forces, particularly the Black and Tans and the Auxiliaries, were projecting on world opinion, and there was growing resistance to the policy of sending more troops into Ireland. This being so, the extension of our activities was likely to force the enemy to evacuate some of his troops—say, from West Cork—to meet a new emergency elsewhere and thus give us more scope for training enthusiastic Volunteers, for treating our wounded, and for resting those who were exhausted. Only a division of the size we were contemplating, controlled by an experienced and active O/C and staff, could achieve all this.

Measures to deal with the enemy policy of executing prisoners of war and of burning the houses of our supporters were discussed, and decisions similar to those made at our Brigade meeting of 9 April met with approval. In particular, it was decided that on a specified date an attack should be made on all Crown forces that were encountered in our Divisional area. Shortly after these decisions, and just as night was falling, the meeting concluded. It had been a very formal meeting, and the business to be dealt with was handled in the most expeditious manner. It was decided to set up Divisional Headquarters in the Coolea area, near Ballyvourney.

The Daring Removal of Mines from Derrinard Bridge

In an effort to impede the movement of British military forces in the Schull Battalion area, bridges were destroyed and roads effectively cut at strategic points until the area was almost completely isolated so far as motorised troops were concerned. At the time in question the only enemy force left in the area was a strong garrison of Royal Marines that occupied the heavily-fortified Coastguard Station at Schull. In order to maintain contact with this unit the military at Skibbereen decided to rebuild some of the bridges that had been destroyed, especially the bridge at Derrinard, near Ballydehob.

During the course of the month of April some lorry loads of soldiers from Skibbereen set to work to restore the bridge at Derrinard, and forced local people to assist them at the task. At a given moment in the course of the work the local people were ordered to depart temporarily from the scene, and there was a strong suspicion among them that during their absence some device was laid with a view to preventing further demolition of the bridge or to kill those who attempted it. About this time reports had filtered through that Volunteers in other areas had been killed or maimed by trap-mines laid in refilled trenches and rebuilt bridges, but there was no information available as to the type of mine or explosive being used. In order to prevent further casualties, orders were issued from Headquarters to the effect that in future refilled trenches and rebuilt bridges were not to be interfered with, but that instead new cuttings were to be made some distance from the refilled ones. This order involved a number of difficulties. Not merely did it mean added hardship for the local Volunteers who had to keep repeating the strenuous work of cutting new road trenches, but it also meant running the risk of being surprised at the work by the enemy and shot. The result was that the local Volunteer officer, Captain Tom Hickey of Skehanore Company, decided that an effort should be made to probe the secret of the mined bridges, and the one at Derrinard was selected as the most suitable for the experiment.

On the night chosen for the task, the men of Skehanore Company gathered at Derrinard bridge, some of them carrying old-fashioned farm lanterns. Before the work of digging began strict instructions were given to the men to examine each stone encountered very carefully before disturbing it. They were also instructed that if they noticed anything unusual they were to raise the alarm immediately and the men were to retire with all speed to a safe distance. After some time a small wooden box was discovered under a heavy stone. Thereupon Hickey, having instructed his men to retire, ventured alone to the spot where the box lay partly exposed. Prising the lid back slowly and cautiously, he inserted his hand and felt the familiar form of two Mills bombs. The safety pins had been removed so that the bombs would explode a few seconds after the stone had been lifted off the spring levers. Hickey called for help, and Jack Harte volunteered to give the necessary assistance. After some difficulty the two men succeeded in removing the stone sufficiently to enable the springs to be held down by the hand. The bombs were then removed from the box one at a time and made safe by having the detonators removed. As there were no safety pins available to keep the spring levers in position, there was no other way to render the bombs harmless. The work of excavation was continued, and shortly afterwards another box was discovered and this was found to have two Mills bombs also, and they were set in exactly the same position. The same operation was employed to remove the bombs from this box as from the first one.

The four Mills bombs that were salvaged were kept for future use, but one of the boxes was sent by post to Colonel Hudson who was the commanding officer of the military barracks at Skibbereen, and it was his men who had laid the trap-mines at Derrinard bridge. Enclosed in the box was a note thanking the Colonel for the contents of the box and requesting him to send a further supply. The second box was sent to Brigade headquarters with a full report, and this was the first piece of reliable information obtained regarding the trap-mines that were being laid by the enemy at that time.

About a week after this episode Derrinard bridge was restored once more by the British military and this time four boxes each containing two Mills bombs were laid. This time the boxes were painted in a dull grey colour and as a result were almost indistinguishable from the stones surrounding them, and the bombs were laid with the springs at the side instead of on top. Again the greatest care was taken when excavating the boxes, and the bombs were successfully removed. Only six of the bombs were effective as two of them were rendered useless as a result of being immersed in water.

Further Casualties

On 29 April two officers of the Timoleague Company, Jimmy Hodnett and Con Lehane, were called to examine some prisoners who were being held under guard in a house outside Clogagh. The owner of the house, Mrs O'Donovan, provided the two men with a meal and as they were preparing to leave she asked them to wait until she got a bottle of Holy Water from the bedroom. They complied and presently the good woman gave the two officers a liberal sprinkling from the bottle and sent them on their way with her blessing. On the road local scouts reported the approach of some men who could not be identified in the darkness of the night, and Lehane and Hodnett decided to investigate. At some distance they could hear voices which at first seemed to betray local accents and Hodnett called out to them. There was a pause and then in a pronounced Cockney accent they were greeted with the words, 'Come on up, chum!' Almost instantaneously a hail of fire followed the words. The two Volunteers returned the fire, but in the exchange Hodnett was shot in the ankle. He managed, nevertheless, to crawl over the fence by the roadside and made his way across a few fields to Staunton's where he asked for transport to take him to safety. The wounded man had scarcely made his request when he fainted, much to the distress of the householder.

But he soon regained consciousness, and with his handkerchief he bound up his damaged ankle. It was considered too dangerous to put a car on the road that night, but a horse was provided and Jimmy rode him bareback to Jim O'Riordan's of Gaggin mountain three miles away. Having rested there for a while, he was conveyed to Kealkil where he remained until the end of hostilities. He always attributed his lucky escape to Mrs O'Donovan's benediction and liberal aspersion of Holy Water.

A few weeks after Hodnett's narrow escape at Clogagh, his companion, Con Lehane, was surprised and captured by the Essex at nearby Ballycatten on the Bandon-Timoleague road. The military had come into the district in great numbers to carry out a raiding mission and they had the western side of Kilbrittain parish surrounded. Leaving Lehane in the charge of an armed guard, the rest of the military continued their raiding operation. At this juncture a local girl happened to come on the scene and seeing the dire straits of Con, she immediately occupied the soldier in conversation in the hope of drawing his attention from his prisoner. Lehane waited for his opportunity and as soon as the guard momentarily relaxed his vigilance the action started. The powerful Timoleague blacksmith hurled himself on the British soldier and in a flash had him overpowered. Disarming the guard and relieving him of fifty rounds of ammunition, Con vanished into the night.

But the news of Lehane's fortunate escape was dampened by the loss of an excellent officer of the Timoleague Company. He was Con Murphy of Clashflugh, a participant at Crossbarry and earlier engagements. On the same day on which Con Lehane was captured, Murphy was shot down at Cloondereen by an Essex raiding party : he had been returning from a meeting of the Bandon Battalion staff at Maryborough, Kilbrittain. His remains lie at Clogagh with those of Charlie Hurley, Paddy Crowley, and several other outstanding Volunteers.

* * * * * *

On 7 May a sub-Divisional meeting was held at Hurley's of Shanacrane East, eight miles north-west of Dunmanway. It was presided over by Liam Lynch, O/C of the Division, and was attended by officers representing the First and Third Cork Brigades and the Kerry First and Second. The main purpose of the meeting was to finalise arrangements for the landing and distribution of the arms that were to arrive from Genoa and to be landed at Squince

Strand near Union Hall.[3] A second purpose of the meeting was to build up closer relations between the Brigades of the Division and to organise a Divisional Training Camp. In dealing with this latter project Lynch decided that the Clydagh Valley lying to the south of Rathmore and near the Cork-Kerry border would be the most suitable venue for the camp, and it was proposed to hold two three-week training sessions there. It was decided that three senior officers from each Brigade should attend. At a subsequent date it was decided to begin the first training session on 3 July, and Tom Barry, Denis Lordan, and I were to take part in it.[4]

The Seizure of Bicycles on 10 May

For some time the enemy had been seizing bicycles in their raids on houses in our area, and it appeared likely that if they continued unhindered at this work, they would end by removing all bicycles from our control, and thus deprive us of the fastest means of transport normally available to us. To anticipate the enemy in this matter an order was issued from the Brigade Council meeting of 9 April directing Battalion O/Cs to have all available bicycles in their areas collected on 10 May and safely dumped. In carrying out this order exception was to be made of bicycles whose owners could be depended upon not to let their machines fall into enemy hands.

On the day appointed the order was carried out in every parish of the Brigade area where bicycles were available, and the thoroughness with which it was executed was an index of the high level of efficiency that had been attained by our organisation at the time. At least three thousand of the five thousand Volunteers on our rolls took part in the operation. In pairs or at most in groups of three the Volunteers cllected the bicycles in the areas assigned to thm. The object was to have the entire operation completed in the shortest possible time and, in fact, to have it done before the enemy was likely to have heard about it.

The plan was successful in its primary objective, but it indirectly cost the lives of two staunch Volunteers, Geoffrey Canty of New-

3. Some weeks later, to our great disappointment, word was received that the landing of these arms was cancelled.
4. In fact, the three of us set out for the Camp on 2 July. When, however, we arrived at Gougane Barra, a dispatch from Divisional Headquarters awaited us with orders to return to our base and await further instructions. No explanations for the change of plans was given. A week later news of the Truce reached us.

cestown, and Frank Hurley of Laragh. Canty was one of a party collecting bicycles who was shot as he endeavoured to get away from the main Bandon-Dunmanway road at Murragh. Hurley had gone with two local Volunteers to collect bicycles near Bandon. As the trio entered Scott's yard they ran into a patrol and were captured. Hurley was armed with a revolver and a few rounds of ammunition, but his two comrads were unarmed. Near Bandon the men were ordered to enter Castle Bernard Park. This very probably struck Hurley as ominous, and remembering the fate of Captain John Connolly, who as a prisoner had been murdered there by the Essex soldiers, and of others captured and shot nearby, he must have thought that he was to meet a like fate. The situation appeared desperate, and given the kind of person Frank was, it could be understood that he would make a gallant bid to escape by making a bolt into the nearby wood. In his dash for freedom Hurley was shot down, and his death deprived the Brigade of a great and inspiring leader.

It should be mentioned that on the day of the seizure of the bicycles, Tuesday, 10 May, the Battalion Commanders and many of the Battalion Staffs were absent from their areas and attending a Brigade Council meeting at O'Riordan's of Coosane in Kealkil district of the Bantry Battalion area. The main purpose of the meeting was to finalise arrangements for a midday attack on the enemy to take place on 14 May as a reprisal for the execution of armed Volunteers captured in action. While most of the Battalion Staffs and indeed many Company Captains were aware that the attack, or some form of reprisal, was being planned, its time and the particular form it would take were not announced until this meeting.

The Reprisals of 14 May

During the four days that followed the operation to seize all available bicycles in the Brigade area, the Battalion Staffs, in conjunction with the Company Commanders, arranged to put into effect the wide range of retaliatory attacks planned by the Brigade Council for 14 May. The Schull Battalion was an exception for the reason that all active enemy forces had already been cleared out of its area and the only British force remaining there was a small inactive unit of Royal Marines that manned Schull Coastguard Station. The Brigade Staff undertook to plan and lead two of the attacks : one to be carried out in Bandon and the other in Dunmanway. In the event, not all the attacks planned were put into effect, because the enemy failed to appear at the time and place expected, but successful attacks were carried out in Bandon, Innishannon, Kilbrittain, Courtmacsherry, Clonakilty, Dunmanway, Drimoleague, and at Furious Pier, near Rossmacowen. Of these the most elaborately planned was the attack staged at Dunmanway, while the most spectacular was carried out in Bandon.

The Dunmanway attack was intended to be the beginning of a campaign that we hoped would have the effect of clearing the Auxiliaries from the town which was the centre and vital point of the area. Over a period of several weeks it had been observed that a Crossley tender carrying a number of Auxiliaries arrived in the square in Dunmanway every Saturday at noon. The men remained for an hour to drink in one of the local pubs and to do some shopping. They were members of the infamous 'K' Company of the Auxiliaries, a hundred strong, that occupied the workhouse that was situated a mile to the east of the town. The R.I.C. barracks was located only a hundred yards from the town centre and was a strongly-fortified building with a garrison of twenty R.I.C. men and Black and Tans.

In planning the action we decided to have two sections of Volunteers converge simultaneously on the town centre at noon to attack the Auxiliaries there. The first section, under the command of Ted O'Sullivan, Brigade Vice-O/C, was to consist of eighteen armed men, six with rifles, and twelve with shotguns. It was to enter the town from the north via Cat Lane and take up a position at the point where the lane opens on to the square. To support this armed section there was to be an additional party of sixty Volunteers drawn from various Companies north of the Bandon river.[5] The duties of this party included scouting, maintaining contact with the other units on different roads, and especially blocking all roads to cover the retreat of the men after the attack. The second section, under the command of Paddy O'Brien, Battalion Adjutant, consisted of twenty-one armed men, six with rifles, and fifteen with shotguns. This second section was to enter the town from the south, pass the Railway Hotel and East Green, and take up its position at the southern corner of the square. It was to be supported by a party of thirteen Volunteers with duties similar to those of the party supporting the first section.[6] Finally, eight men

5. The Companies in question were Aultagh, Togher, Derrynacaheragh, Coppeen, Kenneigh, and Behagh.
6. The men of this party were drawn from the Companies of Clubhouse, Ballinacarriga, Shanavagh, Enniskean, and Ballineen.

from the town Company were to do duty in the square, and to report on the situation there to the leaders of the two sections when they arrived on the scene. At the final briefing on the night prior to the attack watches were synchronised in order that the two sections would arrive at their respective positions just as the Angelus bell was ringing at noon on the following day.

It was originally intended that I would take charge of the Dunmanway operation, but, unfortunately, two days earlier I had fallen from a side-car at Coosane Gap and dislocated a knee. On the day of the attack I was lying in bed at Farrell's of Clogher feeling very despondent. What worried me was the fact that I was unable to join the men for whom I was responsible in the very risky operation. I had helped to plan for Dunmanway. I was obsessed by fears that one or more of the Volunteers involved in the attack would be killed or captured in action while I lay in comparative safety and comfort away from the scene of danger. No matter how I tried to dispel them thoughts of this kind never left me during the long hours of that Saturday afternoon. What a relief it was when Ted O'Sullivan, who had taken command of the operation in my place, came to me later in the evening to announce that we had had no casulaties and to give the following report of what transpired.

The two sections synchronised their approach to the square in Dunmanway town with perfect accuracy, and they both occupied the positions decided upon as the Angelus bell began to peal. The scouts on duty near the square reported that the Crossley tender with its party of Auxiliaries had not yet arrived, so the sections waited. After about fifteen minutes two armed policemen emerged from the R.I.C. barracks and approached the square. Fire was immediately opened on them, but they dodged into a doorway close to the barracks and made their escape. As soon as the sound of rifle fire was heard, the supporting units outside the town immediately put their orders into effect and felled the already partly-sawn trees across the roads. This, of course, meant that now the Auxiliaries could not drive into Dunmanway if they attempted to do so, and there was nothing left for the two sections to do but to withdraw. To attack the R.I.C. barracks in the town was out of the question as it was impregnable. For the men on protection duty the most dangerous operation was to fell a tree and hold the Auxiliaries at the bridge over the Bandon river between the square and the workhouse. This task was efficiently performed by Jim Buttimer, Aultagh, and Tim Corcoran and Tom O'Donovan, both of Behagh.

Judging by the results, this operation in Dunmanway might be written off as a failure, but it had, nevertheless, a special importance. It represented the largest daytime mobilisation of our armed forces in a strongly-fortified enemy position. One hundred and twenty Volunteers were on duty that day; they had the town encircled and all roads leading to and from it were completely blocked in daylight. Significant, too, was the fact that neither the R.I.C. nor the Auxiliaries made any attempt whatsoever to attack the sections of Volunteers as they retired from the town. It is true that army vehicles were grounded, but the enemy could have pursued our men on foot to attack them. In fact, they thought it wiser to remain in the security of their fortified quarters.

* * * * * *

The 14 May attack carried out at Bandon was, perhaps, the most spectacular. A model T. Ford car was requisitioned on the previous day from Mike O'Reilly, the undertaker in Bandon, and was driven out of Hurley's forge at Baxter's bridge. From there it was taken by two Volunteers to a rendezvous on the Bandon side of Tinker's Cross and handed over to Tom Barry, who was to lead the attack. It was planned to mount the Lewis machine-gun captured at Crossbarry on the Ford car the next morning, break the glass of the windscreen as a precautionary measure, and fold down the hood. When all was in readiness, Barry was to enter the car with Seán Lehane, Pete Kearney, Mick Crowley, and Billy O'Sullivan and drive into Bandon town. The car was to be driven into the square and to approach the front of the military barracks garrisoned by the Essex Regiment. There fire was to be opened on the barracks with the Lewis gun and rifles. This done the car was to be driven across to the Devonshire Arms Hotel on the other side of the square and fire was to be opened on the Black and Tans who had set up a barracks in the hotel. As soon as this operation was completed, the car with its occupants was to be driven with all possible speed away from the town in the direction of Kilbrittain.

In point of fact, the plan had to be abandoned. As the car with its party of five Volunteers approached the military barracks, a contingent of Essex soldiers was seen in a field adjoining the Grammar School, and they were subjected to a hail of bullets from the Lewis gun and from rifles. No attempt was made to return the

CHAPTER 27

A MORAL VICTORY AT GLOUNDAW

The inevitable weed of treachery and betrayal that reared its head too often in the heroic garden of our enterprise emerged once more into prominence just a week after the concerted operations of 14 May. The event took place in the Ballinspittle Company area, and the villain was none other than a member of the Ballinspittle Company and a very much trusted friend of the Company Captain, Jack Ryan. In fact, he shared the complete confidence of his commanding officer, and indeed of the other members of the staff.

This Volunteer sent frequent reports dealing with the plans and activities of the Volunteers in the Ballinspittle area to a person in Kinsale who immediately transmitted them to the local R.I.C. barracks; thence they were relayed to the headquarters of the Essex Rgiment in the town. The result was that a number of strange incidents occurred. One such incident took place on 21 May.

The Ballinspittle Company planned to attack the Royal Marines at the Coastguard Station on the Old Head of Kinsale on 21 May. On the preceding day Jack Ryan with the treacherous Volunteer went to Ballinadee to collect three rifles, two revolvers, and a supply of ammunition. They returned with these and dumped them in a hayrick, and finalised their plans for the action next day. Ryan instructed the Volunteer to meet him on the following morning to collect the arms, and then proceed with him to Barrell's Cross where they were to meet two other members of the Company, Lawrence O'Donovan and Mick Galvin. All four were then to move off, and carry out the attack on the marines.

Saturday morning came, but the traitorous Volunteer failed to put in an appearance at the time and place arranged. Instead he sent a young fellow along to give Ryan a hand with the weapons, and help him to convey them from the dump to the rendezvous at Barrell's Cross. He also sent a plausible excuse to account for his failure to keep his appointment. Thereupon Ryan borrowed a horse and cart, and having put the arms and ammunition into it, set out to meet the other two Volunteers.

Exact information regarding the Volunteers' plan had been sent by the traitor in advance to Kinsale, and it eventually reached the military there. Major Percival, who was in charge, took immediate steps to meet the threat. With half a Company of Essex soldiers he fire or to follow the car as it turned and raced back into the country.[7]

The moral effect of the 14 May attacks both on the people in general and on the Volunteers in particular was tremendous. Nearly a dozen attacks were made at various points inside enemy strongholds, and that in broad daylight. The enemy in the line of fire who were not killed took to their heels, ran for shelter, and did not reappear until long after our forces had left the scene of action. In no case did we suffer any casualties, and everywhere our men and their leaders carried out their duties with admirable efficiency and courage.

7. I am indebted to Mick Crowley, who took part in the attack Bandon described above, for facts concerning the operation.

left Kinsale military barracks on foot, crossed the Bandon river by boat, and landed at the dock opposite the town. Thence the soldiers marched in extended formation through the fields with the obvious intention of being in position at Barrell's cross, four miles away, before the Volunteers arrived there. Fortunately, Ryan was keeping a sharp look-out as he made his way towards the Cross, and chanced to observe Percival's soldiers a field away from him converging on the Cross. The horse and cart were moving along a sheltered part of the road when Ryan made his timely discovery of the enemy's prsence. So, jumping from the cart Ryan dumped the three rifles and ammunition in a deep ditch beside the road. Next, he instructed the young fellow accompanying him to drive on in the cart, while he drew his two revolvers and prepared to meet the enemy.

To his right, and approximately two hundred yards from him, Ryan saw a party of fifty armed military advancing towards the road in extended formation. The soldiers had still to cross a fence to enter the field separating them from the road, and this fact offered Ryan his only hope of escape. For to his left the ground dropped steeply to the river and offered no means of evading capture. Vaulting the fence on his right, Ryan dashed for higher ground still further to his right in the hope of avoiding the Essex soldiers' line of fire. He had gone about two hundred yards unseen by the enemy when an Essex officer appeared on a fence to his left and immediately opened fire with a revolver. Ryan held his fire as he raced for the shelter of a fence in front of him. But the sound of the Essex officer's firing brought the military along at the double and they began to close in on Ryan both from the left and the rear. Fortunately, Ryan was an excellent athlete and exceptionally swift of foot. He raced on unharmed and as he reached the fence towards which he was running turned to face the officer who was following him. Firing first with the gun in his right hand, he found that the spring-pin failed; but being equally accurate with both hands, he fired with the gun in his left hand and dropped the officer. Then, crossing the fence he dashed away, and under cover of a ditch escaped the rifle fire of the military and made his way to safety.

It was generally believed that the officer whom Ryan shot was none other than Major Percival himself. This man while on operational duties wore a coat or vest of mail under his tunic, and when hit by Ryan's bullet was temporarily knocked out, but not seriously injured. A few nights after the episode Ryan went by night to the scene of his escape and recovered the rifles and ammunition which had remained hidden in the ditch where he had dumped them.

Personally, I have always considered Jack Ryan's feat on that morning of 21 May one of the finest individual actions in the whole campaign in West Cork. He continued to the end in command of his Company, but when the crisis had passed, he had to pay the penalty exacted of so many of his brave comrades. Many nights spent sleeping in the open, irregular meals, and long spells without food took their toll during the long months he was 'on the run' in the area around Ballinspittle that offered so little cover. He was stricken with what was then the dreaded disease of tuberculosis.[1]

* * * * * *

Frank Neville of Raheen, Quartermaster of Crosspound Company,[2] was another brave Volunteer who fell victim to the betrayal of a traitor—this time a local spy and not a member of the Volunteers. As in the case of Jack Ryan, Neville cheated death by a combination of quick thinking, great courage, and exceptional rapidity of movement.

The Nevilles of Raheen were typical of the many families of West Cork whose admirable self-sacrifice and whole-hearted support was an absolutely indispensable element in sustaining the efforts of our Brigade during the long years of struggle. But the Neville family had an added distinction. With homes such as those of the O'Mahonys and Delaneys of Belrose, the Fordes of Ballymurphy, the Kellehers and Drews of Crowhill, and the O'Sullivans of Raheen, it constituted what could be called the nerve-centre and headquarters of the Brigade for months on end during the years beween 1919 and 1921.

One young member of the Neville family, Ned, had, besides the part he took in fighting activities of the local Company, the very responsible task of helping to construct and protect the main arms' dumps of the Brigade at Raheen. There, at times, as many as fifty and more rifles, revolvers, ammunition, and mines were stored by

1. Ryan was advised by his doctor that the only hope of saving his life lay in emigrating to Australia. So, he left for that country in 1926, and in a matter of a few years made a complete recovery; so complete indeed that he successfully worked a large holding of his own in Goulbourn, and raised a family there. He returned to his old home twice since 1926, and at present is reported to be enjoying excellent health.

2 Frank Neville was subsequently appointed Assistant Quartermaster of the Brigade.

Ned and his companions. The weapons had to be cleaned and oiled, and from time to time had to be transferred to new dumps lest tracks made to the old ones should betray their location to the ever-watchful foe. All this work involved the gravest risk as the enemy was particularly anxious to discover our arms' dumps and were constantly searching for them.

On one occasion when the arms at Raheen had been cleaned and oiled after an attack and safely dumped, Frank Neville, Ned's brother, was engaged in making a gap in a fence between his farm and the adjacent one of the Jagoe family. Suddenly the order, 'Hands up!' was barked at him, and lifting his head he saw three British officers in the act of jumping off the fence from the other side. Here in his own words is Neville's own account of what transpired :

> One of the officers asked me my name, but another intervened and said, 'Neville is his name. We know all about him and his pals, O'Sullivan and Kelleher. We have our intelligence working well around here now.' They accused me of all the happenings in the district in which I had engaged— ambushes, attacks and the dumping of arms in a local farmer's hayshed. The information this officer had was correct, and it was easy to see that he had been supplied with an account of the facts by an informer.
>
> I was then moved down to Jagoe's farm to the south of the place in which I was caught. I felt relieved at this because if the officers carried out raids to the north all the dumps would have been discovered. There was a big box of explosives in a potato pit in a field quite near and a big dump full of arms and ammunition in another field not far away.
>
> There was a big gang of the Essex (soldiers) at Jagoe's yard. Two of them took charge and marched me away and each of them had the muzzle of his rifle in the small of my back. I was forced along th lane past Drew's and Kelleher's while the soldiers all the time hurled abuse at me. They said that the D Company, No. 2, were a tough crowd and would beat the I.R.A. with all our buckshot and road mines even with their bare fists. When we had marched about half a mile, we reached Desmond's Lane and there met another big gang of Essex. Two or three of them then began to beat me up. After that I was moved along a lane leading into Hawkes's place where the lorries were stationed. There I saw that two other local men, one a Volunteer, were being held

by the soldiers.

When I arrived one of the officers whom the others addressed as Major Percival pointing to me said, 'Put him in the last lorry. He is for Cork.' Then referring to the other prisoners he said, 'The other two are for Bandon.' The lorries then moved away, the last, in which I was, going very slowly so that the others in front soon disappeared from view. The soldiers said very little now. About half way between Tuough Bridge and Ballinacurra there is a wood on the right with a deep glen down to the river and a hill on the other side with a short lane at the left leading into some fields. There the lorry stopped and I was told to get out. A soldier got out from the front. He had a short Webley in his hand. He pointed to the lane and said, 'You get up there!' As he said that I took a step to the other side of the road. Immediately he aimed the gun at my chest and fired. I just managed to tip his hand as he fired and then bounded back along the road as fast as I could. He was still firing, but I kept going and got in over a fence on the right side of the road. There was another fence which hid me from the soldiers who had by this time come out on the road. I could hear them talking and cursing. I ran up along the fence and came to a big wide gap. I crawled across it. A short distance away from the gap there was another fence. I got on top of it and fell over on the other side. When I tried to rise, my legs were quite gone and I felt all wet along my back and chest. I thought I had been wounded, and opening my clothes felt for what I thought was blood, but it was sweat. As I knew then that I was not hit my legs came to life again, and I dashed off through the bushes. There was good cover there, and besides it was now nearly dark. Making my way to O'Sullivan's of Raheen, I met Pat and after a while Dick Barrett, Jack Kelleher and Dan O'Mahony came. They took me to O'Mahony's of Belrose, and there I collapsed from shock. After a while I recovered and we went to Jimmy Murphy's which was a safe home. I stayed there that night and the next day. I felt very shocked and was uneasy about the Raheen dumps. I decided to remove all the stuff. So with Pat O'Sullivan, Denny Delaney, Ned and Frank Drew I dug another big dump in a glen at Kelleher's farm near Aherla Road. Another was made in an old house at Crowley's farm, Belrose, but as we did not think it a safe place, it was never used. Pat

O'Sullivan, Ned, and Frank Drew and I spent three or four nights removing all the stuff from Raheen to the new dumps. Shortly afterwards the British made a big raid, and with the help of a local spy located all the old dumps at Raheen. But they found nothing except a Peter the Painter, which I had in a small private dump near the house at home. Percival was in charge of these raids. It transpired that it was a local man who had given them a great deal of information. Shortly afterwards this man fled the country when he found that we were on his track.

The Challenge at Gloundaw, 28 May

Early in the month of May, Gibbs Ross and I arranged to meet Tom Ward, O/C of the Bantry Battalion, to examine the possibility of mounting an offensive against the enemy in his area. Except for the two attacks on the R.I.C. in the previous February, the Bantry district had seen very little action against the strong enemy garrisons located there, namely, the military and R.I.C. in Bantry, the Auxiliaries in Glengarriff, and the R.I.C. in Drimoleague. This inactivity, it is true, can be explained by the fact that the Bantry Battalion had suffered a serious setback in November 1920 when its staff was captured. The loss of such experienced officers as Maurice Donegan, Seán Cotter, Ralph Keyes, and Con O'Sullivan was deeply felt, and though all Companies in the Battalion continued the usual activities, operations of the kind formerly planned and executed by the imprisoned leaders no longer occurred. We sought to remedy this situation.

In discussing the matter with Tom Ward we considered the Auxiliaries in Glengarriff and the military in Bantry. Of the two we thought that the Auxiliaries rather than the military should be our target for the reason that the latter were not nearly so aggressive and besides, we were doing quite well in receiving a weekly supply of .303 ammunition from the military barracks in Bantry as a result of the efforts of the I/O, Tom Reidy, ably assisted by Sonny Minahane. To cope with the Glengarriff Auxiliaries we could think of several good ambush positions on the Glengarriff-Bantry road, and one position in particular was considered by us to be ideal. Nevertheless, two major difficulties presented themselves. From intelligence reports we gathered, first, that there was no regularity in the Auxiliaries' movements and, second, that when they travelled they were liable to move in a convoy of anything from six to ten tenders. The first fact presented the likelihood of

our having to wait considerably more than twenty-four hours in
the ambush position before encountering the enemy, and the second
gave rise to the need of mobilising the full Brigade Column for the
operation. Now, to maintain such a large force in ambush positions
for more than twenty-four hours meant, as we knew from experience, bad military tactics. Besides, in an area where food and
supplies were already strained, the question of billeting and feeding
the men posed a major problem also.

At this point in our deliberations Tom Ward came up with the
suggestion that the Auxiliaries from Dunmanway who had been
penetrating into his area at Drimoleague and Castle Donovan
should be made the object of an attack. He conceived the idea of
luring the Auxiliaries into the ambush position by staging an
attack, even a token one, on the R.I.C. barracks at Drimoleague.
In the event of such an attack a force of Auxiliaries would most
likely speed to the rescue and could be ambushed by a full Column
well placed to deal with them. And the place he considered best
for the purpose lay at Gloundaw, midway between the towns of
Drimoleague and Dunmanway, four miles west of the latter.   .

Ward's suggestion seemed so good that we were determined to
pursue it further. Accordingly I sent Ward to contact Dan O'Driscoll of Drimoleague and Willie Hayes of Knockbue, and directed
that all three should inspect the proposed site of the ambush, make
a rough map of it, and bring back, together with the map, a
detailed report. This was duly done and the findings were so satisfactory that a few days later, at dawn on 27 May, Seán Lehane,
Tom Ward, Dan O'Driscoll, Willie Hayes, and I inspected the site
and selected a spot most favourable for an attack. We plotted the
section positions, the place for laying the road mine, and for locating the Lewis gun captured at Crossbarry. We decided that Dan
O'Driscoll should lead the party that would attack the R.I.C.
barracks at Drimoleague.

Next, we went to Drominidy where units of the Column had
been mobilised under their respective Battalion Commanders and
were billeted in various houses in the locality. There we held a
council of war to explain in detail to the section commanders the
plan of the ambush. The section positions were indicated and
arrangements were made to meet a convoy of anything from six to
ten lorries of Auxiliaries. The barracks at Drimoleague was to be
attacked on the following morning by a party of five men under
the command of Dan O'Driscoll. They were to take up a position
about two hundred yards to the left of the barracks, behind a

fence running parallel to the railway line, and to open the attack at 8.30 a.m. We could expect the Auxiliaries from Dunmanway to move towards the ambush position shortly afterwards. Our plans were now complete. It was 2.00 a.m. when we lay down to rest.

We rose at 4.00 a.m. and had a good breakfast. At five o'clock the Column was on parade. It was a beautiful summer morning and the men were in excellent spirits, eagerly looking forward to the engagement. It was a heartening sight to see them, eighty riflemen standing to attention in sections, the great majority of them seasoned fighters with mines, bombs and the Lewis machine-gun with five hundred rounds of ammunition. They were facing battle with the same courageous spirit as of old. A final check was made and when all sections reported that everything was in order, we moved off from Drominidy and were in action stations at Gloundaw by 6.30 a.m.

The ground was high on both sides of the road so positions were occupied there without any fear to our men from crossfire. The usual care was taken of flanks and rear—a lesson we had well and truly learned at Crossbarry. At one end of the ambush position, commanding a clear view of the road from Dunmanway, a section of twenty men under the command of Pete Kearney guarded against any surprise attack or encircling movement. Similarly, at the other end, Seán Lehane with fifteen men guarded the approach. In this section was included Billy O'Sullivan with the Lewis gun. He had been a machine-gunner in the World War, and now as he adjusted the sights of the gun to command a clear sweep of two hundred yards of the road, he prepared to give a warm reception to any enemy force, small or great, that came within his field of fire. Sam Kingston was in charge of the mine at one end of the ambush position, and Paddy O'Brien had a like duty at the other end. The inner sections were commanded by Jim Hurley, Seán Hales, Jack Corkery, Denis Lordan, John Lordan, and Neilus Connolly. For this ambush we had a good supply of hand grenades and home-made bombs; those in charge of them were armed with revolvers.

Meanwhile, Dan O'Driscoll and his companions were in position just two hundred yards from the R.I.C. barracks in Drimoleague and ready to open the attack. At 8.30 a.m. a Black and Tan opened the door of the building and walked towards the centre of the village. He was fired on just as he reached a point in front of the position occupied by the Volunteers. He fell wounded to the ground. Thereupon the attackers fired another round at the windows of the barracks and then quickly withdrew. At the same time a good cyclist, Patrick O'Mahony, was speeding on his bicycle to Gloundaw to bring us news of the action that had begun in Drimoleague. As soon as we received the welcome news a state of alert was ordered in all sections. An hour passed and nothing happened. By 10.30 we felt that something had gone wrong as the enemy had not appeared. However, we remained in our positions all day satisfied that even if our presence had been reported to the enemy we could still meet any effort on his part to surround us.

During the course of the day we were joined by Tom Barry and Mick Crowley. Barry had only returned from Dublin on the previous night and had no knowledge of our plans for the ambush before we left. But once he got news of the situation he hurried to join us in the hope of being in time to take part in the fight. It was a vain hope. At six o'clock in the evening, having spent almost twelve hours in the best ambush position we had ever found, we were compelled to withdraw. So, I handed the Column over to Tom Barry, and with Gibbs Ross prepared to head north to Brigade Headquarters at Hurley's of Coomhola. Just as I was about to leave a rather amusing incident occurred.

In the Column that day was a stalwart from Barryroe, Dan Santry. He was armed with a rifle and revolver, and I asked him for his revolver to equip a bomb-thrower whose rifle had been given to a late-arrival from the local Company. Dan very gladly gave his revolver, but when we were about to withdraw from our ambush position, he approached me and demanded the return of his weapon. Quite candidly I told him that I did not know to whom it had been given. That did not satisfy the bold Dan. 'I gave you my Webley this morning, and now I want it back,' he gruffly insisted. In the end there was nothing for it but to parade the Column, examine all returned revolvers and allow Dan identify his own particular Webley. He succeeded all right, and when I observed the affectionate way in which he handled the revolver my impatience in face of his insistent demand disappeared : the gun seemed to mean so much to this brave and honest fighter that I was glad to be able to placate him.

While I climbed towards the north-west, the Column, now led by Tom Barry who had taken over command from me, moved south to Lissane Upper and on the following night to Maulatrahane. Later it headed for Kealkil and from there continued into the mountain fastnesses above Borlin Valley. Intelligence reports coming in now seemed to indicate that British forces were slowly encircling the area from Cork, Bandon, Dunmanway, Bantry, Macroom as well as from Kerry, so it was decided to cross from Borlin Valley over Conigar mountain into Valleydesmond and then descend to Gougane Barra. With the aid of a local guide the Column crossed over Conigar at night and after a gruelling march got safely into Valleydesmond and continued on to Gougane Hotel. There for the second time during the war the Brigade Column was warmly received and generously accommodated by the Cronin family. Having rested for a day in and about the hotel the Column proceeded via the Pass of Keimaneigh back to Kealkil and thence to the mouth of the Borlin Valley again.[3] A night and a day were spent in this district and then the Column marched south to the Caheragh area where it was demobilised and divided into Battalion units which returned to their respective areas.

A few days after our disappointment at Gloundaw we learned what happened on the morning of our planned ambush. As soon as the Black and Tan was shot and the attack on the R.I.C. barracks began, the Auxiliaries in Dunmanway were notified by telephone— we had left the wires untouched precisely for this purpose. On receiving the news the Auxiliaries immediately boarded six lorries and were on the point of moving out from the workhouse in which they were stationed when a man—his identity was never discovered —was seen approaching and speaking to the officer in the first lorry. Quite obviously the officer was being alerted about the intended ambush because the Auxiliaries immediately dismounted from the lorries and returned to their quarters. As further intelligence reports reached us we were in a position to fill in the picture. We learned that the O/C of the Auxiliaries in Dunmanway telephoned the King's Liverpools in Bantry informing the commanding officer, Colonel Jones, of the ambush prepared at Gloundaw and suggesting that troops from Bantry and Skibbereen should move in and surround our position. Although the enemy had more than five hundred troops at their disposal in the outlying districts they refused to meet us. This information helped considerably to neutralise our disappointment at our failure to engage the enemy at Gloundaw. Examined in depth it showed the mentality of the enemy at this stage of the struggle, and it also showed the strength

---

3. In point of fact the enemy encirclement which gave rise to the above manoeuvres took place rather in the mountain district between Ballyvourney, Carriganimmy, Rathmore, and Glenflesk and did not endanger our Column. Cf. Florence O'Donoghue, *No Other Law*, pp. 171-72.

of our position. Though they knew exactly where we were located, the enemy, despite all his resources, refused to come out and meet us.[4]

* * * * * *

Before the end of May orders arrived from G.H.Q. with instructions to send a senior officer from our Brigade to Dublin for special training in the latest type of automatic that had appeared. This was the Thompson gun and it was considered to be very suitable for guerilla warfare. As effective as the Lewis or Hotchkins models, it was much lighter in weight and could be transported as easily as a .303 rifle. Seán O'Driscoll, then Vice-Commandant of the Schull Battalion and later to succeed Seán Lehane as O/C there, was deputed to go. After ten days' training he returned to Brigade Headquarters with the message that a cargo of Thompson guns was actually *en route* from America, and that a small boat would attempt to land some of them at Dunworley Strand near Seven Heads at the east of Clonakilty Bay. We were asked to maintain a constant look-out for the vessel, and to be prepared to help land the guns when they arrived. The Barryroe Company was entrusted with this mission, and its Captain, Mick Coleman, with six men, all local fishermen and expert oarsmen went on duty day and night for six weeks in the hope of sighting the expected ship and landing the arms.[5]

4. The enemy forces available to meet us at Gloundaw were as follows: Dunmanway Auxiliaries—120; Bantry Military—200; Skibbereen Military —100. In addition to these forces there were also others that were further removed from Gloundaw but capable of taking part in an offensive against us. These were as follows: Bandon Essex Military—200; Macroom Auxiliaries—100; Clonakilty Essex Military—100.

5. About the middle of July this operation was called off; it was learned later that the vessel with the cargo of Thompson guns proceeded to Cork and discharged its cargo there.

CHAPTER 28

LIGHT AND SHADE

At one of the conferences which Tadhg O'Sullivan and I attended at G.H.Q. during our Easter-week visit to Dublin, an announcement was made that experienced officers and men from the more active areas would form columns and operate them in less active areas in order to carry the war further afield and to relieve enemy pressure on their home front. This was a decision which both Tadhg and I welcomed with enthusiasm. It was further suggested on the occasion of the conference that our Brigade should take officers sent to us from other areas in order to train them and, above all, to give them experience with the Column in active service. As a result three young officers, two of them from Galway and one from Limerick, arrived towards the beginning of June at our Brigade Headquarters, then located at Nugent's of Dunbeacon, for training. They were James Hogan, later Professor of History at University College, Cork;[1] Michael Hogan, who became a colonel in the regular army later; and Dave Reynolds. who was subsequently Major General in the army of 1922. All three men were to return after training to south and east Galway in order to form fighting units and with them develop the war there.

Unfortunately, the visit of these officers was untimely. The Brigade Column had been disbanded and as we had decided not to mobilise it in full strength again during the summer months, except for some very special operation, the visitors were unable to benefit by doing active service with it. Furthermore, they had come to Brigade Headquarters at a time when it was located at the remote seaside hamlet of Dunbeacon that offered few, if any, of the conditions required for a practical course in military training. We gave the visitors whatever hospitality we could, and did our best to find some means of meeting their requirements, but after three days of fruitless effort we had to admit our inability in the circumstances to provide the kind of practical training that was sought. There was nothing left but to send the young officers back to their bases.

An Evening's Entertainment among Friends

In spite of the stress and strain of the war, indeed perhaps

---

1. It should be mentioned that James Hogan had already had experience of fighting in a Column in East Clare and had taken part in Glenwood ambush early in 1921.

because of them, the few occasions for relaxation which came our way were all the more eagerly accepted and enjoyed. One such occasion presented itself on 8 June, a time when Brigade Headquarters was located at Caheragh. We had received a cordial invitation from the inimitable Seán Lehane, O/C of the Schull Battalion, to an evening's entertainment in his area at Ballydehob. How very willingly we accepted it! It had been almost two years since I had a dance or an evening free to join one. So, accompanied by Tadhg O'Sullivan, Flor Begley, Gibbs Ross, and Seán Buckley, I set out for the village. On our arrival we were warmly welcomed and ceremoniously presented to the host of the evening Corney Kelly, the local stationmaster at Ballydehob. As I walked in and around the village of Ballydehob that evening, I experienced a feeling of exhilaration to think that it was now possible to move freely about the place without the slightest fear of arrest or capture. All active enemy had been cleared from the Schull peninsula by this time, and the very thought of this fact made it possible for us to enjoy ourselves all the more: I certainly enjoyed every minute of that evening with its songs, dances and stories and, of course, the gracious and generous hospitality of our host. Tadhg O'Sullivan, normally the staid, stolid and taciturn soldier, was for once carried away by the excitement of the occasion; he relaxed and yielded himself to the mood of the hilarious gathering.

News of the successful social function at Ballydehob spread rapidly, and within a week we found ourselves heading for another round of entertainment, this time near Skehanore, still in the 'free Republic area'. We were treated to a picnic organised by local members of Cumann na mBan on Jerh Murphy's farm near Cross House between Skibbereen and Ballydehob, and afterwards were brought to a dance at John O'Regan's house, half a mile away in Kilcoe. Yet another memorable evening was provided by Cumann na mBan girls in a sunny spot overlooking Roaringwater Bay and 'Carbery's Hundred Isles'. The sense of freedom and relaxation we experienced among such good friends meant a great deal to us at that time, and when we came to bid farewell to them we did so with regret. Everywhere we sensed a great spirit of optimism. We could see no other outcome of the long struggle but victory, and though we did not know when the hour of liberation would come, we felt that its coming was now inevitable.

Yet these bright hopes were somewhat dimmed in the days that followed, and we were grimly reminded that if Skehanore, Ballydehob, Dunmanus and Goleen were free, the situation was still very different outside the 'free Republic area'. On 18 June I attended a meeting of the Skibbereen Battalion at Walsh's of Maulatrahane on the Skibbereen-Drinagh road and after the meeting I went with Tom Barry, Denis Lordan, Seán Buckley, and Tadhg O'Sullivan to the neighbouring house of Charlie O'Sullivan to stay overnight there. It was a period when the enemy appeared to have abandoned its policy of raiding houses, so that it was only natural that we should feel reasonably safe. However when, towards midnight, we went to bed, Stephen O'Brien, the Battalion Adjutant, mounted guard outside.

At 3.00 a.m. we were roused by O'Brien who informed us that the enemy were surrounding the house. We dressed quickly, but in our haste to get away we left two trench coats behind us. As we reached the haggard at the back of the house we could hear the soldiers hammering at the front door with the butts of their rifles. They had not, however. covered the rear of the building by the time we were emerging and we got safely away. When we had departed the soldiers entered the house, searched it and having found our two trench coats took them away with them when they left.

Later, when Tom Barry found that his coat had been taken, he worked himself up into a state of righteous indignation, though the remarks he used to express his feelings were more forceful than righteous. Eventually he sat down and wrote a letter to Colonel Hudson, O/C of the King's Liverpools, whose men had carried out the raid. He demanded the return of the two trench coats, pointing out that they were not contraband of war. At the time we thought Barry's letter a very good joke, and soon forgot all about it. However, some days later the Colonel actually called on Dick Connolly, acting manager and editor of the *Southern Star,* informed him of the letter he had received from Barry, and said that he quite agreed with the sentiments expressed in it. He handed back the two coats and requested that they be delivered to us. This was one of the few chivalrous gestures we experienced at the hands of the enemy, and we would not have been human if we did not appreciate it. Colonel Hudson had previously shown the better qualities of an officer when he expressed his appreciation of our treatment of some of his men on the occasion of our occupation of Skibbereen in February. We always regarded him as a worthy commander who managed to carry out his military duties in a humane way and always respected the rules of war. He was very unlike many of the officers sent by the British Government to our country who carried out a terror campaign in our midst. For example, the officers of the Essex Regiment in Kinsale and Bandon showed an utter disregard for the ethics of war on many occasions. Their trail of destruction and reprisals was checked at Crossbarry, and the aftermath proved that the cruelty and barbarity of these villains, far from breaking the spirit of our people, rather tempered the steel of their opposition while winning for the British Government the obloquy of world opinion.

The Burning of Bandon and Skibbereen Workhouses

After a night's journey I arrived at daybreak on 21 June in Rossmore, and billeted at Mickey Harrington's of Caherkirky. I promptly fell asleep, but was wakened three hours later by Tim O'Donoghue, Vice-O/C of the Clonakilty Battalion, with urgent news from Brigade Headquarters informing me that the enemy were sending hundreds of extra troops into our area and that the billeting stations to be occupied by these troops were the two work-houses in Bandon and Skibbereen. These two substantial stone buildings stood in their own grounds and could easily be converted into two impregnable fortresses for the enemy. Indeed the fear that this was about to happen galvanised us into immediate action.

At the time in question the two workhouses were occupied by that unfortunate section of our people who as a result of poverty or illness were forced to spend their old age in circumstances that were neither comfortable nor happy. Were the enemy to occupy the buildings the inmates would receive scant consideration, and we were determined that they would be spared this inhumanity. As the responsibility for caring for the unfortunate people in the workhouses rested with the Board of Guardians which was now in our control, we could see to it that they were provided with alter-native accommodation. We quickly formed our plans.

Orders were issued mobilising sections of the Column from the nearest Battalions to destroy the two workhouse buildings and to contain the enemy while the work was in progress. By late afternoon on the following day seventy men assembled at Kilmoylerane near Ballinascarthy which was a central point from which to strike. As soon as dusk fell we were on our way to the objectives. One half of the Column under Tom Barry headed for Bandon while I led the other half to Skibbereen.

My main problem was to ensure sufficient uninterrupted time for the operation we had in hand. To this purpose one section of the Column was detailed to hold the approaches between the head-quarters of the King's Liverpool Regiment in the town and the workhouse on its outskirts. This section under the command of the Brigade Engineer, Mick Crowley, occupied some houses and took up positions behind the fence on the Cork road. With the remaining fifteen men I marched on to the workhouse, roused the gatekeeper, and told him of our mission. The inmates were quietly instructed to collect their few belongings and they were assured that when this was done they would be taken to a place of safety. Fortunately, they were fewer in number than we had anticipated and there was no panic. The chapel was an integral part of the building and was so centrally situated that it could not escape the blaze. The chaplain, Father David Crowley, was called and he quickly removed the Blessed Sacrament as well as the sacred vessels and vestments to safety. Having done so he returned to us to provide an invaluable service in comforting the old people in their fright and anxiety. We were indeed very grateful to him for his understanding and courageous help that night. In an hour we had the whole building ablaze from end to end, and the fire was so vast that it lit up the night sky for miles around. Although this illumination was clearly visible in the town of Skibbereen, the enemy made no move to leave his fortified quarters with the result that we could withdraw at daybreak to Maulatrahane without incident.

As we marched away in the early dawn of that morning from Skibbereen none of us could have anticipated that this had been our last operation carried out together. Little did I personally suspect that I would never march with the Column again or share with its members the fierce excitement of battle or enjoy the wonderful companionship and protection that were to be found in its ranks, the optimism of the men in face of difficulties, their enthusiastic courage when confronted with danger, and the wild thrill of victory that their concerted efforts had so often wrested from a ruthless foe. Least of all did I think that within fourteen months the four officers leading in the file, all close friends, namely Neilus Connolly, O/C of Skibbereen Battalion, Seán Hales, O/C of Bandon Battalion, Mick Crowley, Brigade Engineer, and I, would be divided, and opposed to each other in an unfortunate civil war, Connolly and Hales on one side, Crowley and I on the other.

* * * * * *

Meanwhile, Tom Barry with his party had entered Bandon, and approached the workhouse at the eastern end of the town. While he and his men occupied positions in South Main Street and Shannon Street to deal with whatever troops might rush from the adjacent enemy posts to inhibit the Volunteers in their work, Jim O'Mahony, Adjutant of Bandon Battalion, and some men of his unit evacuated the inmates and staff of the workhouse to nearby dwellings, and then set the building on fire. Here again as at Skibbereen the enemy refused to leave their fortresses and try to save the property which they had intended to commandeer for their extra troops.[2]

To add to the embarrassment of the British forces in Bandon another building, this time one situated right in the centre of the town, was destroyed by the Volunteers of the Bandon Company about a week after the burning of the workhouse. The Allin Institute was a Protestant social hall commanding the main bridge crossing the river in Bandon town, and it was earmarked for enemy occupation. It was a rather substantial building and had a considerable strategic importance because of its position. On the night of 29 June a party of Volunteers daringly burnt the building to the ground.

On the day after the burning of the workhouse at Bandon and Skibbereen I received a dispatch summoning me to a meeting at Ballinagree about seven miles directly north of Macroom to meet Liam Lynch, Divisional O/C, and Seán O'Hegarty, O/C of Cork Number One Brigade. As the Ballinagree district was entirely new country to me, I asked John Lordan of Newcestown, who had an intimate knowledge of the locality, to accompany me. We called first to Kilmurry where the ever-reliable Pake Sheehan guided us to Canovee. Thence we crossed the River Lee by a means that must have been unique in its way. Mick Murphy of Coolnacarriga had an unusual horse which was trained to go of its own accord from the adjoining farmhouse to the river, and cross it if anyone on the opposite bank beckoned to it. Then it would return with one or two passengers straddled on its back, and would cross and recross the river as often as it was required. We gladly availed ourselves of the services of this friendly animal on both our outward and return journeys.[3]

2. Cf. Tom Barry, *Guerilla Days in Ireland,* pp. 287-88, for an account of the Bandon workhouse operation.
3. It must be put on record that the co-operation we received at all times from the Seventh Battalion of Cork Number One Brigade, in particular from Dan Corkery, O/C, and Charlie Browne, Battalion Adjutant, as well as from the men of the two Companies of the Battalion on our border was equal to any we found within our own Brigade. So far as the two Companies mentioned was concerned, we were indebted to their respective Captains, Pat O'Leary, Kilmurry, Billy Powell, Crookstown, and their brother officers and men. The people of the district merited our gratitude for the welcome they showed us at all times.

The Ballinagree meeting proved to be brief. It was mainly concerned with continuing our policy of protecting in every way possible those of our men who were captured while bearing arms and also the homes of our men from reprisals. Though we could not directly put a stop to breaches of the rules of war perpetrated by the enemy, we were determined to counter them indirectly. In fact, we were so successful in this policy that an end was eventually put to the shooting of prisoners and the burning of houses by the enemy.

The Capture of Lord Bandon

A number of our men had been captured in various raids conducted by British forces up to the middle of June 1921. Some of these men were due to be courtmartialled, and it was understood that in most cases the outcome would be the death sentence for those involved. Matters came to a head when some outstanding Volunteers who had been captured by the British were awaiting trial and almost certain death sentences. Among them was Bill Daly of Shannonvale, who had been wounded in action and captured at Jones's Bridge near Clonakilty during the previous March. Anticipating that these men would be summarily executed unless counter measures were taken, we decided to act quickly.

At Brigade Headquarters, then located at Johnny Sweeney's of Maughanaclea, Kealkil, we decided to send orders to the Commandant of the Bandon Battalion, Seán Hales, instructing him to arrest Lord Bandon and other prominent British supporters, preferably administrative officials such as magistrates, and to hold them as prisoners pending further instructions.[4] It was decided to send similar instructions to the Commandant of the Clonakilty Battalion for the arrest of R. Bence Jones, Deputy Lieutenant to Lord Bandon. Our intention was to take these officials as hostages, and to inform the British military authorities that if any of our men were executed at least one of the captured officials would be shot.

On 21 June plans were completed for capturing the Earl of Bandon, Charles C. King, J.P., and several other pro-British person-

---

4. Lieutenant Mick O'Driscoll of Coomhola was entrusted with the task of bringing the orders from Brigade Headquarters to Seán Hales at Skeaf, Timoleague, a distance of approximately thirty miles. Armed with a revolver and provided with a bicycle, O'Driscoll set out on the journey. He was given four hours to deliver the orders to Hales and to report back at Brigade Headquarters. Actually he reported back some ten minutes before the end of the time allowed—a wonderful achievement in the circumstances.

ages. According to intelligence reports, a guard of military or Black and Tans was posted each night in the vicinity of Castle Bernard, the residence of the Earl of Bandon even though at this time martial law and curfew law were in force in and around Bandon town. On the night of 21 June Volunteer scouts were detailed to keep Castle Bernard and the surrounding grounds under close observation and to report the movements of any parties of military or police that were noted. A party of Volunteers under the command of Seán Hales waited at Knockbrown, about four miles from Bandon, until the early hours of the morning of 22 June and then proceeded to within a mile of Castle Bernard where they were informed by one of the scouts on duty during the night that, though no British forces had been seen entering the Castle or its grounds, it was not certain that there were no military or police actually in the Castle.

Seán Hales decided that he would lead his party of nine men right up to the building, enter it by force if necessary and capture the Earl even if he had to fight his way in and out. The party then approached the Castle from Old Chapel side in extended formation and just as dawn was breaking they moved up to the Castle building proper. Six of the party took up positions covering the windows of the back and front and three approached the main door. They knocked but received no response. Next, an effort was made to gain a forcible entry by bursting the door lock with a sledge-hammer, but this was not effective. Denis Lordan at the rear of the building moved up to the conservatory and finding the door open, entered, walked through the conservatory into another compartment leading towards the front door whence he coud hear the noise of the blows of the sledge. Passing through a few rooms he came to the main hallway and shouted to his comrades that he would open the door for them, which he did. Leaving four men posted outside of the Castle, Hales and the remainder of his men began to search the rooms for the occupants but failed to find anybody. At this Hales remarked, 'As the bird has flown we will burn the nest.' No preparations had been made to burn the Castle, so the men simply piled up some furniture in a few of the rooms, threw the curtains torn from the windows on top of the piles and set the curtains alight.

While these measures were being taken two of the party found their way into another wing of the Castle and there located Lord Bandon and members of his household staff. By this time the fire was beginning to take a grip of the building, so the Earl and his household were quickly removed outside. Leaving the male and female members of the staff in safety in one of the out-houses, the Volunteers marched off with the Earl of Bandon as their hostage. As Bandon military barracks was only about half a mile away as the crow flies it was necessary for the Volunteers to get away from the vicinity of Castle Bernard with all possible speed : the fire in the Castle would soon attract the attention of the military and bring them to the scene without delay. Hence the Volunteers moved south from Bandon in great haste and placed their hostage in security in the early hours of the morning.

Next morning General Strickland, the British O/C in Cork, received a message informing him that we were holding Lord Bandon and several other pro-British officials as hostages, and that they would be executed unless the lives of Bill Daly and other captured Volunteers were spared. The British authorities yielded, and not merely was Daly saved, but an end was put to the enemy policy of executing prisoners of war, at least so far as the active areas of Munster were concerned.[5]

5. It is significant that on the same day, Lord Bandon's Deputy Lieutenant, R. Bence Jones, Lisselane, Clonakilty—who escaped capture by being absent from home—had an interview with General Strickland. A few hours afterwards Denis Bowdren, the solicitor engaged in the defence of Bill Daly and other captured Volunteers, was called to Victoria barracks in Cork, and informed that the carrying out of the death sentence on Bill Daly and other Volunteers condemned to death had been postponed.

CHAPTER 29

A NARROW ESCAPE

The enemy's final big round-up in West Cork began towards the middle of June, and centred on the area around Ardfield on the western side of Clonakilty Bay. Commencing at dawn on 15 June, strong contingents of the Essex Regiment swept southwards in extended formation from Clonakilty military barracks. The line of troops stretched for a mile and a half, and advanced with the obvious intention of isolating the Ardfield district and of fine-combing it as they drove towards the cliffs and the sea in the vicinity of Dunnycove Bay.

Three prominent Volunteers of the Clonakilty Battalion were in the Ardfield district at the time, namely, Jim 'Spud' Murphy, Captain of the Clonakilty Company, and Tom, and Jim Lane. Murphy was still recuperating from a wound in the thigh which he sustained in an engagement with the Black and Tans at Clonakilty early in the preceding month. The three men were fortunately given some warning of the net which was being cast to entrap them before it was too late, and they were able to think of some means of escape. To break through the line of advancing troops was out of the question. On the other hand, failure to break through meant being forced eastwards towards the cliffs and the sea.

Conscious of the contracting line of military moving towards him 'Spud' Murphy led the way in the direction of the cliffs making use of every available cover. Before he and his companions reached the sea they observed a destroyer anchored in the bay about four hundred yards off Dunnycove Point. This meant that there was no possibility of escape by sea. Murphy, however, knew every foot of the neighbouring coastline and encouraged his companions with the thought that if they could climb down the cliff face they had at least a slight chance of being able to outwit the enemy. The venture would have been difficult and hazardous at the best of times : with a wounded companion it was so dangerous as to be justified only by desperate circumstances. The three men knew there was no alternative and they decided to take the chance. There followed many anxious moments as they helped each other down the cliff face, but they made the descent without mishap and came to a concealed cave accessible only to the initiated. When the three men reached this spot the tide was still ebbing, but as the evening advanced the water rose rapidly and reached a height of four feet by the time the darkness of night made it safe for the fugitives to leave their sanctuary. When they emerged the troops had disappeared.

During the following three days Jim 'Spud' Murphy and Jim Lane remained in the Ardfield district On Saturday evening, 18 June, the two men moved on to Lissavaird where they stayed the night, and on the following day, when they learned that Ross-carbery was clear of the enemy, they decided to pay a visit there. They covered the six miles' journey on horseback and reached their destination at 8.30 in the evening. Not unnaturally, on their arrival they called first to Cathy O'Regan's licensed premises. In the bar, when they entered, they found a solitary customer, a local man employed by a prominent loyalist landowner. He invited the visitors to a drink, paid for it, and immediately afterwards took his departure.

Miss O'Regan chatted with the men while they were having their drink and invited them to an evening meal .She also told them that the Auxiliaries had been in the town on the previous evening, but had not arrested anyone. Before going to the kitchen to prepare the meal she went first to close the shop door, and glancing down the street saw to her horror that the Auxiliaries had returned again. A convoy of eleven tenders had halted at the end of the street. Already some of the Auxiliaries had dismounted and were coming straight towards her shop. Here is how Jim 'Spud' Murphy described what followed :

Hastily closing the door, Miss O'Regan warned us of the danger. Thereupon we rushed through the kitchen into a large yard at the back. As we did so we could hear the rifle butts pounding on the front door. Racing through the yard we reached a door in the wall at the far end leading into a lane which ran parallel to the street at the back of the houses. But as we did so we heard the voices of Auxiliaries in the laneway and then realised that we were completely sur-rounded. At this we climbed a wall separating Miss O'Regan's yard from the next house and made our way across the roof of a shed into another yard which, though we did not know it at the time, was the property of two elderly spinsters also named O'Regan. Reconnoitring this yard, we found a large outhouse at one end with a fixed ladder leading to a loft, and we decided we had no option but to make of it a temporary hiding-place for the night. It was almost dark by this and we felt we were fairly safe for the time being. The Auxiliaries could still be heard shouting in the street and speaking to each other in the laneway. So we spent the night with our backs to the wall of the loft facing the doorway and wondering what the dawn would bring us.

About 7.30 on the following morning we heard someone quietly mounting the ladder leading to our loft. Jim Lane released the safety catch on his rifle and pointed the muzzle towards the door. I sat rigidly beside him with my two revolvers directed to the same target. Slowly the door opened and one of the Misses O'Regan appeared. She had no idea we were there, and she had come to collect some old clothes from the loft. Recovering quickly from her surprise, she turned to leave saying that she would be back in a minute. When she returned she brought a bottle of whiskey and two tumblers—a sight that in other circumstances would have brought joy to our hearts. 'We are in a tight corner, Jim,' I said to my companion, 'we will need all our wits about us to get out of this alive, so be careful!' We took a stiff peg each and handing the bottles back to Miss O'Regan warned her not to return unless there was any fresh news, and even then to give us some signal to indicate that she was coming. With a humorous twinkle in her eye she said that when she came she would call the chickens and that this would be a sign to us.

'The long hours of the day dragged on. At about 2.30 in the afternoon we heard a loud, 'Chuck-chuck, chuck, chuck!' and knew that Miss O'Regan was returning. She told us that the Auxiliaries were still in possession of the town and surrounding it. Searching, she said, had continued all day, and her own house had been ransacked twice. She felt that after these two searches the Auxiliaries were not likely to come again. With typical courage she now invited us to come into her house and rest. So we followed her across the yard and upstairs to a room from the window of which we could command a view of the square. From this vantage point we could see that the Auxiliaries had lined up all the men of the town, and also a number of farmers who were rounded up when returning from the creamery. They were all being roughly searched and interrogated. In spite of our extreme tension and imminent danger of being captured, we lay down on the bed and fell asleep immediately. Our slumber was very soon disturbed and we woke to find Miss O'Regan shaking us and telling us that the house searching had begun again, and that the Auxiliaries would probably be knocking at her door in a matter of minutes. She had, however, one bit of welcome news : the sentry who had been on duty at the back of her house was no longer there : he had probably gone away for a meal. We decided to make an attempt to escape from the back of the house.

I asked Miss O'Regan to open the door in the back wall of her yard leading out into the lane. I also told her to open the gate at the other side of the lane leading into a potato garden. She hurried away to do so while we moved quickly across the yard. Casting a quick look up and down the lane we darted across and into the garden closing the gate as we did so.

The potato garden into which Jim Lane and I entered was typical of those in West Cork. Rich green stalks in ridges rose to a height of two and a half feet with a deep furrow between the ridges. So luxuriant were the stalks that in spreading they made a bower over the furrow or trench. Slipping into one of these little bowers in the middle of the garden we lay flat and were completely concealed from view. Lying there we could still hear the Auxiliaries talking loudly in the street beyond the adjacent houses. To the west of the town there rose a steep hill called Ardagh and on its slopes we could see a party of Auxiliaries taking up positions overlooking the town. It was all too evident that they were convinced that their quarry was somewhere in hiding, and they were determined to capture it.

It was a glorious afternoon and to lie in the cool shelter of the potato stalks was a welcome change from the confined space of the loft. But we had not been long enjoying the pleasant setting in which we found ourselves when four Auxiliaries who had completed the third ransacking of the Misses O'Regan's house came out to the lane and entered the potato garden where we were hidden. They had a general look round and then walked along the headland. Finding nothing suspicious they relaxed, and one of them became very interested in the clusters of wild flowers that were growing in profusion on the garden wall. He picked a bunch of these beautiful wild flowers while one of his comrades came and stood at the end of the furrow in which we were hiding. Idly he glanced along the ridge and stooped to pluck a few blossoms from a stalk. Little did he know how close he was to death at that moment. Jim Lane, an ex-Munster Fusilier, had him covered with his rifle and at the first suggestion of his discovering our position would have dropped him cold at thirty yards range. Instead the man turned away and joined his comrades as they were leaving the garden.

Later still that evening a Christian Brother, who was a brother of Kathy O'Regan, the owner of the garden, entered and glanced curiously around. I gave a low whistle and attracted his attention to the furrow in which we were lying. He was very surprised to see us as he had thought that we had already escaped from the town. The good Brother gave us two bars of chocolate which he had in his pocket and offered to bring us out some food and drink. Tempting though the offer was, I declined it considering the risk too great. I told the Brother that in view of the grave danger it would be best if he did not return to the garden : the possibility of his attracting attention to our presence there was too great. Before leaving the Brother warned us that the town was still surrounded and that there was little hope of escape yet.

As night fell Lane and I arranged to sleep in turn while the other kept watch. Tuesday dawned bright and clear and the day passed without incident. Nobody entered the garden. We spoke in whispers and agreed that for the moment anyway we were safe in the garden and that it was still too risky to leave it. Tuesday night came and we were bothered by thirst to such a degree that sleep did not come easily. To while away the time Lane, in reminiscent mood, spoke in whispers of his experiences in France during World War One and of the long nights he spent looking out over no man's land. On just another moonlit night as ours he was on sentry duty at La Basse, and what struck him then was the loneliness and utter desolation all around. He spoke, too, of the Battle of the Marne and of the holocaust, the useless holocaust, at the Somme. The conversation not unnaturally turned to the present campaign, of the men who were soldiering in the war and the hopes they had of success. Though I had not a soldier's professional experience to draw from, I had, nevertheless, given some service to the Brigade Column from its inception. I spoke of the Kilmichael ambush and of the victory won there by unseasoned and inexperienced and hastily-trained soldiers. I also referred to the attack on Burgatia House and of the sortie which caused a diversion that enabled the Column to withdraw.

Tuesday night passed and another dawn brought its hopes and fears. On Ardagh Hill we could still see the Auxiliaries in position and concluded that the town was still surrounded. Through that warm June day we suffered much from thirst and welcomed the cool evening breeze that blew in from the Atlantic at sundown. In weighing up our prospects on Wednesday night we felt that another twenty-four hours would be the most we could endure and that we must make an attempt to escape on Thursday night no matter what the risk. We had an intimate knowledge of the country round about and had little difficulty mapping out an escape route. Our big problem was to break through the cordon of the enemy.

The prospect of action buoyed us up during Wednesday night and we looked forward to the warm welcome we knew we would get in the house to which we planned to call on our route to freedom. What we did not know at the time was that the 'bush telegraph' had been busy for the previous few days. Our narrow escape was the talk of every house in the locality. With no definite news of our whereabouts being available, many and strange stories about our escapades began to circulate. While everyone hoped we had eluded the enemy, the ring of Auxiliaries was felt to bode no good and it was feared that we might still be captured.

Thursday night came at last and we were quite exhausted. The heat of the day together with the pangs of hunger and thirst convinced us that there was nothing for us now but an attempt to break through the enemy cordon at all costs. Impatiently we waited for a waning moon and at 3.00 a.m. we crossed the wall of Kathy O'Regan's garden into the adjoining property. Leaving the shelter of the walled potato garden for what proved to be an open field brought the first test. Crouching in the shelter of a ditch we moved cautiously towards the main road between Fred Calnan's and the bridge at the Clonakilty end of the causeway. We paused here for five minutes; then scanning the road from the shelter of the ditch and finding it clear we quickly crossed the road, and finding the tide out dropped on to the sloblands. Moving quickly but with due care we regained solid ground again at

Rosscarbery Pier, and at that point, for the first time in four days, felt that our chances had improved. We walked through the fields in a direct line for Downeen and Milcove, a mile south-west of Rosscarbery. Daylight was slowly breaking in the east as I spotted a light in a cottage window. In response to my knock the door was opened by Sadler Hayes who was himself avoiding Rosscarbery because of the occupation of the town by the enemy.

The owner of the cottage, a namesake of Sadler, gave us a warm welcome, but we were anxious to move on, and asked whether there was any chance of securing a boat in the neighbourhood. At this Hayes said that he had a boat down at the cove and that he would gladly take us across Rosscarbery Bay in it to a district where we knew we would be safe and given a good welcome. The four of us went straight to the boat and rowed the two miles' stretch of water across the bay and landed at Fisher's Cove inside Galley Head. Bidding a grateful farewell to the boatmen, Jim Lane and I headed straight for Jerry 'Rounds' O'Donovan's from whose house we had started on our perilous journey on the previous Sunday. It was now 5.00 a.m., and as we cheerfully banged on the door an upstairs window was raised, and to an indignant 'Who's there?' we replied ' "Spud" and Jim Lane.' In a few seconds Jerry came down and opened the door. He was very glad to see us as he had been fearing the worst and thought it unlikely that he would ever see us alive again. He lost no time in celebrating what he called our 'resurrection'. He produced a bottle of brandy and two glasses, and bade us make a start with that while he set about preparing a meal for us. As the man was still in his nightshirt, I jokingly suggested that he should get decently dressed before serving the breakfast.

The stimulant and a good meal did much to restore our spirits, and forgetting all about rest and sleep, we took to the road and made for Lar O'Leary's which was three miles away. Lar was a farmer living with two sisters, and he was driving the cows in for milking when we walked into his yard. It was 8.00 a.m. and his sisters were still resting, but Lar was able for the occasion. As in the case of 'Rounds' his delight at seeing us knew no bounds. Though he had not the facilities for celebrating that we had already experienced at Fisher's Cove, Lar led his visitors into the kitchen and called out loudly,

'Mag and Nell, "Spud" and Jim Lane are back here alive and well. Get up quickly and, Mag, bring me down a pound till I stand them a drink.' Quickly the two sisters dressed and came to add their welcome to Lar's. Mag handed over the pound, and the three set out for Coughlan's Bar at the Chapel Cross, Ardfield. Proudly Lar led the two of us into the premises and planking the pound note down on the counter he said, 'Miss Coughlan, give "Spud" and Jim a gallon of porter!' We spent a pleasant and relaxing hour in Coughlan's and then at Lar's pressing invitation all three of us continued to Joe O'Mahoney's pub half a mile down the road. Here the balance of Mag's pound was spent in a further celebration. It was a very happy morning but in the end exhaustion from exposure and lack of sleep prevailed. Leaving Lar we walked another mile and a half to William Whelton's of Dunowen and went to bed. We slept undisturbed from Thursday afternoon until Saturday morning when we were called to join the Column at Ahiohill, ten miles away.

While we hurriedly took breakfast that Saturday morning, our host prepared the horse and trap that was to drive us to our destination. When, however, we arrived at Ahiohill we found that the Column had already moved off, but we followed and caught up with it at O'Hara's of Kilmeen Cross. Even there, nine miles north east of Rosscarbery, the story of our disappearance on the previous Sunday night had been the chief topic of conversation all the week, and our reappearance that Saturday afternoon was the cause of all-round rejoicing. Tom Barry's welcome was in the best military tradition. Referring to the horse which he had lent me earlier and which I had lost at Rosscarbery, he greeted me and immediately added, ' "Spud", where is my horse?' But he never again referred to the loss of his gallant steed.

On Saturday night the Column moved on to attack, if possible, the Auxiliaries in Rosscarbery. Positions were taken up on the Dunmanway road outside the town. After the usual precautionary reconnoitring by scouts, two sections of the Column under the command of Tom Barry and 'Spud' Murphy entered the town. Seeing a number of Auxiliaries standing beside a Lancia tender they opened fire, and from the shelter of the tender the fire was returned. This firing was of short duration. It was evident that the enemy had no desire to engage in a night action, and they refused to be drawn from the shelter of their billets. Later in the night the Auxiliaries withdrew, taking with them two horses, one of which had been lent by Tom Barry to 'Spud' Murphy. As a result this horse was given the name 'Spud' and it was frequently to be seen on the road in Dunmanway until the end of hostilities. Seeing that no good purpose was being served by remaining in the area, the Column withdrew to the Glounbrack district, seven miles north of Rosscarbery where it was demobilised. This was the last encounter of the Column with the enemy.

* * * * * *

While the events narrated above were taking place, I came from Kealkil to Rossmore. Tom Barry joined me there and then we attended a Bandon Battalion Council meeting at White's of Rathrout, Ballinadee, on 29 June. After this we set off for a Clonakilty Battalion meeting. Jim O'Mahony, Vice-Commandant of the Bandon Battalion, accompanied us and also Jerh McCarthy. Once the Column had been demobilised both Jim and Jerh felt themselves at a loose end and were glad to come with us, while we were happy to have their company in such a dangerous area. They were both loyal comrades and great soldiers in any emergency. Our destination was Rossmore, seventeen miles distant, and we took the journey in our stride that bright June evening. The next day we discovered that the meeting had been convened in the Reenascreena district which was a further seven miles from Rossmore, but as we were feeling very fit the extra distance did not worry us.

When we crossed Baldwin's Bridge and approached Currivreeda —to bypass Bandon—a thoughtless remark of mine to Barry sparked off a night's adventure. As we left Currivreeds for Clancoole I jokingly remarked, 'Tough on you, Tom, to be so near Bandon and yet so far from it!' He stopped dead and facing me replied, 'Why shouldn't we go in now that we are so near and have a go at the curfew patrol?' That landed the ball back in my court and though the challenge was indeed a rash one, I accepted it, and we immediately changed direction.

Entering the town through Glueyard Lane and Warner's Lane, we arrived unnoticed at the Little Bridge at 8.40 p.m.—twenty minutes before curfew. We took our stand on the south, or post office, side of the bridge. Directly opposite us on the other side four men were to be seen having an evening chat. I recognised two of them as old G.A.A. friends and we exchanged a friendly greeting. Then they wisely moved away. Two of them had shops nearby and quickly put up the shutters and closed the doors. At this critical period the people of Bandon knew only too well that any visit by Volunteers boded ill for the peace of the town, so that the action of the two traders was quite natural in the circumstances.

As nine o'clock rang out we prepared for action, but there was absolutely no movement to be seen anywhere. Looking down the length of Shannon Street we could see the railway bridge on our right and the main bridge across Bandon river directly in front. It was across the latter bridge that we expected the curfew patrol to pass at any moment. Our hope was that the patrol would not be preceded by an armoured car as frequently happened. If a car accompanied the patrol our chances of survival would have been very slight; for the only way of retreat open to us was the way we had come, by Warner's Lane, and this offered no cover whatever.

We remained where we were until 9.30 p.m. and when the enemy did not appear our enthusiasm waned and we decided to leave the town and resume our trek to Rossmore. Halting at O'Leary's of Clancoole we had a welcome tea, and then set out with renewed vigour to cover the remaining thirteen miles to our destination. In retrospect our venture into Bandon seems foolhardy, but it was not without its moral value, for our visit became the talk of the town next day : the fact that four armed Volunteers, two of them well known to the townspeople, could dare enter Bandon would soon be known to the enemy and its significance would not be lost on him.

CHAPTER 30

THE NAVAL OPERATION AT FASTNET ROCK

Ever since the time we first found ourselves in a position to come to close quarters with the enemy, we quickly realised that one of the most effective means of coping with enemy mechanical transport was the road mine. For the manufacture of such mines explosives were the first necessity, and from an early date in the war we were fortunate in being able to capture twenty-five hundredweight of explosive material in the form of gun-cotton from the Royal Engineers on Bere Island. Now in June 1921 the prospect of acquiring more gun-cotton presented itself when certain enterprising Volunteers in the Schull Battalion area happened to turn their gaze to Fastnet Rock. Intelligence reports confirmed the fact that for security reasons the British had stored large surplus quantities of explosive material in the lighthouse rather than in any of the mainland bases.

The idea of a raid was first proposed by Ricky Collins, Captain of the Goleen Company, who had been employed as lighthouse keeper on Fastnet Rock for six years, i.e. between 1912 and 1918. No one could have been more competent to lead an expedition of the kind contemplated, but, unfortunately, Ricky was captured in a raid by the Auxiliaries before his suggestion could be put into effect. However, John O'Regan of Schull then came forward and offered his services for the proposed expedition.

The Fastnet Lighthouse is ten miles from the mainland and about three miles south-west of the nearest land at Cape Clear Island. No serious resistance would be expected on the lighthouse itself, but many serious dangers had to be faced before there could be question of reaching the rock at all. There were forty-seven armed British Marines in the Coastguard Station at Schull and a British naval vessel kept a nightly patrol on the coast between Castletownsend Bay and Bantry Bay. The weather was another danger. Even in the finest weather Fastnet Rock is notorious for its heavy swells. Finally, shore arrangements would have to be perfected for the safe disposal of the gun-cotton in the event of its being captured and successfully landed.

To make an unobserved landing in the darkness of the night from a heaving boat on Fastnet Rock called for a man of iron nerves, local knowledge and good seamanship. In John O'Regan, the Battalion Commander had the man required for the mission.

As a boy and as a young man O'Regan had lived on the sea, knew all its most fickle moods and had an unrivalled knowledge of the coast and every one of 'Carbery's Hundred Isles'. He was quite well acquainted with Fastnet but hitherto had always landed there in daylight.

Seán Lehane, Commandant of the Schull Battalion, was the man responsible for the projected raid on Fastnet Lighthouse. When all the plans were completed, he decided that the attempt would be made on the night of 28 June. John O'Regan was given the task of piloting the boat and of being the first to make the dangerous jump from the heaving deck to the slippery wave-washed rock. In fact, the success of the expedition depended largely on his seamanship and cool, calculating daring.

The evening of 28 June saw John O'Regan, with Alex McFarlane as companion, piloting the motor-boat, *Golden Port,* owned by William Cadogan, out of Schull Harbour on the first stage of the adventure. At Gun Point on Long Island Sound, Michael O'Donovan, Captain of the Leamcon Company, had been mobilised with the other Volunteers who were to form the raiding party. Among these were Seán Lehane, Seán O'Driscoll, Charles Cotter, Jim Hayes, and Thomas J. Hickey. When all were aboard the boat left Long Island Channel at dusk and headed out for the open sea.

Very soon John O'Regan was convinced that the state of the swell which was running that night was such that the party had not sufficient experienced seamen on board to make a successful landing on the dangerous Fastnet Rock. Accordingly it was decided to land on Cape Clear. There Seán Lehane announced that the raid would be postponed until the following night. So leaving the others on the island, John O'Regan and McFarland brought the *Golden Port* back to Schull in order to avoid any suspicion being aroused by the absence of the vessel.

O'Regan was anxious to make his presence seen in Schull. With this in view he made a point of delaying after the Holyday Mass to chat with some friends in the congregation that collected outside the chapel door. That same evening O'Regan went to Gun Point on Long Island Sound, and picked up Tim Murphy of Colla, Michael Murphy of Gun Point, William Daly of Lowertown, and the Company Captain, Michael O'Donovan. Then in the motor-boat, *Irene,* owned by O'Regan, they sailed to Cape Clear. The boat was then returned to Long Island Sound by Michael O'Donovan and Tim Murphy. Meanwhile, Lehane had obtained the twenty-four foot Cape Clear fishing boat *Máire Cáit* from the owner, Thade O'Regan, whose son had by this time joined the party. This brought the raiding party to twelve. It included four Cape Clear fishermen, Dan Leonard, Dan O'Driscoll, Dan Daly, and John O'Regan.

The June sun was going down in a ball of fire on the western horizon as Dan Leonard steered the *Máire Cáit* out of North Harbour, swung her first north-west and then west into the dying sunset. As dusk deepened into darkness, the British destroyer that patrolled the coast from the Old Head of Kinsale to Bantry Bay appeared on the skyline and the intermittent sweep of her searchlights could be seen searching the sea and the coast. Veering off to keep out of the range of the probing beam, the *Máire Cáit* waited in silence and watched the destroyer circling Fastnet Rock and making for Mizen Head on her way to Bantry Bay. The raiding party knew that they would have two or three hours in which to accomplish their mission—if no alarm was raised—and without further delay they now headed straight for their objective.

Shortly after midnight the boat approached Fastnet Rock. The sea had become choppy under a rising wind which caused the waters of the swell around the rock to rise and fall as much as six to eight feet. There was no landing pier. Instead there was a large rock in which was fixed an iron ring. The boat moved slowly in and dropped anchor. Poised on the prow of the heaving boat, John O'Regan with a tope tied around his waist balanced himself like an acrobat to the rise and fall of the boat, timing himself for the right moment to make the hazardous jump from the vessel to the slippery rock. In broad daylight this would have been a matter of grave risk, but in the darkness of the night it was so dangerous that only a very brave man would attempt it. All lights had to be extinguished before the boat came near the rock, and it would have been fatal to light them now. O'Regan could not even see the iron ring and had to remember from his previous knowledge just exactly where it was in order that when he jumped he could grasp it.

At a given moment O'Regan jumped. His companions could not see whether he had made it or not as a wave of spray swept over the rock at the time O'Regan made his leap. It did not seem humanly possible that the man could avoid being swept into the sea, but as the boat sank his companions saw him with his hands gripped round the ring. In a moment the boat was made fast. Waiting only to kick off his heavy sea boots and to observe that the others were landing, O'Regan made for the two-ton steel door of the lighthouse. Fortunately, it was not locked. He opened it, entered, and raced up the spiral stairway leading to the room where the lightkeeper was on duty. The lightkeeper put up no resistance and all danger of the alarm being raised was removed. As a precautionary measure the wireless set was dismantled. Then began the all-important work of loading the boxes of gun-cotton into the boat below.

The lightkeepers were allowed retain sufficient gun-cotton to cope with about forty-eight hours of continuous fog. After such a period of fog the supplies of the lighthouse would automatically be replenished, and then the deficiency in the supply of gun-cotton would be made up. Seventeen boxes of gun-cotton and three boxes of detonators and primers weighting over half a ton were now loaded on to the *Máire Cáit* by means of the lighthouse derrick. Within an hour the boat was out at sea again and heading for Gun Point in Long Island Sound. As she neared the coast the searchlights of the destroyer could be seen far astern as she rounded Mizen Head on her return patrol, but she was too far away to pick up the *Máire Cáit*.

At Long Island Sound Mick O'Donovan and the men of the Leamcon Company were waiting to begin unloading the spoils. As soon as the boat came ashore the boxes were landed and the whole consignment was safely dumped under a large heap of sea-weed in O'Donovan's field near the beach. It was so well camou-flaged that it escaped detection in the raid that was carried out by the British military on the following day.

The first streaks of dawn were appearing in the east as the *Máire Cáit* set out on her homeward journey to Cape Clear Island carry-ing on board the four fishermen who had done so much to make a success of the Fastnet raid. They would begin another day with their boats and their nets on the sea as though nothing had happened to break the routine of their simple lives. On the main-land, too, Seán Lehane and his men would disperse and return to their various occupations. They rose manfully to the demands that were made on them and gave of their best in achieving the objec-tives placed before them, but of recognition and appreciation for their heroic services they thought nothing. Such were the men of the Schull Battalion to whose memory I should like to pay tribute here in affection and gratitude.

CHAPTER 31

THE TRUCE

The end came abruptly and indeed unexpectedly. On 9 July I attended an important meeting of the ·Dunmanway Battalion Council at the house of the local school-teacher, John McCarthy, in Togher. We were in the process of making sweeping changes in the command of the Dunmanway Battalion, and had arranged to have Seán Lehane, the well-established leader of the Schull Battalion, transferred and made Commandant of the vitally important Dunmanway area, when we were suddenly interrupted. John McCarthy hurriedly rushed in to us with a copy of *The Cork Examiner* of that day announcing the cessation of hostilities and stating that a truce would come into effect on the following Monday, 11 July.

We received the news in silence. It was a dazed silence in which we mentally digested the unexpected information. No trace of emotion, not the slightest sign of enthusiasm, betrayed themselves in the reaction of my colleagues. The announcement might as well have been a routine matter of fact, an ordinary report in the regular daily and even hourly flow of communications that by this time had become part of our lives.

Had I been ásked my opinion beforehand, I should have opposed a cessation of hostilities at this time, unless a clear and definite assurance of a satisfactory outcome were part of the arrangement. It seemed to me that our struggle had brought us to a position of strength which warranted high expectations so far as conditions of peace were concerned. I had personal experience of the efficiency of the military machine we had built up in West Cork, and I was aware that the progress and achievement of the other two Cork Brigades were in no way inferior to our own.

I was acquainted also with the Kerry Brigades, and knew about the spectacular development made particularly by the First and Second Brigades during the previous six months. The leaders were well known to me—the strong-willed Paddy Cahill, Tadhg Brosnan, and Austin Stack, who were to Kerry what Tomás MacCurtain and Terence MacSwiney were to Cork; the fighting pioneers, Tom McEllistrim and Jack Cronin of Ballymacelligott; and the young intrepid officers, Humphrey Murphy and John Joe Rice. Equally with young Kerrymen I was inspired by the example of those three great Kerry leaders who had fallen in the fray, The O'Rahilly of

Ballylongford, Tom Ashe of Kinnaird, and Dan Allman of Rockfield.

I knew something, too, of County Limerick and the deeds of the East Limerick fighters under Donnchadh Ó hAnnagáin, men such as Tom Malone, the Crowleys and the Clancys, as well as the example set by Con Colbet and Ned Daly in 1916 and continued by the two Brigade O/Cs of West and East Limerick who had died in action during the struggle, namely, Seán Finn and Seán Wall. South Tipperary, indeed Tipperary as a whole, was standing up manfully to relentless enemy pressure despite the loss of the great Seán Treacy. Again, Waterford inspired confidence, particularly in view of the fairly recent fights at The Burgery and Tramore, while the three Clare Brigades had been exemplary ever since 1916. Indeed, relatively more families in Clare than in any other county were in the thick of the struggle, and if I name two, the Brennans and the Barretts, it is because they were the main leaders there from the beginning.

Dublin, though further away, was in a sense closer to me because of what I had learned about it in the course of my four visits to G.H.Q. between October 1919 and Easter 1921. I had considerable dealings with Cathal Brugha, Dick Mulcahy, and Mick Collins in connexion with matters of policy affecting the country generally and West Cork in particular. My visits to Dublin enabled me to meet, and to form an opinion about, officers from the different Brigades throughout the country, and particularly the many heroic men of the Dublin Brigade who held the streets of the capital agaist all the odds. To name all of them would be impossible, but the personalities that stand out in memory, apart from the three already mentioned, were the great McKee, Peadar Clancy, Oscar Trayor, Liam Tobin, Frank Thornton, Tom Cullen, Jimmy Slattery, and Pat McCrea. My opinion of these men was very high. I knew they had to bear the continuous strain of fighting in the city. And they had no mountains or rocks like those of Coolenagow to fall back on as we had and get some rest. Their daily lives were a nightmare and yet they soldiered on unflinchingly.

Besides my personal contact with a number of the leaders of Brigades, particularly those of Munster, I had a lively interest in the development of the Volunteer organisation throughout the country as a whole. With my comrades of West Cork I followed the progress made in the different counties and was enthusiastic about the successes achieved at Ballytrain in Monaghan, Camlough in Armagh, Lisburn in Antrim, Trim in Meath, Clonfin and Ballinalee in Longford, Hugginstown in Kilkenny, the daring rescue operation in Sligo, Four Roads and Scramogue in Roscommon, and the many successful fights, such as those of Touranmakeady, Kilmeena, Carrowkennedy, and Ballyvary in Mayo.

Briefly, my knowledge of the internal organisation of the Volunteers throughout the country, of the efficiency of the movement as a guerilla army, and its mounting achievements in face of the ruthless British murder machine, the fact that it had succeeded in making it impossible for the British Government to rule in what was practically seven-eighths of Ireland's territory—all these considerations led me to be optimistic as to its capability of exacting from the enemy, in the end, the terms of peace on which we had set our hearts, namely, the complete independence of Ireland in its totality, and the establishment of an Irish Republic.

But neither my comrades nor I were under any illusion as to the attitude of the British Government towards our aspirations at the time of the Truce. Whatever advances it may have been prepared to make on the Home Rule policy of pre-1916 days, there was as yet no question of its contemplating separation of our country from the Crown. In other words, the gap between the terms of peace we sought were so far removed from the terms the British Government was prepared to accept that we saw no immediate prospect of a peace settlement. In consequence, we viewed the Truce as a mere breathing space, a stage on the journey towards our goal.

When I had time to reflect further on the Truce, and its significance came home to me, I experienced very mixed feelings about it. I would not have been human if I did not welcome it as a respite after the incessant strain of the war, and particularly of the period of almost two years during which I was 'on the run'. To be able to move about freely again without fear of sudden arrest or capture and of the tortures I knew to be the inevitable fate of Volunteer leaders falling prisoner to some of the British units seemed like a luxury. But the duration of the Truce appeared likely to be short, a fortnight perhaps, four weeks at most, and then we would have to face a resumption of war conditions. Would we then be able for it? I could foresee that an instant change would occur in the way of life of our fighting men from the moment the Truce came into effect. From being hunted by a relentless foe and being forced to endure the nerve-racking hardships of guerilla warfare with its long marches and spartan conditions, the Volunteers would suddenly find themselves feted as heroes by town and country alike. Instead of the frugal fare of the camp, they would enjoy the plenty provided by a grateful people, particularly in the towns. Nothing would be good enough for the brave soldiers who had forced the enemy to call a halt, and had put an end at least for the time being, to the day and night shooting, to the continual raiding and searching, and to the general acts of terrorism that had been a constant nightmare for the people in all areas since the previous July, and indeed in some areas even long before that.

The effect of the relaxation which the Truce would bring was bound to threaten discipline. While the struggle continued we had been able to maintain a reasonably high standard of control all round, and this was to the great credit of the Battalion and Company commanders. But once the pressure of the war was removed, even for a short while, discipline could easily break down, and the difficulty of restoring it when hostilities were renewed could well be a formidable task. There appeared to me to be a real danger that the military efficiency we had built up with such effort might be very much impaired by the time the Truce ended.

Such were some of the thoughts that preoccupied me on that eventful Saturday afternoon as I left John McCarthy's of Togher and jogged along through Coosane Gap in a pony and trap with Tom Barry. We were on our way to Crowley's of Trinamaddree near Ballylickey, the last location of Brigade Headquarters. When we arrived there we found that a dispatch from the O/C of the First Southern Division was awaiting us. It instructed the two of us to proceed to Divisional Headquarters at Glantane, Lombardstown, and announced that Tom Barry had been appointed to the post of Liaison Officer to the area of Munster and Kilkenny for the Truce period, and that I was to take up a post on the recently expanded Divisional Staff.

While this order from Divisional Headquarters caused me no surprise for the reason that Liam Lynch had spoken to me about it at previous meetings, it brought both Barry and me back to reality and prevented us from being carried away from the task in hand by the startling news we had received earlier that day. I immediately set about contacting Ted O'Sullivan, Vice-Commandant of the Brigade, in Baurgorm and having found him handed over control of the Brigade. With his usual thoroughness Ted made arrangements to have a car ready to collect Barry and me at Crowley's of Trinamaddree at noon on Monday, 11 July, the day on which the Truce was to begin.

That day brought my activities with the West Cork Brigade to an end, as indeed it did for Tom Barry also. There was no ceremony to mark the occasion and there were no farewells, save a handshake and Godspeed from those good comrades of the Brigade Staff, Ted O'Sullivan, Gibbs Ross, Tadhg O'Sullivan, Seán Buckley, and the unforgettable piper of Crossbarry, Flor Begley. Barry and I motored to Bandon and there saluted Mrs Fitzsimons and her sister, Miss Bannon, and also Con and Mrs O'Donoghue, all of whom had given such loyal service to the movement during the struggle. This was the first opportunity that came my way of expressing my sympathy to the last-named couple on the death of their eighteen-year-old son, Jim, who had filled the role of Assistant Brigade Adjutant in Bandon so thoroughly and satisfactorily after my forced departure from the town in 1919. From Bandon I continued on my way to Kilmacsimon Quay to visit my family. What a joy it was to see my mother and father again after months of separation, and above all to see them at a time when the menacing clouds of war had rolled away and the bright hope of peace filled the air for them. I sensed the relief they were experiencing now that hostilities had ended and they looked forward expectantly to an era of peace at last.

But for me there was sorrow mingled with joy in that visit. Of my five brothers there was but one in touch with home, Jim, who was now the youngest. Two of the others were prisoners of war in British jails, Miah in Ballykinlar and Jack in Bere Island. Ted was away from home in Skibbereen, while Pat lay in his grave in Castletown cemetery. I could not help thinking of the time less than two years earlier, before I had been forced 'on the run', when our united family shared together the simple joys of rural life in the quaint hamlet of Kilmacsimon Quay by the busy waters of the Bandon. But those days were gone and with them part of myself.

Evening advanced and it was soon time for me to leave. Bidding farewell to my parents and telling Jim to keep the boat in action at the Quay river crossing, I set off in the direction of Cork on my way to Lombardstown. As I passed through Innishannon village, memories of my boyhood crowded in on me. Here was the centre in which I had founded, and taken active part in, the Valley Rovers Hurling and Football Clubs, and it was here also, early in 1918, that I organised a Company of Volunteers and was elected its first Captain. Though this latter event had occurred but three years before, an age seemed to separate me from it now. Memories cascaded through my mind. The light was fast fading from the scene and the beautifully-wooded valley of the Bandon through which I drove was growing dim. As I passed on I felt with a pang that I had come to end of an era.

NUMERICAL STRENGTH AND STAFF OF THE THIRD CORK BRIGADE

Numerical Strength of the Companies of the Third Cork Brigade (July 1919)

First (Bandon) Battalion

Ballinadee	35
Kilbrittain	45
Timoleague	12
Barryroe	55
Clogagh	20
Bandon	12
Innishannon	22
Crosspound	30
Kilpatrick	16
Mount Pleasant (Farnivane) .	20
Newcestown	35
	302

Second (Clonakilty) Battalion

Clonakilty	25
Ardfield	22
Bealad	15
Kilmeen	20
Lyre	18
Ahiohill	25
	125

Third (Dunmanway) Battalion

Dunmanway	25
Ballinacarriga	30
Shanavagh	30
Ballineen	22
Kenneigh	30
Behagh	30
Aultagh	40
Togher	36

243

Fourth (Skibbereen) Battalion

Skibbereen	30
Castlehaven	20
Myross	16
Leap	40
Bredagh	20
Lisheen	25
	151

Fifth (Bantry) Battalion

Bantry	50
Caheragh	20
Drumsullivan	15
Kealkil	15
Coomhola	20
Glengarriff	20
	140

Sixth (Beara) Battalion

Castletownbere	24
Bere Island	40
Rossmacowen	30
Adrigole	16
Inches	40
Ardgroom	45
Ballycrovane	36
Urhan	30
	261

* * * * * *

Numerical Strength of the Battalions of the Third Cork Brigade (11 July 1921)

Bandon	1023
Clonakilty	620
Dunmanway	742
Skibbereen	728
Bantry	950
Beara	644
Schull	563

Staff Personnel of the West Cork Brigade
Brigade Staff Officers (including special services)

1919 (6 January)
Brigade Commandant, Tom Hales, Ballinadee.
Brigade Vice-Commandant, Hugh Thornton, Bandon and Dublin.
Brigade Adjutant, Michael McCarthy, Dunmanway.
Brigade Quartermaster, Denis O'Shea, Skibbereen.
Brigade Intelligence Officer, Denis O'Connell, Skibbereen.

1919 (16 August)
Brigade Commandant, Tom Hales—Captured 27/7/20.
Brigade Vice-Commandant, Seán Hayes, T.D., Caheragh.
Brigade Adjutant, Liam Deasy, Innishannon.
Brigade Quartermaster, Pat Harte, Clonakilty—Captured 27 7/20.
Brigade Intelligence Officer, Seán Buckley, Bandon.
Brigade Acting Adjutant, Flor Begley, Bandon.
Brigade Assistant Adjutant, Jim O'Donoghue, Bandon.
Brigade Engineer, Mick Crowley, Kilbrittain.

1920 (6 August)
Brigade Commandant, Charlie Hurley, Kilbrittain—killed 19/3/21.
Brigade Vice-Commandant, Ted O'Sullivan, Bantry.
Brigade Adjutant, Liam Deasy, Innishannon.
Brigade Quartermaster, Dick Barrett, Upton—Captured 22/3/21.
Brigade Intelligence Officer, Seán Buckley, Bandon.
Brigade Acting Adjutant, Flor Begley, Bandon.
Brigade Assistant Adjutant, Jim O'Donoghue, Bandon—Killed
   2/12/20.
Brigade Assistant Quartermaster, Frank Neville, Upton.
Brigade Engineer, Michael Crowley, Kilbrittain.
Brigade Communications, Con Crowley, Kilbrittain—Captured
   21/11/21.
Brigade Police Officer, Seán O'Donovan, Clonakilty—Captured
   1/1/21.

1920 (1 October)
Brigade Training Officer, Tom Barry, Bandon.

1921 (6 February)
Brigade Police Officer, Sam Kingston, Skibbereen.
Brigade Communications, Tim Warren, Ballineen.

1921 (7 April)

Brigade Commandant, Liam Deasy.
Brigade Vice-Commandant, Ted O'Sullivan.
Brigade Adjutant, Gibbs Ross, Schull.
Brigade Quartermaster, Tadhg O'Sullivan, Timoleague.
Brigade Column Commander, Tom Barry.
Brigade Intelligence Officer, Seán Buckley.
Brigade Acting Adjutant, Flor Begley.
Brigade Assistant Quartermaster, Frank Neville.
Brigade Engineer, Mick Crowley.
Brigade Medical Officer, Dr Con Lucey.
Brigade Assistant Officer, Eugene Callanan.
Brigade Police Officer, Sam Kingston.
Brigade Communications, Tim Warren.

FIRST BATTALION (BANDON)

1917

Battalion Commandant, Tom Hales, Ballinadee.
Battalion Vice-Commandant, Denis Lordan, Kilbrittain.
Battalion Adjtant, Hugh Thornton, Bandon.
Battalion Quartermaster, W. P. Walsh, Bandon.

1918

One change—Liam Deasy succeeds Hugh Thornton.

1919 (January)

Battalion Commandant, Seán Hales, Ballinadee.
Battalion Vice-Commandant, Denis Lordan.
Battalion Adjutant, Liam Deasy, Innishannon.
Battalion Quartermaster Flor Begley, Bandon.
Battalion Engineer, Pat O'Sullivan, Upton.

1919 (August

Flor Begley succeeds Liam Deasy, Tadhg O'Sullivan, Timoleague, succeeds Flor Begley.

1920 (January)

Charlie Hurley, Kilbirttain, succeeds Denis Lordan.
Jim O'Mahony, Kilbrittain, succeeds Flor Begley, promoted to Brigade Staff.
John Lordan, Newcestown, succeeds Charley Hurley.
Charley O'Donoghue, Mount Pleasant, Assistant Adjutant.

Dan Holland, Barryroe, Assistant Quartermaster.
Dick Russell, Innishannon, Communications.
Pat Deasy, Ballinadee, Signals—Killed 28/11/20.
Pat O'Sullivan, Upton, Engineer—Killed 15/2/21.
John J. O'Mahony, Kilbrittain, Police Officer—Captured 21/11/20.

1921 (April)
Battalion Commandant, Seán Hales.
Battalion Vice-Commandant, John Lordan, Newcestown.
Battalion Adjutant and Intelligence Officer, Jim O'Mahoney.
Battalion Quartermaster, Dan Holland.
Battalion Assistant Adjutant, Charley O'Donoghue.
Battalion Engineer, John O'Callaghan, Newcestown.
Battalion Communications and Signals, Dick Russell, Innishannon.
Battalion Intelligence Officer, Sonny O'Sullivan, Bandon.

SECOND BATTALION (CLONAKILTY)

1917
Battalion Commandant, Jim Walsh, Lyre.
Battalion Vice-Commandant, Joe Flynn, Clonakilty.
Battalion Adjutant, Mick Aherne, Clonakilty.
Battalion Quartermaster, Pat Harte, Clonakilty.

1919 (July)
Battalion Commandant, Seán O'Donovan, Clonakilty.
Battalion Vice-Commandant, Dan Harte, Clonakilty.
Battalion Adjutant, Batt Murphy, Shannonvale.
Battalion Quartermaster, Stephen O'Neill, Clonakilty.
Battalion Engineer, John 'Flyer' Nyhan, Clonakilty.

1919 (September)
Dan Harte succeeds Seán O'Donovan.

1921 (January)
Battalion Commandant, Jim Hurley, Clonakilty.
Battalion Vice-Commandant, Tim O'Donoghue, Rossmore.
Battalion Adjutant, Batt Murphy, Shannonvale.
Battalion Quartermaster, Paddy O'Keeffe, Clonakilty.
Battalion Column Leader, Jim 'spud' Murphy, Clonakilty.
Battalion Communications, Sonny Hurley, Kilkernmore.

Third Battalion (Dunmanway)

1917

Battalion Commndant, Con Ahern, Dunmanway.
Battalion Vice-Commandant, Michael McCarthy, Dunmanway.
Battalion Adjutant, Paddy O'Brien, Ballinacarriga.
Battalion Quartermaster, Liam O'Driscoll, Shanavagh.

1919 (April)

Battalion Commandant, Seán Murphy, Aultagh.
Battalion Vice-Commandant, Liam O'Driscoll.
Battalion Adjutant, Paddy O'Brien.
Battalion Quartermaster, Mick O'Dwyer, Enniskean.

1919 (August)

Battalion Commandant, Paddy O'Brien.
Battalion Vice-Commandant, Michael McCarthy.
Battalion Adjutant, Paddy O'Brien.
Battalion Quartermaster, Mick O'Dwyer.

1919 (November)

Battalion Commandant, Seán Murphy.
Battalion Vice-Commandant, Michael McCarthy—Killed 28/11/20.
Battalion Adjutant, Paddy O'Brien.
Battalion Quartermaster, Mick O'Dwyer.

1921 (January)

Sonny Dave Crowley, Kenneigh, succeeds McCarthy.

1921 (9 July)

Battalion Commandant, Seán Lehane, Schull.
Battalion Vice-Commandant, Sonny Dave Crowley.
Battalion Adjutant, Paddy O'Brien.
Battalion Quartermaster, Seán Murphy.

Fourth Battalion (Skibbereen)

1917

Battalion Commandant, J. B. O'Driscoll, Castlehaven.
Battalion Adjutant, Florence O'Donoghue, Skibbereen.

1919 (June)

Battalion Commandant, Michael J. O'Brien, Skibbereen.
Battalion Vice-Commandant, Samuel Kingston, Bredagh.
Battalion Adjutant, Florence O'Donoghue.
Battal'on Quartermaster, Paddy O'Sullivan, Skibbereen.

1919 (August)
Samuel Kingston succeeds M. J. O'Brien.

1920
Battalion Commandant, Samuel Kingston.
Battalion Vice-Commandant, Neilus Connolly, Skibbereen.
Battalion Adjutant, Stephen O'Brien, Skibbereen.
Battalion Quartermaster, Paddy O'Sullivan, Skibbereen.

1921 (February)
Battalion Commandant, Neilus Connolly.
Battalon Vice-Commandant, Pat O'Driscoll, Myross.
Battalion Adjutant, Stephen O'Brien.
Battalion Quartermaster, Paddy O'Sullivan.

FIFTH BATTALION (BANTRY)

1917
Battalion Commandant, Michael Murray, Bantry.

1918
Battalion Commandant, Dan O'Mahony, Bantry.

1919 (16 August)
Battalion Commandant, Ted O'Sullivan, Milleeny, Bantry.
Battalion Vice-Commandant, Maurice Donegan, Bantry.
Battalion Adjutant, Seán Cotter, Bantry—Captured March 1920.
Battalion Quartermaster, Michael O'Callaghan, Bantry.

1920 (January)
Seán Lehane, Scart, succeeds Maurice Donegan.

1920 (March)
Maurice Donegan succeeds Seán Lehane.
Michael Harrington, Bantry, succeeds Seán Cotter.

1920 (June)
Seán Cotter succeeds Michael Harrington.

1920 (August)
Battalion Commandant, Maurice Donegan—Captured 21/11/20.
Battalion Vice-Commandant, Tom Ward, Durrus.
Battalion Adjutant, Seán Cotter—Captured 21/11/2.
Battalion Quartermaster, Michael O'Callaghan.

1920 (November)
Battalion Commandant, Tom Ward.
Battalion Vice-Commandant, Denis Keohane, Caheragh.
Battalion Adjutant, Michael Harrington.
Battalion Quartermaster, Michael O'Callaghan.
Battalion Intelligence Officer, Tom Reidy, Bantry.
Battalion Transport, Miah Houlihan, Bantry.
Battalinn Engineer, Dan McSweeney.

SIXTH BATTALION (BEARA)

1918
Battalion Commandant, Charlie Hurley, Kilbrittain, employed at Castletownbere.
Battalion Adjutant, Michael Crowley, Castletownbere.
Battalion Quartermaster, Sonny Mark O'Sullivan, Castletownbere.

1918 (August)
Battalion Commandant, Michael Crowley succeeds Charlie Hurley—Captured August 1918.

1919 (August)
Battalion Commandant, Peter O'Neill, Eyeries, resigns because of ill-health, January 1921.
Battalion Adjutant, Michael Crowley.
Battalion Quartermaster, Sonny Mark O'Sullivan.

1920 (August)
Liam O'Dwyer, Eyeries, becomes Battalion Vice-Commandant.

1921 (April)
Battalion Commandant, Liam O'Dwyer.
Battalion Vice-Commandant, Mícheál Óg Ó Súilleabháin, Adrigole.
Battalion Adjutant, Michael Crowley.
Battalion Quartermaster, Sonny Mark O'Sullivan.
Column Leader, Christy O'Connell, Eyeries.

SEVENTH BATTALION (SCHULL)

Battalion formed July 1920 from units of Skibbereen and Bantry Battalions on the peninsula.

1920 (13 July)
Battalion Commandant, Seán Lehane, Scart, Bantry.
Battalion Vice-Commandant, Denis Murphy, Schull.
Battalion Adjutant, Gibbs Ross, Durrus.
Battalion Quartermaster, James Hayes, Schull.

1921 (January)
Seán O'Driscoll succeeds Denis Murphy.

1921 (April)
Jim Hayes succeeds Gibbs Ross (appointed Brigade Adjutant).
Jack McCarthy, Durrus, succeeds Jim Hayes.

1921 (9 July)
Battalion Commandant, Seán O'Driscoll, Ballydehob.
Battalion Vice-Commandant, Thomas J. Hickey, Skehanore.
Battalion Adjutant, Denis O'Mahony, Ballydehob.
Battalion Quartermaster, Ned O'Sullivan, Gloun.

Company Captains of the West Cork Brigade
up to the time of the Truce

Note—The vacancies that caused successions were in most cases due to enemy captures. In other cases to ill-health and retirement. Also promotion to more important posts.

First Battalion

Ballinadee
1. Tom Hales
2. Seán Hales
3. Con O'Donoghue
4. P. O'Brien

Ballinspittle
1. Bob Fitzgerald
2. Denis Collins
3. Jack Ryan
4. Michael Galvin

Kilbrittain
1. Denis Lordan
    Captain pre 1916
2. B. J. O'Driscoll
    Captain 1917/18
3. Jim O'Mahony
4. Jack Fitzgerald
5. Mick O'Brien
6. Jacky O'Neill
7. David O'Sullivan
8. Denis O'Brien
9. Michael McGrath

Trimoleague
1. Con Lehane
3. Jim Hodnett
3. Con Murphy
4. Jack Driscoll
5. Dan Minihane

Quarry's Cross
1. Maurice O'Donovan
2. Daniel Callaghan
3. Tim Mahony

Kilpatrick
1. John Lordan

2. Mick Lordan
3. Willie Coveney
4. Jim Doyle
5. John Crowley
6. Michael Riordan

Crosspound
1. Redmond Walsh
2. Paddy Coakley
3. Paddy O'Leary
4. Tom Kelleher

Innishannon
1. Liam Deasy
2. Bat Russell
3. Con O'Sullivan
4. Miah Deasy
5. Dick Russell
6. Sonny Crowley
7. Tom Kiely

Barryroe
1. Jim Moloney
2. Mick Coleman
3. Dan Santry

Clogagh
1. Eugene Walsh
    Captain 1916/17
2. Tim Sexton
3. Dan O'Donovan
4. Paddy Dempsey

Bandon
1. Pat O'Dwyer
2. Mick O'Herlihy
3. John Galvin
4. Denis Mehigan
5. Con McCarthy

Newcestown
1. Jack Allen
   Captain 1917/18/19
2. Dan Canty
3. John Lordan
4. Bill Desmond
5. Dick Hurley
6. John O'Callaghan

Mount Pleasant or Farnivane
1. Frank Hurley
2. Con O'Brien
3. Tim Fitzgerald
4. Charlie O'Donoghue
5. John Condon
6. Batt Russell
7. Tom Russell

Second Battalion

Clonakilty
1. Stephen O'Neill
2. John Nyhan
3. Jim 'Spud' Murphy
4. Dan Nugent
5. Tom Lane
6. Jerh Crowley

Ardfield
1. Con O'Leary
2. Denny O'Sullivan
3. Michael O'Donovan

Kilkernmore
1. Pat O'Sullivan
2. John O'Sullivan
3. Paddy Barry

Rosscarbery
1. John Hodnett
2. Paddy Collins
3. James Hayes

Reenascreena
1. Paddy Murray
2. Dan O'Callaghan

Kilmeen
1. Tim O'Donoghue
2. Jim O'Hara

Ahiohill
1. Con O'Mahony
2. Jack Walsh
3. Mick Walsh
4. Denis Dunlea

Lyre
1. Johnny Cullinane
2. John Cahilane
3. Matt Donovan

Ring
1. Lar Nugent
2. William Whelton
3. Michael Hegarty

Third Battalion

Dunmanway
1. Michael McCarthy
2. Ned Young
3. Denis McCarthy
4. Joseph Keane
5. Jerh Daly

Knockbue
1. Willie Hayes
2. Tim Riordan
3. John Lucey

Derrinacahera
1. Tim J. Hurley
2. Denis Hurley
3. John Sullivan

Togher
1. Jim Burke
2. Pat O'Sullivan
3. Tim Farrell

Aultagh
1. Jim Crowley (Sean)

2. Jerome Hourihan,
3. John O'Neill
Coppeen
1. Jerh O'Mahoney
2. Phil Chambers
3. John Cronin
4. James Crowley
Behagh
1. Tom O'Donovan
2. Tim Crowley
3. Pat Corcoran
Kenneigh
1. Jim Crowley (Doctor)
2. Sonny Dave Crowley
3. John Nyhan
4. Dan Coakley
Ballineen
1. Tim Warren

2. Jack Hennessy
3. William Cullinane
Shanavagh
1. Michael O'Neill
2. John H. O'Neill
3. Michael Carey
Ballinacarriga
1. Paddy O'Brien
2. Dan Hourihan
3. Michael Con O'Driscoll
Clubhouse
1. Michael O'Donovan
2. Michael Connolly
3. Pat O'Connell
Kilbarry
1. Michael Fehilly

Fourth Battalion

Skibbereen
1. Neilus Connolly
2. Tim O'Sullivan
3. Paddy Fehilly
4. Con Bohane
5. John Leonard
Bredagh
1. Samuel Kingston
2. Pat Joe Hourihan
3. J. Minihane
4. P. Hourihane
Drinagh
1. Jim O'Donovan
2. Andrew McCarthy
3. John Hurley
Corran
1. Batt McCarthy
2. Pat Joe Crosbie
3. Denis O'Mahony
4. Pat Tobin
Leap
1. Dan O'Donovan

2. John O'Donovan
3. Stephen Holland
Glandore
1. Johnny Keane
2. Pat Fortune
3. Pat Hurley
Myross
1. Pat O'Driscoll
2. Pat Sheehy
3. Denis O'Donovan
4. Michael O'Driscoll
Castlehaven
1. Con Buckley
2. James Browne
3. Joe Walsh
Baltimore
1. Michael Cotterell
2. Pat Cadogan
3. Denny O'Neill
4. John O'Neill
5. John Crowley

Fifth Battalion

Bantry
1. R. P. Keyes
2. Jim O'Sullivan
3. Jerh O'Sullivan
4. Jerh McCarthy
5. Cecil Keyes

Glengarriff
1. Jack Downey
2. Timothy McCarthy
3. Michael O'Brien

Coomhola
1. Denny Jer O'Sullivan
2. Denis Cronin
3. Michael Driscoll

Kealkil
1. Patsy Sweeney
2. John Wrynne
3. William Dillon
4. Paul Sullivan

Pearson's Bridge
1. Jerh Mullins
2. Tim O'Connor
3. Pat Crowley

Drumsullivan
1. Denis Cadogan
2. Denis Hurley
3. Con Manning

Inchingerah

1. Con Keane
2. John Keohane
3. Con Regan
4. Con Collins
5. Dan T. Sullivan

Caheragh
1. Denis Keohane
2. Denis Daly
3. Seán Mac Aoitir
4. Denis Burke

Durrus Road
1. Pat Lehane
2. Seán Collins
3. Pat Murnane

Drimoleague
1. Dan O'Driscoll
2. Paddy O'Sullivan
3. Denis Brennan
4. Pat Collins

Durrus
1. Tom Ward
2. Tim (Casey) McCarthy
3. Denis O'Leary
4. Dan O'Mahony

Kilcrohane
1. Patrick Coghlan
2. Tim Mahony
3. Dan D. Daly

Sixth Battalion

Castletownbere
1. Charlie Hurley
2. Billy O'Neill
3. John Cronin

Lehanmore or Garnish
1. Kevin M. O'Sullivan
2. John O'Sullivan

Allihies
1. Murt O'Shea

Eyeries
1. Seán O'Driscoll

2. Christy O'Connell
3. Pat O'Neill

Urhan
1. James T. O'Sullivan
2. James O'Sullivan

Inches (part of Eyeries)
1. Corney O'Sullivan
2. Jerh O'Neill
3. Jerh McAuliffe

Ballycrovane
1. Robert O'Dwyer

2. John O'Dwyer
Kilcatherine
1. Michael Lynch
2. Peter Murphy
Adrigole
1. Jack O'Sullivan
2. Florry B. O'Sullivan
3. Matt Sullivan
4. Eugene O'Sullivan
Rossmacowen
1. John M. O'Sullivan
2. Tim Spillane
Bere Island
1. Con Lowney
2. Jim Sullivan
3. Pat Sullivan
4. Dan Harrington
Ardgroom
1. William O'Connell

2. John Sheehan
3. John Sheehan
Note—Lauragh and Ardea Companies (Kerry) were attached to Beara 1916 and 1917. They were then transferred to Kerry No. 2 Brigade. In August 1921 the two Companies were again transferred to Beara Battalion. In effect Lauragh and Ardea were very much in Beara where they rendered much assistance to Columns moving out and in during the War of Independence. The Captains were :
Lauragh
Tom Smyth
Ardea
Timothy Riney

Seventh Battalion

Schull
1. Jerry McCarthy
2. Charlie Cotter
3. Tim Murphy
Gloun
1. Ned O'Sullivan
2. Paddy Tucker
   Daniel O'Sullivan
Leamcon
1. Michael O'Donovan
2. Michael Murphy
3. William Daly
Goleen
1. Ricky Collins
2. Tim Mahoney
Lissgriffin
1. Patsy Wilcox
2. Denis Hegarty
3. Tom Neill
4. Denis O'Sullivan

Dunmanus
1. Mark Lucey
2. Maurice McCarthy
3. Mort O'Sullivan
Dunbeacon
1. John Shanahan
2. Tom Hayes
Skehanore
1. Thomas J. Hickey
2. Tim Regan
3. Joe Kelly
Ballydehob
1. Seán O'Driscoll
2. Joe Kelly
3. Pat Tucher
4. James Harte
5. John Duggan
6. John McCarthy
Lisheen (from Skibbereen)
1. Dan O'Brien
2. Willie Crowley

NUMERICAL STRENGTH OF ENEMY GARRISONS IN THE THIRD CORK BRIGADE AREA
(July 1919)

First (Bandon) Battalion Area

Bandon	. .	30 R.I.C.
		150 Military
Kilbrittain	. .	8 R.I.C.
		200 Military
Timoleague	. .	6 R.I.C.
Innishannon	. .	6 R.I.C.
Ballinspittle	. .	6 R.I.C.
Courtmacsherry	.	6 R.I.C.
Mount Pleasant	.	5 R.I.C.

Second (Clonakilty) Battalion Area

Clonakilty	. .	16 R.I.C.
Castlefreke	. .	4 R.I.C.
Rosscarbery	. .	6 R.I.C.

Third (Dunmanway) Battalion Area

Dunmanway	. .	9 R.I.C.
Ballineen	. .	9 R.I.C.

Fourth (Skibbereen) Battalion Area

Skibbereen	. .	18 R.I.C.
		50 Military
Leap	. . .	5 R.I.C.
Union Hall	. .	4 R.I.C.
Castletownsend	.	5 R.I.C.
Baltimore	. .	5 R.I.C.
Ballydehob	. .	5 R.I.C.
Schull	. . .	6 R.I.C.
Goleen	. . .	5 R.I.C.
Drimoleague	. .	6 R.I.C.

Fifth (Bantry) Battalion Area

Bantry	. . .	15 R.I.C.
		200 Military
Kilcrohane	. .	8 R.I.C.
Glengarriff	. .	6 R.I.C.
Whiddy Island	.	4 R.I.C.
		12 Military

Sixth (Beara) Battalion Area

Castletownbere	. 13	R.I.C.
	80	Military
Bere Island .	. 150	Military
Eyeries . .	. 16	R.I.C.
	50	Military
Allihies .	. 6	R.I.C.

ATTENDANCE AT GLANDORE TRAINING CAMP
(9-15 August 1919)

First (Bandon) Battalion
Liam Deasy, Bandon Battalion Staff.
Flor Begley, Bandon Battalion Staff.
Mick O'Herlihy, Bandon Company.
Denis O'Brien, Newcestown Company.
Pat O'Sullivan, Crosspound Company.
Denis Delaney, Crosspound Company.
Paddy Crowley, Kilbrittain Company.
Jack Fitzgerald, Kilbrittain Company.
Tim Sexton, Clogagh Company.
Jim Moloney, Barryroe Company.
Dan Santry, Barryroe Company.

Second (Clonakilty) Battalion
Patrick Harte, Clonakilty Company.
Stephen O'Neill, Clonakilty Company.
John Nyhan, Clonakilty Company.
Tim O'Donoghue, Kilmeen Company.
Jim O'Sullivan, Kilmeen Company.
John Goggin, Ardfield Company.

Third (Dunmanway) Battalion
Michael McCarthy, Dunmanway Company.
Paddy O'Brien, Ballinacarriga Company.
Liam O'Driscoll, Shanavagh Company.
Michael O'Dwyer, Shanavagh Company.
John Murphy, Aultagh Company.
Jim Crowley, Aultagh Company.
Denis O'Donovan, Behagh Company.
Thomas O'Donovan, Enniskean Company.

Fourth (Skibbereen) Battalion
Sam Kingston, Bredagh Company.
Pat O'Driscoll, Myross Company.
J. B. O'Driscoll, Castlehaven Company.
Michael J. O'Brien, Skibbereen Company.

Fifth (Bantry) Battalion
Ralph Keyes, Bantry Company.
Maurice Donegan, Bantry Company.

Ted O'Sullivan, Bantry Company.
Seán Cotter, Bantry Company.
Michael O'Callaghan, Bantry Company.
Seán Lehane, Bantry Company.

Sixth (Beara) Battalion
Liam O'Dwyer, Eyeries Company.

BRUTAL TREATMENT BY THE ENEMY
OF CAPTURED VOLUNTEERS

Statement of Timothy O'Connell, Ahakeera, Dunmanway

I was arrested on the morning of 2 January 1921 about a mile from the scene of the Kilmichael ambush.

I happened to be in bed in a friend's house when someone downstairs shouted 'Tans!' I hopped out of bed and had a look through an upstairs window. I could see two lorries stopped on the road about a few hundred yards away. The occupants of both lorries were out on the road studying the countryside through binoculars. I slipped on my trousers and coat, the latter being the coat Pat Deasy had worn when he was mortally wounded in the ambush at Kilmichael about five weeks earlier. The bullet hole was plain to be seen, and God help me if the Auxies could only guess the truth.

I ran from the house a short distance, and tried to put the house between me and the enemy. I then made across the fields for a short cut to some cover and away from the road, when suddenly fire was opened on me from all directions. I then discovered that the whole place was surrounded and any hope of escape gone. I still kept going, dodging in and out through bushes and any cover I could find, but to no avail. I knew I hadn't a hope of escape, so I lay down by a low stone fence to escape their fire which was still kept up. They were shouting at me to come out. I knew that if I showed myself then I'd get riddled with bullets. They moved up to where I lay, and hauled me to my feet. The first question they asked me was, 'Where were you hit?' I said that I wasn't hit. At that they seemed disappointed to have missed me at such short range, crack shots and all as they were supposed to be.

The next move was out to the road and on to the lorry. But before I was hoisted on to same I was given a few hefty wallops for good measure. The morning was awfully cold with showers of sleet, and to make matters worse I was only poorly clad, trousers, coat and shirt : I did not have time to put on boots. However, I didn't mind the cold much as I was getting an odd wallop which helped to keep the blood in circulation!

The lorries moved from Shanacashel where I was captured to Coppeen. They hadn't gone far when, meeting a cyclist, a man who knew me quite well, they stopped and asked him if he kne the prisoner. 'No,' he said, 'I never saw him before.' That happened on three occasions before we reached Coppeen, and all these three people knew me. Their reason for denying me was that they thought I had given a wrong name, and they didn't want to get me into more trouble.

Before reaching Coppeen village, the lorries came to a halt. I was ordered down, and told to stand up by the fence. Five or six of them stood on the road with rifles at the ready, and naturally I expected the volley any second. I closed my eyes and waited, but it didn't come. We continued on to the village where they again stood me against the wall of Mr P. Murphy's shop. I could see them in conversation with him, and looking my way at the same time. Eventually one of them came over to me and said that I could thank this man (Mr Murphy) for saving my life as they would have left my brains on the wall, if he hadn't given them my name—which, of course, was the same as I had given—my right name.

They moved from Coppeen southwards towards Castletown for about a mile, turned off at the next crossroads, to the right for another mile or so where they arrested an old man whom they terrified by placing grenades in his pockets with lengths of string attached to pull the pin and blow him up : they specialised in and enjoyed this kind of stuff. They moved again back to Shanacashel to the house I had run from, and searched the place thoroughly, but found nothing. From there they moved to the townland of Lisheenleigh, where some of our boys, including the Company Captain, Jim Crowley, had been sleeping in an empty cottage. This house lay about a quarter of a mile off the road. They stopped the lorries at the nearest point to the above and moved across the fields to their objective, but came back empty-handed and sorely disappointed. I heard them say that the men they were after had just gone as the blankets were still warm.

Th next and final move was from there to the headquarters in Dunmanway workhouse. I was led to the guardroom where I had to take off all my clothes and was thoroughly searched. They found nothing except a scapular which they pulled off my neck and threw on the fire. I was ordered to dress and was taken to the back of the building where a hand-pump was shown to me. I was ordered to get to work turning this to supply the house with water. This job lasted non-stop for over an hour, and by then my palms were raw and bleeding. I was almost too weak to stand. It was now lmost twenty-four hours since I had any food, or even a cup of tea.

Although there were other prisoners there at the time, I was brought back to the guardroom where I lay on the floor until about midnight when three Auxies came in and ordered me to get on my feet. I was marched out of there, one leading and two others followig just behind. We climbed a stairs leading to the top storey at the back of the building. I was led into the room, and when about half way through the room, the leader, a great big savage, suddenly turned round, and before I could realise what was going to happen he lifted me off the floor with a punch. He didn't drop me. I kept on my feet and took at least a few more before I went down. I made no attempt to get up until one of the other two came at me with a bayonet, and after that I stood up with my hands high to guard my face. Once again the savage moved in with a few more haymakers, and put me down for the second time. The blood was almost choking me by then. Once more I was forced to stand up to face the puncher and take more punishment. Finally, I went down to stay. I asked them to shoot me. The big fellow said, 'No, we wouldn't have your blood on our hands,' even though by then they had most of what I had on their hands and clothes as well as pools on the floor.

In the end one of the Auxies dragged me to the top of the stairs where I made an attempt to get to my feet. At this the big one caught me with a kick, and sent me tumbling down almost half way. I then got up, and managed to walk to my cell, an unlit poke of a room where I lay on the floor until morning in agony. My face had swollen to a lump of jelly, both my eyes were almost closed, and my nose was broken. I was brought some breakfast, but I couldn't eat it as my teeth had gone right through my lips, and I couldn't open my mouth, save a small space in one corner. Through this small opening they fed me with soup, and it was almost a month before I could chew or swallow any solid food.

A few days after I was beaten up, I was taken before the big shots, Latimer, De Havilland, and Sparrow, and questioned. All my answers to their questions were to the effect that I didn't know anyone they mentioned, or what they were talking about—even though I knew plenty which they would have given anything to know. Before I was taken away I was told I had until six o'clock next morning to make up my mind to give them the information I had. On the way back to my cell, I was brought into another small room, the walls of which were smeared with blood as well as marks which looked like bullet holes. I was told how a few Shinners who refused to give information were shot against those walls, and that my turn wasn't far away.

Next morning at the stroke of six I was brought before the big shots. Each of them had a gun in his hand. One of them stood behind me with a gun to my neck. They started with the usual question whether I had made up my mind to give the information they wanted. I said I didn't have any to give. They kept at me for half an hour or so, but I refused to answer. One of them wanted to shoot me there and then, but was stopped by the others, and I was then taken back to my cell, and asked no further questions.

I was again moved to the guardroom, still under close arrest, and one day—I can't understand how it could happen—my mother and a neighbouring girl happened to get into the guardroom. How they got past the guard is still a mystery to me. I sat on a chair in the centre of the room, and both of them sat on a stool just inside the door, and there was no more than six feet between us. Neither of them recognised me for about ten minutes, when suddenly the girl spotted something that gave her a clue. At that she turned to my mother and said, 'That's Tim!' Then my mother rushed towards me shouting, but she was manhandled immediately and thrown through the door.

A week or so after that, three of us were taken to Cork as hostages, and arrived back in Dunmanway late that night. I had joined the other prisoners by this time, and they waited up until we arrived back, and had a grand fire to greet us—the weather was shocking cold. Naturally we got as close to the fire as possible, and in about ten minutes my false face fell off in the form of a great scab about an inch thick. So I looked almost normal again.

One Monday morning shortly afterwards, I was called out along with two other prisoners, the Barrett brothers of Coppeen. Three lorries were lined up, each full of Auxies. We were ordered on board, one of us on each lorry, and were told that if one shot was fired at the lorries all three of us would be shot immediately. The first stop was the military barracks at Bandon which had been attacked the previous night. We were ordered off the lorries, and kicked through the gate. Then the Auxies told the military that they had arrested us on the road, and gave it to be understood that we had taken part in the attack on the previous night. Naturally the military decided to get their own back on us. So we were marched to the far end of the barracks where the baths were, ordered to strip off all our clothes, and stand underneath the showers. Then the cold water taps were turned on. It was a bitterly cold morning and the water was almost freezing. We had to stand under the jets of cold water until we were almost lifeless, and the military didn't pull any punches during the proceedings so that we emerged from the showers with more black eyes.

We were brought back again to the barrack square where we were shown an empty coffin which, we were told, was meant for one of us. We were to be shot at intervals of one hour beginning at three o'clock. After a short while four military came from the back of the barracks with a stretcher on which lay a body. They asked us whether we recognised the corpse. We replied that we did not. We were then ordered to place the body in the coffin. One arm was bent and stiff, and I went to push it down by the side. As I did so one of them hit me and knocked me down, while another of them pushed the arm down with his boot, and not too gently either. We put the lid on the coffin which we were then told to pick up and bring to a lorry waiting outside the gate of the barracks. Later we learned that the body was that of Volunteer Daniel O'Reilly who had been killed in the attack on the previous night.

We were held in Bandon military barracks for a week or so. Every day new prisoners were being brought in, and soon the number mounted to thirty. Then on the Saturday night about midnight fourteen of us were handcuffed in pairs and moved to Kinsale in an open lorry under heavy rain. The late Brigade Quartermaster, Dick Barrett, was one of us. On arriving at Kinsale we were ordered down off the lorry, and marched across the fields to Charles Fort. On our arrival there it was discovered that the keys of the handcuffs were left behind in Bandon. So we had to sleep on the cold floor in pairs without as much as one blanket until some time next day when the keys arrived and the handcuffs were removed.

On the following Sunday we were put on the train for Cork military barracks. There we were housed in a sheet-iron hut with plenty of air holes. We did not even have a smoke, as our pockets had been turned out before we were locked up. After a week or so there we were transferred to Cork jail which happened to be about the best and safest place so far, for we were rid of Auxies, Tans, and military. I spent another three weeks or so there, and was then moved down the river to Spike Island. New prisoners arrived every day until there were a couple of hundred, all of whom were handed Internment Forms stating that they were to be held for the duration of the war—all, that is, except myself.

Naturally, I had doubts as to what they intended to do with me next. However, I didn't have too long to wait. After a couple of months or so a wire reached the camp with orders for my removal back to Cork military barracks. This didn't sound too cheerful. Our O/C in Spike, Henry O'Mahony, sent for me on hearing the news. He asked me to give him an account of my activities up to the time I was arrested. I told him everything, and he came to the conclusion that I was to be courtmartialled. He gave me instructions to follow if his hunch proved to be correct, i.e. to re-apply for legal aid, witnesses, etc. He feared that I would be accused of taking part in the Kilmichael ambush. As well as advice he gave me some of his own clothes and cash to help me on my way. I have never forgotten that kind act of Henry.

At midnight an armed guard arrived and marched me down to the harbour, I was put aboard the boat that was sailing up to Cork. A car and two officers were waiting for me when we landed, and they brought me in the car to the barracks. They had erected two extra huts there by then, all full of prisoners, and the only one I knew was Dick Barrett (I forgot to mention that he was released from Kinsale, and had been re-arrested). He was asleep when I entered the hut. It was about 5.00 a.m., and he could not imagine where I had come from at that hour. I sat down beside him and told him the story. He thought it sounded bad.

There was one prisoner in that hut whom I didn't know then, one of the Clonmult survivors named Paddy Higgins. He had been wounded in the fight and taken prisoner. After a week or so both he and I were called out, and marched across the square to the courtmartial quarters. He was led in while I was kept outside the door. He was in for less than fifteen minutes when he came out, and was put on a lorry bound for Cork jail : he had been sentenced to death. I was marched back to the hut without being asked a question. This happened about three times in all, and on each occasion the prisoner was sentenced, but I was never taken inside the door of the murder room. A couple of weeks went by before my next move, which was back to Bandon. I spent another couple of weeks there, and was moved finally back to Dunmanway workhouse where the Auxies were lodged. On 11 May I was released conditionally, and ordered to report back every Saturday morning at eleven o'clock. Once I was outside that building, I prayed that the next time I would come face to face with that gang of murderers I would have a gun in my hands.

(Signed) TIM O'CONNELL

(Signed) JAMES CROWLEY, Company O/C (Witness)

Sworn Statements of Tadhg Ó Seaghdha and Jeremiah Fehilly

I the undersigned hereby make the following voluntary declaration and testify on oath to its accuracy.

While travelling by train from Bantry to Dunmanway on 18 February 1921 I was interrogated at Drimoleague Station by Auxiliaries and Black and Tans and the cut of my trousers was objected to as resembling that of the military. Six or seven with drawn revolvers entered the carriage with me and travelled to Dunmanway. Here I was put on a lorry and taken to the Workhouse which had been turned into a Barracks. I was put into a dirty little room where I found about fourteen other prisoners. A bucket of broken-up biscuits was given to us for supper; our request for water was refused. We slept on the floor.

Next day I was interrogated by an officer who asked me to tell him names of officers of I.R.A. I refused and he ordered me to face the wall. He put a revolver to my back and asked me three or four times would I reveal the names or take the consequences. This threat having failed another man in plain clothes, apparently another officer, started to hit me with his fists and to kick me, finally kicking me out the door. The officer said, 'Take him away and starve him.' I was then taken back to the cell again. The Auxiliary who took me back warned me under threat of being shot not to speak to the other prisoners, and he put me in a corner by myself.

After about ten minutes I was taken out and put into a kind of pantry, about six or seven foot square, off the guardroom. On the way the Auxiliary who was taking me was asked by some of his comrades what was up. He said the prisoner was going to be shot for refusing to give information. I was kept there from about Saturday noon till Monday. On Sunday I was again taken before the same officer and he asked me if I had considered the matter. This was in his own sleeping-room and he walked around with a revolver in his hand. I said that I was prepared to take the consequences. Seeing that his threats were unavailing, he tried to start a political discussion. He then ordered me to be taken back and warned me that if I didn't reveal the names of the Volunteer officers in my district I would never leave the place.

I forgot to mention that when first arrested I was taken to the guardroom and thoroughly searched and relieved of everything, including a gold watch and five pounds ten in cash, and a Post Office account book. I got a receipt for the watch and cash. But

before leaving Dunmanway and also in the other places where I
was subsequently imprisoned my repeated requests for the watch
and cash were ignored. When interned at Spike I wrote a letter to
Commander Kenworthy, M.P., on the subject; this letter was never
posted but was sent to G.H.Q. by a censor at Spike. However, it
secured the return of my watch and cash, but not of my Post
Office book, which I have not yet recovered.

On the afternoon of Sunday, 20 February, after my interview I
was lying down on the floor of the pantry as I was very unwell,
when I heard someone come into the guardroom and asking for
the keys of my cell. 'Are you going to give him a punching?' he
was asked. 'Yes,' he said. He came in and stood over me, cursing
and swearing, but did not hit me; probably he was afraid when
he saw I was sick. I had already asked to see a doctor, but he did
not come until evening and I was taken out of the pantry to see
him. He said in my hearing that I was seriously ill and he ordered
me to be provided with blankets and to be put lying down. I was
changed into a larger but not cleaner room. During all this time
I got nothing but hard biscuits and black tea. The doctor visited
me in this room on Monday and ordered me to be taken to
hospital immediately.

About midday on Monday I was brought out to be interrogated
by some officers. While being questioned I felt weak and asked for
a chair, whereupon I was thrown down on the ground. While
sitting on the floor an Auxiliary—I hardly saw him I was so weak
and dazed—bent my head down to the ground three or four times
so that I felt bent in two : he then asked me if I felt better. An
officer then ordered me to be taken away. While going towards the
door, I was again kicked. While standing near an archway outside waiting for the guard to bring me back I got a weakness and
fell on top of my head. When I recovered consciousness I found
myself back again in my cell.

That evening the doctor (a civilian) returned and again ordered
me to be taken immediately to hospital, declining all responsibility
if I were not. I was again questioned, that evening while lying
down in my cell, by six or seven Auxiliaries who came into my cell.

The officer in charge (as I afterwards found him to have been)
came and intimated that I would be taken home that evening.
About 7.30 or 8.00 that evening an orderly came for me and took
me to the guardroom. While walking slowly towards the guardroom I heard a discussion going on in a room nearby and I
distinctly heard someone saying that they already had a bad-

enough name and that such things as the shooting of Canon Magner would have to be lived down. Which led me to believe that they were discussing my fate. I was kept in the guardroom till after nine. I was told that the cause of the delay was that they had no car available, but I heard several cars passing in and out while I was there. Finally an officer came and told me they had decided to send me back again to the cell that night and to give me an extra blanket and to send me to hospital next morning; he also ordered me to be given some stimulants. So I was taken back. I asked my guard to get me a priest as I felt rather weak, but he only laughed at the idea.

I was then taken to the Union Hospital where I remained four days with a guard over me. On the 26th I was removed to Bandon, then to Victoria Barracks on 1 March, then to Cork Prison, then back again to Victoria Barracks, then again to Cork Prison, then to Spike, and finally to Bere Island where I now am.

Beyond vague abuse no charge was ever made against me; I was never tried. I told the officer in Dunmanway that I am an American citizen, which I am, and this statement, I believe helped to save my life.

> (Signed) Tadhg Ó Seaghdha
> (Signed) A. Ó Raithile (Witness)
> 24 June 1921

I the undersigned hereby voluntarily make the following statement and testify to its accuracy on oath.

I was arrested near my father's house near Rosscarbery on 26 January 1921 by the Dunmanway Auxiliaries. I was asked my name and on giving it was struck a blow. I was taken to the yard and placed with my back to the wall. Two, or perhaps three, officers interrogated me and demanded information concerning the I.R.A. In case of refusal, they said, I had only minutes to live. They brought out my mother to have one last look at me. They produced a note-book which they had found in the house; it belonged to a brother of mine and contained only recitations. On the front leaf they had written this bogus entry : 'Attack Ross Barrack. Blow up bridges, and cut telegraph wires.' They took my Sunday suit of clothes, saying that it was a uniform; they also stole six pounds out of the house and took some fowl away with them.

On finding their efforts to get information unsuccessful, th ordered me into a lorry and I was taken to Rosscarbery Barracks. On coming off the lorry and entering the barrack, an Auxiliary officer caught me and knocked my head against the wall. I was then put into a cell. The local sergeant, Twomey by name, came in with some Auxiliaries, Black and Tans and ordinary police. In their presence he accused me, without giving any proofs, of my crimes. The others then demanded information from me concerning these things. I had none to give. So they stripped me naked and examined all my clothes, tearing them in several places, and my body. All the time they kept threatening me with revolvers, brandishing them and pressing them against my mouth and ears. I was then allowed to dress. Before leaving they told me I had only half an hour to live.

At the end of half an hour they came back and asked me if I was ready and had my prayers said. I said yes. They then ordered me out on the lorry, saying, I wasn't to be shot till I reached Dunmanway that night. They struck my head against the wall on going out.

About nightfall we arrived in Dunmanway. I was put into the guardroom. I was announced as a murderer, etc. After a while the sergeant of the Auxiliaries asked me if I could box. I said no. He then told me to stand up. He then went for me, hit me, knocked me down. While I was down four or five more of them jumped on top of me and kicked me. I was made to get up and was similarly knocked down and treated several times. After that I was made stand for half an hour with my nose to the wall. I was bleeding, bruised, and battered.

I was then taken out before Colonel Lattimer. There were seven or eight in the room with him. He asked me if I knew a certain man. I said I didn't. He called me a liar, jumped up and hit me in the face with his fist. As soon as he did this all the others started hitting me and kept at me for a good while, striking me down, hitting me when down and making me get up again.

I was then taken to the mortuary. There were more of them inside there when I went in. They told me I was to be shot. I said I was ready. At this they got angrier and said I was to be ripped with bayonets, cut with an axe, buried alive. However, I received only a few strokes.

I was then taken back before the colonel. He said he had got statements from a neighbour of mine and from my brother to the effect that I was an officer in the I.R.A. and had organised ambushes, etc. (This neighbour and my brother were arrested on the same day, but after arrest were kept entirely separate from me.)

Was I to make a liar of my brother and this man? I denied the statements. One of them then caught me and held me by the head down between his legs, while the colonel and another Auxiliary kept flogging me with leather belts.

I was then put into a small room where there was another prisoner, Tim Keating. He told me he heard me being beaten and heard my falls in the guardroom. Next day I was taken out as a hostage. We went all round Reenascreena and Ross. At one place there was a man, whom I and everyone knew to be half-foolish, standing behind an idle house about two hundred yards from the road. They stopped the lorries when they saw him and two officers with revolvers went towards him. When he saw them he ran and they fired repeatedly after him but missed him. The men in the lorries then shouted to the officers to lie down and they started firing the Lewis gun and rifles at the man as he was running. But he escaped into a house. The two officers went after him when the firing ceased, and brought him on to the lorries. But seeing he was foolish they let him go.

On my return I was put into a loft which had been used as a laundry. Next morning Tim Keating was brought in. We were there together about four weeks. A few nights afterwards when we were in bed, two Auxiliaries came in and called me out. I was taken out in my shirt and trousers before the colonel. He was wearing my suit with a Sinn Féin tie and badge. He asked me if I knew it. I said it was my suit. He said it was my uniform. He said to me that they had come to put an end to murder and to the murder gang that was travelling round the country and that they were very kind and generous to all who would assist them; and that they knew I would give them very valuable assistance; and I had suffered a lot and that if I gave them this assistance I would suffer no more, but would be let out in a few days, and would get money and everything I'd want; and no one would know about it except themselves and me. I said I had no information to give. The colonel and the officers with him then began striking me, throwing me down several times; they kicked me and hit me on the head with revolvers. They kept asking me questions and after each they struck me. I was all covered with blood, my eyes were blackened, and my shirt was torn off me. I was then brought back and on reaching the top of the stairs leading to the loft I was thrown down the stairs on my head. Four or five more who were below jumped down on me when I reached the ground. Tim Keating heard my fall and saw my appearance when I returned.

The following Sunday two Auxiliaries came in after dinner. They asked us if we knew who kidnapped their two pals. We said no. They then began belting us in turn for a long time; using their fists and feet. That night again the same two returned and did the same again. On several nights when bringing in our supper they hit us, and once our supper was spilled. We were kept once on water and biscuits for eight days. (On the occasion of my interview with the colonel, either he or an officer said they would try hunger on me now.)

On the occasion of an attack on Drimoleague Barracks we were both taken out as hostages on separate lorries. Colonel Lattimer told us that in case the lorries were attacked we were to be shot; and he appointed a man in my lorry to carry out this threat. Fortunately for us the attack was over. We left Dunmanway about 4.00 in the morning. I was made to carry a searchlight round Drimoleague for them and we were both made to work at removing stones from the front of the Barracks. They looted Drimoleague and those who came back into the lorry where I was had cigarettes, pipes, tobacco, whiskey, brushes, and other things. The colonel was in charge and travelled to Drimoleague in a Ford car.

The same morning we went to Bantry where we got breakfast. Then we came back to Drimoleague, and then on to Skibbereen. Ross, then to Glandore, then Leap, then to Drinagh and into Dunmanway. At Glandore, the Auxiliaries raided Shorecliffe House (the Irish College). I saw them removing beds and bedding, Irish costumes, tableaux, silver teapots, kettles, etc. There was only a caretaker in the school at the time, as it is open only in summer. These things they brought back in the lorries. Some days afterwards Keating and I and two other prisoners were put to work, in what was formerly the Catholic chapel, at putting up a stage, the scenes and tableaux being those taken from Glandore College.

One Sunday I was carried out as a hostage first on a lorry and then astride the engine of a Ford car. They held up men coming to or going from Mass and ordered them to repair certain bridges. We passed a priest on horseback and the Auxiliaries jeered and shouted at him, and said to me that those damned fellows were the cause of all the trouble.

During part of the time the prisoners used to get their dinner together in the kitchen. I used to be put standing up on a bag of coal in a corner, the Auxiliaries used to throw slurs and jeers at me while there. One morning at breakfast one of them gave me a low in the stomach.

On the day of the Macroom ambush the Auxiliaries told Keating and me and the other prisoners that five or six members of the J Company had been knocked out and that their own men (K Company) were out there that day, and if anything happened them every one of us would be shot. When we were working that evening in the kitchen, they were all mad drunk. As I was scrubbing the floor, they kept throwing lumps of coal at us. When I had finished I was struck on the head with a fire-shovel. They used to go for drinks and come back again. Their language was full of curses and very dirty. One of them took out a revolver and stuck it up to my mouth and said 'We were talking about the Lord Jesus Christ before, but this can talk too' and threatened to shoot me. Another one of them then came in and carried him out.

The laundry or loft in which we were was a rotten verminous place. We never got a bath. There was no fire of course. We could not stand up straight unless we stuck our heads up between a big rafter and some wires. The last week I spent in Dunmanway I was put with about eight or ten others in a bigger cell. The whole time I never saw a priest.

Early on 28 February three others (hostages) and myself were taken in lorries to Cork. We got no breakfast and nothing to eat till we reached Union Quay Barracks, Cork.

About four o'clock in the evening we got our breakfast there. We were then taken up to the Victoria Barracks. I was called out of the lorry and taken in. I spent about a fortnight there between the guardroom and the cage. Then I was taken to the gaol, then to Spike and then here to Bere Island, where I now am.

(Signed) JEREMIAH FEHILY, Bere Island

(Signed) A. Ó RAITHILE (Witness)
15 July 1921

I have read the above deposition and hereby confirm those statements of events which are asserted to have come within my experience. They contain some items which I had forgotten or omitted to include in my own deposition.

(Signed) TIMOTHY KEATING, Bere Island

(Signed) A. Ó RAITHILE (Witness)

18 July 1921

ENGLISH PRESS ACCOUNTS OF CROSSBARRY AMBUSH

The Daily Mail (21 March 1921)
Four Irish Ambushes
Nine Soldiers and Three Police killed
Last Stand by Burning Lorries
Electric mine. Lorries blown up and set on fire.
(From our special correspondent, Dublin, Sunday)

This has been a week of ambushes. Following the three on Saturday in Cork, Waterford and Dublin, there was another tonight near Rochestown, Cork. Eight policemen were fired on and two were wounded.

The ambush at Crosskerry [*sic*], Cork, yesterday and the fighting which followed were on an unusual scale. The Crown forces had apparently heard that an ambush was being prepared and a large force left Bandon to sweep an extensive part of the county. The party which took the road towards Cork consisted of a patrol of the Essex Regiment and a few police and travelled in eight motor lorries and Crossley tenders. On nearing Crosskerry the troops dismounted and two lorries and a tender moved on some distance ahead. When they reached the bridge on the outskirts of the village there was a terrific explosion from an electric mine concealed in the road. Part of the arch of the bridge collapsed and the three lorries were literally blown up.

Fire was opened immediately from both sides of the road and seven soldiers and one policeman, Constable Kenward, were killed while several others including a constable were wounded. Constable Kenward was an Englishman who recently joined the R.I.C. and had been stationed in Bandon only a short time.

The attackers were concealed in groves surrounding two farmhouses. Several of the other lorries dashed off for reinforcements while the remaining members of the ambushed party took cover beside their burning lorries and replied to the attackers' fire. When reinforcements about a hundred strong arrived from the Hampshire Regiment they found the first party almost all killed or wounded. They quickly engaged the attackers in a running fight through the furze and over the gorse-covered hills. The Crown forces endeavoured to carry out an encircling movement. At one time it looked as though seventy to a hundred rebels would be trapped but they were saved by their intimate knowledge of the country and their skilful use of cover. A small rearguard, however, were caught, seven of these were killed and several wounded and captured.

The fight lasted for four hours and covered a large area. Crown forces took possession of all roads and stopped traffic and in the afternoon fires were seen at several farmhouses in the neighbourhood.

The London Times (Monday, 21 March 1921)
Black Irish Week-End. Heavy Ambush Death-Roll.
Stubborn Fights.
(From our own correspondent, Dublin, 20 March)

On Saturday evening General Headquarters in Dublin issued the following report of a fight between forces of the Crown and armed rebels in Co. Cork.

At about 8.00 a.m. today while a party of the Essex Regiment, the Hampshire Regiment and the Royal Irish Constabulary were operating on foot near Crossbarry, six miles north-east of Bandon, their transport which was some little distance from them was attacked by a large body of rebels. A fierce resistance was put up by the small party in charge of the transport but before the main body could come to their rescue three other ranks of the Royal Army Service Corps, three other ranks of the Essex Regiment and one R.I.C. driver were killed and the transport burned. After the arrival of the main body and reinforcements of police and Auxiliaries who vigorously engaged them the rebels fled leaving six of their dead. Seven wounded were carried away by their comrades. Six unwounded rebels and a quantity of arms, ammunition and bombs were captured by the Crown forces. The total casualties of the military and police were six other ranks and one R.I.C. driver killed; two officers, two other ranks and one R.I.C. wounded; one sergeant of the Essex Regiment missing. (The wounded R.I.C. man, Constable Kenward, is unofficially reported to have died.)

A Six Hours' Fight. Farmhouses Burned.
(From a correspondent. Cork, 20 March)

Yesterday morning while thirty soldiers were motoring to the Bandon district to conduct searches on a large scale they ran into an ambush laid by nearly five hundred men and a battle followed which continued for six hours. The troops were travelling in three lorries and when they approached a road bridge at Cross Barry, midway between Kinsale Junction and Upton Stations on the Cork, Bandon and South Coast Railway, they were suddenly forced to stop by the blowing up of the Bridge. The next instant a hail of bullets was rained on them by ambushers who were all under cover. Machine guns, rifles, revolvers and bombs were used against them and in the early stages of the encounter the Crown forces suffered heavily. The soldiers, however, took the best cover available and returned the fire inflicting heavy punishment on their assailants.

Reinforcements were summoned from Bandon and Cork and in a short time nearly three hundred military arrived on the scene with ambulances, and a counter offensive on a big scale was opened against the Republicans, who continued to fight for hours until they were forced to beat a retreat, hotly pursued by the soldiers. Passengers on the Cork, Bandon, and South Coast Line had a full view of the fight for several miles. During the operations several farmhouses appeared to be blown up.

Another account states that the battle opened only a short distance from Upton Railway Station which was recently the scene of the ambush of a train resulting in the deaths of several passengers. The military who were ambushed were only a small part of the total number of soldiers conducting searches in the district, and when firing began troops converged from all directions on the scene. When the battle ended there was intense military and police activity in the whole district. For miles around houses and farm produce are reported to have been burned.

LIST OF MEN WHO FOUGHT AT CROSSBARRY

Staff Officers
Liam Deasy, Brigade Adjutant.
Tom Barry, Column Commandant.
Flor Begley, Assistant Brigade Adjutant.
Dr. Con Lucey, Brigade M.O.
Eugene Callanan, Assistant Brigade M.O.
Tadhg Sullivan, Column Quartermaster.
Mick Crowley, Brigade Engineer (Section Commander).

First Battalion
Ballinadee Company
Seán Hales, Knocknacurra (Section Commander).
William Hales, Knocknacurra.
Bob Hales, Knocknacurra.
Con O'Donoghue, Rathrout.
Jack O'Donoghue, Rathrout.
Denny O'Donoghue, Rathrout.
Jim Crowley, Kilanetig (wounded).
Tim Crowley, Horsehill.
Matt Healy, Rathrout.
Jack Corkerry, Cloghane.
Kilbrittain Company
Johnny O'Leary, Howes Strand.
Denis Lordan, Maryboro (Section Commander).
Peter Monahan (killed).
Jack Roche, Kilbrittain.
Denny O'Brien, Clounboig.
Paddy O'Sullivan, Glanduff.
Timoleague Company
Con Lehane, Timoleague.
Con Murphy, Carhue.
Jimmy Hodnett, Carhue.
Mick Deasy.
Tim Keohane.
John O'Driscoll, Timoleague.
Dan Minnihane, Timoleague.
Barryroe Company
Bill McCarthy.

Dan Holland.
Michael Coleman.
Denis O'Brien, Butlerstown.
Denis O'Sullivan.
Con Callanan.
Clogagh Company
Dan O'Donovan, Burrane South.
Con Daly, Ballinascarthy (killed).
Paddy Dempsey.
Mick O'Donovan.
Dan O'Donovan, Clogagh.
Bandon Company
Denis Mehigan, Dangan.
Mick Kearney, Bandon.
Bill Buckley, Bandon.
Con McCarthy, Bandon.
Farnivane or Mount Pleasant Company
Frank Hurley, Laragh, Bandon.
Con O'Brien, Laragh, Bandon.
Jerh O'Brien, Tullyglass.
Newcestown Company
John Lordan, Coolinagh (Section Commander).
Jim Lordan, Coolinagh.
Bill Desmond.
Dan Canty, Farnalough.
Stephen Staunton.
Jer Desmond.
Denis O'Callaghan, Lauravoulta.
John O'Callaghan, Lauravoulta (Little John).
Denny O'Brien, Tullyglass.
Dan Corcoran, Bengour (wounded).
Kilpatrick Company
Jim Doyle, Kilmore.
Jer Doyle, Kilmore.
John Crowley.
Crosspound Company
Tom Kelleher, Crow Hill, Upton (Section Commander).

Second Battalion
Clonakilty Company
Jim 'Spud' Murphy. Clonakilty (Section Commander).
Dan Nugent, Clonakilty.

Jack Barry, Clonakilty.
Ardfield Company
Con O'Leary, Brownstown, Ardfield.
Dan O'Sullivan, Cahir.
Kilkernmore Company
Eugene McSweeney, Castlefreke.
Jack McSweeney, Castlefreke.

Third Battalion
Aultagh Company
John O'Donovan, Aultagh.
Clubhouse Company
Peter Kearney, Lettergorman (Section Commander).
Patsy O'Connell, Edencurra, Dunmanway.
Pat O'Donovan, Nedinagh.
Behagh Company
Mick Hurley, Gortnamuckly, Dunmanway.
Knockbue Company
Denis O'Leary, Drimoleague.

Fourth Battalion
Corran Company
Jerh O'Leary, Corran, Leap (killed).
Drinagh Company
Jack Dempsey, Dromindy.
Bredagh Company
Tim J. McCarthy, Lissane, Drimoleague.
Baltimore Company
Seán O'Neill, Baltimore.

Fifth Battalion
Coomhola Company
Michael O'Driscoll, Snave, Bantry.
Daniel Lucey, Cooryleary, Bantry.
Kealkil Company
Jack O'Connor, Kealkil, Bantry.
Bantry Company
Patrick (Sonny) O'Sullivan, Milleney, Bantry.
Parson's Bridge Company
Patrick Keohane, Pearsons Bridge, Bantry.
Caheragh Company
Willie Norris, Caheragh.
Denis O'Driscoll, Caheragh.

Sixth Battalion
Adrigole Company
Michael Óg O'Sullivan, Inchintaglan, Adrigole.
Matt O'Sullivan, Lackavane, Adrigole.
Castletown Company
John McCarthy (Whistler), Castletownbere.
Rossmacowen Company
Dick Spencer, Rossmacowen (wounded).
Ardgroom Company
Tim O'Shea, Droumard, Ardgroom.
John Sheehan, Barrakilla, Ardgroom (wounded).
Eyeries, Kilcatherine and Inches Companies
Christy O'Connell, Eyeries (Section Commander).
Seán O'Driscoll, Eyeries.
Tim O'Dwyer, Eyeries, Caileroe.
Pat O'Sullivan, Eyeries, Bawrs.
Murt McCarthy, Inches.
Jerry McAuliffe, Croumlane.
Dan O'Sullivan (Seer), Gorth.
John O'Sullivan, Kilcatherine.

Seventh Battalion
Ballydehob Company
Tim Allen, Ballydehob.
Schull Company
Tom McCarthy, Schull.

Unattached to Companies in the Battalion Area
Jerh McCarthy, Dreeney, Skibbereen (U.C.C. Company).

Scouts
Ted Finn, Crossbarry.
J. Collins, Crossbarry.
Tadhg Twomey, Crossbarry.
Paddy Cronin, Crossbarry.
Denny Doolin, Crossbarry.
Neilus Begley, Killeens.
Bill Hartnett, Killeens.
Danny Buckley, Inagh.
Miah Buckley, Inagh.
Paddy O'Leary, Ballyhandle.
Jack Falvey, Ballymurphy.

Denny Delaney, Belrose.
Jerome O'Mahony, Belrose.
Jim Lordan, Dunkerreen.
Pake McCarthy, Upton.
Battie Cronin, Clashinimud.

CUMANN NA mBAN IN WEST CORK

No history of the West Cork Brigade would be complete without its tribute to the work done by the women's auxiliary of the Volunteers known as Cumann na mBan. From 1917 until 1921 this organisation was an integral part of the army and without it that army could not have succeeded. The duties of members of the Cumann were manifold and included such activities as intelligence work, the carrying of dispatches, even the carrying of arms and ammunition through enemy-occupied areas, nursing the sick and wounded, providing cigarettes and suchlike amenities to those who were captured and were awaiting transfer to prison camps, providing for the needs of the Volunteers generally and particularly of those 'on the run'. The bravery and generosity of the members of the Cumann were heroic, and it would be impossible to repay the debt of gratitude and appreciation which is due to them. Here it is my wish to pay tribute to the great women of that brave and generous band, and to single out for special mention some of the leaders who were most prominent during the struggle.

Bandon Battalion—Daisy Walsh, Kilbrogan Hill; Anna O'Mahony (*née* Hurley); Molly Walsh (*née* O'Neill); Mary Lordan; Nora Crowley; Moll Lynch (*née* O'Donoghue), Ballinadee.

Clonakilty Battalion—Katie Murphy; Lena Crowley.

Dunmanway Battalion—The Nyhan sisters of Castletownkenneigh; the O'Brien sisters of Girlough; Mary O'Sullivan (*née* Buttimer) of Ahakeera.

Skibbereen Battalion—The Kingston sisters of Tureen; the Buckley sisters of Gortbrack; Annie Connolly (*née* Walsh) of Moulatrahane.

Bantry Battalion—Bridie McSweeney of Bantry; Kate Ann Coughlan; Molly O'Donoghue.

Beara Battalion—Mrs Nora O'Sullivan (*née* O'Neill); Bella O'Connell.

Schull Battalion—Kathleen O'Connell; Lizzie Murphy (*née* Ross); Helena Hegarty.

BRIGADE COUNCIL MEETINGS
(1919 to 11 July 1921)

1919
6 January—John Collins's, Kilnadur, Dunmanway.
March—John O'Donoghue's, Ballinvard, Rossmore.
May—Frank Hurley's, Laragh, Bandon.
June—Mick Walsh's, Gaggin, Bandon.
July—Frank Hurley's, Laragh, Bandon.
August—Village Hall, Caheragh.
November—Village Hall, Caheragh.

1920
January—John O'Brien's, Girlough, Ballinacarriga.
February—Frank Hurley's, Laragh.
April—Frank Hurley's, Laragh.
May—Paul Kingston's, Tureen, Skibbereen.
July—John O'Donoghue's, Ballinvard, Rossmore.
August—Mrs. O'Mahoney's, Belrose, Upton.
September—John Murphy's, Ardcahan, Aultagh.
31 October—Denis O'Leary's, Coppeen.
21 November—Dan Kelly's, Gloun, Aultagh.
10 December—Neilus Cotter's, Curradrinagh, Aultagh.
29 December—John Hurley's, Buninumera, Ballinacarriga.

1921
6 February—Lyons's vacant farmhouse, Ballinvard, Rossmore.
April—Charlie Foley's, Maulnadruck, Newcestown.
10 May—James O'Riordan's, Coosane, Kealkil.
19 May—Timothy Seamus Hurley's, Shanacrane East.
June—Patsy O'Neill's, Maryboro', Kilbrittain.

SOURCES

(a) **Manuscript Sources**

1. Notes on military actions of the West Cork Brigade compiled by the late Major Florence O'Donoghue.

2. Memoirs on the Mount Pleasant, Durrus and Drimoleague ambushes by the late Commandant Ted O'Sullivan.

3. Copies of the Statements prepared for the Bureau of Military History by Captain Christopher O'Connell, Eyeries, Co. Cork; Captain Denis Lordan, Cork City; Captain James Murphy, Dundalk (late of Clonakilty, Co. Cork).

4. Records of the Fifth (Bantry) Battalion, Cork III Brigade, Irish Republican Army, compiled in 1969 by Captain Ralph Keyes, Bantry, Co. Cork.

5. Records of the Fourth (Skibbereen) Battalion and of his imprisonment in Belfast and Strangeways Jails by Commandant Neilus Connolly, Skibbereen, Co. Cork.

6. Letters dealing with activities of the Fourth (Skibbereen) Battalion and Glandore Training Camp by Commandant Sam Kingston, Dunmanway, Co. Cork.

7. Records dealing with the history of the Third (Dunmanway) Battalion and the ambush at Kilmichael by Commandant Paddy O'Brien, Dunmanway, Co. Cork.

8. Records of the Seventh (Schull) Battalion, the fight at Schull Barracks and the naval operation at Fastnet Rock by Commandant Seán O'Driscoll, Skibbereen, Co. Cork.

9. Records of the Upton and Crossbarry ambushes and general activities of the West Cork Brigade by Commandant Florence (Flor) Begley, Bandon, Co. Cork.

10. Record of Ballycrovane attack and other activities of the Sixth (Beara) Battalion by Commandant Liam O'Dwyer, Eyeries, Co. Cork.

11. Letters concerning his capture and escape, and an account of the arms dumps at Raheen by Captain Frank Neville.

12. An account of the escape of Volunteer officers at Maulatrahane by Captain Stephen O'Brien, Leap, Co. Cork.

13. An account of the removal of trap-mines from Derrinard Bridge by Captain Thomas J. Hickey, Dublin (late of Ballydehob, Co. Cork.

14. Report of the escape of Captain Jack Ryan by Leiutenant Denis Collins.

15. Statements of Leiutenant Jeremiah Fehily, Volunteer Tadhg Ó Seaghdha and Volunteer Timothy O'Connell concerning the brutal treatment meted out to them as prisoners at the hands of their British captors.

16. Statement concerning the arrest, trial and sentence of several Volunteers captured under arms, and also of his own arrest and trial written by Captain Dan O'Driscoll, Drimoleague, Co. Cork.

17. Records of the Kilbrittain Company compiled by Denis Crowley, Company Adjutant, Kilbrittain, Co. Cork.

(b) Printed Sources

Barry, Tom : *Guerilla Days in Ireland* (Dublin, 1949).

Bennett, George : *The History of Bandon* (Cork, 1862).

Browne, Charlie : *The Story of the 7th* (Cork, 1972).

Deasy, Liam : (1) 'The Schull Peninsula in the War of Independence' in *Éire-Ireland. A Journal of Irish Studies,* 1 (1966), Summer, pp. 5-18; (2) 'The Beara Peninsula Campaign' in *Éire-Ireland. A Journal of Irish Studies,* 1 (1966), Fall, pp. 63-78.

Devoy, John : *Recollections of an Irish Rebel* (New York, 1929).

Holt, Edgar : *Protest in Arms. The Irish Troubles 1916-28* (London, 1960).

Longford, The Earl of, and Thomas P. O'Neill : *Eamon de Valera* (Dublin, 1970).

Macardle, Dorothy : *The Irish Republic. A Documented Chronicle of the Anglo-Irish Conflict and the Partitioning of Ireland, with a detailed account of the period 1916-1923* (Dublin, 1951).

Martin, F. X., o.s.a. : *Leaders and Men of the Easter Rising: Dublin, 1916* (London, 1967).

O'Brien, William, and Desmond Ryan : *Devoy's Post Bag 1871-1928* (Dublin, 1948).

O'Donoghue, Florence : (1) *No Other Law* (Dublin, 1954); (2) *Tomás MacCurtain* (Tralee, 1958).

O'Malley, Ernie : *On Another Man's Wound* (Dublin, 1936).

Ryan, Desmond : *The Fenian Chief. A Biography of James Stephens* (Dublin, 1967).

Williams, Desmond : *The Irish Struggle 1916-1926* (London, 1966).

INDEX

Ahern, Rev. Denis 151

All-for-Ireland League 2

Allen, William Philip 2

Ambushes, Tactics of 32, 34, 39, 40, 63-7, 106-8, 112, 114-5, 116, 126, 127, 129, 132-3, 139, 143-5, 146, 154-6, 158, 165, 168, 169, 170-2, 175-6, 183, 219-21, 229-30, 232-49, 283-5

Ammunition and Arms, How acquired 9-10, 19, 20, 21, 28, 29, 31-2, 35, 38-40, 42, 55, 63-5, 87-9, 93, 105-6, 107, 108, 112-15, 119, 124 and fn 3, 129-30, 133-5, 152, 156, 182, 189, 206, 230, 241, 269-71, 311

Arms Dumps 20, 22, 38, 55, 64, 89, 114, 119, 147, 158, 178, 184, 194, 200, 206, 211, 278, 279, 280, 281, 282, 283

Arms Fund 139, 140, 162 and fn 6, 164, 211

Ashe, Thomas 16

Asquith, H. H., British Prime Minister 226

Ballycrovane Coastguard Station and Pier 113, 119, 120, 124, 230, 249

Bandon, Lord 295 and fn 4, 296, 297

Bandon Volunteer Pipe Band 11-14 *passim*, 232, 239, 253

Barrack Attacks 30-1, 67, 81, 85-6, 92, 95-105

Barrett, Dick 90-1, 111, 128, 131, 134, 140, 141, 164, 168, 173, 227, 229, 232, 249, 250, 251, 252, 255, 282, 339, 340

Barry, Tom 141, 143-4, 155-6, 158-60, 162, 165, 169-73, 177, 178, 181, 183, 188, 192, 198, 201-2, 203, 208, 212, 215, 218, 227-47, 249, 252, 261-2, 266-7, 272, 276, 286, 291, 292, 305, 306, 315

Battle of Kinsale 231

Beaslai, Piaras 46, 47, 257

Begley, Flor 7, 11-13, 60, 67, 69, 91, 103, 131, 168, 220, 227, 232, 239, 245, fn 7, 246, 252, 253, 290, 316

Belfast Jail 43-5

Billeting and Protection 128, 161-2, 172, 190, 192, 204, 206, 212, 216, 217, 218, 245, 247, 299, 304

Black and Tans and Auxiliaries 163, 164-5, 167, 172, 186, 192, 203-5, 209, 216, 228, 245, 246, 250, 268, 274-6, 283-5, 287, 299-305 *passim*, 308

Blythe, Ernest 38

Breen, Father John 267

Brigade Council Meetings 57-8, 62, 69, 76, 84, 85, 110, 112, 129, 158, 162-3, 207, 209, 212, 263, 268, 272, 273, Appendix H

Brigade Headquarters 54, 60, 80, 84, 91, 95, 96, 98, 105, 108, 111, 131, 144, 164, 168, 173, 177, 179, 181, 203, 227, 232, 234, 249, 250, 265 and fn 1, 280, 286, 289, 290, 292, 295, 315

British Destroyers 116, 124, 298, 310-11

Brugha, Cathal 81, 126, 131, 132, 133, 180, 313

Burke, Col. Rickard O'Sullivan 52

Cahill, Paddy 132, 312

Callanan, Eugene or "Nudge" 196 244

Canty, Dan 10, 99, 144, 235

Cassidy, Father 47-9

Cecil, Lord Robert 226

Clancy, Peadar 46, 80, 131, 143, 313

Clune, Most Rev. Dr., Archbishop of Perth 180, 195

Coholan, Most Rev. Dr., Bishop of Cork 193

Collins, Michael or Mick 16, 38, 42, 46, 50, 52, 53, 54, 57, 76, 80, 81, 131, 132, 195, 256, 257, 258, 259, 313

Communications 38, 58, 59, 60, 61, 62, 83, 84, 110, 121, 128, 138, 143, 157, 171, 189, 190, 219, 247 and fn 9, 272, 274, 286, 287 and fn 3, 294, 312, 316

Connolly, Con or Neilus 41, 42, 43, 50, 114, 115, 212, 285, 293

Connolly, John 212, 273

More Interesting Titles
The Shooting of Michael Collins

John M. Feehan

Was Michael Collins killed by an accident of war or was he
ruthlessly murdered? Both of these possibilities are calmly and
carefully examined by the author, who has rejected the
traditional theory that he was killed as a result of a ricochet
rifle bullet and leans towards the possibility that he was shot by
a Mauser pistol.

When the first and second editions of this book appeared
they sold out instantly and caused a newspaper controversy
which lasted many months.

In this sixth edition the author has rewritten large sections
of the book incorporating new and rather startling information
which came his way. This new and rewritten edition is sure to
arouse exceptional and absorbing interest in this baffling and
bewildering mystery.

THE SECRET PLACES OF THE WEST CORK COAST

John M. Feehan

There are moments in the life of every human being when he
becomes haunted with the longing to leave behind the tension
and turmoil of daily living, to get away from it all and to
escape to a clime where true peace can be found. There are
many practical reasons why most of us cannot do this so the
next best thing is to read the story of one who tried.

John M. Feehan sailed, all by himself, in a small boat
around the coast of West Cork and the result is a book which is
not only a penetrating spiritual odyssey, but also a magnificent
account of the rugged coastline, the peaceful harbours, and the
strange characters he met in this unspoiled corner of Ireland.
He writes with great charm, skill, sympathy and a mischievous
roguish humour often at his own expense. His sharp eye misses
nothing.